A PIECE
OF THE ACTION

A PIECE OF THE ACTION

A Plan To Provide Every Family With A $100,000 Stake In The Economy

Stuart M. Speiser

VAN NOSTRAND REINHOLD COMPANY

NEW YORK   CINCINNATI   ATLANTA   DALLAS   SAN FRANCISCO
LONDON   TORONTO   MELBOURNE

Van Nostrand Reinhold Company Regional Offices: New York Cincinnati Chicago Millbrae Dallas

Van Nostrand Reinhold Company International Offices: London Toronto Melbourne

Copyright © 1977 by Stuart M. Speiser

Library of Congress Catalog Card Number: 77–2514
ISBN: 0-442-27010-0

Manufactured in the United States of America

Published by Van Nostrand Reinhold Company
450 West 33rd Street, New York, N.Y. 10001

Published simultaneously in Canada by Van Nostrand Reinhold Ltd.

15 14 13 12 11 10 9 8 7 6 5 4 3 2 1

Library of Congress Cataloging in Publication Data

Speiser, Stuart M.
A piece of the action.

Bibliography: p.
Includes index.
1. Capitalism. 2. Employee ownership—United States—
1971–   3. United States—Economic conditions.
4. Kelso, Louis O. I. Title.
HB501.S83 1977   330.1   77–2514
ISBN 0–442–27010–0

CONTENTS

PREFACE

This is a book about a dream—a dream called *universal capitalism* that first occurred to a San Francisco lawyer named Louis Kelso. As I use the term in this book, "universal capitalism" means a system that will give everyone a chance to be a capitalist, mainly by enabling people who have no savings to own corporate stock. The stock would pay for itself out of its own earnings. I also use "capital diffusion" and "broadening of capital ownership" as synonyms for "universal capitalism."

I want to apologize in advance for using some obsolete terms: "capitalism," "socialism," and "communism." They're still used in economics textbooks and you see them in the newspapers every day, but they don't have precise meanings any more. Since there are no accurate one-word descriptions of the world's economic systems, the best we can do is to use "capitalism," "socialism," and "communism" to label systems that are more like what those terms traditionally meant than anything else.

We used to think of capitalism as a system based on private ownership and initiative, with independent decisions by producers and consumers determining prices and policies. Socialism was supposed to be based on government planning and decision-making, government ownership and operation of the means of production, and redistribution of income by the government to provide social welfare. Communism was supposed to be an advanced form of socialism. According to Marxists, it was the last stage in the historical sequence of slavery, feudalism, capitalism, socialism, and communism, and in its ultimate form the authority of government, being unnecessary, would wither away. In the meantime, each communist nation would be ruled by a dictatorship of the proletariat, meaning that there would be only one political party, and it would have all the power.

By the 1970s, none of these three systems existed in pure form anywhere, and in most nations the three were scrambled together in hybrid forms that almost defy definition. The United States is supposed to have a capitalist system, but here we find extensive government participation in economic decision-making, large social welfare programs, and massive redistribution of income. The strong labor parties of European nations such as Sweden, West Germany, Holland, and Denmark are members of the Socialist International, but that organization, which is a descendant of Karl Marx's First International, no longer strives for government ownership of the means of production. In communist nations such as Soviet Russia, there is a great deal of income inequality, with three quarters of industrial workers being paid by piece rates. And many communist parties throughout the world claim to have abandoned the idea of dictatorship or one-party rule.

Obviously, the world's economic systems are moving toward fusion. Universal capitalism follows this trend by trying to combine the best features of capitalism and socialism.

If we don't adopt universal capitalism or find some other way to bring the benefits of capital ownership to all Americans, what will happen? In many of the other democracies, voters have already rejected capitalism and have elected governments that call themselves socialist. The majority of voters in those countries had no hope of ever attaining the main prize of capitalism—income from the ownership of capital—so they finally learned how to use their political power to change the economic system in a way that they thought would benefit non-capitalists. In the 1976 election, the overwhelming majority of Americans voted for either the Democratic or Republican parties, neither of which had any platform that would give the average American a chance to become a capitalist. Will this go on forever? How long will most Americans vote against any chance of their becoming owners of capital? If we don't find some way of getting everyone in on capital ownership, isn't it inevitable that American voters eventually will elect a government dedicated to some form of collective ownership?

If these questions seem strange to you, try to visualize a democratic nation that chose capitalism as its economic system and then designed its capitalism to be consistent with democracy. In such a nation, the right to own capital, like the right to vote, would be open to every citizen. If someone came along after 200 years and tried to change that nation's system in a way that would limit capital ownership to a pinnacle class of less than 15 percent of the population, what would his chances be? Somehow, America and all the other democracies started out the other way, with a capitalism that is not consistent with democracy. Now, after 200 years, what can we do to correct this oversight and still retain the advantages of capitalism?

Much of this book revolves around Louis Kelso's efforts to provide answers to these questions. Mr. Kelso and his associates generously made their files available to me and granted numerous interviews. However, this book is not an authorized version of Kelso's theories. I have tried to distill from Kelso's works the principles that I think can be synthesized with traditional economics, because I believe that the best hope of achieving universal capitalism is to build a bridge from Keynes to Kelso and get all of our mainstream economists into the quest. In this process, I have reshaped some of Kelso's theories and discarded others, all without any concurrence by Mr. Kelso, who undoubtedly would disagree with many of these modifications.

I am indebted to many others for their assistance, particularly Professor Lawrence R. Klein and Dr. Abel Beltran-del-Rio of Wharton Econometric Forecasting Associates; Dr. Robert Hamrin, staff economist of the Joint Economic Committee of Congress; Professor Hans Brems of the University of Illinois; Winnett Boyd, president of Arthur D. Little of Canada, Ltd.; Father Philip S. Kaufman, O.S.B., of Saint John's University, Minnesota; and Gershen Konikow, founding president of Professional Planners Forum. However, the views expressed in this book are entirely my own.

All the major sources that I relied upon are listed in the Bibliography. If you get stuck on the meaning of any terms or acronyms, there is a Glossary following the Appendix.

Non-American readers should note that I often use the American term "corporation," which is our word for what the British call a limited company, not a government-owned British corporation. I also use "stock" for "shares," and "stockholder" for "shareholder." "Billion" means a thousand million, as in the European "milliard," and "trillion" means a thousand billion. All dollars are U.S. dollars.

As we embark on the adventure of a new idea, it seems appropriate (and, I hope, not sacrilegious) to borrow the last two sentences from the preface written in 1936 by John Maynard Keynes for his classic work, *The General Theory of Employment, Interest and Money:*

> The ideas which are here expressed so laboriously are extremely simple and should be obvious. The difficulty lies, not in the new ideas, but in escaping from the old ones, which ramify, for those brought up as most of us have been, into every corner of our minds.

New York, N. Y.
March 24, 1977

60 MINUTES

It was Sunday, March 16, 1975. I had just flown home from California and was leafing through the accumulated mail as I tuned in Channel 2. "60 Minutes" was about half over, and Morley Safer was talking about Vietnam, a subject that I had had my fill of. As the screen showed coffins being loaded onto a military airplane, Safer concluded:

> In the end, we were just richer than the French. We could afford to take our dead home to bury them in native ground.
> So little of us remains round the decay of that colossal wreck, boundless and bare. The lone and level sands stretch far away.

I went to the kitchen to get a cup of tea, and when I returned to the set, they were showing a picture of cargo being loaded onto an ocean freighter. Mike Wallace was talking:

WALLACE: Buried in the Senate version of the massive tax-cut bill the Congress is putting together to aid our sick economy is a little-known, little-understood provision that could significantly change the relationship between you and the company you work for. That provision would make some of you part owners, along with your employers.

The author of the plan is a maverick economist who has caught the imagination of the chairman of the Senate Finance Committee, Russell Long. Long believes the plan might just be the way to break the boom-and-bust cycle that periodically produces a depression in the United States. Here's how the plan would work.

The men who work on this dock in Oakland, California, work for the Matson Lines, and they earn a good wage here. But if they lose their jobs, they'll earn nothing or they'll go on welfare because all they own is the sweat of their brow, their labor.

But the folks who own the equipment on these docks—that crane, these ships—the stockholders of the Matson Company, they don't have to show up here, and yet they earn a yearly income just the same because they own capital instruments. They own this equipment.

Well, there's a fellow across the bay in San Francisco who says that all the workers on this dock—indeed, all wage earners everywhere—should own a piece of the outfit that they work for, should own a piece of the action.

His name is Louis Kelso. He's a millionaire corporation lawyer who puts together multimillion-dollar business deals. Kelso argues that if capitalism is good for the rich, then everyone should be able to play. Otherwise, warns Kelso, our society as we know it will wither and die.

Ah, yes—Kelso. I remembered reading a short article about him in *Business Week* a few years ago, something about issuing stock to workers and using this as a way to finance business operations. I also remembered reading in a recent aviation magazine that Senator Russell Long was trying to force Pan American Airways to adopt Kelso's method of financing if they wanted the government to help them out of their financial squeeze. I didn't know whether there was anything to Kelso's theory or how it worked. I had filed this information in the back of my mind along with a dozen other economic theories. I just assumed that if any of these theories were valid, the people in charge of our economy would check them out and put them into operation sooner or later.

Now Wallace was interviewing Kelso:

KELSO: The death of the economy is the first step in the death of a civilization. This economy has stopped growing.

WALLACE: For years, Kelso has been hopping around the country like an itinerant preacher delivering his sermon. He tells anyone who'll listen what he told the economic leaders assembled by President Ford: that proposals for more tax cuts and more welfare will never solve the economic mess we're in. They don't go to the root of the problem, he said.

Americans, says Kelso, are a nation of industrial sharecroppers who work for somebody else and have no other source of income. If a man owns something that will produce a second income, says Kelso, he'll be a better customer for the things that American industry produces. But the problem is how to get the working man that second income.

KELSO: How do you use the logic of corporate finance, the logic that the corporation insists upon as minimal—that is, the logic of investing in things that will pay for themselves—how do you use it for the individual? How do you bring the economic game down from the corporation to the human scale?

WALLACE: Here is what Kelso would do. He would have every company set up something called an *employee stock ownership plan*—an *ESOP,* for short—an employees' trust. That trust would then go to a bank and borrow money to buy stock in the company the employees work for when that company wants to expand. And, says Kelso, it wouldn't cost the employees a penny out of their paychecks to buy the stock to build a new plant because the loan would be paid back out of profits produced by that new plant. That's the way business always operates: borrow, and pay back out of profits.

Why would a company want to do this? Because it's a cheap way to finance its growth. Under our tax laws, you see, an employee stock ownership plan is a tax-exempt trust. With Uncle Sam getting no cut, if the new plant cost $1 million to build, the company would only have to funnel $1 million of its profits back through the ESOP to pay off the loan. If there were no tax-exempt ESOP, it would take more than twice as much of the profits to pay off the loan and the taxes.

Kelso says the government would make up those lost taxes because as the employees start getting dividends from their stock, they'll all be in a higher personal income tax bracket. But more important, the cost of government, he says, will shrink as fewer people need to get government handouts.

KELSO: We know how to build goods and services, but we don't know how to produce customers. You're attacking poverty by attacking its causes—that is, by making the average man more productive (because he not only has a job; he has a capital estate that's growing, a capital estate that will support him, whether he's too old to work or sick or technologically unemployed or whatever)—and there isn't a single trace of labor power that isn't being targeted on by some piece of machinery.

WALLACE: Here's an example of what Lou Kelso means. Just half a dozen years ago, it took 600 men two weeks to unload and reload a ship like this. Well, today, with all this new equipment—cranes, straddle carriers, containers —it takes 100 men two and a half days to do the same job.

This kind of automation has been going on across America for twenty years. And Kelso has been arguing for ESOPs for nearly twenty years. But few businesses have seen fit to adopt his plan. The ones that have are mostly small.

I liked this Kelso. He was a peppery, white-haired little fellow wearing a polka dot bow tie, and he spoke with conviction and sincerity. He also seemed to be making some sense. His pixieish appearance made me think of Edmund Gwenn playing Santa Claus in the film *A Miracle on 34th Street*. Indeed, his idea that capitalism should include everyone sounded like it could only come from Santa Claus. I put the mail aside and found myself starting to root for this feisty lawyer and his vision of a new age of universal affluence and happiness. Maybe I was being selfish; he was a lawyer trying to do something good for everyone. After Watergate and the Nixon administration, we lawyers were sorely in need of a win.

> WALLACE: This is the Los Angeles warehouse of Infant Specialties, one of the 150-odd companies in America which have adopted ESOP, the employee stock ownership plan. A year ago, the seventy-five employees of this company were told that they were going to become part owners, stockholders, in Infant Specialties, and without putting up a penny of their own money. The man who did it for them, the man who took over this company a year ago, is John Carter.
>
> How much did you pay for this company a year ago when you bought it?
>
> CARTER: Just $1 million.
>
> WALLACE: How much of your own money did you put up?
>
> CARTER: I and some colleagues put up $250,000.
>
> WALLACE: So you borrowed the other $750,000.
>
> CARTER: That's right.
>
> WALLACE: You went to an ESOP. Why?
>
> CARTER: I wanted the employees to buy this company. I wanted them to pay off this loan because I wanted to be sure that they were working on my side and make my investment a good investment.

WALLACE: So they will own their stock? They'll own 75 percent of this company in eight years?

CARTER: Even more! Right!

WALLACE: Of course, Carter's rosy predictions may not pan out. The business could go sour, but the employees wouldn't have any personal liability. As in any other bankruptcy, the creditors would just seize whatever assets the corporation has.

The picture changed to a shot of Kelso sitting in the office of Senator Russell Long.

WALLACE: Russell Long, chairman of the Senate Finance Committee, is Lou Kelso's most ardent supporter on Capitol Hill. He is pushing to make the ESOP a major form of corporate financing.

LONG: Now, what you're trying to do here deserves a trial. It has been very successful where tried, but so far hasn't been tried on a big scale that it ought to be tried on.

KELSO: In the "big world"—right, right.

LONG: Yes. And I think we're going to get that.

This was getting exciting. Senator Long was not noted for addiction to crackpot ideas, and now that Wilbur Mills had faded from the scene, Long was easily the most influential man in Washington on tax legislation. Quickly, I began to tick off possible obstacles to Kelso. How would labor leaders feel about turning workers into stockholders?

WALLACE: Getting ESOP into the big time means winning over big labor, and that's a formidable stumbling block. Kelso outlined his plan to the Executive Board of the National Maritime Union, who looked at him with some suspicion.

NATIONAL MARITIME UNION EXECUTIVE: When I first read your plan, I saw the whole thing as a union-busting plan. If we're going to be representing workers who are now going to be part of management, they're going to be stockholders in the company, why are they going to need us as union leaders?

KELSO: The union will represent the workers as workers in all of the aspects that it represents them today: wages, hours, working conditions. And it will represent them as stockholders, as owners. I can't believe, for example, that Penn Central could have gotten away with what it did if its employees had owned a significant piece of Penn Central.

This sounded a little unrealistic, but with all the troubles of the economy today, I felt that the opposition of labor leaders could not destroy a plan that seemed to promise so much to the employer *and* employees.

Then the scene shifted to a college campus.

WALLACE: Labor is not alone in its hostility toward Kelsoism. The traditional economists don't like him very much either.

Louis Kelso complains there is a conspiracy of silence about him in the economic fraternity. They won't talk about him, he says; but worse still, they won't argue with him.

Well, there is one economist who will: Nobel Prize-winning economics professor here at the Massachusetts Institute of Technology, Paul Samuelson.

Here comes the end of the pipe dream, I thought. It was just like Mike Wallace to take us through ten minutes of utopia and then shatter the whole thing with a haymaker by Professor Samuelson. The only question was: How would he do it? Would Samuelson pull out a long computer readout sheet, showing at the bottom line that Kelso's plan would bankrupt the United States in 23.0849 months? Or would the professor pull down a dusty volume from his book shelf, pointing out that Kelso's plan had been tried in Upper Bavaria in 1872 under the regime of Finance Minister Bruno von Dummkopf, who spent the end of his life in an insane asylum while his nation attempted to recover from a financial panic? The camera zeroed in on Samuelson's horn-rimmed glasses as he got ready for the kill.

WALLACE: You consign Kelso to—?

PAUL SAMUELSON: Oh, I—I have not met Mr. Kelso. I don't object to anyone pushing his thing, I'm sure he's sincere.

WALLACE: He remains an amateur crank?

SAMUELSON: Your words.

WALLACE: No, no! *Your* words!

SAMUELSON: I think that Kelsoism at this point of scientific knowledge has—is amateur crank, like other interesting forms of alchemy.

WALLACE: Samuelson never made it clear just why he so disdainfully dismisses Kelso's ESOP plan. His main objection seems to be that the ESOP plan is predicated on loopholes in the tax laws.

SAMUELSON: It really has a Marie Antoinette-ish ring to it. "Let them own capital!"

The camera then cut to Kelso.

WALLACE: Paul Samuelson calls Louis Kelso an amateur crank. How come?

KELSO: I'm in the position of Pasteur (not a doctor) coming in and saying to the doctors, "If you'll do it a different way, the thing will work." And they said, "Pasteur's a crank. He's a chemist. He should stay the hell out of medicine and not mess around." This is exactly what this professional credentialism of the professional economists amounts to. When it comes to saving the society, which is in very grave danger, or saving their faces, they will never make the wrong decision. They will save their faces.

Now Samuelson was back on the screen.

WALLACE: All right. My understanding of Kelsoism is that it's designed to enable men who are born without capital to buy it, to pay for it out of the income it produces, to own it, and thereafter to receive income from that capital. Devoutly to be wished?

SAMUELSON: Oh, yes. And it would be nice to have lollipops grow on trees for the picking.

WALLACE: The only thing that you object to, really, in Kelsoism is the fact that it uses a tax loophole to give the workers stock in the company?

SAMUELSON: That is my primary criticism. Now, you tell me that Senator Long is interested in this. I'm distressed. I'm distressed because Senator Long is an influential senator in connection with the closing of tax loopholes and the opening of them.

Tax loopholes? Even I knew that this was hardly a scientific criticism of an economic theory. Wages, pensions, and profit-sharing plans are tax loopholes, too, in the sense that the employer gets a tax deduction for paying them to employees. But what has that got to do with the validity of Kelso's theories? And who ever heard of a tax loophole for the benefit of blue-collar workers? Suddenly, I recalled that Samuelson and many of his academic colleagues had labored mightily at President Ford's Economic Summit Conference in September 1974 and had brought forth as their combined wisdom the ultimate tax loophole: a tax rebate of $100 to $200 for every taxpayer in the country.

But surely Wallace was only prolonging the agony. The program still had a few minutes to go, and no doubt he would bring Samuelson back to lower the boom and spoil the evening for all those who longed for an economic miracle.

Meanwhile, Wallace was talking to Senator Long.

> LONG: What he calls a "tax loophole" is there already. It was there when I became a senator, twenty-six years ago. There are all sorts of things like that in the tax code. I could dredge up a hundred of them for you very easily. The question is: Do they achieve a desirable social purpose? I think that the idea of encouraging the people who work for a company to own an interest in the company is sufficiently socially desirable to give it favorable tax treatment.
>
> We're going to be asked to bail out a lot of companies like the Penn Central, Lockheed, and others. Right now, we're being asked to help Pan American. And I'm telling Pan American Airways, when I—if you fellows want us to put government money behind your company and save your big airline for you, I want you to have an employee stock ownership plan for those employees who right now are out lobbying to try to help save that company.
>
> WALLACE: Lou Kelso says that this will stimulate the economy. And what will it do to the current recession?
>
> LONG: It will bring more production to your economy and therefore more wealth to your economy.

The scene changed once more, back to Kelso.

> WALLACE: It's almost like Alice in Wonderland, sitting here at a time when unemployment rates are rising, when

inflation has been skyrocketing, when the economy is apparently in recession and conceivably going into depression. And you're talking as though—

KELSO: The problems are solvable.

WALLACE: Right.

KELSO: Well, we've had forty years of Mr. Samuelson's brand of economics, and it brings us right back to where we started: another depression. It's perfectly obvious that something's missing. And I say that the thing that's missing is we're pretending that you can solve the income-distribution problems solely through employment. In the meanwhile, the scientist, the engineer, and the manager is hell-bent on destroying employment. That's how he measures his success: how much employment he can destroy.

WALLACE: By putting in machines?

KELSO: By substituting machines for men, right.

WALLACE: So let the unemployed own machines, and everybody's going to be happy.

KELSO: Right. Unemployment is not so bad if you can afford it.

WALLACE: This week, the U.S. Senate will begin debate on the pros and cons of Louis Kelso's ESOP.

And that was it. Samuelson did not return. He left on the record a personal attack on Kelso and absolutely nothing by way of scientific or professional criticism. Was this the strongest case against Kelso that could be mustered by the giant of establishment economics with all the facilities of MIT behind him? If so, might there be something to the theories of Louis Kelso–Edmund Gwenn–Santa Claus?

I decided to try to find out. The rest of this book is the story of how I pursued the answer to that question for more than a year and what I found out.

MOOD INDIGO

The leaders of nations are assembled to prove to consumers that they control the economy, rather than blind forces.
> Secretary of State Henry A. Kissinger, Chateau de Rambouillet, France, November 16, 1975

Whether consumers believe it is another question.
> Tom Brokaw, NBC News, Chateau de Rambouillet

What's Wrong with the American Economy?

Even before the Kelso-Samuelson telecast, I had been worried about the economy in a vague way. Obviously, something was wrong. But like most people, I felt that the solutions should be left to the experts. "60 Minutes" gave me second thoughts about the experts and about the system itself. I decided to read everything I could find that gave any hint about what was wrong and how it could be fixed. As it turned out, there was plenty of reading material on what's wrong but practically nothing intelligible about how to fix it. This chapter is a scrapbook of published statements about U.S. economic problems in 1975 and 1976. As you read it, you will see why I decided to take a closer look at Kelso.

I had first read a little about Kelso in the late 1960s, but I did nothing about it. Like almost everybody else at that time, I felt that the economy was in great shape. Why tinker with it? Capitalism or free enterprise or the American way was working beautifully. There were decent jobs available, it seemed, for practically everyone who wanted to work. There was plenty of capital around for old and new businesses. And fortunes were being made in the stock market nearly every day.

In his 1975 book *Money* John Kenneth Galbraith sums up this era:

The twenty years from 1948 through 1967 may well be celebrated by historians as the most benign era in the history of the industrial economy, as also of economics. The two decades were without panic, crisis, depression or more than minor recession. . . . It was a very difficult time for critics of the capitalist system.

But by the time of the Kelso telecast in 1975, all this had changed. Instead of having faith in the economic system and its experts, things had reached the point where the secretary of state had to reassure the world that "blind forces" were not in control of the economy—and nobody really believed him. How did all this happen?

In putting together my scrapbook, I didn't bother with antiestablishment papers such as the *Village Voice* or *Rolling Stone;* I didn't have to. I started with the people who were most likely to minimize the economy's defects and stand for the status quo. I found that the economics establishment itself was bewildered and worried—worried enough to talk about it.

The title of this chapter comes from the title of an article by Vermont Royster, the star of the editorial page of the *Wall Street Journal*. In his regular column, "Thinking Things Over," on December 31, 1975, Royster said that he had found a general lack of faith in the future of America as the country moved into the bicentennial year. He had just finished a trip around the country and had recorded some of his impressions:

Most of the people, moreover, are well aware of their general good fortune. If you ask them, singly or in groups, they will confess it. Only in the worst parts of the inner cities will you find visible signs to mar the picture of a country still vigorous on its 200th birthday.

All the more curious, then, to find in so many places a sort of blue mood settling over the country, especially among the vast numbers of the middle-class who have been, and still are, the chief beneficiaries of the American dream.

Royster was not alone in his "Mood Indigo." The entire editorial page of the *Wall Street Journal* for that last day of 1975 was covered with similar statements. The main editorial proclaimed the failure of Keynesian economics, concluding on this tenuous note:

So there is room for hope as well as nervousness. But we should not forget that we are dealing with something we do not understand as well as we once believed.

The other major editorials dealt with "Thoughts on Our Economic Bewilderment" and "Putting a Lid on Social Programs," which concluded with this statement:

Now many first-rate minds are searching for ways to close the gap between soaring outlays for entitlement programs and reduced federal revenues to pay for them. The gap would vanish if the economy were to recover rapidly next year, the experts note. But with a sputtering recovery, they expect it to widen.

The *National Observer*, also published by Dow Jones, carried this front-page story on January 24, 1976:

Watergate, Inflation, Crime, Drugs, and Other Ills
Leave Blue-Collar Workers Asking:
"Where Can We Turn?"

Talk to the folks who work in this country's factories and dime stores, who drive its taxicabs and build its houses, and it soon becomes apparent that it's not just an American sense of community that the nation's working class perceives as "gone for good." Morality, public and private. Economic health. Opportunities for the ordinary bloke to get ahead. The political system's potential for producing effective leadership. The chance that retirement will bring even reasonable comfort. Such things seem severely diminished in working-class Americans' eyes these days, and the perception of such trends has sent optimism scurrying from the factories and neighborhood bars of blue-collar America. In place of optimism is frustration.

Bill Moyers is one of the most perceptive commentators on the American scene. Early in 1976, he returned from a four-month nationwide tour for his public television series and had this to say about the mood of the country in an interview in *People* magazine:

What is the people's No. 1 concern?
Obviously, it's the economy. The stock market is up now, but underneath there is a profound perplexity about why capitalism can't close the last gap, why it

hasn't been able to accomplish all it has been called upon to do. This is still a bearish period in our history.

Certainly this mood of despair is not as bad as it was during the Depression?

There is a difference. In the 1930s, people tended to think that whatever their problem was, it was the result of their own failure. Now the feeling is that the institutions are failing, that individuals aren't to blame. The problems of today are so vast and interlocking that people are beginning to realize that perhaps fundamental institutional reforms are necessary for our society to correct itself.

Many public opinion polls taken in 1975 and 1976 echoed these feelings. Probably the most significant was the 1975 questionnaire sent to authors of learned articles in the *Encyclopaedia Britannica,* thousands of experts in every major field of human endeavor. The results made me gulp:

Nearly 40 percent thought that democracy as we know it will not survive this century in the United States.

When asked about the quality of life in the United States for the next generation, 22 percent thought it would be better, 42 percent thought it would be worse, and 31 percent thought it would be about the same as it is for this generation.

Nearly two out of three thought that widespread famine was inevitable in the underdeveloped countries.

This pessimism was not limited to intellectuals or blue-collar workers. T. Rowe Price, the conservative seventy-seven-year-old pioneer of investment counseling, was interviewed for *Money* magazine in December 1975. His punch line was:

I'm very worried about the great U.S.A. and the capitalistic world. You can have everything else right, but if inflation makes your currency go to nothing, all those right things are meaningless.

This was the opinion of a man known for his faith in growth stocks, a man whom many others still looked to for investment advice.

And the conservative economist who may be the last man in America who still parts his hair down the middle, Dr. Arthur F. Burns, chairman of the Board of Governors of the Federal

Reserve System, started talking the same way in 1975. In speeches at the University of Akron and the University of Georgia, he made it clear that the economy was in need of basic structural reforms.

Unemployment and Inflation

What drove Dr. Burns and other conservatives to this radical conclusion was their realization that neither wages nor prices ever come down anymore, even during recessions. The traditional fine tuning of government control knobs, which had kept inflation and unemployment at reasonable levels since World War II, had simply stopped working.

Our national economic policy, which is stated in the Employment Act of 1946, is supposed to solve these problems. The act requires the federal government to "use all practicable means" to promote maximum employment, production, and purchasing power. But it does not indicate how much unemployment should be tolerated or how much inflation. This is left up to the president and his three-man Council of Economic Advisers. When we have to struggle with both high unemployment and rapid inflation and we wind up with *stagflation,* there is a strong incentive for the administration to concentrate on control of inflation at the expense of employment. Even 9 percent unemployment, which is considered very high, seems to affect only 9 percent of the work force, but inflation clobbers everybody. How can unemployment be reduced when inflation is raging out of control? Our national economic policy runs into a stone wall, and we go back to the dole of the 1930s. The only difference is that now we are doling out a lot more money, more than any administration dares to try to raise through taxes.

Many economists and politicians have suggested that government-created public service jobs, such as the Works Progress Administration of the 1930s, are preferable to the dole. President Ford did not agree, and in 1976, his administration resisted congressional attempts to establish large public-service job programs. This set up an angry confrontation between

Ford's Council of Economic Advisers and Senator Hubert Humphrey, chairman of the Joint Economic Committee of Congress. At public hearings in January 1976, Humphrey castigated the Ford administration for failure to come up with any public-service job programs. But Alan Greenspan and Paul MacAvoy, two of the council members, told Humphrey that it takes about $50,000 of federal money to create one job paying $8,000 a year and that after three years only one or two new jobs remain out of ten supposedly created. Humphrey asked them whether they had anything to recommend other than the dole, which he thinks is the worst-possible solution ("anything is better than the dole!"). But Greenspan and MacAvoy had to admit that they had no other solution and that it seemed to be beyond the power of the present economic system to find a cure for unemployment that would not also trigger ruinous inflation.

In 1976, the Humphrey-Hawkins Full Employment and Balanced Growth Act was introduced. Its goal was to reduce adult unemployment to 3 percent within four years by making the federal government the employer of last resort. But many liberal economists found themselves in the uncomfortable position of agreeing with Professor Milton Friedman's *Newsweek* analysis:

> [Humphrey-Hawkins] is full of pious promises but contains no measures capable of fulfilling those promises. It would not reduce unemployment but simply add to government employment and reduce private employment, in the process making us all poorer and very likely igniting a new inflationary binge.

Support for Humphrey-Hawkins was so shaky that the Democratic majority did not bring it up for a vote in 1976, despite its potential value as a campaign issue if Congress had enacted it and President Ford had vetoed it.

It makes you wonder. Aren't most of us working against the national economic policy of "maximum employment?" Personally, I don't know a single owner or manager of a business who is trying to create more employment. Even in boom times, most managers try to eliminate jobs and substitute machines for human beings wherever they can. This leaves it to the government to increase employment, and as Greenspan and MacAvoy admitted, the government simply does not have the tools to create real jobs. Could there be something wrong with the national economic policy?

The story doesn't end with Greenspan and MacAvoy shuffling back to get some more money printed for the dole. Who bears the brunt of the failure of national economic policy? The minorities, the urban poor, the people at the bottom of the economic ladder. When we tolerate unemployment rates of 8 or 9 percent, this translates to 40 percent of black teen-agers, a whole generation growing up outside of our production system. And what happens then to crime rates, to racial friction, to violent destruction of property, to the American dream? A study released by the Joint Economic Committee in 1976 showed that a rise of only 1 percent in unemployment had far-reaching effects, such as sharp rises in the rates of suicides, heart attacks, liver diseases, mental illness, and imprisonment.

Many economists thought that they had a tool to deal with the inflation-unemployment problem: the Phillips curve (named after Professor A. W. Phillips of the London School of Economics). It was supposed to show the price increases that would have to be accepted to bring unemployment down to a specific level. However, as it developed, Phillips should have stuck with his fast ball, because his curve did not work. The Phillips curve is just one example of how the laws, curves, and principles of traditional economics fail to solve the stagflation problems of the 1970s.

It seems pretty clear, then, that regardless of which party is in power, there will be no quick solution of the stagflation problem—unless somebody comes up with a brilliant new idea.

Are There Any New Ideas?

You would think that a presidential campaign during troubled economic times would bring forth an outpouring of new ideas. Indeed, the entrants in the 1976 presidential sweepstakes took aboard economic advisers of impeccable academic standing: John Kenneth Galbraith (for Morris Udall), Walter W. Heller (for Sargent Shriver), Milton Friedman (for Ronald Reagan), Lawrence R. Klein (for Jimmy Carter), and so on. The list filled nine inches of double columns in the business section of the *New York Times* for Sunday, December 28, 1975. However, the lead article in that section, "Candidates in Search of Economic Wisdom," came to this jolting conclusion:

> The economy will be the biggest issue in 1976, strategists say, and the candidates are seeking wisdom. Still, they've yet to come up with a single new, imaginative idea.

One of the first candidates to issue a detailed economic policy statement was Sargent Shriver. It included this bit of logic, which should make you sleep easier tonight:

(a) If we can reduce unemployment, we will be able to reduce the federal budget deficit, which is caused in large part by unemployment.

(b) Our best means of reducing unemployment is to spend more federal funds, which increases the deficit.

(c) Therefore, the way to reduce the deficit is to increase the deficit.

This looks like something out of a Bob Hope script, but the men who wrote it are not clowns. Shriver has had a brilliant career as a lawyer, businessman, organizer-director of the Peace Corps, and ambassador to France. When his campaign economic adviser, Walter Heller, was chairman of the Council of Economic Advisers under Kennedy and Johnson from 1961 to 1964, inflation and unemployment were kept at reasonable levels. We must assume that the policy of reducing the deficit by increasing the deficit is the best that these highly skilled professionals can turn out under the present system. Maybe that's why conservatives such as Arthur Burns are starting to talk about restructuring the system.

Writing in the *New York Times Magazine* in February 1976, Russell Baker summed up the situation:

> In Washington, almost everybody of importance, man and woman, has run out of imagination. Wit's end seems not far off. All that remains to talk about is how the money is dwindling away and whether the next bank-loan

payment can be met. The business of the Republic has become a glum quibble among bookkeepers. We are in the hands of men who make no music and have no dream.

John Kenneth Galbraith has always been one of my heroes, mainly because he has the rare ability to make interesting reading out of economics. When I decided to look into Kelso's theories I turned immediately to Galbraith's works and was happy to learn that he was coming out with a new book, *Money: Whence It Came, Where It Went.*

Money, which was published in 1975, is fascinating reading. Galbraith shows how we got into this mess. He explains that Keynesian economics has the fatal flaw of inelasticity, which makes it practically useless against inflation. (Keynes, by the way, was Galbraith's great hero.) He says that the final straw was reliance on monetary policy (control of money supply), which was not up to the job of controlling inflation. I absorbed the beautifully written history lessons and eagerly approached the last chapter, hoping that the great professor would point the way out of the wilderness.

It was a big letdown. Galbraith is much more than a historian, and he does set down his ideas for recovery. But the only real change he recommends is revival of wage and price controls. He keeps going back to his successful experience as a price administrator during World War II, but he disagrees with the opinion of most other economists that wage-price controls will work in this country only in wartime.

Galbraith explains the market power of big corporations and big unions, which puts them beyond the natural forces that would otherwise check inflation. He says that the only way to halt inflation is to curb this market power by government wage and price controls of the "big" sector. He would leave the smaller areas of business and labor (including agriculture) out of the control system because he thinks that they do respond to market forces and that they are not the real problems. He states his case eloquently, but the fact is that he is practically alone in his belief that controls can work in democracies in peacetime. Obviously, such controls are much more effective in countries in which the government does not have to bother with the inconveniences of democracy and freedom. Examples: India and Brazil.

Threat to Democracy

In June 1975, India was facing severe problems that sounded very familiar: rapid inflation, unemployment, poverty, corruption in government, and increasing crime. Prime Minister Indira Gandhi was also facing a personal challenge to her election campaign practices. At that point, she simply ended democracy in India. She jailed more than 1,000 political opponents, effectively silenced all cricitism, and proceeded to seize almost absolute government power.

And what did this accomplish for India? In the first six months of the Gandhi dictatorship, she was able to claim that she halted inflation, brought labor and management together to eliminate strikes and lockouts, made inroads into unemployment and poverty, and cut back sharply on crime, violence, and corruption. She also claims to be enforcing the collection of taxes from the rich for the first time in India's history.

Of course, India is not the United States. Indian democracy was only twenty-five years old when Indira Gandhi folded it up, and its 600 million people have problems that are not shared by the American people. But the fact that the ending of democracy also seems to have solved India's severe economic crisis is frightening. If things get worse in the United States, we may be led to the conclusion that the only way we can get out of the hole is to suspend democracy. If you think this can't happen, take a look at the views of eight leading world scholars in a sixteen-page study, "Is Democracy Dying?" published in *U.S. News & World Report,* March 8, 1976.

In the 1960s, Brazil suffered some of the worst inflation in the world, long before it hit Western democracies. Yet, in 1975, the Brazilian military had been in control of the government for nearly ten years and had managed to bring inflation and other economic problems under far greater control than their democratic predecessors had.

These examples make us realize that when our free-enterprise–capitalistic–private property economy is threatened by inflation, unemployment, and other problems, we are also facing potential threats to democracy-liberty-freedom.

Nineteen seventy-five turned out to be a bad year for democracy-liberty-freedom. An organization in New York called Freedom House, headed by former Maine Senator Margaret Chase Smith, keeps a worldwide scorecard of political and civil rights. Their report for 1975 showed losses of freedom for 743.2 million persons in eight countries, which brought the worldwide percentage of persons living in freedom down from 35 percent in 1974 to 19.8 percent in 1975. If you deduct from this 19.8 percent the many millions who are living in theoretical political freedom but who have little or no economic freedom, you come to realize that the United States is one of a shrinking number of islands of free enterprise in an ocean of government-controlled economies. And if you follow the trends of the Freedom House reports, you can see that government control of the economy is often followed by reductions in political and personal freedom. For example, in 1975, Freedom House moved Sweden, a democracy, down one notch on the political freedom scale because "political rights were somewhat hampered" and the country was governed by an "entrenched bureaucracy."

Many well-intentioned people who believe in democracy but who feel that capitalism must fail eventually, point to Sweden as an example of successful democratic socialism. Sweden is a nation of only 8 million people, mostly homogeneous; but even on their ideal scale, they are having trouble maintaining democracy in a welfare state. Inflation and heavy transfer payments are taking their toll. In 1976, Prime Minister Olof Palme tried to shift the entire burden of health insurance and pensions to corporations and the self-employed, thereby reducing workers' taxes by about 10 percent in an election year. As a result, the 500,000 self-employed Swedes must pay taxes of 101.2 percent of all income over $35,000. Yes, that's 101.2 percent, meaning that you lose money by making more than $35,000!

Even though most of the rest of the world is turning toward socialism (democratic or otherwise), there is still no great movement in that direction in the United States. The overwhelming defeat of George McGovern by Richard Nixon in 1972 showed that. The great majority of U.S. economists and politicians are struggling to find a way to make capitalism work. And it appears that most Americans would prefer to stick with capitalism as long as it continues to bring them a high standard of living and a realistic hope for a better future.

There is no point in changing over to democratic socialism until we find out whether capitalism really works. To do this, we have to understand what capitalism really is and whether it can be made to work for everyone. But there was no political candidate in 1976 who defined capitalism, suggested any national economic policy for capitalism, or tried to tell us how capitalism could work for everyone.

Just How Bad Are Things?

There are still plenty of respectable authorities around who feel that America will pull out of its slump and get back into the growth pattern of the 1960s. They say that we have been hit by three unforeseeable catastrophies back to back: Vietnam, Watergate, and the quadrupling of oil prices. They claim that our survival of these catastrophes shows how strong our basic system really is and that we just need a few years to adjust to these problems.

Those who still have faith in the system like to point out that despite all our troubles, the official U.S. poverty level of about $5,000 annual income per family of four would be considered affluent by most of the people in the world today, even though our poverty statistics are based on the cost of a "nutritionally adequate food plan" designed by the Department of Agriculture for "emergency or temporary use when funds are low." To me, that's not very relevant. There is no point in comparing a family in the United States with one in Honduras. The real test is what the economy is producing for the American family today—by our standards, weighed against our potential, our desires, our driving forces.

I am not a pessimist by nature, but my 1975–1976 scrapbook tells me that things may actually be a lot worse than they
seem on the surface. We seem to be falling into a trap of trying
to live with inflation, accepting it as inevitable because our
economists and politicians can't come up with a cure. In fact,
we've built even more inflation into the system by providing
automatic increases in social security payments and automatic
wage raises to many workers whenever the consumer price index goes up. This quote from a Sylvia Porter column of October 1975 will give you an idea of why we can't live with
inflation:

> If prices were to continue soaring at the 12.2 per cent rate
> of 1974, the value of the $1 that bought you 100 cents of
> goods and services in the marketplace at the start of 1975
> would be worth only 51 cents in 1980, only 36 cents in
> 1983, only 26 cents a mere 10 years from now, only 5 cents
> by the year 2000! Today's price level would double as
> early as 1980, triple by 1983, quadruple within the decade
> and be 10 times as high in 2000 as now.
>   You couldn't make stable plans for the future—to
> educate your children, to save for your independence, to
> do anything, really. Living month to month, your very ex-
> pectations of the disaster of relentlessly galloping infla-
> tion would help make the disaster a self-fulfilling
> prophecy.
>   A certain result would be the death of the private
> enterprise system as we have known it.

Even the most optimistic politicians don't talk about
eliminating inflation; they just hope they can bring it down to 3
or 4 percent and keep it there. But if you think that would be a
great accomplishment, consider the calculations offered by the
distinguished management expert Professor Peter F. Drucker in
his 1976 book *The Unseen Revolution:*

> Continuing inflation, even at a low rate (say 2 or 3 per-
> cent a year) erodes the value of the provisions for retire-
> ment. A 3 percent inflation rate halves the value of the
> average pension dollar, that is, the dollar which a worker
> in his early forties puts in to get retirement benefits
> at age sixty-five. Double-digit inflation actually destroys
> a pension fund within a few short years. Provisions for
> the future are meaningful only if the purchasing power
> of money can be assumed to be reasonably stable.

Even if inflation is cut to half the 1974 figure, you can
see that we are still in plenty of trouble, especially because
everything we do to fight unemployment seems to force inflation back up toward double digits. And Professor Galbraith
points out in *Money* that the countries of Central Europe that
suffered ruinous inflation after World War I fell into "Fascism,
Communism or in most cases—Poland, Hungary, East Germany—both."

The bicentennial celebration was surprisingly peaceful
and happy throughout the country, and it lifted our spirits. As
Mary McGrory wrote of the Washington festivities:

> All the ugliness and meanness of the sixties was washed
> away in a flood tide of jubilation. Pride and joy, which
> had not shown their faces in these parts for 10 years,
> suddenly reappeared and took over. Patriotism, which
> had been reckoned the last refuge of scoundrels during
> the Vietnam-Watergate era, came back to a hero's wel-
> come.

As I watched the tall ships and the fireworks bursting
around the Statue of Liberty, I felt confident for the first time
that nobody would have the nerve to put New York into bankruptcy. This kind of bicentennial logic affected many of us; it
made us turn our binoculars the long way and look back on all
that our country had accomplished in 200 years. It also made us
look forward with the same long view toward the next 100
years, a more pleasant aspect than the next ten years. Politicians
and futurists were telling us that the United States had the
resources to wipe out poverty and that we would certainly do it
by 2076. But nobody had a game plan for 1977.

Supposedly, we were in a strong economic upswing in
1976. But youngsters graduating from college had great difficulty finding decent jobs, and most young married couples
could not even think about buying a house. The *average* new
house sold for $50,000 in 1976, the kind of house that would
have sold for about half that in 1967. General Motors announced that the *average* price of their 1977 autos would be
$6,000. The Census Bureau announced that the number of
Americans below the poverty line rose by 2.5 million in 1975,
the largest increase in any year since the bureau started keeping

poverty statistics in 1959. Unemployment remained well over 7 percent, and inflation was not far behind, with everybody waiting for the next wave of inflation to come on as soon as we made a real effort to cut unemployment. The official inflation rate of 6 to 8 percent did not even try to measure the hidden inflation reflected in the erosion of quality. (Think of the parts of your automobile that are now made of cardboard and the inside sections that are not painted.) In calling 1976 a year of recovery, what we've really done is switch labels. Just a couple of years ago, unemployment and inflation figures of 7 percent would have been labeled "disaster." In 1976, they were labeled "economic upswing."

If these are the good times, what will the next bad times be like?

Today's inflation even makes our measuring standards obsolete. The 1975 financial statements of major businesses gave a distorted picture of profits and financial health because they did not show the effects of inflation on inventory or on the cost of replacing facilities and machines as they wear out. For example, if a machine cost a company $100,000 in 1966 and had a service life of ten years, the company would deduct from its profits $10,000 a year for ten years so that when the machine wore out in 1976, they would have a depreciation reserve of $100,000 to replace the machine. But in 1976, the same machine would probably cost $200,000 or more to replace. This means that the company overstated its profits by at least $100,000 by not allowing for the true replacement cost of the machine.

In 1975, the Securities and Exchange Commission (SEC) proposed a change in accounting rules to force disclosure of replacement costs for both inventory and depreciation. This reform was vigorously opposed by accountants and corporate financial officers but was finally adopted as an SEC requirement for corporations with assets of $100 million or more, starting with 1976 reports. A 1975 analysis by Dr. Larry Long and Angela Falkenstein of Legg Mason, a highly regarded Washington securities research service, showed that making allowance for true replacement costs would reduce 1974 total corporate profits from the reported $73.3 billion to $23.8 billion (in 1974 dollars). Legg Mason went a step farther and translated these figures into constant 1965 dollars (i.e., using the purchasing power of the dollar in 1965 instead of its reduced purchasing power in 1974). In constant 1965 dollars, they found that true corporate profits for 1974 would be only $14 billion, less than one-fifth the amount reported to the public. So when you see a story about "record profits" of an industry or a company, you'll probably get a more accurate picture if you divide the current profits by 4 or 5.

The constant-dollar measuring standard can be very embarrassing to anyone claiming economic success today because it often shows how little real progress (if any) has been made since the mid-1960s. James R. Schlesinger, in his first major statement since his removal as secretary of defense, wrote in *Fortune:* "In constant dollars, defense investment has shrunk to less than half of the 1968 level and 35 percent below the pre-Vietnam level."

Schlesinger pointed up one of the most frightening aspects of inflation: it is shooting down unbuilt U.S. bombers and sinking unlaunched U.S. ships at a pace that is bound to make the Russians happy. Schlesinger, a man who measures his words very carefully, feels that because of this shrinking defense investment, "At no point since the 1930s has the Western world faced so formidable a threat to its survival." He told a chilling story of our navy's response to the *Mayaguez* incident: The first ship on the scene developed serious power problems, and two aircraft carriers assigned to the engagement never got there at all because of mechanical breakdowns of old equipment.

Even though we are talking about a defense budget of over $100 billion in 1977, the highest in U.S. history, inflation brings the real effect down to a deterrent that looks weaker and weaker against the Russian military buildup. Schlesinger and lots of other knowledgeable people are very worried about what the Russians might do to exploit this weakness. In their eyes, our survival as a nation may depend on our ability to get our economy back on the track so that we can afford to match Russian defense budgets and provide a real basis for détente.

Even though bankruptcy seems to be our fastest-growing industry today, perhaps things are not so bad as they seem. We know more about the nation's problems than our parents did because we are bombarded by three hours of mostly bad news every night on television. We are better educated, more involved in government and politics, and we have many more research tools, indexes, and information services to tell us how serious our troubles are. Maybe if we'd had all these tools in 1930, we would have given up capitalism right there and missed out on the golden decades of the 1950s and 1960s. Also, we expect and demand much more from our government and our country than anyone ever has before. This new phenomenon, labeled "the revolution of rising expectations" by Harvard sociologist Daniel Bell, also goes under the name of *egalitarianism,* meaning equality of results, instead of mere equality of opportunity or legal rights.

Of course, the end result of a completely egalitarian approach to the economy would be the reduction of every family's income to the lowest common denominator. Even the liberal wing of the Democratic party does not support egalitarian leveling of the economy, but liberals do push in the *direction* of egalitarianism by supporting massive redistribution of income to achieve a better break for the underprivileged. At the conclusion of *Money,* Galbraith says that he thinks we will have to move toward "a more consciously egalitarian income distribution," although he seems to relate this to equity rather than complete equality of result.

Appearing on David Susskind's program in December 1975, novelist Gore Vidal provided an unusual slant on television's role in egalitarianism. He said that American television, which was supposed to be a pacifier for the poor, actually is making the "class war" worse because the television commercials showing fine things that the poor can't afford make the gap much more visible to them. Vidal also thinks that successful violence shown on television news programs has inspired bolder moves by the poor and has increased the threat to the richer elements of our society.

The egalitarian thrust will probably be held off as long as capitalism continues to produce a reasonably high standard of living for the great majority of Americans. But when the standard of living starts to slip and stays off track for any long period, you can expect egalitarians to push forward with greater demands for leveling what is left of income.

Transfer Payments

Already, egalitarianism has increased the pressure for redistribution, or *transfer payments.* In 1975, transfer payments by the federal government were being made at the rate of $146 billion per year, escalating to about $168 billion in 1976. This represents over 40 percent of the entire federal budget. The biggest chunk of transfer payments is $95 billion per year for social security and federal pensions (up from $33 billion in 1969). Other transfer payments include veterans' benefits ($11.9 billion in 1975, against $7 billion in 1969), unemployment compensation to working people who lose their jobs ($13.6 billion in 1975, up from $2.9 billion in 1969), welfare payments to needy people other than those who have recently lost jobs ($15.6 billion in 1975, compared with $3.9 billion in 1969), and medical care for the elderly and poor ($24 billion in 1975, compared with $9 billion in 1969). More than half of the national budget is now spent on federal domestic social programs. About one-third of the national budget is spent by the Department of Health, Education, and Welfare. In 1965, transfer payments were equal to 6.9 percent of total wages and salaries earned in the United States. In early 1975, transfer payments amounted to 21.4 percent of wages and salaries, so transfer payments *tripled* in proportion to wages between 1965 and 1975.

I don't know whether all these expenditures are necessary or desirable, but it seems clear that no administration, Democratic or Republican, is going to make much of a dent in these figures very soon. They have been assumed as fixed costs of maintaining our society. They can be reduced only by improving the economy or changing the system so that they will not be necessary. Otherwise, any government, regardless of party, is going to have to meet these bills through increased taxation, continued erosion of the value of the dollar, or both. As the

1976 elections approached, I realized that the voters had no real choice, no way to avoid these huge transfer payments.

The huge growth of transfer payments has had some very serious side effects. Harvard economist Martin Feldstein concluded in 1975 that the American system of unemployment insurance actually *creates* more unemployment. He thinks that it encourages recipients of aid to remain unemployed longer and makes it easier for companies to lay off workers, especially in seasonal and cyclical industries. Feldstein says that although unemployment benefits are supposed to be pegged at about 35 to 50 percent of a worker's wages, they really amount to much more because the benefits are exempt from taxes, the employee is relieved of the expenses of going to work, and the worker's family may become eligible for other benefits.

In 1975, New York State Senator William T. Smith II headed a state commission to study transfer payments. He reported that the average gross earnings of employees covered by unemployment insurance in New York State was $10,433. A worker in that bracket with a wife and two children would have net income of $8,110 after deducting taxes, transportation, meals, and union dues. If that worker was laid off, the income from various forms of government benefits available to him and his family would total $10,342 net after taxes, over $2,000 more than he would take home if he worked. Smith's report concluded:

> A state can ill afford to set welfare benefits at levels which are as high or higher than what a significant portion of our working population receives in wages. It is unreasonable to expect taxpayers in our state to finance tax-free benefits for others which nearly equal or exceed their own incomes.

These facts were brought home to New Yorkers when first New York City and then New York State faced financial crises in 1975, rescued at the last minute by federal action that still leaves the basic problems unsolved.

With transfer payments accounting for more than 40 percent of the federal budget, you would expect that they were making distribution of income more equitable. But a 1976 staff study by the Joint Economic Committee of Congress concluded otherwise:

Redistribution of income, rather than wealth, is already being attempted through the many income support and income transfer programs now in operation. Though such programs are necessary to remove some of the hardship of poverty and to fulfill basic needs, they are still only marginally effective. Despite them, the distribution of income has remained virtually unchanged since World War II; the top quintile of the population holds just over 40 percent of the income and the lowest quintile has 5 percent. Even these figures understate how rich the rich really are, for the top quintile of families have about 80 percent of total personal wealth. Clearly, income will not become more equally distributed in this country until the base of wealth holdings is broadened.

Along with the ballooning of transfer payments has come the increased burden of government payrolls. Economists at the Ford Motor Company made a study of this trend toward government employment in 1975. They reached the conclusion that as of 1975, there were more Americans being supported by tax dollars than there were workers in the private sector to support them. We had only 71 million nongovernment workers, compared with 80 million "tax dependents" consisting of government employees; military personnel; the disabeled, retired, and unemployed; and those on welfare. Of course, government workers also pay taxes, and some of them contribute productive services. But the plight of New York City and the precarious position of many other city and state governments, as well as that of the federal government, make it clear that this trend cannot continue much longer without reaching a breaking point.

One of the most sensitive spots is social security. Many articles and television programs during 1975 alerted us to the fact that the social security system was in deep trouble. I was startled to learn that the social security trust fund is not like the reserves that insurance companies set up to pay future claims. In fact, social security is not really insurance; it is more like an intergenerational transfer program. There is a trust fund that used to accumulate benefit money fifteen to twenty years in advance of payment, but this has slipped to the point where the contributions of today's workers are needed to pay benefits to those now retired or disabled.

Inflation is one cause of the social security trust fund's problems, but there is another. Since the start of social security in 1935, Americans have increased their average life span and have been retiring earlier. Today, the majority of Americans live past working age and draw retirement benefits. This puts greatly increased pressure on those who are working now to support higher social security payments, as well as government pensions and veterans' benefits, which are also affected by this change in the age of the population.

We who are working today will have to rely on the willingness of the next two generations to continue to make large payments so that we can collect our benefits. Despite an increase of 42 percent in the social security bite since 1973, inflation forced President Ford to ask for still another boost in his 1976 budget message. And if inflation continues, nobody can tell you how much of your future earnings you will have to pay in taxes to support those now retired, particularly in view of the fact that social security benefits increase automatically as the consumer price index rises. A 1976 report by the chief actuary of the Social Security Administration reported that the system would be $4.3 *trillion* in the hole by the year 2050 unless taxes were raised or benefits were cut substantially.

Shortage of Capital

Now let's take a look at what has been called the *capital crunch*. This is a problem that you probably have not had to face up to directly unless you are on the board of directors or the financial staff of one of our larger corporations. But it is so critical that *Business Week* devoted a special issue to it on September 22, 1975, entitled "Capital Crisis—The $4.5 Trillion America Needs to Grow." The $4.5 trillion figure is their estimate of the capital needs of American industry for the decade 1975–1984, and at the moment, nobody knows where all this money is going to come from because the previous decade (1965–1974) required only $1.6 trillion in capital. *Business Week* said bluntly, "It is indeed naive to imagine that the capitalist-mixed economy can long survive a capital crisis." This was echoed in a 1975 news-paper advertising campaign by International Telephone and Telegraph Corporation, with the big black headline, "What Happens to Capitalism If We Run Out of Capital?"

What's more, America is way behind the other major in-dustrial nations in the percentage of its gross national product (GNP) devoted to capital formation. Here are some recent fig-ures showing percentage of GNP devoted to capital investment: Japan, 35 percent; West Germany, 25 percent; France, 24 per-cent; Italy, 20 percent; Great Britain, 18 percent; and the United States, 13 percent.

Some experts blame the capital shortage on the explosive growth of government transfer payments; some blame ecologists who have forced environmental policies that will cost industry many billions; others just blame inflation.

And what is the solution? The best that American business has been able to come up with is a proposal to reduce or wipe out the corporate income tax so that corporations can accumu-late the capital needed to keep the economy growing. Of course, this proposal was immediately labeled a big-business giveaway, just another version of the *trickledown* theory, which asks us to believe that what is good for business eventually becomes good for everybody. But trickledown can't be sold to voters or legisla-tures today; nobody believes in it anymore.

The only way to eliminate the corporate income tax is to show that this would *directly* benefit many people, not just the few who now own most of the corporate stock. But the trickle-down boys can't show that; the most they can claim is that corporations with more capital can create more jobs (assuming they don't use all the capital to buy machines that eliminate workers). As we'll see in Chapter 3, there is one man who advo-cates elimination of the corporate income tax for the *direct* benefit of people who are not now corporate stockholders: Louis Kelso.

If you doubt that we are running into a capital shortage, just take a look at the capital positions of the two principal providers of capital for the U.S. economy: banks and insurance companies. Some of the largest banks in the country were put on danger lists by the comptroller of currency during 1974 and 1975 because they had inadequate capital to meet the prospects of large losses on questionable loans then on their books. In 1976, U.S. casualty insurance companies were in perhaps the worst position they had ever been in from the standpoint of capital available for their own businesses, to say nothing of providing capital to other businesses.

The weak market for stocks during the 1970s forced many major corporations to rely too heavily on debt. This was acknowledged by Robert N. Flint, vice president and comptroller of American Telephone and Telegraph Company in his testimony before the Joint Economic Committee in December 1975. He said that between 1965 and 1975, the Bell Telephone System had been forced to increase its debt-equity ratio from 33 to 50 percent. AT&T would prefer to obtain a greater portion of this capital through the sale of stock, but under 1976 market conditions, this did not appear likely. Instead, they will have to go further into debt if they are to meet their construction expenditures of more than $10 billion a year.

If America's largest corporation (which has a legal monopoly over a vital service) is troubled by the capital crunch and has had to increase its debt dangerously, what are the prospects for the rest of American industry over the next ten years? And where will we get the research and development money that brought breakthroughs like the Polaroid camera, the Xerox copier, the transistor, along with millions of new productive jobs and billions of dollars in foreign sales?

What are the economists doing about this? Could there be some other source of capital that they are overlooking? Or could there be something wrong with the system that is causing them to look in the wrong places?

But never fear. The Brookings Institution has the answer. The huge demand for business capital can be offset by a decline in demand for funds by the federal government, they say. Translated, this means that the federal government would have to run a budget *surplus* of an average of $11.5 billion a year for the period from 1974 to 1980. The Brookings economists are not fazed by the fact that the 1976 federal budget *deficit* was over $65 billion, with no surplus in sight even in the eyes of the most optimistic administration economists. If you believe that our present economic system can achieve such surpluses, as Brookings predicts, then you will not worry about the capital crisis. Personally, I am still worried about it. In fact, I am even more worried that one of our most prestigious economic institutions has offered this as their proposed solution to the capital crisis.

What Choices Do We Have?

With stagflation and so many other economic problems plaguing the country, it is not surprising that we have started to look for some new ideas. In 1975 and 1976, a book called *Winning Through Intimidation* was prominent on the bestseller lists. The author told us how we could make money and be successful by outintimidating everyone else. He did not explain how a nation composed of expert intimidators would survive its own daily intramural confrontations. But perhaps the success of this self-improvement book is a measure of our desperation. In any event, as a lawyer, I gained comfort from this passage:

> Attorneys are not subject to intimidation like buyers, sellers and other normal people, simply because their law school brainwashing teaches them that no one has a higher station in life than a legal counselor. With that kind of self-image, how can an attorney possibly be intimidated?

Despite this gloomy economics scrapbook, I don't think that we are morally or financially bankrupt yet. The fact that there is so much discussion of the problem shows that we have a strong yearning to find a way of improving our economic system.

Economics is a highly complex subject, and it is easy to become absorbed in details and lose track of the main issues. Therefore, I think it will be helpful from time to time throughout this book to present the major issues to you in a simplified, condensed manner. I've chosen a form we are all familiar with: the multiple-choice question. Here is your first.

> Since the American economy is plagued by problems of inflation, unemployment, capital shortage, more tax de-

pendents than private-sector workers, crushing burdens
of transfer payments, erosion of the work ethic, threatened insolvency of the social security system and of many
city and state governments, and weakening of national
security:
__ (a) Our economists and politicians are so stupid that
they cannot use the devices built into our economic system to solve these problems.
__ (b) The system needs changing.

If you chose *a,* you have relieved yourself of the burden of
reading the rest of this book. I don't believe that our leading
economists and politicians are stupid. I think it is obvious that
the system needs changing. But what changes should we make,
and how?

Louis Kelso says that economists and politicians have been
looking in the wrong places. They have been focusing on jobs
and salaries and ignoring capital and wealth. John Maynard
Keynes took wealth as an almost unchangeable fact; he saw the
solution of the 1930s depression in the creation of jobs. In his
classic *General Theory of Employment, Interest, and Money,*
Keynes said:

> In so far as the distribution of wealth is determined by
> the more or less permanent social structure of the com-
> munity, this also can be reckoned a factor, subject only to
> slow change and over a long period, which we can take
> as given in our present context.

Most influential American economists are followers of
Keynes, and they, too, look upon wealth and capital ownership
as a permanent part of the social structure, rather than as a
potential tool for income distribution. Therefore, you won't find
any extensive discussion of the concentration or distribution of
wealth in any of the standard economics textbooks. Yet, if you
look into the subject, you will find that the percentage distribution of wealth in the United States is about the same as in
India.

Not everyone has missed the significance of this concentration of wealth. In *Money,* Professor Galbraith noted the predic-
tion of Karl Marx: "In the ultimate crisis capitalism, now
attenuated by concentration in the hands of the few, would be

destroyed." And historian-commentator Alistair Cooke, in his monumental book *America,* gave us this warning:

> What is fiercely in dispute between the communist and non-communist nations today is the quality and staying power of American civilization. Every other country scorns American materialism while striving in every big and little way to match it. Envy obviously has something to do with it, but there is a true basis for this debate, and it is whether America is in its ascendant or its decline.
>
> I myself think I recognize here several of the symptoms that Edward Gibbon maintained were signs of the decline of Rome, and which arose not from external enemies but from inside the country itself. A mounting love of show and luxury. A widening gap between the very rich and the very poor.

There are a few other people besides Alistair Cooke who are keeping their eyes on this widening gap between the rich and the poor. They include Louis Kelso, Senator Russell Long of Louisiana, and the U.S. Census Bureau, which keeps a head count of people who fall below the poverty line. In 1976, the bureau released its poverty line report for 1974, which showed that "inflation widened the gap between America's rich and poor in 1974 and plunged 1.3 million more persons into poverty." The Census Bureau also reported the dumbfounding fact that *all* of those 1.3 million people who fell below the $5,000 income line were employed. Families headed by nonworkers (persons on welfare, pensions, or social security) made income gains or lost no ground to inflation. This little-noticed report contains a great moral for our times: If you want to avoid poverty, stay out of work.

Traditional economics is full of acronyms, such as GNP for gross national product, and DJI for Dow Jones Industrials. Let's coin a new one: RPG, for rich-poor gap. Unlike the GNP or the DJI, you don't need any tickertapes, computers, or information services to interpret the RPG. You will know when the RPG reaches the critical level—when you hear the sound of rocks smashing your windows.

Sorry to have kept you so long with this depressing scrapbook, but you are about to have all your ideas about economics turned upside down, and it wouldn't make much sense to go through that exercise unless you are aware that we are in very deep trouble and that our choices appear to be narrowing down to socialism, communism, or a new twist on capitalism.

THE NONGRUBBY REVOLUTION

The nations of our time cannot prevent the conditions of men from becoming equal; but it depends upon themselves whether the principal of equality is to lead them to servitude or freedom, to knowledge or barbarism, to prosperity or wretchedness.
Alexis de Tocqueville, *Democracy in America*

Meeting Kelso

Soon after the March 1975 Kelso-Samuelson "60 Minutes" telecast, I decided to telephone Kelso and try to meet him. I told him that the telecast had aroused my curiosity, that I didn't know anything more about his theories than what he had said on "60 Minutes," that I was anxious to learn more, and that I thought the best way would be to meet him and discuss it over lunch. It happened that he was coming to New York in April, so we made an appointment.

When he showed up at my office on April 21, 1975, he was still wearing a blue polka dot bow tie, and he looked as peppery as he had on television—even more so. In fact, with his pixieish manners and speech, he struck me as one of the few lawyers I have ever met who seemed genuinely to enjoy all his work.

Before we went to lunch at the Sky Club, at the top of the Pan Am Building, he gave me about an hour's lecture on his economic theories and a thumbnail history of the Kelso movement. He almost bubbled over as he spoke. It was an exciting presentation *and* an entirely logical one. I kept looking for the "amateur crank" stuff, but by the time we left for lunch, he still had not said anything that sounded crankish to me.

He had to leave after lunch to catch a helicopter to New Jersey, where he was designing a stock ownership plan for employees of a large manufacturing company that needed about $20 million in working capital. I told him that I wanted to make a careful study of his theories and that if I became convinced he was on the right track, I would try to come up with some ideas on how I might be able to help. He gave me three books that he had written on universal capitalism and a lot of other literature on the subject. We agreed that I would read it all and that we would get together again in May, when he returned to New York for further work on the New Jersey deal.

We met again on May 22, 1975. This time, I met him at his suite in the Waldorf Astoria Hotel in the evening. He told me that his objective was nothing less than a "capitalist revolution" that would bring capital ownership to all people for the first time—a revolutionary idea by the standards of Adam Smith and all the economists who had followed him. Then, looking around the luxurious suite and walking me over to the well-stocked mahogany bar, he said, "But this won't be a grubby revolution. Nobody will have to eat worms!" Because this was to be my first revolution, I was happy to learn that it would be a nongrubby one.

Kelso is a very successful corporation and tax lawyer, and he sees no reason to change his elegant life-style simply because he is trying to do something for the nonaffluent. We went to dinner at the Four Seasons that night, and I was impressed by Kelso's knowledge of French wines and fine cuisine. He was rapidly becoming my first choice for the man I would most like to spend a revolution with.

At our Waldorf meeting, I told Kelso that I had read the three books and the other literature and found it all fascinating. His reasoning seemed sound to me: that capital ownership by the masses had never been tried and that it was the only thing that could keep us from joining most other nations in the slide toward state ownership of capital. I told him that his ideas for practical achievement of universal capitalism also seemed logical but that there was one missing link: In all of the many hundreds of pages he had given me to read, there were practically no statistical projections to back up his theories.

It happens that in my law practice I have long been involved with fatal accident cases, and it is part of my job to prove how much money the deceased accident victim would have earned if he had lived out his life expectancy. This gets pretty complicated when you have to predict what a man's earnings will be twenty-five or fifty years from now. You have to consider such things as industry and company structures, earnings levels likely to prevail in various jobs, and inflation. To aid juries in making the necessary calculations of lost earnings, we use economists as expert witnesses. In their testimony, they rely on economic statistics as the basis for their projections. This use of statistics to solve economic problems and make economic projections is called *econometrics*. In 1970, I wrote a book called *Lawyers Economic Handbook,* which covers the use of econometrics and the trial testimony of economists in proving financial losses caused by fatal accidents. I can confidently claim that it is the outstanding book in the field; the fact that it is the only one ever written on this subject should not be held against me.

Since World War II, econometrics has become even more exotic, with the development of *econometric models* of the entire national economy. These models are systems of very complicated mathematical equations, and when they are used in combination with high-speed computers, they can very quickly make calculations that would otherwise take years of pencil pushing. Professor Lawrence Klein of the University of Pennsylvania's Wharton School has been the leading figure in development of these large-scale models, which are now used by governments and industries throughout the world to forecast far-reaching effects on whole economies.

I asked Kelso why he had not published any econometric studies to back up his beautiful theories. He told me that he had tried to develop such statistics but that every attempt had been thwarted. The government and academic economists who control the major econometric models were not interested in investigating his theories, and the private services capable of making these studies wanted too much money for the job. He had tried raising money from foundations and in 1965 had even gotten Congressman Jerry Ford interested in his theories up to the point of seeking econometric verification, but Kelso had not been able to raise the large sums needed to conduct these complicated studies on his own.

At dinner, I asked Kelso whether he thought that econometric studies would prove the validity of his theories. He said, "Yes, I'm sure that they would because mathematics is logical, and the computer is logical, and my theories are based entirely on sound logic." Would he agree to submit his theories to econometric testing? "Yes, of course, I would welcome any kind of impartial econometric testing. But I don't see why I should be called upon to pay for it out of my own pocket. I'm satisfied that I'm right, and I don't have the time to convince academics or bureaucrats that they should try to find out if I'm right. I don't have any more time to spend trying to convince foundations to put up the money for private testing. I'm spending my time installing practical stock ownership plans for the benefit of corporations and their employees. These working models are the best proof that my theories are not only valid as theories but that they work in practice."

I was delighted to find that Kelso would agree to econometric testing. The stock ownership plans he was installing in various corporations were important working models, but only econometric testing could show the potential effects of his theories on the economy as a whole for a long period in the future. It was this broad picture that bureaucrats and legislators needed —not the *microeconomic* effects on individual companies, but the macroeconomic data on the entire American economy.

I told Kelso that I would like to take a crack at getting the testing done. He welcomed the idea and told me about some correspondence he had, going back many years, with an econometrician named Dr. Abel Beltran-del-Rio, who worked under Professor Lawrence Klein at Wharton Econometric Forecasting Associates. Wharton EFA, a nonprofit organization owned by the University of Pennsylvania, is probably the leading econometric forecasting service in the world, thanks to the eminent position of Professor Klein. Beltran-del-Rio had expressed interest in having WEFA test Kelso's theories at Kelso's expense. I asked Kelso to send me copies of the correspondence and told him that I would see what I could do.

Kelso still had work to do on the New Jersey deal. He planned to return to New York in June, so we made a date to meet then.

In June, the nongrubby revolution convened at the Carlyle Hotel, with Kelso hosting another fancy dinner. I was beginning to wonder whether my stomach would get through this revolution without succumbing to rich French sauces.

By this time, I had become hooked on universal capitalism. I had a gut feeling that Kelso was right, but it would not be easy to prove it to the people who would have to assume responsibility for making radical changes in our economic system. I decided to concentrate on that problem: How do we find out whether Kelso is right?

It seemed to me that the best way to tackle this problem was to write a book about universal capitalism. That would force me to organize a systematic research program to cover the subject thoroughly, which is something you can never be sure you've done until you sit down to write a book. Another reason for deciding to write this book was that I really had to push myself to plow through the three books Kelso himself had written. All three are well organized and beautifully written, but because they use the language of economics textbooks and philosophical essays, they make difficult reading for most people, who, after all, are not economists or philosophers.

It was at our dinner at the Carlyle, the hangout of the Kennedys and international jet-setters, that I told Kelso about my desire to write a book. I had been afraid that he might resent this intrusion by an outsider, but he welcomed the idea with his usual bubbling enthusiasm. I told him that I wanted to do a very thorough research job and asked him if he knew of anyone with some knowledge of the subject who might be available to work with me because I had to continue practicing law while writing the book. He suggested Jeff Gates, a third-year student at the University of California's Hastings Law School in San Francisco, who had written some articles on Kelso for the law school newspaper.

Within a few days, Jeff Gates flew to New York, we made a deal for him to work with me on the book, and we began the fascinating job of checking out Kelso. The job was to take us all over the United States and to parts of Europe, seeking out dozens of key people in the universal capitalism story, including Senators Russell Long and Hubert Humphrey; Professor Mortimer Adler, the Great Ideas man of *Encyclopaedia Britannica,* who had coauthored two books with Kelso; Professor Paul A. Samuelson; Professor Lawrence Klein and Dr. Abel Beltran-del-Rio, the Wharton EFA people; many professors, businessmen, and bureaucrats you have probably never heard of; Maurice Macmillan, member of Parliament, son of former Prime Minister Harold Macmillan, and a leader in the British universal capitalism movement; former intimates of John Maynard Keynes; and consumer advocate Ralph Nader. And of course, I interviewed Louis Kelso and his principal supporting cast, including Patricia Hetter, a scrapper disguised as an attractive political science writer; Norman Kurland, a combative Washington lawyer who quit the Walter Reuther antipoverty crusade to enlist in the Kelso movement; Winnett Boyd, president of Arthur D. Little of Canada, who designed Canada's first jet engine, was chief designer of the world's largest nuclear reactor, and then set out to design a Kelso-style plan to save Canada from socialism; Joe Recinos, a Guatemalan-American converted to universal capitalism, who rides buses through Central America preaching the Kelso gospel; Wayne Thevenot, for thirteen years an assistant to Senator Russell Long, who made the Kelso-Long connection and then signed on to devote his life to the Kelso movement; and Joe Novak, a New York lawyer who played an important role in the universal capitalism story in 1972 as tax consultant to the treasury secretary of Puerto Rico.

Before telling you the story of what I found, I think it's about time that I gave you some idea of what Kelso is all about. You got a little taste of it from the "60 Minutes" transcript in Chapter 1, but as you will soon see, that revealed only the tip of the iceberg. The real scope and significance of universal capitalism are not that easy to summarize. What you will read now has been put together by me after wading through thousands of pages of material, much of it written by Kelso, Adler, Hetter, and Kurland. I have tried to capture all their basic ideas without getting bogged down in their technical terminology.

A word of advice: As you start to read this, set yourself to discover what makes people rich; for the moment, don't bother trying to find out what makes people poor. Also, don't focus on symptoms; try to look for the basic diseases that are causing the symptoms. You are not going to read about aspirins or Band-Aids; this stuff involves major surgery. And it will help you to keep in mind these measuring standards: democracy, freedom, justice, economic reality, human nature, and logic. As you judge Kelso's theories by these standards, do the same for the present U.S. economic system (mixed capitalism), and see how the two compare in your mind.

Four Forms of Capitalism

Let's start out by looking at the four forms of capitalism, as described by Kelso and Adler: primitive, state, mixed, and universal.

Primitive capitalism can be traced back to the start of the Industrial Revolution and the publication of Adam Smith's classic *The Wealth of Nations* in 1776. Smith, a Scottish professor of moral philosophy at the University of Glasgow, believed that men seeking their own betterment are led by an "invisible hand" which forces them to advance the interests of the whole society, even though they neither know it nor intend it. It is this invisible hand that guides the "free market" through competition among self-seeking men who know what is best for them and what society needs. Smith thought that free competition would force prices to their "natural" level and would divide the wealth of the nation (its total annual production of goods and services) among the three contributors to production: laborers, who receive wages; landowners, who receive rents; and capital owners, who receive profits. Smith called this system "perfect liberty," but it became known as *laissez-faire capitalism*.

Smith was greatly impressed by the division of labor; indeed, his book opens with his famous description of a pin factory in which ten workers divide up the pin-making process by specialization and turn out 48,000 pins a day, compared with the few that each could have produced working alone. He saw this division of labor, combined with the profit motive and the invisible guiding hand, as the keys to the continuous growth of national wealth. And Smith believed that this wealth would trickle down to the lowest ranks of the laborers, again through the magic of the free market. He believed that government should prevent formation of monopolies but otherwise should keep hands off the economy.

In spite of Smith's misplaced faith in the guiding hand, the free market, and trickledown, *The Wealth of Nations* is a monumental work, and it would be unfair to leave the record so negative. Although Smith is considered the father of industrial capitalism and his influence has been used by greedy men for purposes of exploitation, his own objectives were very different. He was concerned for the poor workers, who were sorely oppressed by *mercantilism,* the economic system of his time (the reign of George III). Mercantilism imposed tight regulations on business and labor, including maximum wage laws to keep British labor costs below those in other countries. The benefits of mercantilism were reaped by a few insiders who monopolized and manipulated the eighteenth-century English economy.

Smith's laissez-faire was a plea for the government to take its hands from the throats of the workers and the honest businessmen so that together they could fashion a better system: creation of wealth for everyone through efficient organization and production. He saw the rich-poor gap of his time, called it a disgrace, and hoped that his ten years of work on *The Wealth of Nations* would narrow it. His great book did help to end mercantilism and is responsible for many of the benefits of the Industrial Revolution and the free-enterprise system.

But we must return to Smith as the symbol of primitive capitalism, which is controlled only by the invisible hand. Today, 200 years after the publication of *The Wealth of Nations,* most of us have felt the invisible hand—in our pockets. We know that the guiding hand of primitive capitalism is not strong enough to turn man's natural greed into a force that is beneficial to society. We know that laissez-faire has never produced a distribution of wealth or income that has enabled the majority of people in any nation to live decent lives. We know that it always concentrates ownership of capital and wealth in a very few hands, the blessed few whose greed Smith wanted to harness as the engine of plenty for all mankind. Some of Smith's theories remain as part of the foundation for today's capitalism, but we know that the Scottish professor's well-intentioned eighteenth-century primitive capitalism must be modified to meet twentieth-century concepts of economic justice.

The first proposed modification of primitive capitalism was *Marxism*. You might think that Marxism was more than a modification, that it called for complete destruction of capitalism. But Kelso and Adler don't see it that way; they call Marxism *state capitalism*. They point out that industrialized Marxist societies still use capital and that Marx expressed his admiration for the productive capacity of capitalism and its ability to bring a high standard of living to large numbers of people. They say that Marx was right in his condemnation of primitive capitalism, which caused misery and class warfare, in his description of the proletariat as nonpropertied wage slaves, and in attributing many of the evils of primitive capitalism to its concentration of capital in the hands of a few, who then exploited the rest of society. But Kelso and Adler say that Marx made a major mistake in his proposed cure. Instead of trying to preserve the benefits of primitive capitalism while cutting away its rotten parts, Marx threw the baby out with the bath water. His cure for concentration of capital in the hands of a few was to concentrate it completely in the hands of the state.

Kelso and Adler say that instead of eliminating private property in favor of state ownership, Marx should have tried a more logical cure: deconcentration by spreading ownership to all the people. But Marx chose state capitalism, and now his followers are stuck with total concentration of both economic and political power in the hands of a few bureaucrats, a system that has consistently crushed democracy and freedom wherever it has been installed. It has also killed the incentive that Adam Smith correctly perceived, the basic human drive for betterment, which has made capitalism the most productive system man has ever devised and brought about history's highest standards of living.

One of the things I like about the logic of Kelso and Adler is that they always test economic theories by the standards of political democracy. In pointing out the wrong turn that Marx made in his attempt to erase the evils of primitive capitalism, Kelso and Adler said in *The Capitalist Manifesto:*

> The Marxist error here is flagrant. If we recognize that a republic in which only a few men are citizens is politically unjust, we can also see that the remedy is to make all men citizens, not to abolish citizenship. Hence when we recognize that an industrial economy in which only a few men are capitalists is economically unjust, we should be able to see that the obvious remedy is to enable all men to become capitalists, not to make it impossible for anyone to be a capitalist.

Karl Kautsky, a German disciple of Marx who was considered a leading interpreter of Marxist economics in the first third of the twentieth century, felt that the best way to carry out Marx's ideals was to spread capital ownership to the masses. Kautsky predicted that the concentration of total economic and political power in the state would be fatal to freedom and contrary to Marx's real objectives. But most Marxists ignored Kautsky, especially the influential Marxists who wielded total power over their countrymen thanks to state capitalism.

Marx theorized that the dictatorship of the proletariat would be a temporary stage, during which man's acquisitive drive would be extinguished. Then the state would wither away, leaving in its place a perfect classless society, free of greed. *The Russians,* a 1976 book by Hedrick Smith, former Moscow correspondent for the *New York Times,* sheds some light on how the "Communist nobility" is managing to pass the time while waiting for their greed to wither away. According to Smith, there is a privileged class in Soviet society, about 1 million people who are on the *nomenklatura,* or secret roster selected by Party bosses. They live much better than the average Russian, who is called upon to share the distribution of scarcity. Smith describes in great detail the goodies that the elite bestow upon themselves, including food, clothing, housing, transportation, and recreation of the highest luxury class. He also says there is a thriving countereconomy, estimated to be about 10 percent or more of the Soviet GNP, that involves illegal private enterprise ("creeping capitalism" as some Russians playfully call it) .

Primitive capitalism (Adam Smith) managed to hold out against state capitalism (Karl Marx) well into the twentieth century. But the Russian Revolution of 1917, which brought Lenin to power, and the worldwide depression of the 1930s made modification of primitive capitalism inevitable in those countries that were not to succumb to Marxism. The modification adopted by the United States, England, and other democracies has many names. Kelso and Adler call it *mixed capitalism*. It is capitalism mixed with socialism, Marxism, or both. The nametags don't matter. The essence of mixed capitalism is redistribution, the attempt to overcome the evils of primitive capitalism by taxing the income and property of the haves and distributing tax money to the have-nots to the extent necessary to keep the rich-poor gap from reaching the window-smashing point.

Primitive capitalism sowed the seeds of its own destruction by choking off the mass purchasing power needed to consume its ever-increasing productive capacity. It had to be modified to survive, and it is no surprise that the modifications focused on government intervention to boost consumption by creating jobs and consumer credit and redistributing income to provide artificial purchasing power. Kelso and Adler claim this was a big mistake. But they weren't around to advise Keynes or Roosevelt, and nobody else saw the light, so I think that we have to be thankful that Keynes, Roosevelt, and their followers did bring government into the game and gave capitalism another chance for survival.

It looked for a while as though mixed capitalism would work, but in the 1960s and 1970s, its basic contradictions came to the surface. Kelso bangs away at these contradictions, which he saw clearly and started yelling about way back in the 1950s, when most of us thought that mixed capitalism could be made to work through fine tuning of government control knobs.

Kelso says that lack of mass purchasing power has been a basic defect of capitalism since the Industrial Revolution, when capital became important in production and its ownership became concentrated in few hands. Technology and automation greatly increased productive capacity, but because the ownership of the tools of production was concentrated in the hands of a few people, those few could satisfy their needs, and even indulge cravings for luxury, without making much of a dent in the productive capacity of the economy. How many steaks can factory owners eat? How many cars can they drive?

The trickledown theory was supposed to take care of this problem, but it never did. The trickle was never strong enough to keep most people above the levels of squalor and serfdom. We've made a strong try at supplying the missing purchasing power through massive consumer credit. But Kelso says that this is one of the big contradictions of mixed capitalism. Consumer credit seems to close the purchasing power gap today but actually makes it larger tomorrow. Houses and cars and television sets represent wealth, not productive capital. They produce no income, and if you buy a house and a car on credit, you wind up paying for three houses and one and a half cars after the interest is figured in. Consumer credit actually puts most families further in the hole and cuts down on their real purchasing power in the future.

Kelso pinpoints many other artificial devices designed to stimulate purchasing power: subsidized farm production; skyrocketing employment by federal, state, and local governments; defense spending and stockpiling; foreign aid subsidies in the form of credit for purchases in the United States; public works jobs and featherbedding jobs. He says that if these artificial props were removed, the unemployment rate would be up around 30 percent and that our truly productive employment is less than 70 percent of the work force right now. But these make-work programs are necessary under mixed capitalism, and so is direct redistribution (transfer payments for social security, unemployment benefits, food stamps, and welfare).

As we saw in Chapter 2, we are reaching the breaking point on transfer payments, if indeed we haven't already passed it. The main device we have used is to print more money. The inevitable result is inflation and erosion of the value of every dollar that each of us has in the bank.

Full employment has become our national policy and expectation. Yet, full employment is incompatible with automation, which is aimed at destroying jobs as quickly as possible. Our industrial and tax systems are designed to foster automation, and the performance of our executives is judged by how many jobs they can turn over to machines. So long as we attempt to produce through capitalism and distribute through labor, we will continue to pay more money for less productive work, and we will continue to manufacture our own ruinous inflation. Kelso and Adler pegged this as "Mixed Capitalism's Insoluble Problem: Inflation" way back in their 1958 *Capitalist Manifesto*. It is now being acknowledged by Keynesian economists, but they continue to look for the solution in more redistribution, which seems to offer only more vicious stagflation.

We have been playing the redistribution game since the 1930s. Yet the average working American is rarely more than one paycheck away from financial difficulty, and he can't even look forward to a dignified retirement. As redistribution builds to a crescendo, we are sliding closer to concentration of total economic and political power in the same hands. Mixed capitalism is also creeping socialism and embryonic Marxism. It concentrates tremendous economic powers in the central government, which also wields the political power. If we learned anything from Watergate, it was the danger of concentrating too much power in the central government. But how long can we expect Americans to continue voting for capitalism, when most of them have no chance to ever become capitalists?

Mixed capitalism also perpetuates the class warfare that Marx saw as the central thrust of history. It sets up a continuous struggle between those who are trying to support themselves without government help and those who exist on government redistribution. No wonder then that the eminent economist Joseph Schumpeter called the American mixed economy "capitalism in an oxygen tent."

Looking ahead twenty-five to fifty years, it is hard to visualize much economic freedom surviving under mixed capitalism. The loss of economic freedom would likely be followed by loss of political freedom, resulting in a totalitarian state—unless you believe in democratic socialism, which Kelso condemns as a contradiction in terms, and which seems to be a long shot at best, considering human nature and socialism's history of power concentration.

So, we come to the only form of capitalism that has never been tried: *universal capitalism*. Its chief proponent, Louis

Kelso, makes some strong claims for it. He says that universal capitalism has the following characteristics that make it unique among all economic systems:

It is completely democratic and therefore is the economic counterpart of political democracy.

It keeps political and economic power in separate hands, avoiding the concentration that can lead to totalitarian government.

It can bring us the classless society while maintaining democracy, individual freedom, and high standards of productivity and living.

It is aimed at eliminating both the robber baron and the entrenched bureaucrat, leaving the people in charge of their own government and their own economic destiny.

It combines the emotional appeal of Marxism with the self-betterment drive of Adam Smith's capitalism, all built on economic freedom and economic justice.

Professor Milton Friedman calls Kelso's theory of universal capitalism "Karl Marx turned on his head." Louis Kelso says that you *have* to turn Marx on his head to have his theories make sense.

Let's stand on our heads and take a look at Kelso's universal capitalism.

KELSO'S VISION OF UNIVERSAL CAPITALISM

Mr. Kelso's conception of capitalism as the economically free and classless society which supports political democracy and which, above all, helps political democracy to preserve the institutions of a free society is, to my mind, the most revolutionary idea of the century.

Professor Mortimer J. Adler

Overconcentration of Capital Ownership

Can you think of any better way to ensure the survival of capitalism-democracy-freedom than to spread the benefits of capital ownership to all Americans, instead of to just a few? That is what Kelso wants to do. No country has ever tried to make capital ownership universal. And although the United States proclaims itself a political democracy, it has never tried to be an economic democracy as well. In fact, the American economic system is designed to produce the opposite result: overconcentration of capital ownership.

Let's define *productive capital* as the nonhuman elements that go into production of goods and services, including land, structures, machinery, materials, computers and vehicles. *Wealth* is a little different; it includes personal possessions, such as homes, yachts, and autos, that produce no income. For the moment, let's forget about the yachts and mansions and concentrate on productive capital, the things that produce income, and let's dare to think about who owns it.

During the first century of this nation's history, land was the most important kind of productive capital, and the population was about 85 percent rural, mostly owners of small farms. Today, the population is 75 percent urban, mostly wage earners who own little or no productive capital. The productive capital is now owned primarily by corporations, and most of the stock in the corporations is owned by a small minority of the population.

There are millions of Americans who own a few shares of stock and millions who are involved in stock ownership indirectly through pension funds that are invested in stock. But Kelso claims that 5 percent of Americans own 95 percent of all personally held stock (i.e., stock owned by individuals rather than by corporations, pension funds, or institutions) in U.S. corporations. Some people dispute these figures, but there is no doubt that the wealthiest 1 percent of Americans own at least 50 percent of all personally held corporate stock and that the overwhelming majority of Americans, probably well over 90 percent, do not receive any significant income from dividends paid on stock. To Kelso, this very small number of Americans who receive significant *income* from capital ownership is the important figure.

Kelso's theory of universal capitalism is built on the premise that the income from broadly diffused ownership of capital can bring general affluence. He claims that, contrary to the title of the famous book by Professor Galbraith, America is not an "affluent society," that Galbraith formed his concept of affluence by comparing the United States with preindustrial economies, and that by today's standards, the United States is a grossly underdeveloped country. Kelso believes that everyone wants to be affluent, that this desire is legitimate, and that general affluence is achievable in an economy endowed with natural resources, manpower, and know-how, as ours is.

Neither the United States nor any other Western industrial nation enjoys genuine affluence. Indeed, the leaders of these countries do not even consider general affluence to be a potential goal of economic policy. In their eyes, affluence is the product of capital ownership and therefore is only for the very rich. For this reason, political leaders are afraid to talk about affluence as an economic goal. No wonder they keep pushing the puritan work ethic. It perpetuates the belief that capital ownership is only for the entrepreneur and the very wealthy. Political leaders seem to have no idea how affluence can be brought to everyone. And the people don't ask their leaders for capital ownership. They ask for jobs and welfare, and at most, that is what they get, along with ever higher taxes and inflation.

Indeed, entrepreneurs and the very wealthy, who are mostly conservatives, hire liberal economists who focus their studies and writings on employment rather than on capital ownership. They would say to Kelso, "How dare you talk about spreading capital ownership when most Americans are struggling for mere survival?" As Professor Samuelson said on "60 Minutes" "It really has a Marie Antoinette-ish ring to it. 'Let them own capital!' " That's why you will find practically no mention of widespread capital ownership or general affluence in economics textbooks.

Kelso points out that if the United States were truly affluent, it would not be necessary to resort to artificial stimulation of purchasing power through huge consumer debt. He also challenges Galbraith's statement that affluent societies neglect public facilities. Kelso maintains that only an affluent society can afford to pay attention to public improvements and preservation of the environment. This is borne out by the terrific struggle of government and industry to cope with environmental problems today, particularly those efforts requiring billions of dollars in additional capital investment, which have helped cause the capital crunch we discussed in Chapter 2. Furthermore, a genuinely affluent society would not have to fuel inflation by redistributing income in order to maintain the semblance of a decent standard of living.

Kelso wouldn't get much of an argument from most Americans on the question of whether they live in an affluent society today. But how would he bring affluence to everybody?

Kelso's Financed Capitalist Plan and its Reservoir of New Capital

Kelso is a very practical corporation lawyer. He doesn't dream about pie in the sky, about theoretical stock ownership in nonexistent corporations. He doesn't talk about taking capital away from those who own it now, regardless of how they came to possess it. He zeroes in on a reservoir of real capital that is created every year in the United States: the *new* capital that American corporations acquire through purchase of capital items to be used in their businesses. The new capital for 1976 was about $120 billion, and as we saw in Chapter 2, there are estimates that the total for the decade 1975–1984 will be about $4.5 *trillion*.

Kelso says that ownership of this handy reservoir of capital can be spread throughout the society without any disruption of the present system because this newly created capital is not owned by anyone now. Ownership would be represented by shares of stock in the corporations making the capital expenditures. Kelso uses corporate stock as the basis for capital diffusion because corporations own most of the productive capital and because corporate stock is the most convenient means of broadening capital ownership. The corporations whose stock Kelso would diffuse are mostly the big winners; they can justify large capital expenditures and show projections of future profits that will pay for the capital items being acquired. We're not talking about new start-up ventures, but about the profitable giants in whose corporate assets most of the nation's productive capital is concentrated: for example, General Motors, AT&T, Exxon, IBM, Xerox.

As we'll see shortly, the present corporate finance and tax systems are rigged so that the bulk of the new capital created in the future will be owned by those who already own most of the corporate stock, even though they do not have to put up the money to acquire it. Kelso's *Financed Capitalist Plan* would simply change the rigging so that the new capital would be owned by New Capitalists, that is, by those who own little or no capital now. But it would not be a gift from the present stockholders to the New Capitalists. The new capital would still be paid for; in fact, it would be made to pay for itself out of the corporate income it creates, just as it is designed to do under the present system. The only real change is a change of ownership from the rich to the poor.

Kelso maintains that productive capital in the hands of the major successful corporations will pay for itself over a reasonable period no matter who owns it, an old capitalist, a wooden Indian, or a New Capitalist (see Figure 1). Whoever has access to long-term credit can sit back and let this capital pay for itself and then reap the benefits of capital ownership. Kelso's Financed Capitalist Plan would open up access to long-term credit for acquisition of capital ownership, and it would make this credit available to the New Capitalists.

The New Capitalists

This is probably a good time to touch on one of the most intriguing parts of Kelso's Financed Capitalist Plan: the question of which Americans will become New Capitalists. Actually, Kelso doesn't try to answer this question completely, even though *The New Capitalists* is the title of one of the books he wrote with Mortimer Adler. In the latest version of his plan, Kelso designates "low income families" as the recipients of diffused capital ownership because the poorest families have little or no capital now and are most in need of more income. But not everyone would agree that the poorest families should automatically receive the benefits of capital ownership. Should capital ownership go to welfare families or only to working families? Because capital ownership is a privilege rather than a constitutional right, should it be extended only to those who do something in return, such as staying out of jail? And is it wise to dump capital ownership into the laps of people who have no

Kelso's Wooden Indian Theory

FIGURE 1

P roductive capital used by major successful corporations will pay for itself out of its own earnings no matter who owns it, an old capitalist, a wooden Indian, or a New Capitalist who cannot afford to pay for it out of savings. Whoever has access to long-term credit can own this productive capital and let it pay for itself.

Capital investment pays for itself...

...no matter who owns it.

Long-term credit is the key.

experience with handling large sums of money? There are a lot of tough decisions involved. The new federal legislation needed to establish the Financed Capitalist Plan would have to specify the beneficiaries or at least set guidelines for their selection.

We'll get around to discussing these questions in Chapter 12, but I mention them here so you'll know that the Financed Capitalist Plan does not require any automatic selection of beneficiaries and is not based on employment. (In Chapter 8, we will examine Kelso's employee stock ownership plan, which *is* based on the employment relationship.) First, we have to determine the validity of Kelso's claim that capital ownership can be diffused to millions of people who now have little or no income from capital. If we get past that hurdle, we can look into the more pleasant problem of deciding how to divide up the pie.

How the Present System Perpetuates Overconcentration of Capital Ownership

Kelso has spent most of his career as a lawyer for big corporations and wealthy people. He knows that the key to wealth is accumulation of capital ownership through self-liquidating credit—making capital instruments pay for themselves out of their own earnings.

It is important to remember that America's corporate finance and tax systems are artificial creations. In fact, the corporation itself is the most artificial creation in the whole economy. These man-made mechanisms are like plumbing systems. They are intended to serve the best interests of the society, but nobody was watching when the present system was installed. Nobody realized that there might be a better design that could make the economy even more productive and spread affluence throughout the society. So don't be frightened by the changes in the rigging that will be necessary to implement the Financed

Capitalist Plan. There is nothing sacred about the present rigging; it is just another plumbing system.

The Financed Capitalist Plan can be adopted without interfering with any constitutional or legal rights. Both the means and the ends are designed to bring about economic justice. Because it is part of the genius of Louis Kelso to use existing institutions and mechanisms wherever possible, the innovations involved in the plan are much less drastic than the income tax, social security, and civil rights legislation. He simply rerigs the plumbing to make sure that it serves all of us, instead of just a privileged few. Kelso's new rigging is no more radical than the bill passed by the New York State legislature in 1975 that outlawed pay toilets. Just as there is nothing sacred about pay toilets, and public plumbing facilities can be made available to all, so with capital ownership.

To understand the changes involved, let's start out with a simple concept: *participation*. Kelso was probably the first to say that it is the duty of a free society to enable all its citizens to participate in production both through labor and through capital ownership. Most Americans get some opportunity to participate in production through labor, but this just keeps them on a treadmill. To become affluent, they also need to participate in production through capital ownership; but the game, as it now stands, is rigged against them.

Because of the way that business corporations are financed and taxed, it is inevitable that the monopoly of productive capital ownership will continue and will probably get worse. The money to pay for new capital (the $120 billion of new capital for 1976 that we've been talking about) comes from two main sources: borrowing, which is to be repaid by the corporations out of future profits, and reinvestment of past profits, which are bottled up in corporations for this purpose instead of being paid out to stockholders as dividends. Only a tiny fraction (no more than 5 percent) of this newly formed capital is paid for by sale of newly issued common stock. Even this small amount of stock can be bought only by people wealthy enough to risk a cash investment (see Figure 2).

There is nothing in the American system of corporate finance or taxation that is designed to spread ownership of pro-

Present System
of Financing
Capital Outlays

FIGURE 2

In the 1970s, 95 percent of new corporate capital items were paid for by borrowing and by use of internal funds (including retained earnings and investment tax credits) ; only 5 percent were paid for by newly issued common stock. Therefore, out of $120 billion spent by corporations for capital items in 1976, 95 percent will be owned automatically by the present corporate stockholders, and 5 percent will be paid for by new stockholders who can afford to buy stock for cash. None of this $120 billion expenditure created ownership by New Capitalists.

In this way, the present system perpetuates overconcentration of capital ownership. The wealthiest 1 percent of Americans now own more than 50 percent of individually owned stock, and the great majority of Americans have no significant participation in capital ownership.

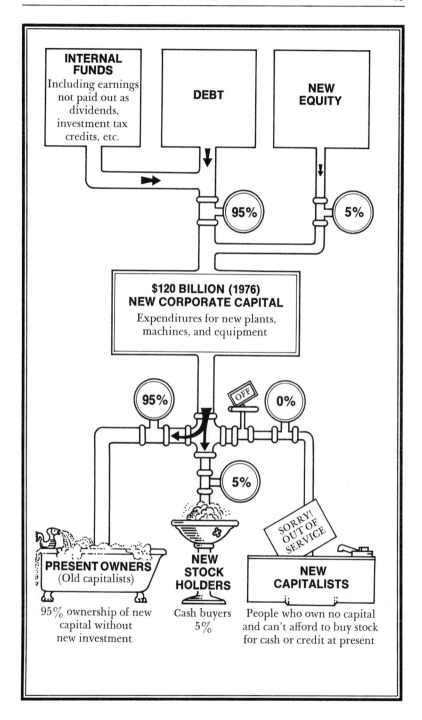

ductive capital. The leverage obtained by using the corporation's credit to pay for newly formed capital out of future earnings gives the present stockholder an automatic increase in
capital holdings. Without putting out any additional money,
the present stockholder enjoys the benefits of the huge corporate
credit mechanism. But the individual who is not a big stockholder and who is dependent on wages for his wealth is taxed
more and more without accumulating any productive capital.

Interest paid by a corporation is tax-deductible, which
helps corporations to use debt for capital outlays. There is also
the *investment tax credit,* an artificial stimulant applied by the
government in years when capital spending is lagging. It allows
corporations a tax credit for capital outlays. (A tax credit, by
the way, is about twice as valuable as a tax deduction because a
credit is subtracted directly from taxes; whereas a deduction is
subtracted from taxable income.) In 1975 and 1976, the investment tax credit was 10 percent, which allowed major corporations to save about $8 billion each year. That amounts to an $8
billion gift from all U.S. taxpayers to the present stockholders
because the $8 billion tax saving is added to the corporate assets,
which the stockholders own.

Because of the interest charges, it is more expensive to pay
for capital items by using debt than by issuing or selling common stock. But the present stockholders don't mind the extra
interest expense because they come out better in the long run
when the corporation uses debt. Most large stockholders are
wealthy and have high incomes, so they are not interested in
receiving large dividends on their stock. They would rather
have the corporation use the rigged plumbing system to acquire
new capital items through accumulated earnings and debt because they know that the corporations will pay back the debt
from increased profits realized through operation of the new
capital assets. This will increase the value of the stockholders'
stake in the company, but they will pay no taxes on this increased value unless they sell their stock; and even then, it will
be only a capital gains tax, which is roughly half of what the tax
would be on dividends.

Everything is rigged to *absorb* most of the newly created
capital into the corporation, which means it is owned automatically by the present stockholders. Nobody complains about this,

certainly not the present large stockholders who control the corporate voting power, and certainly not the millions who are not stockholders because they believe that they can't be stockholders without having the savings necessary to buy stock in the market.

Kelso points out an insidious side effect of this process. The plumbing system is rigged to keep billions of dollars of accumulated earnings bottled up in the corporations for capital expenditures, and this reduces the income available for mass consumption of what the corporations are producing. The wealthy stockholders don't want it as dividend income because they would have to pay up to 70 percent of the dividends in income tax. But if this capital ownership were spread throughout the society, it would be owned by many lower-bracket taxpayers who would be very happy to pay the income tax on dividends in order to get more income. Kelso says that by bottling up this potential purchasing power, the major corporations are killing their own mass markets, committing "customercide."

Kelso considers this monopolization of capital ownership more serious than any antitrust case that has ever been prosecuted by the Justice Department, but the subject is never even discussed in terms of monopoly. It has turned this country into a nation of industrial sharecroppers because the great majority of the American people work only for subsistence wages and do not share in ownership of productive capital to any significant degree. Most Americans fit Marx's description of the proletariat: unpropertied wage slaves.

How the Financed Capitalist Plan Would Work

Let's get back to the $120 billion reservoir of new capital created by American corporations in 1976. As we saw, about 95 percent of this ($114 billion) came from use of corporate credit to borrow against future earnings and from reinvestment of past earnings. Only about $6 billion will come from sale of newly issued common stock, and that stock will be bought only by the wealthiest segment of the population, who already monopolize capital ownership.

Now suppose that ownership of this $120 billion could be channeled to 20 million New Capitalists. That would mean $6,000 in capital ownership per family for 1976 ($120 billion divided by 20 million families). Over a period of five years, the 20 million New Capitalists each would become owners of at least $30,000 worth of stock in leading American corporations, assuming, of course, that arrangements were made for these corporations to pay for the new capital by issuance of common stock at market value. (Actually, each family could own more than $30,000 worth of stock. The $120 billion figure represents the corporate capital outlay for 1976 only, and higher totals have been forecast for subsequent years. But to be conservative, let's leave it at the 1976 figure for five years.)

Please note that I'm using the figure of $120 billion merely to illustrate the potential of the Financed Capitalist Plan. Although that is the actual capital outlay of U.S. corporations for 1976, not all of it would be available for ownership by New Capitalists in 1976. A good portion of it, perhaps as much as 50 percent, would represent replacement of old capital that has been depreciated on the books of corporations. Kelso agrees with those who say that present stockholders should retain ownership of new capital which replaces depreciated old capital. Also, as we'll see in Chapter 11, there may be good reasons why we should not go all out to diffuse ownership of all new capital in the early years of the plan. If you're worried about the accuracy of these figures, you can simply assume that the plan is to be strung out over a longer period; assume ten, fifteen, or even twenty years, which is no longer than the time allotted for repayment of the average home mortgage loan.

On the other hand, the figure of $120 billion for 1976 is low in comparison with capital outlays predicted for the decade 1976–1985: an average of at least $400 billion per year (if the $4.5 trillion ten-year forecast is accurate). Also, Kelso predicts that there will be a greater percentage of real capital growth in the form of new plants and capital items once the plan is put into operation. The plan will not be started in 1976 and probably not for several more years, so we can assume that the $120 billion figure will represent less than half the total corporate capital outlay for the year in which the plan is started. So we're back to our assumption that we will diffuse ownership of $120 billion new capital each year for five years to 20 million New Capitalists, each of whom receives a total of $30,000 in stock over the five-year period.

OK—this sounds great, but how are the 20 million New Capitalists going to become the owners of $120 billion worth of stock each year? Is someone going to stand on street corners and hand out the stock to them? Will it be given away through welfare offices? These 20 million New Capitalists can't even begin to pay for the stock. How will the $120 billion get into the hands of the corporations so that they can use it for their capital needs?

Here's where Kelso's genius and practical experience come in. He knows how capital is formed and paid for. Most of the time, corporations expect to pay for new capital items out of *future earnings.* We are not talking now about people buying yachts or television sets; we are talking about new factories, machines, computers, typewriters, things that are bought in order to make money in the future for corporations. And in the world of big profitable corporations, these capital outlays are not made unless there is a carefully budgeted projection showing that they will pay for themselves within a reasonable number of years.

As we have seen, the future earning power of major corporations is used by existing stockholders to monopolize ownership of newly created capital. But Kelso thinks that this future earning power can be used to broaden capital ownership. He says that diffusing capital ownership in this way will make capital spending work like a pump to supply purchasing power throughout the society.

In addition to using the credit power of major corporations, the plan would involve the banks, the Federal Reserve System, and a new government agency to be called the Capital Diffusion Insurance Corporation (CDIC), which would insure bank loans in much the same way that the Federal Housing

Administration (FHA) insures home mortgages and the Federal Deposit Insurance Corporation (FDIC) insures bank depositors against losses in the event of a bank failure.

Some laws would have to be amended so that corporations would be either encouraged or required to obtain their new capital through issuance of stock, rather than through debt or accumulated earnings. For purposes of this discussion, let's assume that corporations are required to pay all their earnings to stockholders as dividends (they would be permitted to retain only those reserves needed to keep the business operating) and that corporations will issue stock to the New Capitalists at market value in payment for capital outlays, instead of incurring debt for this purpose (see Figure 3). (We'll discuss these assumed changes more fully later in this chapter.)

A priority system would then have to be set up to determine who will acquire ownership of this $120 billion in corporate stock (i.e., who will be the first New Capitalists). For the sake of simplifying the arithmetic, let's start off with 20 million households or families as the New Capitalists because this figure corresponds roughly to the number of working families now below the poverty line.

The head of each of these families would go to a bank and arrange to buy $6,000 worth of stock on credit (a *nonrecourse, self-liquidating loan*). There would be no risk to the stock buyer or to the bank on these loans because the bank would be insured by CDIC.

The stock acquired by each of the New Capitalist families would be held in escrow until it is paid for out of dividends received on the shares purchased. Remember that we have changed the law so that corporations must pay out practically all their earnings in dividends. Kelso uses a figure of 20 percent annual return on invested equity capital *before taxes*. Accountants have various ways of calculating the return on invested capital, and some might dispute Kelso's figure. But most major corporations do earn something close to 20 percent per year before taxes on invested capital, so let's use that figure. If the actual return is less, then more time will be needed for the stock to pay for itself.

Now another change in the rigging will have to be made by another amendment of existing law. The plan requires that the whole 20 percent per year return on capital be paid out to shareholders (at least to the 20 million New Capitalists) as dividends. Under the present system, corporate income taxes would take about half of this 20 percent, and that would slow down repayment of the stock purchase loan and postpone the day when the New Capitalists would start receiving the income from the stock. To accomplish this change, the corporate income tax must be either wiped out entirely or made inapplicable to the corporate earnings paid out as dividends on the stock distributed through the Financed Capitalist Plan. This could be done by allowing the corporations a tax deduction for the dividends paid on the stock owned by New Capitalists. (We'll discuss the tax adjustment later in this chapter.)

Assuming that the average 20 percent return on capital is paid as dividends each year, Kelso estimates that the newly issued stock would be paid for in about seven years, allowing for payment of interest on the loans made to buy the stock and also for payment of a reasonable loan insurance fee to CDIC for insuring the banks against defaults. The stock would then be owned outright by the 20 million New Capitalists, and they would start to receive the dividends themselves (see Figure 4).

Let's return to the example in which each of the 20 million New Capitalist families would receive $6,000 worth of stock each year for five years, for a total of $30,000 worth of stock. Assuming that the 20 percent average return continued, each New Capitalist family eventually would receive income of $6,000 per year from the stock. Of course, the program could be continued for more than five years, and each New Capitalist family might receive $50,000 to $100,000 worth of stock or more. The amounts would be a matter of policy and could be controlled by Congress.

As you can see, there is a built-in lag of about seven years before the Financed Capitalist Plan produces income for the New Capitalists. However, we must start somewhere. If Kelso's plan had been installed twenty years ago and it had worked out as he says it will, millions of families would now be receiving this income from the pool of newly created capital needed by corporations each year, and we would be much less dependent on redistribution and welfare. Kelso's Financed Capitalist Plan is a get-rich-slowly scheme because it is designed to pay for itself,

The Financed Capitalist Plan

FIGURE 3

The Financed Capitalist Plan is one of Louis Kelso's ideas for saving the free-enterprise system by making capitalism universal. It would change the present method of financing capital outlays by making major successful corporations pay for all capital items through issuance of new common stock at market value. All this stock would be available for ownership by New Capitalists through long-term nonrecourse self-liquidating credit guaranteed by a federal agency (see Figure 4 for details). Corporations would be required to pay out practically all their earnings as dividends and would not be allowed to use internal funds or borrowings to pay for new capital items, as they now do for 95 percent of capital outlays.

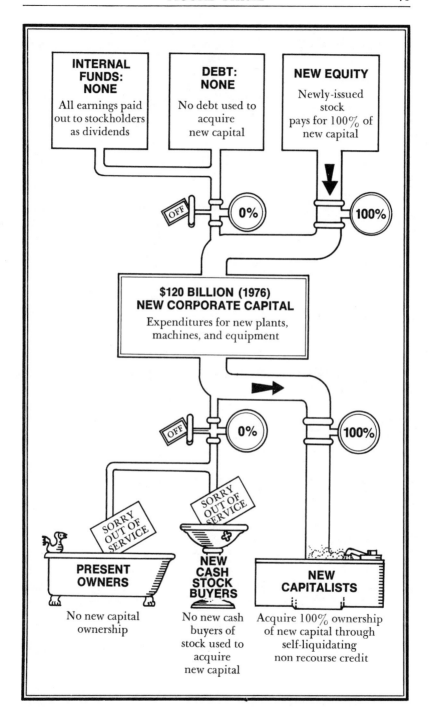

Step by Step Outline of the Financed Capitalist Plan (FCP)

FIGURE 4

Participating Corporations

1. Participants are the major successful corporations which account for most of the $120 billion annual capital outlays.

2. New legislation requires them to participate in the FCP by paying for 100 percent of capital outlays by issuance of common stock at market value (no debt or retained earnings may be used) and by making all this common stock available for the FCP.

3. They receive payment for full market value of their common stock when issued, and use the funds for capital outlays.

4. They are required to pay out to stockholders (or at least to New Capitalist stockholders) nearly all earnings, in form of dividends, retaining only enough to operate business.

5. Either the corporation income tax is eliminated, or the participating corporations get tax deductions for payment of dividends to New Capitalists. In either case, annual dividends should average about 20 percent of invested capital, since these corporations now earn about 20 percent before taxes on invested capital.

New Capitalists—Before Stock Pays for Itself

6. Eligibility is determined by Congress. Priority goes to those who own little or no capital now.

7. Eligible persons go to commercial banks and become New Capitalists by signing applications to acquire their allotted shares of stock of the participating corporations.

8. To provide maximum diversification, stocks of all participating corporations are pooled, and New Capitalists receive a certificate of ownership of proportionate shares of each corporation (similar to mutual fund concept).

The Banking System

9. Banks lend the full amount of each stock purchase, and turn the money over to participating corporations in full payment for stock.

10. To enable commercial banks to make large sums available for New Capitalist loans at low interest rates, banks are permitted to rediscount New Capitalist loans with the Federal Reserve System.

11. Bank loans are *nonrecourse*; the New Capitalists are not responsible for payment. Banks hold stock in escrow until loans have been repaid out of dividends. If dividends are not sufficient to repay loans, banks can sell the stock to obtain repayment. If stock sale doesn't produce enough to repay loans, banks can look to a new government agency, Capital Diffusion Insurance Corporation (CDIC) for insurance against losses.

12. Banks pay an annual fee to CDIC for insurance against loan losses. Fee estimated at $\frac{1}{2}$ percent per year, similar to rate charged by FHA to insure banks against losses on mortgage loans.

New Capitalists—After Stock Has Been Paid for

13. Bank loans for New Capitalist stock are *self-liquidating*; they are designed to have the stock pay for itself out of its own dividends. Increased dividend rate of 20 percent permits repayment of loans with interest in about seven years.

14. After bank loans are repaid, stock is released from escrow and turned over to New Capitalists, who then own it and receive dividends.

15. If Congress desires to provide income to New Capitalists before loans are repaid, half of dividends could be used to repay loans and half could be paid directly to New Capitalists. This would stretch out loan repayment over about 14 years—still a lot shorter than repayment period for home mortgages.

Effects on Economy

16. Creates millions of New Capitalists, and gives everyone the opportunity to participate in capitalism through ownership of productive capital.

17. Brings capitalist income to millions of New Capitalists, who will then have purchasing power to match our huge productive capacity.

18. Provides new source of capital for corporations now facing future capital shortages.

just as corporations make their new capital instruments pay for themselves now. But the flow of income to needy families could be speeded up by modifying the plan so that part of the dividends would go to the bank for repayment of the stock purchase loans and the rest would go directly to the New Capitalist families. For example, half the dividends could go to the bank and half to the New Capitalists. This would stretch out the loan repayment to about fourteen years, which is still much less than the average repayment time for FHA-guaranteed home mortgages.

Once the Financed Capitalist Plan got under way, it could provide its own momentum to make the economy grow faster and thereby accelerate the diffusion of capital ownership and income throughout the society. The amount of credit that could be made available for the plan would be limited only by the economy's need for productive capital. As the economy grew, there would be more need for new capital formation, and more capital would be spread to the new Capitalists.

Through this process Kelso sees the economy feeding on itself and growing at much greater rates than the 4 to 8 percent per year considered acceptable today. He reminds us that between 1940 and 1945, the boom years of World War II, the American economy grew by over 100 percent at an average rate of 20 percent a year, even though 16 million people were taken from the labor force for military duty and there were shortages of some raw materials. He visualizes a second economy several times the size of the present economy once the credit power of the corporation is harnessed and all the people who need increased purchasing power are turned into New Capitalists.

When Kelso's second economy arrives, annual expenditures for new capital formation will multiply, perhaps by several times. The 1976 capital expansion ($120 billion) was produced by a creeping growth rate of about 5 percent. Kelso envisions growth rates as high as 15 percent, with annual new capital formation of $300 billion or more. Of course, this would greatly accelerate the rate at which ownership of new capital could be pumped out to New Capitalists. At the same time, the need for welfare and transfer payments would diminish. According to Kelso, all this would be noninflationary and

possibly even deflationary because the money would be going
into productive capital; that is, the money would be used to
purchase capital items that would increase the supply of goods
and services.

If you think Kelso's ideas on capital growth rates are wild,
let's go back to the figures that leading traditional economists
agree on. In Chapter 2, we looked at the anticipated capital
needs of industry for the decade 1975–1984. *Business Week* editors and many other economists figure this at $4.5 trillion. If the
Financed Capitalist Plan were applied to the entire $4.5 trillion
of new capital outlays and divided equally among 45 million
American families, do you know how much income-producing
capital that would give each family? Your pocket calculator
probably can't handle trillions, so I'll write it out for you:

$$\frac{\$4,500,000,000,000}{45,000,000 \text{ families}} = \$100,000 \text{ capital ownership per family}$$

Yes, each of 45 million New Capitalist families would receive
capital ownership of $100,000 and, eventually, an income of
about $20,000 per year from that capital, without any present
capital holdings being confiscated (see Figure 5). This would
cover more than 80 percent of American families.

There is nothing rigid about the figure of 45 million families or the earlier figure of 20 million families. They merely
illustrate the potential of Kelso's plan. The number of families
and the amount of capital to be acquired by each would be
governed by national policy. Of course, the Financed Capitalist
Plan would be available only to those who need it. There would
always be a limit to the amount of stock that could be acquired
under the plan. These levels could be fixed by Congress or by a
government agency.

Kelso's revolutionary ideas clash with the ancient supersti-
tion that only a privileged few are destined to own capital, but
they are not without precedent. Kelso points to the Homestead
Act, which in 1862 opened up the frontier, helped America to
become a nation of landowners, and thus created millions of
small capitalists. In those days, land was the most important
kind of productive capital, and the government gave it away

Potential Benefits of the Financed Capitalist Plan

FIGURE 5

If the entire reservoir of $120 billion in corporate capital outlays for 1976 were used for the Financed Capitalist Plan, 20 million New Capitalist families or households could acquire $6,000 each in ownership of newly issued stock. If the plan were continued at that pace for five years, each New Capitalist family would own $30,000 worth of stock and would receive $6,000 a year in dividends (assuming a 20 percent return on investment before taxes).

If the estimate of $4.5 trillion in new capital expenditures for the decade 1976–1985 is accurate, there is potential new capital ownership of $100,000 for each of 45 million New Capitalist families in one decade, with each family receiving $20,000 annual dividend income.

These figures are used to illustrate the potential of the plan. It may not be realistic to assume that the entire $120 billion of 1976 new corporate capital expenditures or the entire $4.5 trillion estimate for the next decade (even if accurate) could be used. But even if the plan were implemented gradually, these potential results might be achieved over longer periods of time.

In One Year (1976):

20 MILLION FAMILIES

After five years each New Capitalist family
would own $30,000 in stock and would
receive $6,000 annual dividend income,
assuming a 20% dividend rate.

In One Decade (1976–1985):

45 MILLION FAMILIES

Each New Capitalist family will
receive $20,000 annual dividend income,
assuming a 20% dividend rate.

under the Homestead Act. This broad ownership of productive capital lasted for several generations, until industrialization changed the picture.

Under the Homestead Act, the government had to decide who got what land; and under FHA, the government had to create a new credit device to finance billions of dollars' worth of new homes and had to decide who would get these homes. Against this background, Kelso's Financed Capitalist Plan does not look all that revolutionary. It seems strange to us because it dares to invade an area that has always been considered taboo by our leaders and economists: the basic wealth represented by capital ownership. But once we open our eyes to the question of who should own the capital created by the credit power of corporations, it is not difficult to find the answer in such precedents.

Once the number of New Capitalists has been determined, it will be necessary to decide who will get stock in which corporation. Kelso has not spelled out the answer. At this stage of our study of the Financed Capitalist Plan, I believe it is simpler to assume that each New Capitalist will get the same thing. That is, the newly issued stock of all the corporations involved will be pooled, and a certificate of ownership of $6,000 worth of this stock, in proportion to each corporation's share of the $120 billion in new capital, will be issued to each New Capitalist. It would be similar to a mutual-fund certificate.

Kelso doesn't think that this is the ideal solution. He would rather give each New Capitalist the right to select specific corporate stocks. He believes that would inspire a stronger feeling of ownership. I think he's probably right, but I don't see how 20 million New Capitalists could be allowed to make their own selections without running into big problems of duplications and priorities. Also, I think there is some value in treating all New Capitalists alike; in that way, there won't be some who get very rich from one zooming stock and some who wind up with next to nothing from bad stocks. However, this is a policy decision that can be made at a much later stage, and Kelso agrees that it does not affect the feasibility of the plan.

Now that we've completed our quick look at the Financed Capitalist Plan, it's time for your second multiple-choice question.

Assume that U.S. corporations will spend about $120 billion in 1976 on new capital items and that in most cases these capital items are projected to pay for themselves in a few years through extra income which the corporations will receive from their operation. This newly created capital of $120 billion:

__ (a) Should be owned by the present owners of most of the stock of U.S. corporations, even though they do not pay anything for acquisition of this capital, even though this capital is expected to pay for itself after the corporations lay out the cost from accumulated earnings and borrowings against future earnings, even though this will perpetuate the corporate finance and tax rigging that encourages corporations to create new capital without creating any new stockholders, and even though this will aggravate the existing concentration of capital ownership and income in a pinnacle class, thereby further reducing the mass purchasing power needed to consume the productive capacity of the economy and further widening the rich-poor gap.

__ (b) Should be owned by wooden Indians.

__ (c) Should be owned by 20 million New Capitalists, each of whom would receive ownership of $6,000 in productive capital, provided that a practical means can be found to issue new corporate stock to them, to pay the issuing corporations for the stock immediately, and to finance the payment of the stock price over a period of years out of dividends paid by the corporations from their future earnings.

If you chose *c*, you voted for the Financed Capitalist Plan.

Changes Needed to Implement the Plan

Let's back up and take a look at the four changes in the current system that will be needed to start the Financed Capitalist Plan: a new government agency to guarantee loans, a way of persuading corporations to pay for capital items by issuing new stock to the New Capitalists, a requirement that corporations pay out most of their earnings in dividends, and elimination of the corporate income tax, at least as to the shares of stock involved in the plan.

Capital Diffusion Insurance Corporation

CDIC is the only really new device in the whole plan. The important thing about CDIC is that it would not hand out any money or even lend any money; it would simply insure banks, for a fee, against losses on loans the banks would make for acquisition of stock under the Financed Capitalist Plan. Because Kelso has set up such a conservative structure for the plan, these losses are not likely to be large. The plan is based on the capital expansion of the largest and most successful corporations, each of which would have to present feasibility studies showing that the new capital items would pay for themselves out of future earnings within a reasonable number of years. This is exactly what the corporations do now when they finance new capital acquisitions through loans.

It is typical of Kelso that he has tied the plan to the credit power and earnings of major successful businesses. Others who claim to be trying to help the little guy would lend him money so that he can start a new business and try to compete with established giants. Kelso thinks that venture capital (capital for starting new enterprises) is a game to be played by the very wealthy and that to help the little fellow you have to give him a chance to participate in the big game. Thus, CDIC is not another government handout. Before CDIC could be called upon to reimburse banks for losses, there would have to be a considerable number of bankruptcies among major corporations. The bank loans are to be repaid solely out of dividends (remember, the New Capitalists are not responsible for payment), but even if the dividends are not paid, the bank holds the stock itself as security. Because the portfolio would be fully diversified, taking in all major successful U.S. corporations, the banks could look to the dividends and the underlying stock values of all the winners to make up for any losses.

Kelso suggests that life and casualty insurance companies be given the opportunity to participate in CDIC or to own it entirely if they wish. Because the risk would be minimized by the huge credit power of major corporations, Kelso thinks that the CDIC loan insurance fee should be modest, no more than $\frac{1}{2}$ percent per year, which is about what FHA charges banks for mortgage loan insurance fees. And because the banks' risks would be insured by CDIC, Kelso suggests that the banks should not charge more than 2 percent interest per year on Financed Capitalist Plan loans, making the total financing cost $2\frac{1}{2}$ percent per year. This low cost would help to get the loans paid off rapidly so that the dividends could start to flow directly to the New Capitalists.

Kelso also sees the Federal Reserve System playing a role in the plan. He would allow the banks to discount notes of the New Capitalists by turning them over to Federal Reserve banks in exchange for cash, less a small discount. This would give the banks virtually unlimited power to create credit for new capital formation and capital diffusion; that is, the amount of credit would be limited only by the major successful corporations' legitimate needs for capital expansion.

Kelso says that the present system of financing new corporate capital formation involves double insurance. The banks that lend money to a corporation for capital expansion must have proof that the new capital items will pay for themselves out of future corporate earnings; otherwise they will not make the loans. But the banks have further insurance. If the corporation does not make profitable use of the new capital, or if the corporation's profits disappear entirely, the bank can look to the corporation's other assets (the capital it has accumulated in the past).

But under the Financed Capitalist Plan, the New Capitalists don't supply any such collateral or insurance; they have none to put up, and they don't even become personally responsible for repayment. So there seems to be something missing: the insurance factor represented by the corporation's past capital accumulations. But in fact, it is not entirely missing. The stock of the major successful corporations is held as collateral by the banks, and the stock is a strong insurance factor because it represents a partial claim to the corporations' past accumulations. However, Kelso recognizes that some further insurance is needed, and that is the function of CDIC. Overall, the Financed Capitalist Plan gives the banks much more security than they have under present capital formation loans, and that is why

Kelso pushes for low bank interest rates and low CDIC loan insurance fees.

Getting Corporations to Pay for New Capital with Newly Issued Stock

The major successful U.S. corporations must be induced or required to pay for capital items by issuing the new stock that will be made available for ownership by the New Capitalists. Kelso is flexible about how this is accomplished. Wherever possible, he likes to introduce changes by making them more attractive than the present system. He thinks that access to virtually unlimited financing for capital growth will attract many large corporations to volunteer their stock for the Financed Capitalist Plan. My own feeling is that the plan will not get off to a running start unless all the major successful corporations are brought into it at the outset. One way of doing this would be to eliminate the corporate income tax *only* for those corporations that agree to supply their stock to the plan in payment for their capital outlays.

The idea of forcing corporations to issue stock to pay for new capital items instead of relying on debt and accumulated earnings may seem like a radical interference with business, but there is no doubt that the federal government has the power to do this through the tax laws and in other ways. The U.S. Supreme Court decided back in 1937 that Congress could require corporations to contribute to social security for their employees, by virtue of its police power to provide for the general welfare. The courts are not concerned with the expediency, wisdom, or necessity of legislation; they only question the power of Congress to act, which is clear in this case. Congress would merely have to decide that a national policy of capital diffusion would promote the general welfare of the American people.

If Congress adopted such a policy, present corporate stockholders might argue that the future value of their shares would be diminished by the Financed Capitalist Plan. It is true that they bought their stock at a time when the corporate plumbing system was rigged to assure them that future capital acquired by the corporation would be owned by them; this assurance is one of the things they paid for, and it was reflected in the price of their stock. They might also feel that they are entitled to the benefits of the corporation's credit power, which would be used by the plan to finance stock ownership for the New Capitalists. For this reason it probably isn't entirely correct to say that the Financed Capitalist Plan is based on capital not owned or claimed by anyone now or that the plan will not take anything away from anybody. It is quite possible that the plan might diminish the future value of outstanding stock at least temporarily, even though the stock acquired by the New Capitalists would be sold at market value.

But if we're going to make capitalism work, something has to give. There is no free lunch, as traditional economists are fond of saying. The old system, which gives the present stockholders ownership of 95 percent of future capital additions, is breaking down. There are only a few ways to keep it running. One is the socialist system, which imposes taxes of 98 and even 101 percent on some business profits. What will the present stockholders' shares be worth if the U.S. government is forced to tax productive people and businesses at that level in order to keep the redistribution game going?

That's why Kelso's idea of requiring corporations to issue stock to pay for new capital is reasonable. The present stockholder's position must be compared with his real future expectations under redistribution, rather than with his meaningless dreams of past glory. Stock values have already been eroded by billions of dollars in the 1970s, even with the old plumbing system in place. Kelso feels that any potential drop in stock values will be more than offset by the overall benefits of the plan to the economy. He points out that there is no economic dilution involved when stock is issued at market value for acquisition of productive capital. Each stockholder will have a smaller percentage of ownership but nobody will lose anything; everything will stay in proportion.

Remember, too, that no national policy has ever declared that corporations should be allowed to bottle up their earnings and use them to perpetuate the monopoly of capital ownership. If Congress adopts a new national policy that recognizes the need to spread capital ownership in order to preserve capitalism-democracy-freedom, the old plumbing will have to be rerigged to comply with the higher needs of that new policy.

If corporations were forced to issue large amounts of new stock each year and to pay out their earnings fully as dividends, you would probably see a more stable stock market pegged closely to the actual return on invested capital, which is what stock prices are supposed to reflect after all the gobbledygook of the securities analysts is stripped away. In this respect, Kelso is right on track with Keynes, who regarded the stock market as a gambling casino despite the fact that he did well in his own speculations.

Congress would have to decide which corporations would participate in the plan and whether limits would be set on the amounts of capital they could acquire under it. Because most annual capital expenditures are made by large corporations, and because Kelso wants to make the New Capitalists stockholders in the most successful enterprises, the government would have to keep its eyes on another danger: strengthening the competitive position of giant corporations over smaller rivals who would not be able to benefit as much from the plan. This could be handled through enforcement of the antitrust laws, just as it is under the present system, in which the giant corporations already have access to greater capital resources than their smaller competitors do. Finally, special measures would be needed to make venture capital available to innovators whose access to funds might be impaired by the plan.

Making Corporations Pay Out Earnings as Dividends

Corporations must be required to pay out practically all their earnings as dividends, retaining only the cash needed to operate their businesses. This should be the easiest change because it goes back to the original concept of the corporation as a vehicle for group sharing of risks and profits.

As we have seen, the present tax structure encourages corporations to hold back most of their earnings and use them for new capital formation, thereby escaping the double tax on dividends. Before dividends can be paid today, the corporation must pay corporate income taxes of up to 50 percent on the profits, and then the dividends are taxable at rates up to 70 percent when received by the stockholders. But once corporations are no longer allowed to use accumulated earnings to pay for new capital outlays and the corporate income tax is eliminated, there will be no reason to hold back dividends.

Eliminating the Corporate Income Tax

You will find the elimination of the corporate income tax in the platform of every chamber of commerce and business-oriented political candidate, but it has no chance of enactment so long as it is seen primarily as a benefit to the already-rich. It cannot be sold as trickledown, but it can be sold as part of the package needed to diffuse capital ownership and spread purchasing power throughout the economy.

Kelso says that government revenue losses would be made up eventually through savings in welfare and other transfer payments. The corporate income tax is not a big revenue producer anyway; in 1974, it accounted for only 12 percent of federal tax collections. The revenue loss would be controlled because all the earnings now taxed at the corporate level would be flowing to stockholders as dividends, which could be taxed at whatever rate the government found necessary to maintain adequate revenue.

There is a choice here. The corporate income tax can be eliminated entirely, or dividend payments can be made tax-deductible (as interest payments are now). This could even be limited to dividends paid to stockholders participating in the Financed Capitalist Plan, which would still have the desired effect of getting the entire 20 percent average before-tax return on capital paid to the plan stockholders each year.

Would the New Capitalists Be Willing to Work?

As you look ahead ten or fifteen years to the possibility of millions of families owning $50,000 to $100,000 in capital and receiving capitalist income of $10,000 to $20,000 a year, a question might occur to you: Why would these people want to work? For most people, the opportunity to get more spendable income through working should be enough incentive, especially when inflation cheapens the dollar. Most people with comfortable capital holdings still work; many of them work even harder than those who own no capital. And the new national policy of capital diffusion could be managed so that the amount of capital flowing to each family would not be so high that it would discourage work. This problem would be much easier to solve than the present dilemma of how to create economic growth and employment through redistribution without runaway inflation.

Kelso has a more complete answer to the work question. He visualizes a time when many Americans will not have to work for subsistence, a richly humanistic culture in which many are engaged in the "work of civilization," that is, the arts, religion, humanities, and research for the betterment of mankind. He does not see this coming for at least a generation or two after universal capitalism has been installed because it will take at least twenty-five to fifty years to bring the economy up to its full production potential and diffuse capital ownership sufficiently to wipe out poverty. It seems like a beautiful dream, but I don't have the slightest idea how to determine if it is anything more than a dream. However, I don't think that it is essential to evaluate this vision now. I am concerned about preserving our free society for the next twenty-five to fifty years; that's a big enough project for a starter. Whether most people will be working for a living in 2025 or doing the work of civilization, I don't really care. I'll settle for the United States being around then as a democracy, with capitalism working and people prospering.

Kelso's Other Plans for Universal Capitalism

The Financed Capitalist Plan is the most promising of Kelso's ideas for bringing about universal capitalism, but he has thought of others. Some of his ideas are:

The estate and gift tax laws should be amended to encour-

age wealthy people to give or leave large chunks of stock to nonwealthy people. Kelso believes that estate and gift taxes should be based on the wealth of the *recipients,* rather than that of the givers. For example, he thinks that gifts or bequests should carry no tax at all if they do not make the recipient any richer than $50,000 total capital. In this way, hundreds of thousands of new capital-owning families could be created each year. The present tax laws encourage evasive devices, such as charitable foundations, that do not increase the number of capital owners. It would be more beneficial for society to have these large holdings broken up to create many more capital-owning families. If the billions of dollars' worth of Ford Motor Company stock bottled up in the Ford Foundation had been given instead to all Ford employees, there would be hundreds of thousands more families participating in production as substantial capitalists today.

Corporations should be encouraged to set up more and better employee stock ownership plans. This is the famous ESOP, about which we will have much more to say in Chapter 8. ESOP plays a small role in the basic theory of universal capitalism, but it is the only part of the Kelso plan for universal capitalism that is actually in operation, thanks to the existence of employee-benefit tax provisions receptive to the formation of ESOPs. And as we will see in Chapter 9, the existence of these tax provisions gave Senator Russell Long the power to use ESOPs as an opening wedge for universal capitalism.

The consumer stock ownership plan (CSOP) which Kelso designed to help utilities to raise capital and at the same time distribute stock to their customers in proportion to the customers' consumption. Utilities would be given the right to require their customers to subscribe to their stock in proportion to each customer's use of service. The stock subscriptions would be financed by banks and would be paid for entirely out of dividends. Kelso has not published any studies or statistics showing the feasibility of this plan. It seems to me that CSOP would create a lot of paper work and a lot of stockholders with very small holdings. It would also diffuse capital ownership in a way that would not necessarily benefit those who need it most. However, it is certainly worthy of further study, and in 1976, several large utilities were looking into CSOP proposals.

Judging Kelso's Theories

In Chapter 3, I suggested that you judge Kelso's theories by these standards: democracy, freedom, justice, economic reality, human nature, and logic.

It is obvious that no other economic theory comes close to universal capitalism in its compatibility with democracy and freedom. Universal capitalism is the only economic system compatible with political democracy because it is fully democratic itself. It avoids overconcentration of government power; it is the only way to create a classless society and still maintain democracy, freedom, and a high standard of living; it curbs both the robber baron and the entrenched bureaucrat.

As to logic, I don't know of any other system that tries to kill three birds with one stone: meeting the huge capital needs of corporations by diffusing ownership of newly created corporate capital so that millions of New Capitalists receive substantial capitalist income, which supplies the missing link of capitalism: the mass purchasing power needed to match huge productive capacity. Kelso uses the basic logic that has worked for successful corporations and wealthy people for centuries: making capital acquisitions pay for themselves out of their future earnings.

Let's take a closer look at justice, economic reality, and human nature.

Maybe my legal training has prejudiced me, but I feel that justice is the strongest underpinning of universal capitalism. We have a beautiful Bill of Rights in our Constitution, but most Americans live out their lives without ever using rights such as freedom of the press, petitioning the government, speedy trial by jury, reasonable bail, or freedom to refuse to quarter soldiers in their houses. There are practically no economic rights spelled out in the Constitution, yet we use our economic rights nearly every day. Equal justice under law begins to mean something when you apply it to such economic rights as access to productive credit and participation in capital ownership.

Kelso and Adler were the first to propose a system of economic justice that does not reduce all people to the lowest common economic denominator and does not take away the income or savings of one person to support another. They put forward the unique proposition that *participation* in production through capital ownership is the right of every citizen, a matter of economic justice that is just as important as civil rights. In addition, Kelso and Adler hold that economic justice requires *limitation*. They would put limits on greed when greed interferes with the rights of others to participate in capital ownership, but they would not confiscate existing wealth. They would simply limit the participation under any government-sponsored scheme adopted as part of universal capitalism.

It should be no surprise that Kelso's theories are based on economic reality; after all, he works in the real business world. His X ray vision of the corporate financial structure helped him to find the way to extend capital ownership to New Capitalists by using the same methods of capital formation that corporations use. Even in proposed new legislation such as his Full Production Act, he uses existing agencies such as the Council of Economic Advisers and the Joint Economic Committee. And his imaginative CDIC is patterned after the functions of the FHA and the FDIC.

As for human nature, Kelso takes it as it is. Unlike Marx, he does not try to destroy man's natural acquisitive drive or thirst for freedom. Unlike Adam Smith, he does not depend on an invisible hand to overcome human nature by forcing man's acquisitive drive to work for the benefit of society. Kelso says that it is both natural and legitimate for all people to want to own capital and be affluent. He offers a way to accomplish this through capitalism and still maintain democracy, freedom, and economic justice, a way that combines the emotional appeal of Marxism with the self-interest drive of Adam Smith. Universal capitalism offers man's acquisitive nature a piece of the action instead of a piece of the welfare state, which nobody owns but everybody works for.

Now that we've taken a closer look at Kelso theories, let's add some of the more specific advantages that he claims for universal capitalism:

- It is anti-inflationary and probably deflationary because

billions of dollars will be diverted from unproductive redistribution and transfer payments to productive capital, and increased production is the strongest weapon against inflation. Because of the increased income that they will receive from capital ownership, poor families will need far less redistribution, and this will also cut taxes substantially.

• Research and development of new technology and new products will be greatly increased because there will be capital available for it and national policy will recognize its importance. This will help us to deal with environmental problems, instead of sweeping them back under the rug in the desperate effort to keep employment up rather than shut down plants which cause pollution.

• The corporate capital crisis will be solved by turning capital needs into a pump that feeds capital ownership into the mainstream of society.

• It will give America a decisive weapon in the global struggle against communism: a foreign policy based on exporting economic justice and human dignity to underdeveloped countries, rather than one that forces them to turn to communism as the only alternative to the economic imperialism of multinational corporations.

• It is in keeping with all the great traditions of America, both liberal and conservative. It helps individuals and families to gain independence through private income instead of public handouts. It is conservative in reducing taxes, transfer payments, and the government bureaucracy and in preserving private property and existing financial institutions while helping business. It is liberal because it does more for the little guy than all the government welfare schemes ever dreamed up. This is very important because it shows the potential appeal of universal capitalism to the entire spectrum of political and social opinion. A new national economic policy will require extensive legislation and therefore it will need political support from both Left and Right. Without such support, universal capitalism won't amount to anything more than an interesting theory for academic debate.

I doubt that I can improve on Nicholas von Hoffman's description of this mainstream political quality of Kelso's work, which appeared in *Esquire* in December 1973:

Kelso's plan comes as close as any system that recognizes ownership of private property as a basic right will come to the withering away of the state; it comes considerably closer than many Communist and Socialist arrangements where the state appears to grow to infinite size while the individual withers away. This also must have a great appeal to Americans who're not going to be talked out of their suspicion, fear and detestation of big government. It's a set of proposals that fits in with our cultural values for it keeps competition, it keeps a free market with its freedom to go down the street if you don't like the service you're getting from the man you're doing business with. . . . It succeeds in being both revolutionary and so far within the traditional understanding that either major party could incorporate it in its platforms without suffering ruptures and walkouts.

You probably know Nicholas von Hoffman as the feisty liberal counterweight to conservative Jack Kilpatrick on "60 Minutes." They were paired because they disagree on practically everything. But one thing they have agreed on is Kelso. In his syndicated column of January 20, 1972, Kilpatrick hailed Kelso as the Copernicus of economics, the first man to show us a true picture of our position in the economic universe.

In addition to von Hoffman and Kilpatrick, you can find lots of other pairs of strange bedfellows, all of whom have declared their support of Kelso's theories: for example, populist former Senator Fred Harris and professional conservative Ronald Reagan; California's radical black congressman Ron Dellums and conservative New York Congressman Jackie Kemp, the former pro quarterback; maritime labor leader Harry Bridges and John D. Rockefeller 3d. I don't know any other economic or social idea that can unite so many of us.

Will It Work?

By this time, you must be asking yourself: How could anyone be opposed to universal capitalism? The answer is that nobody in his right mind could be opposed to it *if* we could be sure that it would work out as Kelso has visualized it. But before we toss our caps in the air and claim victory over our economic woes, we have that one little hurdle to clear. And how do we even try to find this out without wrecking the present economy?

With all its faults, the present system gives most Americans a relatively high standard of living. It is in delicate shape right now and might not be able to stand the shock of a foolish experiment. Therefore, it is important to find out whether universal capitalism is a foolish experiment or a godsend.

Most great truths are simple. So is the theory of universal capitalism. But its potential ramifications are complicated and have hardly been explored. Can the credit system stand up under billions or trillions of dollars in self-liquidating loans needed to implement the Financed Capitalist Plan? What would be the effects of major corporations issuing billions or trillions of dollars' worth of new stock when they have been accustomed to handling capital expansion through debt or internally generated funds? Can the government operate without the revenue from the corporate income tax? If this untried plan is put into effect, will it trigger the greatest boom and bust in history?

On the other side of the coin, suppose that cursory study of universal capitalism discloses some problems. How do we know that these problems can't be solved by slight modifications such as gradual implementation? Are there other ideas, new or old, that can be synthesized with Kelso's theories to make universal capitalism work?

We need our best minds and resources working hard to find the answers to these questions. Otherwise, what might be the greatest idea of the twentieth century and the last hope for American capitalism-democracy-freedom will fall between the tables.

KELSO'S ONE MISTAKE: THE TWO-FACTOR THEORY

The guiding philosophy that underlies the [Puerto Rican Pro-prietary Fund] bill is that associated with the two-factor theory of Louis Kelso (and various collaborators such as Mortimer J. Adler). Kelsoism is not accepted by modern scientific economics as a valid and fruitful analysis of the distribution of income, but rather it is regarded as an amateurish and cranky fad.
Paul A. Samuelson, *San Juan Star,*
April 27, 1972

I think that Louis Kelso may well have come up with the most important idea ever originated by an American. I'm positive that he knows more about economics and corporate finance than I'll ever know. It would be presumptuous of me to try to add anything to Kelsonian economics, but I am going to try to *subtract* something, at the risk of losing Kelso's friendship and being branded with the ultimate Kelso epithet, "one-factor man."

Two-Factor Theory

Along with his concept of universal capitalism, Kelso has developed what he calls the *two-factor theory* (*TFT*). This theory has caused all sorts of problems for him. I think TFT is a mistake, but I also believe that it is remarkable to find only one mistake in a revolutionary theory of economics developed by a man who has never earned his living as an economist.

Adam Smith took ten years to write *The Wealth of Nations.* He was subsidized by a wealthy patron and had to devote only part of his time to tutoring and teaching. Furthermore, his teaching brought him into contact with other European economists and philosophers and thus helped him to

develop his theories. Karl Marx worked on *Das Kapital* for at
least twenty years, and only the first volume was completed
before his death. Friedrich Engels helped to support Marx
financially during his lifetime, and he edited and completed the
second and third volumes of *Das Kapital* after Marx died. Marx
concentrated so fiercely on his revolutionary work that he allowed his family to approach starvation rather than interrupt
his writings to go to work for wages. His young son Guido died
from the effects of malnutrition—"a sacrifice to bourgeois misery," according to Marx.

In contrast, Kelso wrote his books in what little time he
could spare from his busy law practice. He did not have Smith's
leisure or access to academics, and he would not sacrifice his
family as Marx had done. All the more amazing that Kelso
could cover so much new ground with so little error.

The two-factor theory starts out simply enough. In an industrial economy, there are two basic factors of production:
labor, including intellectual, technical, and manual work,
which Kelso calls the *human factor;* and capital, including land,
structures, and machines, which Kelso calls the *nonhuman factor.* There is nothing to argue with in that. But Kelso goes
much farther. He says that technology and automation are designed to take the burden of production off labor and move it
onto capital. He claims that the net effect of this change, which
started with the Industrial Revolution and which continues to
gain momentum today, is that labor's contribution to production is constantly decreasing and that capital's contribution is
constantly increasing. He concludes that today capital contributes at least three times as much to production as labor does. In
some writings, he claims that capital's contribution is 90 percent. Yet, under mixed capitalism, the shares of GNP are just
the reverse: 75 percent of GNP goes to labor, and no more than
25 percent goes to capital.

Traditional economists agree only that labor gets 75 percent of GNP. They say that in a free-market economy, the true
value of your contribution to production is measured by what
the market pays you. Therefore, if labor receives 75 percent of
GNP, that is the value of its contribution to production.

Kelso admits that the market pays 75 percent of GNP to

labor, but he says that the market is not free, that government and labor unions team up to *coerce* employers to pay labor three-quarters of national income although its real contribution to production is only one-quarter. Kelso's critics say that he has no proof of this claim, indeed, that he cites no studies or statistics which even attempt to measure the relative contributions of capital and labor. Kelso says you don't need any studies; you can see with your naked eye that capital has become more important than labor. However, he never explains how he arrived at his measurement of their contributions.

Why TFT Is Irrelevant to Universal Capitalism

It took me awhile to discover that this fascinating controversy has absolutely nothing to do with capital diffusion or universal capitalism. It is an irrelevant issue that would be ruled out of the case if Kelso were trying it in court. For proof of this, look back to Chapter 4, in which I presented the theory of universal capitalism without once mentioning the relative contributions of capital and labor. Kelso himself has taken the present 20 percent return on invested corporate capital and projected it as the means of paying for the whole Financed Capitalist Plan. Kelso has also said many times that the man who owns the capital is the one who gets rich, not the man who depends on his own labor, even under the present distribution, which favors labor 3 to 1.

The big problem with Kelso's attempt to measure the contributions of labor and capital is that he winds up advocating that wages be cut back to match the real contribution of labor. In his first book, *The Capitalist Manifesto,* he called for "fully paid out capital earnings to owners of capital, and with an *ultimate reduction of the wages of labor* to what labor's contribution earns, as measured by demand under freely competitive conditions" (italics added). If you ask Kelso about this, he'll

tell you that he doesn't mean to cut wages until capital ownership is spread throughout the society, by which time we will all
be capitalists and it won't be necessary to use wages to keep
living standards high. But the two-factor theory comes across as
a pitch for cutting labor's share of GNP from the current 75 to
25 percent (or even to as little as 10 percent) on the basis of
nonexistent methods of measuring the productive contributions
of labor and capital.

To make matters worse, Kelso has now packaged his entire
universal capitalism theory in the two-factor wrapper. His latest
book is titled *Two-Factor Theory: The Economics of Reality*,
and he named his organization's quarterly newsletter *Two-
Factor News*. When he makes a speech or appears before a congressional committee, he talks about *two-factor economics*.
Anyone searching his works today for the theory of universal
capitalism will first have to wade through the wage-cutting proposal and learn for himself that it is a side issue. Regrettably,
many potential supporters never get that far. They are put off
by the wage-cutting idea, they assume that it is a necessary part
of universal capitalism, or they doubt that Kelso's revolutionary
theory of universal capitalism can be valid if he is so far off base
on wage cutting, which he seems to play as his lead card.

TFT has confused even Kelso's followers. I'm sure that
most of the people who admire Kelso's idea of spreading capital
ownership would not want to spend five minutes on the idea of
cutting wages by half or more in order to give capital its fair
share of national income. As we shall see, traditional economists
who have looked at Kelso's works come away with the notion
that his wage-cutting scheme *is* the two-factor theory, and that it
is the "central tenet" of Kelsoism.

To eliminate this confusion, let's establish the independence of these two concepts right now. Let's use two-factor theory as the label for Kelso's wage-cutting scheme, and let's stick
to universal capitalism as the label for all the rest. Kelso won't
agree with me, but I am convinced that it is critically important
to make this distinction.

How TFT Alienates Traditional Economists

Kelso's unfortunate detour into TFT has caused him to be shunned by the traditional economists. It has put him on the defensive and led him to make extreme statements that he can't back up. For example, he has said that traditional economists completely overlook capital as a factor in production and that they claim that goods and services are produced only by labor. He often describes anyone who does not go along with TFT as a *one-factor man.* The way he says it, you'd think he was describing someone who is missing a vital organ.

But, in reality, traditional economists *do* recognize capital as a factor in production. The definitive traditional textbook, Paul Samuelson's *Economics,* devotes six chapters to this subject (grouped as "Part 4, Distribution of Income: The Pricing of the Productive Factors"). Capital as a factor in production is so elementary that even I picked it up in my *Lawyers Economic Handbook.* (I am relieved to discover that I had taken the precaution of being a three-factor man.)

> Economic theory refers typically to three factors of production, three resources that are used in the production of almost any goods or services throughout the economy. The three resources are land, labor and capital.

The one-factor label would be especially unfair to Professor Samuelson, for he and his MIT colleague Professor Robert Solow engaged in a famous long-running debate with Cambridge University Professor Joan Robinson in the 1960s on the issue of the relative contributions of labor and capital to productivity. Samuelson and Solow defended the role of capital and justified its share of income distribution against the sharp attacks of Robinson, a close associate of Keynes, who became an avowed Marxist. Marx believed that labor was the only real factor in production and that capital was nothing more than "congealed labor."

However, Robinson, Samuelson, and Kelso agree on one point: that the shares of national income paid to labor and capital depend at least partially upon power and politics. As the power and political clout of labor have increased, it is not surprising that labor's share of national income has also increased through higher wages. Nobody claims that the free market is free of such pressures or that it makes a perfect scientific measurement of the contributions of capital and labor. In our democratic society, we want the shares of national income to reflect the views of the majority, as long as this does not damage the production system that brings us a high standard of living.

The Keynesians who have not become Marxists cannot be accused of ignoring the contribution of capital to production. What they *have* ignored is the possibility that capital ownership can be turned into a source of adequate income for everyone. More precisely, they haven't gotten around to studying it yet. They have concentrated on full employment, higher wages, and redistribution through taxes and transfer payments to improve the income of the nonwealthy. These are the tools Keynes left to them, and they are still trying to make these old tools work. However, all these tools are designed to work on only one factor of production, labor, because the Keynesians are not aware that anything useful can be accomplished by tinkering with capital ownership.

But Kelso has come along with a new tool, diffusion of capital ownership, which might be a means of providing adequate income for everyone. Capital ownership has never really been used as a factor in government efforts to improve distribution of income. If Kelso had presented his ideas in that way, he probably would have attracted a lot of Keynesians by now, at least out of intellectual curiosity. But by calling them one-factor men and saying that they completely ignore the role of capital in production, he tends to discourage even intellectual curiosity. Kelso's use of the word *factor* automatically signals traditional economists that he is claiming that they ignore capital as a factor in production and that capital contributes three times as much to production as labor does. They never get beyond this to the point of considering capital ownership as a factor in *income distribution*. That is why I advocate the drastic step of restricting the two-factor label to the wage-cutting scheme so that Kelso's capital diffusion proposals can be examined on their own merits.

Where Would TFT Lead Us?

In fairness to Kelso, let's follow TFT through to its logical conclusion and see where it lands us. He claims that because human beings on the job are doing less physical work all the time, capital instruments are now responsible for practically all gains in productivity. Where does that get you? If you believe in the free market, as Kelso does, then you must accept the wages of labor and the return on capital as the free market's final value judgment. But Kelso says that in this case the free market is not speaking freely, that coercion by government and unions has created a false evaluation.

Let's assume for the moment that this argument is relevant, that we really want this free-market creation of ours to ignore political and social pressures and make a scientific evaluation of the relative contributions of capital and labor. Increases in productivity are obtained by combinations of men and machines, but no system exists for determining the exact contributions of each. How would Kelso go about it?

He gives us a hint in the Full Production Act, which is the climax of his book *Two-Factor Theory*. This is the model statute designed by Kelso to bring about universal capitalism. He makes several references to determining the relative contributions of capital and labor. In the declaration of new national policy, he says that the right to own capital is meaningless unless the share of income to be paid to capital is "freely and impartially determined by the forces of supply and demand in workably free, competitive markets." Section 4 of the act, which deals with the *Economic Report of the President,* requires that the president report to Congress each year on specific matters, including the following:

> the extent to which such production is being achieved respectively through the human factor, and through the privately-owned non-human factor. . . .

the degree to which the value of labor and the value of the non-human factor of production are determined by the forces of supply and demand in workably free competitive markets or are administered, manipulated or controlled by private persons, by private corporations, or by public agencies, or otherwise. . . .

the extent to which wealth and income may be distributed within the economy on the basis of need rather than on the basis of contribution to production. . . .

All this conjures up visions of the president's men going into factories to determine how much capital contributes to production and how much labor contributes. But how? No one has designed such a method, and Kelso does not suggest one. What standards are to be used? If physical effort is to be measured and workers are to be penalized for sweating less than before, how will workers ever be persuaded to accept new machines? Won't the machines be breaking down all the time so that workers can use more muscle and earn more money? Won't the mop-and-pail brigade be paid more than the highly skilled workers who operate complicated but highly productive machines? Won't the minimum wage laws have to be repealed? TFT also disregards education and training, which may enable worker A to produce twice as much as worker B using the same machine.

In the end, the present system of wage determination and collective bargaining would have to be completely dismantled. Furthermore, because none of Kelso's proposals would disturb existing capital ownership, the incomes of the present owners of capital would be tripled and the overconcentration of wealth would be aggravated. I don't see how the U.S. economy could survive this kind of upheaval, all of it unnecessary and irrelevant to Kelso's real goal of diffusion of capital ownership.

Would we really want a society that disregards need in favor of an exact measurement of contribution to production, even if such a measurement were possible? This would tend to make production and private property ends in themselves, which is exactly the opposite of what Kelso and Adler want. Kelso and Adler sincerely want to do more for the working man than most union leaders and politicians. They want to make the workers affluent; they want to raise the working man's standard of living through a combination of wages and capitalist income. But their intentions are obscured by the way in which they present TFT. And that is the tragedy of TFT.

How did these two brilliant men get diverted from their real objective? I can only guess at the answer. I think that when they were writing *The Capitalist Manifesto,* they were concentrating on a theory that would refute Marx. They wanted to show the errors in Marx's labor theory of value (the idea that only labor can create wealth) and in his concept that any wealth not distributed to labor is "surplus value" stolen from the workers by the capitalists. They did succeed in refuting Marx, but in doing so, they also followed his rigidly theoretical format. They used his concept that wealth belongs to the person who creates it. They showed Marx's error in claiming that all wealth is created by labor, but in the process, they stuck themselves with a theory that is just as impractical: that capital is entitled to all the wealth it creates, regardless of all other considerations. This led them to the idea that capital's share of income should be determined by measurement of capital's real contribution to production.

But capital's share of income is whatever capitalism's own free market will pay. To change that would be to go through a meaningless revolution, meaningless because even if the present system is thrown out, there is no measurement to replace it. Certainly, there are abuses of union power, but that is a different subject, dealt with in the Taft-Hartley Act. It has nothing to do with diffusion of capital ownership. And few thinking people are going to be won over to universal capitalism by the prospect of drastically reduced wages, even if they understand that Kelso would do this *only after* capital ownership is spread throughout society.

When everyone owns capital, the pressures now being exerted to raise wages will be counterbalanced by the universal desire for higher return on capital, and the free market will continue to fix the income shares of capital and labor. But under the present system of overconcentrated capital ownership, TFT gets twisted into an argument for a 90 percent share of GNP for the wealthy few. For example, the Russian newspaper *Pravda,* commenting on TFT in its 1959 review of *The Capitalist Manifesto,* said:

The authors urge that the share in distribution of wealth should be directly proportional to the investment of each in the production of common wealth by means of utilization of his own property. In practice it means the decrease of meagre subsistence of the working people, and unlimited increase of the profits of the capitalists.

So TFT is an albatross that Kelso has hung around his own neck. In his well-intentioned effort to bring affluence to workers, he has made himself seem antilabor. And if Kelso continues to use the TFT wrapper, he will chill the prospects for adoption of universal capitalism. This danger is best illustrated by a series of events that took place in Puerto Rico in 1972.

Kelso Comes to Puerto Rico

Near the end of his annual State of the Commonwealth Address on January 14, 1972, Luis A. Ferre, governor of Puerto Rico, made a historic announcement. He would put before the Puerto Rican legislature a bill to create the Proprietary Fund for the Progress of Puerto Rico. The fund would enable Puerto Rican workers to acquire stock in Puerto Rican companies without any financial risk. The stock would be paid for by a combination of government-guaranteed bank loans and government grants. The loans would be repaid out of dividends received on the stock.

January 1972 was a time of great triumph for Kelso. He was the star of a press briefing held at La Forteleza, the governor's mansion, shortly after Ferre's block-busting announcement. Journalists from the world's major press services listened as the "bubbly bright-eyed San Francisco lawyer-economist" explained how the Ferre fund would enable "the little fellow, the one who has never had access to the sources of capital, to get it—and on credit." Governor Ferre was delighted with the gallery reaction to his announcement, and within a few days, there was favorable press treatment as well. The *San Juan Star* called the fund "a scheme which could revolutionize the position of the Puerto Rican worker in his own society." *Time* said that "Ferre's recommendation is a bold call for action in meeting Puerto Rico's social and economic needs."

The proprietary fund had its origin in events that began in 1969. Kelso made a business trip to Puerto Rico as consultant to a Puerto Rican company that was interested in setting up an ESOP. The company never did install a plan, but during the trip, Kelso met Governor Ferre and briefed him on universal capitalism. On his return flight from San Juan to Miami, Kelso chanced to sit next to Joseph Novak, a thirty-eight-year-old Massachusetts-born, Harvard-educated tax lawyer who had been living and working in Puerto Rico for ten years; Novak was on his way to visit his parents at their winter home in Miami.

Joe Novak remembers the flight vividly.

> I was fascinated by the guy sitting next to me. He was poring over the *New York Times*, very agitated, and making lots of angry notes in scrawling black pen all over the paper. I *had* to ask him what he was doing!

By the time the plane touched down in Miami, Novak had learned why the *New York Times* (and most of the rest of the world) misunderstood the economic situation. He got his first explanation of universal capitalism directly from Kelso, and his life hasn't been the same since.

Novak was receptive to Kelso's preachings because he was greatly distressed by Puerto Rico's widespread poverty, although it did not touch him personally. (He comes from a well-to-do family and had established himself as a successful tax lawyer.) Novak is a dreamer, and he yearned for a dramatic solution to Puerto Rico's economic problems. He had looked at other ideas, but none had seemed promising.

When Novak returned to Puerto Rico after his visit with his parents, he started corresponding with Kelso. This brought him a flood of books and articles on universal capitalism, all of which he devoured. Here at last was the central core of an idea that could save Puerto Rico. But how could it ever become a reality there if nothing had been done about it in the United States in the more than ten years since the publication of *The Capitalist Manifesto?*

The answer fell into Joe Novak's lap unexpectedly. He had begun his legal career in New York with Shearman & Sterling, one of the oldest, largest, and most prestigious law firms in the country. But he found that New York practice was not for him and decided to move to Puerto Rico. His colleagues suggested that he look up Wallace Gonzalez, another Shearman & Sterling alumnus who had returned to his native Puerto Rico, where his family was prominent in legal and banking circles. Novak took the suggestion, and he and Gonzalez eventually became law partners. By August 1971, Governor Ferre had appointed Gonzalez secretary of the treasury, Novak had established his own law firm, Ferre had directed Gonzalez to study proposals to overhaul the Puerto Rican tax structure, and Gonzalez asked his old friend and former law partner Novak to help him on the tax-reform project. Novak gladly pitched in because he knew that Puerto Rico was operating under archaic tax laws, but he also had another motive. He had been mulling over Kelso's theories for two years and was more than ever convinced that they could help to solve Puerto Rico's economic problems. Now he had an opportunity to get the ear of the governor, and he decided to try to tie in Kelso's theories with the tax-reform report he had been assigned to write.

Novak worked on the report through August and September 1971, and he also drafted a description of the proprietary fund plan, adapting Kelso's theories to the Puerto Rican economy. He didn't call Kelso in at that point because he had no idea whether Governor Ferre would show any interest in the idea. Finally, he completed his report and sent it to Gonzalez for delivery to the governor on September 20, 1971, along with the proposal for the proprietary fund. Governor Ferre sent word back through Gonzalez that he was excited about the fund proposal and wanted Novak to start drafting a detailed version immediately.

Novak jubilantly telephoned Louis Kelso in San Francisco and told him that here was the first chance to have universal capitalism considered by a real live legislature—with the backing of the governor. Would Kelso come to Puerto Rico to help draft a detailed plan that the governor could use in his State of the Commonwealth address?

After years of writing, speaking, and carrying a revolution on his own shoulders, Kelso was not about to miss the first chance to see his dream become law. He made three trips to Puerto Rico and worked frantically with Novak. Finally, they completed a white paper describing the proprietary fund, and the governor triumphantly presented it to the legislature.

Proprietary Fund for the Progress of Puerto Rico

The proposed proprietary fund legislation went through several versions before Ferre decided on the final one to submit to the legislature. Although Kelso's theory of universal capitalism was the foundation of the bill, the final version did not follow Kelso's Financed Capitalist Plan in all details. The Plan had to be adapted to the Puerto Rican economy, and it was Joe Novak who did most of the adapting. Kelso and Novak did not have a huge pool of unowned newly created capital (comparable to the $120 billion new capital outlay of U.S. corporations) to play with, and they were dealing with a weak economy. So they had to be innovative.

The final bill, thirty-one pages long, is a beautiful piece of legislative draftsmanship. Here is the text of the preamble:

Statement of Motives

Since the enactment of Act Number 184 of May 13, 1948, the first of several successive laws providing special tax incentives to encourage investment in, and development of, the Puerto Rican economy, Puerto Rico has depended primarily upon improved employment opportunities, education and welfare programs for the betterment of its citizens.

However, we believe that the economic goals of our society should change. We should maximize the economic productiveness of every family and individual both through opportunities for useful employment and through more effective opportunities to acquire an additional basic source of income and of economic security, by means of the private ownership of productive capital. It is the duty of the Commonwealth to find the means, consistent with the logic of free enterprise and private property, to accomplish these new economic goals.

This Act is designed to improve the present economic order (where reliance is placed mainly upon employment and welfare to close the purchasing power gap), to permit the participation by all our people in the production and enjoyment of goods and services through employment and through the acquisition of the ownership of productive capital. Moreover, as the incomes of Puerto Ricans grow through the supplementation of labor income by capital income, the growth of industry and businesses in response to the increased purchasing power of our population should provide more effective means to combat unemployment. It is also a goal of this Act to provide additional means for financing the expansion of Puerto Rican industry, commerce and agriculture.

It is another objective of this Act to begin vigorously to eliminate the causes that would in the future increase the welfare burdens upon our economy. As personal and family economic security is fortified through additional incomes derived from privately owned capital, welfare requirements of the future and the tax burdens they would otherwise bring, should decline. The concept of this Act is a new approach, as it involves reaffirming the institution of private property while enabling the many to become owners of productive capital over a reasonable period of time and without impairing their incomes or requiring the investment of their savings.

The Proprietary Fund for the Progress of Puerto Rico is a dynamic concept which will grow and improve constantly in the light of experience in a way that will enable it to attain the goals and objectives of this Act in the most effective manner possible. As it becomes possible to increase the appropriations to the Fund, a larger number of residents of Puerto Rico will be able to participate in the benefits of this Act. In addition, we expect to provide as soon as possible for a governmental investment of not less than $100 per annum for each qualified employee, which would permit the investment of at least $200 per annum for the benefit of each qualified employee who participates in the Proprietary Fund for the Progress of Puerto Rico.

It is the continuing policy and responsibility of the

Commonwealth to promote true equality of opportunities for the economic betterment of all residents of
Puerto Rico, both through employment and through
ownership of productive capital.

Note the fine hand of Louis Kelso, but note also that there is no
mention of two-factor theory or of raising capital's share of income at labor's expense. In fact, there is no mention of TFT in
the entire bill. Remember this; it becomes important.

The fund's structure is intriguing. It was to be a diversified investment fund that would invest in business enterprises
operating in Puerto Rico. The fund could not own more than
25 percent of any business and could not invest more than 5
percent of its assets in any one business. Investments were to be
selected by professional investment managers. The fund was to
have a board of twelve directors, six appointed by the governor
and six elected by the shareholders. Only Puerto Rican residents over eighteen would be eligible to acquire stock. And two
stock purchase plans were provided.

The *Commonwealth Co-Investment Plan* was open only to
the estimated 800,000 Puerto Rican workers who earned between $800 and $7,800 a year. (Novak had wanted to include
jobless people, but Governor Ferre had insisted that the plan be
limited to workers because he felt that they would be more
responsible than nonworkers in handling new capital ownership.) Each of these workers would be allowed to buy $50 worth
of fund stock annually; this would be matched by $50 worth of
stock bought for the worker by the Commonwealth (the government of Puerto Rico) , making a total annual investment of
$100 per worker. Complete financing of the workers' $50 annual purchase of stock was to be provided by local banks
through loans arranged by the fund and guaranteed by the
Commonwealth. The loans were to be repaid out of dividends
paid on the stock acquired; the worker was not to be personally
responsible for repayment of the loan. In the event that dividends were not sufficient to repay any loan within five years, the
Commonwealth was to pay the balance owed to the bank and
then carry the loan itself. As each $50 loan was paid off, the
worker would start to receive the dividends on stock that had
cost $100 originally.

The fund bill requested appropriation of $10 million for

the first year's matching $50 investments, which meant that 200,000 workers would each be able to acquire $100 in fund shares. Priority was given to workers at the lowest end of the scale (those earning annual wages of $800). It was hoped that successful experience with the fund would enable the Commonwealth to increase both the number of workers covered and the amount invested annually.

Of course, the workers could not sell or transfer their stock until it was fully paid for, but the bill went even farther to encourage them to hold onto their stock for income. It provided that a worker who sold any stock would be ineligible to acquire any additional stock for three years.

To get more people interested in the fund, the bill set up the *Supplemental Investment Plan*. This plan was to be open to any resident of Puerto Rico with annual income of $18,000 or less. Each investor would be allowed to buy between $25 and $100 in common stock each year, but unlike the Commonwealth Co-Investment Plan, there would be no bank financing or Commonwealth matching purchases under the Supplemental Investment Plan; these investors would have to buy the stock with their own cash.

To make sure that there would be no large accumulations of fund stock and no misuse of the fund by wealthy people or speculators, the bill limited each stockholder's total holdings to the number of shares he could have acquired by purchasing the amount allowed to each qualified employee or investor each year that the fund was in operation. Thus, if the limits remained at $100 per stockholder per year, after ten years, no stockholder could own stock that had cost more than $1,000 when issued. And to make doubly sure, the bill prohibited anybody whose annual income exceeded $18,000 from buying fund stock either directly from the fund or from a shareholder who wanted to sell.

There were also some favorable tax provisions in the fund bill, most of them designed to get 20 percent or more annual return for fund shareholders. The fund itself was to be exempt from income taxes. It was also to be reimbursed by the treasury for its proportionate share of income taxes paid by the businesses in which it held interests. For example, if the fund owned

3 percent of the stock of a Puerto Rican corporation that paid
$100,000 in income taxes, the fund would get a rebate of $3,000
from the treasury. This device would give the fund its share of
corporate income free of taxes, so that it would be in a position
to pay out to the fund shareholders the maximum amount of
earnings each year to reduce the loans against the stock and get
the dividend income flowing to the low-income workers as soon
as possible. It was a clever way of carrying out Kelso's theory of
eliminating corporate income taxes; it cut out those taxes that
would have slowed down capital diffusion but retained those
taxes that were not related to capital diffusion. The bill also
provided that dividends paid on fund shares would be tax-
exempt, making the dividend income that much more valuable
to each shareholder.

The fund plan was more generous than Kelso's Financed
Capitalist Plan because it would have given Puerto Rican New
Capitalists a free ride on half their shares. Therefore, it provided for a faster payback of the nonrecourse loans. The Puerto
Rican stockholder would be able to use the dividends from $100
worth of stock to repay each $50 bank loan. As Novak figured it
out, even if the annual before-tax return on investment was
only 15 percent, the stock financed under the Commonwealth
Co-Investment Plan would be paid for in four years (assuming
a 7 percent interest rate on the bank loans).

Because of the $50 matching provision, the fund had to
start out on the modest scale of $100 total annual investment
per worker. But Novak calculated that with reasonable success
and gradual increases in annual appropriation, the fund would
produce a total paid-up investment of about $37,000 and a total
tax-free income of about $71,000 for the low-income employee
who participated throughout his working career. During retirement, the worker would have an annual tax-free income of
about $5,600. For an impoverished island like Puerto Rico,
these are big numbers. Nothing like these incomes was in sight
before the proprietary fund bill of 1972, and nothing like them
has been proposed since.

At the same time, the fund was designed to supply capital
to businesses operating in Puerto Rico and to encourage more
businesses to locate there in order to take advantage of the

availability of capital. All this was calculated to create more jobs, cut welfare costs, and help industrialize an underdeveloped economy.

With so many things going for it, the bill was easily approved by the Puerto Rican House of Representatives on March 9, 1972. The House was controlled by Governor Ferre's New Progressive Party (NPP). However, the opposition Popular Democratic Party (PDP) held a majority in the Senate. The president of the Senate was Rafael Hernandez Colon, who was also likely to be the PDP candidate to oppose Ferre in the 1972 election. From Ferre's very first announcement of the fund, PDP leaders expressed concern or opposition. In an election year, they were obviously not enthralled by the prospect of Governor Ferre bringing to hundreds of thousands of Puerto Rican voters the hope of improvement in their economic situation and participation in capital ownership.

The fund bill was sent to the Senate in March 1972, but Senate President Hernandez Colon and his PDP colleagues were in no hurry to put it to a vote. The Senate was due for adjournment at the end of April and would not reconvene until after the November election.

Professor Samuelson Takes a Hand

As Governor Ferre pressed the Senate for a vote on the bill in April 1972, a turning point in the history of universal capitalism occurred.

On Wednesday, April 26, 1972, Hernandez Colon announced to the Senate that he had requested Nobel Prize-winning economist Professor Paul A. Samuelson of MIT to make an analysis of the fund bill. He released the text of Professor Samuelson's analysis to the Senate. It was reprinted in the *San Juan Star* on April 27. The analysis was extremely negative. In fact, it made the fund look like an invitation to financial disaster.

Armed with the Samuelson statement, Hernandez Colon was able to avoid a Senate vote on the fund bill in 1972. Just before it adjourned for the year on April 30, the Senate created a special committee to study the legislation and submit a report. But because the Senate would not reconvene until after the election, this move meant that the report would not be presented until the 1973 session. Given the worldwide prestige of Samuelson and the extremely negative nature of his analysis, Hernandez Colon seemed on very solid ground in preventing the fund bill from becoming law before it had received very careful study. On April 28, 1972, the *Wall Street Journal* reported:

> Whether the measure eventually becomes law next year will depend in large measure on what happens in Puerto Rico's November elections.
>
> Should Governor Ferre win reelection, a new attempt probably will be made to push the measure through. A victory by the opposition Popular Democratic Party probably will mean that further action won't be taken on the measure.

The *Wall Street Journal* was exactly on target. The PDP won the 1972 election, bringing Rafael Hernandez Colon into the governor's office. Nothing more was heard about the proprietary fund bill or the study that the special Senate committee was to make.

Professor Samuelson's analysis, as reprinted in the *San Juan Star,* is his first and only published criticism of the fund bill or Kelso's theories. Indeed, it is the only published analysis of Kelso's theories by a prominent traditional economist that I have been able to find. Such a rarity is worth reprinting here in full.

The Proprietary Fund Criticized

Statement by Paul A. Samuelson on House Bill 1708, concerning the Patrimony for the Progress of Puerto Rico (the Proprietary Fund).

1. This statement is prepared at the request of the president of the Senate of Puerto Rico, soliciting my views on the wisdom of this measure. The views I express are my own and have no relation to the views of any

political parties or factions in Puerto Rico. Moreover, I make no pretense toward expert knowledge of Puerto Rico; I confine myself to problems of broad general economic principle, relating to the distribution of income and to economic development.

2. The general purposes of the bill must strike an economist as being vaguely philanthropic if not grandiose. One would wish for the typical citizen of any land both higher real wages and higher non-wage income. However, the guiding philosophy that underlies the bill is that associated with the two-factor theory of Louis Kelso (and various collaborators such as Mortimer J. Adler). Kelsoism is not accepted by modern scientific economics as a valid and fruitful analysis of the distribution of income, but rather it is regarded as an amateurish and cranky fad. Although it has been put forth in more than one book and has been around for a long time, the principal learned journals of economic science—e.g., the American Economic Review, the Royal Economic Journal, the Harvard Quarterly Journal of Economics, the Chicago Journal of Political Economy—have steadfastly withheld recognition and approval from the doctrines of Kelsoism. Its central tenet is contradicted by the findings of economic empirical science: according to statistical study of macroeconomic trends, by such distinguished scholars as Professor Simon Kuznets of Harvard (Nobel laureate in economics for 1971), Senator and Professor Paul H. Douglas (award winner for his Cobb-Douglas statistical measurement of the aggregate production function), MIT Professor Robert M. Solow, and numerous researchers at the National Bureau of Economic Research under the directorship of Arthur F. Burns, chairman of the Board of Governors of the Federal Reserve System, economic adviser to Presidents Eisenhower and Nixon, the contribution of labor to the totality of GNP is in the neighborhood of 75 percent, with only 25 percent attributable to land, machinery and other property.

Moreover, an increasing proportion of labor productivity is attributable in modern economies, such as Puerto Rico is aspiring to become, to investment of "human capital" in the form of education and skill enrichment. This 75–25 percent breakdown is diametrically opposite to the Kelso presuppositions, which are purely speculative and not based upon econometric analysis of the observed statistics of nations at different stages of development.

3. Because the basic economic principles underlying the proposal are faulty, it is likely in practice to prove a cruel disappointment to the Puerto Rican people. Beyond its fundamental weaknesses, the proposal has so many pitfalls and loopholes that the American Congress would condemn it to oblivion. Let me enumerate only a few of the defects that struck me at first study of the matter. If so many defects appear on the surface, think how many more a careful and informed analysis would reveal.

a. It is a first principle of sound finance that families at low income level must not invest so heavily as more affluent families in venture equities. Although Puerto Rican incomes are higher than they used to be and higher than in many Latin countries, island incomes are lower still than in any of the 50 states. It would be rash for California, our most affluent state, to tempt people into venture equity investment by guaranteed bank loans and various gimmicks of government guarantees and tax abatements. How much more rash for Puerto Rico.

b. You cannot get something for nothing in economic life. The scandal of John Law in ancient France pretended otherwise, and led to fiasco. I fear the same in this case. If the Commonwealth guarantees bank loans to purchase Patrimony stocks, it has thereby less credit to expend in other directions of development. What advantage is there in a dollar of dividends if it slows down the growth of productivity of real wages by tens of dollars?

c. The Commonwealth has a limited tax base. It must not squander that base. It must expend it prudently in developing industry. Every dollar of tax exemption squandered on the Patrimony is that much less of a dollar available for other Bootstrap operations. Here in the states, we have much experience, much of it sad, with venture capital efforts—the disastrous Small Business Investment Companies with their wasted tax exemptions, etc. At the least, very wealthy men who can afford to lose their money should be relied on for such risky ventures. To tempt, or coerce, the masses and the poor into such avenues is to invite, if not disaster, at the least disappointment, economic inefficiency, and waste.

d. Further, the program is open to dangerous pitfalls of corruption, political patronage, and tax avoidance. Thus, if one has tens of thousands of dollars of capital gains in a business, and even if it makes no economic sense for this to be acquired by the Patrimony, there is a tax reason for selling to that body and temptation to lobby with some future government official to have this done. Who will be able to prevent this or even recognize that such a miscarriage of sound finance is taking place? To avoid inheritance tax, some men will send for the priest and at the same time acquire tax-exempt Patrimony shares, only to have their heirs sell off those shares after they have performed their loophole functions.

These are not vague possibilities. As consultant to the U.S. Treasury over the years and as an expert witness before congressional committees, I have had occasion to see every chink in the law exploited in this way, and yet I have never seen a mainland bill so carelessly drafted in terms of providing such tax-avoidance opportunities. The Puerto Rican legislature is warned!

4. In summary, despite the laudable intentions of the Patrimony bill, a careful cost-benefit analysis of its features in terms of scientific economics must raise grave fears concerning its unsoundness for a commonwealth anxious to elevate the standard of living of its citizens.

A Close Look at Samuelson's Analysis

Because Samuelson's statement was published only a few days before the Puerto Rican Senate adjourned, there was no time for proponents or opponents of the fund bill to make a detailed analysis of it. But it remains an important document, for it shows the devastating effect of TFT on the chances for universal capitalism. Let's look at it section by section and see what it really says.

In Section 1, Samuelson disclaims any expert knowledge of Puerto Rico and confines himself to broad economic principles.

Section 2 is the most important part of the article because it reveals that Samuelson was under the mistaken impression that the proprietary fund was based on the two-factor theory and that he therefore completely misunderstood the fund proposal. He says that "the guiding philosophy that underlies the bill is that associated with the two-factor theory of Louis Kelso." Actually, there is not a single mention of the two-factor theory or of the allocation of income between capital and labor in the proprietary fund bill. All the public discussions of the bill made it clear that the proponents were basing the fund's prospect for success on the present 20 percent before-tax return on capital. Indeed, many of the bill's tax provisions were designed to enable the fund to pay out to its shareholders the full 20 percent return that is available now, without using the two-factor theory to increase capital's share of income by cutting wages.

It is clear that when Samuelson refers to the two-factor theory, he is not speaking of Kelso's theory of universal capitalism; rather, he is zeroing in on Kelso's theory of changing the 75–25 percent sharing of income between labor and capital. He cites statistical studies by distinguished economists which show that the contribution of labor to GNP is 75 percent, with only 25 percent attributable to capital; and in the same sentence, he says that these 75–25 statistical studies contradict the "central tenet" of TFT. He ends Section 2 by saying that "this 75–25 percent breakdown is diametrically opposite to the Kelso presuppositions, which are purely speculative and not based upon econometric analysis of the observed statistics of nations at different stages of development." It is clear that Professor Samuelson assumes that the central tenet of TFT, and indeed of Kelsoism itself, is that the 75–25 sharing of GNP should be reversed so that capital receives the 75 and labor receives the 25. Because Kelso's writings now identify his entire body of teaching as two-factor theory and two-factor economics, Professor Samuelson can't really be blamed for reaching this conclusion. But to me, this is the clearest example of the way in which the beautiful dream of universal capitalism can be shattered if Kelso continues to present it as part of the two-factor theory.

If there is any doubt left about Professor Samuelson's belief that Kelsoism requires cutting of wages to benefit capital, we need only look at the beginning of Section 3, in which he condemns the entire proprietary fund bill "because the basic economic principles underlying the proposal are faulty." Again, he assumes that the basic economic principle underlying the fund bill is the two-factor theory.

Professor Samuelson does analyze some specific features of the bill in Section 3. However, it is clear that his entire outlook on the bill was clouded by his incorrect assumption that it was based on TFT. He seems to be saying that he didn't bother to read the bill very carefully because he knew it to be based on an unsound theory that would not support other provisions of the bill no matter how praiseworthy they might be. This is pointed up by his introductory language: "Let me enumerate only a few of the defects that struck me at first study of the matter. If so many defects appear on the surface, think how many more a careful and informed analysis would reveal."

The jarring effect of TFT, even upon so noted a scholar as Professor Samuelson, can be seen from his analysis of specific provisions of the bill, all of which strongly suggest that he misunderstood the purposes of the fund.

In Section 3a, Professor Samuelson warns that "families at low income level must not invest so heavily as more affluent families in venture equities" and that it "would be rash for California, our most affluent state, to tempt people into venture equity investment." He concludes that it would be much more rash for Puerto Rico to do this. All this is true, but it has nothing to do with the proprietary fund. There is not a word in the fund bill indicating that low-income families may invest any of their own money in the fund or that any of the fund proceeds are to be used for starting new businesses (which is what he means by "venture equities").

In fact, if Professor Samuelson had ever spoken with Kelso for even five minutes, he would have learned that Kelso will have nothing to do with venture equities. He believes, as Samuelson does, that venture capitalism is a game for the rich, not for the poor. There is not a word in the proprietary fund bill or the writings of Kelso to indicate any connection with venture equities. The philosophy is just the opposite: to give low-income families a chance to own a piece of successful companies operated by others, instead of trying to turn them into entrepreneurs by providing them capital to start new businesses. Indeed, Governor Ferre mentioned in speeches that he had already approached owners of some of the more successful Puerto Rican businesses and that they indicated their willingness to make large blocks of stock available to the fund. He also said that the fund's officers, who would be professional investment advisers, would invest "only in proven enterprises." I'm sure that Governor Ferre would have agreed to amend the fund bill to prohibit investments in start-up ventures or in any business that did not have a record of consistent profits if anyone had suggested that such an amendment was necessary.

In Section 3b, Samuelson says that the Commonwealth credit used to guarantee bank loans for fund stock detracts from the credit the Commonwealth might expend "in other directions of development." However, he does not mention any other directions of development that would be more beneficial than the spreading of capital ownership among low-income families and at the same time making funds available to businesses operating in Puerto Rico.

Samuelson bases his arguments in Section 3b on the premise that "you cannot get something for nothing in economic life." Neither the proprietary fund bill nor the writings of Kelso claim that something is being offered for nothing. What they do say is that productive capital can be made to pay for itself out of its own earnings, that this is being done now for the benefit of corporations and wealthy capital owners, and that it can be done for the benefit of low-income families as well. This is not "something for nothing"; it is more like some of the existing action for everyone.

In his condemnation of the use of Commonwealth credit for guaranteeing bank loans, he overlooks the fact that the proceeds of the bank loans are invested in Puerto Rico's economic development. It is only the ownership of the capital that differs. Instead of the Commonwealth guaranteeing loans made directly to business and thus increasing capital ownership of people who are already wealthy, the Commonwealth would provide the same capital for Puerto Rican businesses but would channel its ownership to those who are in need and who would spend the dividends in the Puerto Rican economy.

In Section 3c, the professor warns against squandering tax

exemptions on "venture capital efforts." But, as we have seen, the fund has nothing to do with venture capital, and neither does Kelso.

In Section 3d, Professor Samuelson really goes overboard in branding the fund as a program "open to dangerous pitfalls of corruption, political patronage, and tax avoidance." He puts the full weight of his prestige behind these charges, reminding us of his consulting work for the U.S. Treasury and his appearances before Congress as an expert witness, and ends with the punch line, "I have never seen a mainland bill so carelessly drafted in terms of providing such tax-avoidance opportunities. The Puerto Rican legislature is warned!"

I don't know how many statutes Professor Samuelson has read or drafted, but all my experience tells me that he is way off base in these statements. To help you reach your own conclusions, I'll have to tell you something about my experience. My writings on legal subjects fill fifteen volumes, most of them dealing with statutes. Several of these books have been cited by the U.S. Supreme Court and other appellate courts as legal authority. I have been a consultant and an expert witness for legislators who sought my help in drafting statutes. Everything that I have learned about statutes tells me that the proprietary fund bill was not carelessly drafted. I have read both the bill and Professor Samuelson's analysis many times, and I have been unable to find any unusual opportunities for corruption, political patronage, or tax avoidance, nothing approaching the opportunities in such "mainland" bills as our welfare and Medicare legislation.

Professor Samuelson gives two examples of dangerous pitfalls in the fund bill. First, he says that

> if one has tens of thousands of dollars of capital gains in a business, and even if it makes no economic sense for this to be acquired by the Patrimony, there is a tax reason for selling to that body and temptation to lobby with some future government official to have this done. Who will be able to prevent this or even recognize that such a miscarriage of sound finance is taking place?

Here he is referring to Article 20 (e) of the fund bill:

> Gains realized from the sale to the Fund of equity in business enterprises and from the sale to the Fund of the

other types of assets shall be exempt from income tax, provided, however, that whenever the sales price is in excess of One Hundred Thousand Dollars ($100,000), the granting of this exemption shall be subject to the prior approval of the Secretary, which approval shall be based on the Secretary's determination that the same is beneficial to the public interest.

This provision was inserted to encourage owners of profitable businesses to sell stock to the fund without having to pay capital gains taxes on the sale. It is another indication of the desire to attract successful businesses rather than venture equities. The owners of stock in start-up ventures and unsuccessful businesses are not likely to have capital gains. The "Secretary" mentioned in this article is the secretary of the treasury of the Commonwealth of Puerto Rico. Because he would have to give his personal approval in transactions exceeding $100,000, it is difficult to see how this provision could be widely abused.

The other dangerous pitfall is described by Professor Samuelson this way:

To avoid inheritance tax, some men will send for the priest and at the same time acquire tax-exempt Patrimony shares, only to have their heirs sell off those shares after they have performed their loophole functions.

If I hadn't read this under the byline of Professor Samuelson, I would have guessed that it came from the script of a Marx Brothers movie. The dying Puerto Rican worker (perhaps played by Harpo), who earns less than $7,800 a year, goes out laughing, for he first acquires $100 worth of fund stock and passes it through a loophole to his heirs without paying any inheritance tax. But what his ingenious tax lawyer (undoubtedly played by Groucho) didn't tell him was that there is no inheritance tax in Puerto Rico on estates under $60,000. I'd be willing to bet that you could count on the fingers of one hand the number of Puerto Rican workers eligible for the fund who would have taxable estates of $60,000. Furthermore, the Samuelson scenario specifically states that this worker acquires the stock on his deathbed solely to avoid inheritance taxes, which means that this "loophole" would be used only by someone who was not already participating in the fund. I can only conclude that when Professor Samuelson was told about the estate tax exemption, something was lost in the translation.

Apparently, no one told Samuelson about the many safe-guards against corruption that were written into the bill. The fund could not invest more than 5 percent of its total assets in any one business enterprise nor own more than 25 percent control of any business enterprise. Voting rights were vested directly in the hundreds of thousands of workers who would be shareholders, and they would elect half of the board of directors (the other half to be appointed by the governor). Officers and directors of the fund were to be indemnified by the fund against judgments and costs arising out of litigation *except* in cases where the director or officer was adjudged liable for negligence or misconduct. This is a much stricter provision than most American corporations and funds have for indemnification of their officers and directors. In the United States, most officers and directors are indemnified against claims of negligence.

Furthermore, acquisition of fund shares was limited to $100 per year, even on the part of wealthy individuals who might seek to buy up fund shares from low-income families. Then there was the provision to discourage sale of stock by the low-income families, even after it was paid for, by forcing them to drop out of the fund program for three years after the sale of stock.

There was also a provision in Article 16 of the bill for very stiff penalties (up to five years in jail and fines of up to $5,000) for furnishing false information to the fund, which was made a felony. Finally, Article 18 provided for an annual audit examination, and Article 19 required the fund to deliver an annual report to the governor and both houses of the legislature ("a report *sworn to* by its President and Treasurer"). The annual report was also to be published in two general-circulation newspapers.

To sum it up, the people who drafted this statute did their homework; the people who told Professor Samuelson about its "loopholes" did not.

Professor Samuelson's statement ends with Section 4:

> In summary, despite the laudable intentions of the Patri-
> mony bill, a careful cost-benefit analysis of its features

in terms of scientific economics must raise grave fears concerning its unsoundness for a commonwealth anxious to elevate the standard of living of its citizens.

Samuelson indicated in Section 3 that he was writing from "first study" and that he had not made a "careful and informed analysis" of specific provisions of the fund bill; therefore, we can only conclude that the "careful cost-benefit analysis" referred to in Section 4 deals with TFT. Samuelson did make a more careful analysis of what he calls the "central tenet" of Kelsoism, and he cited scholarly articles on the 75–25 income split. Because he believed that TFT was the "guiding philosophy" underlying the fund bill, he must have rejected the specific provisions of the bill as unworthy of careful cost-benefit analysis. Thus, the *Wall Street Journal* (April 28, 1972) reported that Samuelson's analysis had been used to block the fund bill in the Senate and repeated Samuelson's charge that the fund bill was

> based on an economic theory that already had been discredited by most responsible economists. (The proposal was based on the two-factor theory of Louis Kelso, who advised the Ferre administration in drafting the measure.)

How TFT Hurt Kelso in Puerto Rico

There is further evidence of Samuelson's mistaken assumption that TFT was the keystone of the fund bill and of Kelsoism. When Mike Wallace and "60 Minutes" producer Norman Gorin went to MIT to interview Samuelson for the 1975 Kelso telecast, the professor spent the better part of an hour of videotape time talking about the 75–25 income split and how Kelso was all wrong on this according to scientific economics. He cited the same scholarly studies that he mentioned in his *San Juan Star* statement. When Wallace did not run any of this footage or even mention the 75–25 income split, Samuelson felt that his position had not been properly represented. Incidentally, Wallace taped about twenty hours of Kelso interviews and picked up a lot of TFT statements, but he used none of them on the air. It was clear to Mike Wallace—and, through him, it became clear to millions of American viewers—that Kelso's ideas on capital diffusion could be presented and debated without touching on the irrelevant issue of cutting wages to increase the return on capital.

Finally, in a discussion with me in 1976, Professor Samuelson continued to deal with the 75–25 income split as *the* two-factor theory of economics and the fundamental concept of Kelsoism. He still felt that the 75–25 studies by Kuznets, Cobb-Douglas, Solow, and Burns refuted the entire two-factor theory. I tried to convince him that there was a lot more to Kelso that was independent of TFT, but he was so alienated by TFT that he felt he simply couldn't take the time to look into Kelso's ideas any further.

If you have any doubts left about TFT being a millstone around Kelso's neck, you have only to look at a speech made by Governor Ferre in August 1972. Ferre was still struggling to keep the fund bill alive when he made the commencement address at the University of Pittsburgh Graduate School of Business. He explained all the objectives of the fund and what it would do for Puerto Rico. This was exactly the same fund bill that he had presented to the Puerto Rican House of Representatives in March 1972, but this time, there was no reference to Louis Kelso. The only person Ferre mentioned as being instrumental in developing his interest in the fund was former MIT Professor Paul Rosenstein-Rodan. In fact, Ferre had discussed the general subject of broadened capital ownership with Rosenstein-Rodan prior to 1972, but the professor had played no part in drafting the fund bill. Remember that at the January 1972 press conference in the governor's mansion, Ferre had proudly presented Louis Kelso as the architect of the fund. Clearly, Ferre was stung by Samuelson's charge that the fund was based on the "discredited" Kelso two-factor theory.

Kelso, Novak, and Ferre all lost out in Puerto Rico in 1972. And the people of Puerto Rico lost a chance to improve their low standard of living. Nobody can be sure that the fund would have been successful or that it would have helped Puerto

Rico very much even if it had succeeded. But as the four-year term of Governor Hernandez Colon neared its end in 1976, Puerto Rico's GNP was declining at the rate of about 2.5 percent a year; the majority of Puerto Rico's people were living on food stamps; and the unemployment rate was 20 percent, unless those who had given up looking for jobs are also counted, in which case it was 40 percent. Obviously, traditional methods of fighting poverty were not working any wonders in Puerto Rico. Surely things could not have been worse if the fund bill had been enacted. At least, the Puerto Rican poor would have been given some hope for a better future.

To the idealistic Joe Novak, the sinking of the fund bill was a terrible disillusionment. He tried to go back to his Puerto Rican law practice, but his heart wasn't in it anymore. He decided to drop his practice and look for a way to get back into the quest for universal capitalism.

It would be easy to cast Professor Samuelson as the heavy of the Puerto Rican episode. He used his great prestige to knock out a bill that he obviously had not read too carefully, and some of the pitfalls he warned about were nonexistent. But let's not be hasty. If universal capitalism is to be given a fair chance, its proponents will have to get some support from traditional economists such as Samuelson or at the very least draw them into a debate that covers the real issues involved. We must ask this question: Why would Samuelson condemn the fund bill and all of Kelsoism unless he believed that they were based on the erroneous two-factor theory?

There is a temptation to explain Samuelson's position by the NIH factor (not invented here). But the pattern of Samuelson's lifework makes this doubtful. His books draw heavily on the works of other economists, many of whom (e.g., Milton Friedman and Joan Robinson) are poles apart from Samuelson on basic economic philosophy. He doesn't claim to have all the answers. In his textbook, *Economics,* he recognizes "the unsolved problem of an incomes policy to cure stagflation in the mixed economy," and he points out the great inequality in the distribution of income and wealth in the United States.

If you ask Chicago's Professor Milton Friedman for an opinion of Kelsoism, as *Time* did in its edition of June 29,

1970, he'll tell you that it is "a crackpot theory." He explains, "Instead of saying that labor is exploited, Kelso says that capital is exploited. It's Marx stood on its head." Notice that Friedman, like Samuelson, treats all of Kelsoism as a crackpot theory because of TFT. This is one of the few things on which Samuelson and Friedman agree.

I see nothing to be gained by criticizing Samuelson or Friedman for their failure to peel off the TFT wrapper and get to the parts of Kelso that are potentially useful. Instead, let's try to find a way to get them past TFT so that they can help us to find out whether universal capitalism will work. We're going to need all the help we can get, especially from the leaders of traditional economics.

Lessons of the Puerto Rican Experience

There are several lessons to be learned from the fate of the Proprietary Fund for the Progress of Puerto Rico.

1. Because universal capitalism is a novel theory and its consequences are not fully known, legislators will be afraid to enact broad capital diffusion measures if they are opposed or ridiculed by leading traditional economists.

2. Traditional economists will not support bills based on universal capitalism if Kelso continues to insist on combining wage-cutting theories with capital diffusion theories under the label of two-factor theory or two-factor economics.

3. Because capital diffusion and wage cutting are two independent ideas, Kelso should separate them and apply the TFT label to wage cutting only.

4. When wage cutting has been separated from capital diffusion, the stage will be set for traditional economists to investigate capital diffusion as a means of bringing adequate income to everyone.

5. Until that separation takes place, many traditional economists will follow the lead of Professors Samuelson and

Friedman and refuse to make any serious study of capital diffusion.

It's time for another multiple-choice question.

Louis Kelso has developed a theory of universal capitalism under which he has proposed that ownership of new corporate capital be channeled to New Capitalists and that the new corporate capital be allowed to pay for itself in a few years through the present 20 percent before-tax return on capital. Kelso has also concluded that capital contributes at least three times as much to production as labor does; that the present distribution of GNP, which favors labor over capital by 3 to 1, is the result of coercion rather than free, competitive market forces; and that after capital ownership has been spread throughout the society, wages should be cut in order to make the return on capital 75 percent or more, reflecting capital's true contribution to production.

___ (a) These two theories, capital diffusion and wage cutting, should be combined under the label of two-factor theory or two-factor economics so that all persons in favor of spreading capital ownership throughout the society must also favor cutting of wages and must take Kelso's word for the conclusion that capital contributes three times as much as labor because there is no accepted method of determining relative contributions to production other than the prices that the market is willing to pay.

___ (b) These two theories, capital diffusion and wage cutting, should be separated (with capital diffusion to be known as universal capitalism and wage cutting to be known as two-factor theory) so that traditional economists will be in a position to investigate Kelso's capital diffusion theories without becoming involved in wage cutting and so that those who favor spreading capital ownership will not have to attach themselves to a movement that would destroy the present basis of collective bargaining and triple the incomes of present owners of capital.

What are the chances of getting Louis Kelso to choose answer *b?* To understand his position, it is necessary to take a look at the history of the Kelso movement.

FROM THE CANAL ZONE TO THE BOHEMIAN GROVE: THE KELSO MOVEMENT, 1944-1964

You'd better pick some other field if you want to do a snow job on me. This is a field I know as much about as any man alive or dead. There isn't any theory of capitalism, *universal or otherwise—there just isn't a theory about it!*
Dr. Mortimer Adler to Louis Kelso,
Cloverdale, California, 1955

Kelso in Colorado, 1913-1942

Louis Kelso came up the hard way. His father, a Denver musician, had to struggle constantly to keep his family fed and housed. Louis was born in 1913. By 1928, he was working, but he stayed in school. Through the depression years, he took any job that came along, including driving a dynamite truck, and he worked his way through the University of Colorado.

It was during his high school years in Denver that Louis first realized that something was missing from capitalism. He lived near the railroad tracks, and so he noticed that the passenger trains were mostly empty and that the freight cars were not carrying much freight but *were* carrying a lot of people, the beaten people of the depression years, who rode the boxcars from town to town in their desperate search for work. As he studied economics in high school and college, he noticed some other things:

> On the one hand, I saw the vast idle capacity of our factories and farms to produce goods and services and the

capability of bringing into existence even greater productive capacity. On the other hand, I saw hunger and suffering; poverty and unsatisfied human needs and wants were everywhere. Physically, we had the capabilities of satisfying our needs and wants. Those who could produce the goods and services wanted to do so. But the unsatisfied needs and wants continued year after year. We had a physical problem: poverty. We had the physical answer. Clearly, we could not make the answer effective because we did not have the proper business and institutional arrangements.

That's the way Lou Kelso talks. When he says "the proper business and institutional arrangements," he means the economic system.

He took a closer look at that system, and during his college years, he made some startling discoveries.

I naïvely assumed that if I first learned how a "capitalist system" is supposed to work, I could then identify those who were failing to do their part. *I found that there was no theory of capitalism at all.* In fact, the bulk of the literature on the subject was written by enemies of a private-property economy. This motivated my search for the theoretical framework for a universal capitalist economy, one that did for every family and individual what the robber baron variety did for the pinnacle affluent class.

Kelso's entire career was shaped by these early discoveries. Others may dispute his conclusion that there was no theory of capitalism. After all, what about Adam Smith? But to Louis Kelso the boy in Colorado or to Louis Kelso the distinguished author and lawyer in San Francisco, Adam Smith said nothing about how capitalism could come to grips with the problems of America in the 1930s or in the 1970s.

He found more to explain capitalism in the writings of Karl Marx because Marx was the only one who talked about the central issue: deciding who is going to own the capital. Kelso was fascinated by Marx's repeated expressions of admiration for the marvelous productivity of capitalism, which he admitted could not be duplicated by any other system known to man, even though his goal was to destroy capitalism. Kelso gorged himself on the writings of Marx—not exactly a fashionable pursuit in the Colorado of the 1930s, especially for a patriotic lad who wanted to become part of the establishment.

Kelso graduated from the University of Colorado in 1936 with a *cum laude* degree in finance. He stayed on at Colorado and became a distinguished law student, graduating in 1938 after winning top academic recognition as editor in chief of the *Rocky Mountain Law Review*. He passed the Colorado bar that year and began law practice in Denver, specializing in municipal bonds and public tax systems.

In his spare time, he continued to search for a theory of capitalism, hoping that somebody besides Karl Marx had written one. That search proved futile, and so he dared to start making notes for one that he himself might write some day. But the pressures of establishing a law practice and starting a family were very great, and he didn't get very far with the project during his Denver years.

In the Canal Zone, 1944-1945

At the outbreak of World War II, Kelso enlisted in the navy and was quickly commissioned as an intelligence officer. He was trained for a secret mission behind Japanese lines, but in the great tradition of the armed forces (which will make future generations wonder how we ever won the war), he was shipped to the Panama Canal Zone and put in charge of processing counterespionage information from Latin America.

By 1945, this job got pretty dull, and Kelso started thinking about the theory of capitalism again. He had his wife ship him a trunkload of his economics books and notes. He tried working in his room at BOQ (bachelor officers' quarters), but

> it was very noisy in those places. The boys would go down to the whorehouses in Panama City and come home very drunk and noisy, and it was cutting into my hours very seriously. So I went to the captain of the base, and I said, "Captain I've got a problem. I am trying to write a book, and I need some peace and quiet."

The captain, who had been a Cincinnati high school principal in civilian life, was sympathetic. In fact, he was starving for intellectual companionship, and he invited Kelso to join him in his beautiful three-bedroom cottage, complete with cook, maid, and laundry service. In that Panamanian cottage, Kelso wrote the first draft of his theory of universal capitalism. He explains its tentative title, *The Fallacy of Full Employment,* this way: "What that meant is the fallacy of relying exclusively on full employment to solve the income distribution problem."

As the war ended and Kelso prepared to go home in December 1945, he was filled with excitement about his manuscript.

> I was perfectly sure that an idea so obviously sound would just move through the society like wildfire. I have since concluded that if I had had it printed up in Panama in paperback, loaded up a bomber with a million copies, and dropped them all across the United States, it would still have never been noticed at all. It would have been as obscure as it was in my closet.

The Closeted Manuscript: San Francisco, 1947-1955

Right about the time that Kelso returned from the wars, something was happening in Washington that made him decide to leave his precious manuscript in the closet. Congress was debating the Full Employment Act of 1945, a bill that adopted as national economic policy the very theories Kelso blasted in his manuscript. In the end, some legislators insisted that the federal government could not really guarantee everyone a job, and the bill did not pass in its original form. Kelso explains what happened next:

> So they very cleverly solved that, as politicians will. They took off the word "Full" and passed the same law the next year—that is, the Employment Act of 1946—and that is still our national economic policy in 1976.

The thirty-two-year-old lawyer, with a wife and two daughters to support and his career interrupted by the war, had two choices. He could pick up the threads of his law practice and start again to build his family life and fortune, or he could take his manuscript out of the closet and proclaim to the world that the U.S. Congress had made a horrible mistake by adopting a national economic policy that was at variance with the theories of Louis Kelso. The manuscript stayed in the closet, although he did put one copy in a bank vault for safekeeping.

The war had given Kelso his first glimpse of San Francisco, and it was love at first sight. "When I saw San Francisco, I decided I'd been born in the wrong place," he recalls. He decided to move there as soon as possible. It took him about a year, during which he taught constitutional law and municipal finance at the University of Colorado Law School. Then, in 1947, he packed up and moved his family and his legal career to San Francisco. There he joined Brobeck, Phleger & Harrison, one of America's great law firms.

He soon became a partner and went on to achieve extraordinary success as a financial and tax lawyer for some of California's leading corporations. He handled acquisitions for the American Trust Company, which absorbed the Wells Fargo Bank and took its name, becoming the nation's twelfth-largest bank. He did the legal work for the development of the huge Embarcadero Center for the Rockefellers. He represented bankers, securities underwriters, utilities, and wealthy individuals. And he couldn't help but notice that the wealthy, whether corporations or individuals, had a habit of acquiring more capital by letting it pay for itself.

As Kelso went about building his reputation and fortune in San Francisco, he made a point of never mentioning his closeted manuscript. In fact, he had decided to let it age for twenty-five years before trying to get it published. He knew that his revolutionary theories would brand him as a maverick, which is not good for business when you are establishing yourself as a big-time corporation lawyer. Furthermore, he had a sense of the greatness of his ideas which told him that they would still be valid a quarter of a century later. He stuck to his plan for his first eight years in San Francisco. But a turning point in the history of universal capitalism came in 1955: a heated argument between Kelso and Mortimer Adler.

Professor Adler Smokes Out the Manuscript, 1955

Kelso had enrolled in Adler's lecture course on the Great Books in 1951. Adler was then forty-nine and had achieved worldwide recognition as a philosopher and educator. He had taught at Columbia from 1923 to 1929 and then had joined the Robert Hutchins team at the University of Chicago, where he remained from 1930 to 1951. Apart from his teaching, he wrote many books and was one of the originators of the Great Books program in liberal arts colleges and in adult education. Adler persuaded the *Encyclopaedia Britannica* people to publish Great Books of the Western World, a series that includes more than fifty classics by authors such as Homer, Vergil, Dante, Shakespeare, Swift, Tolstoy, Dostoevski, Machiavelli, Rousseau, Adam Smith, Mill, Marx, Newton, Darwin, Freud, Plato, Aristotle, Aquinas, and Kant. He also developed the *Syntopicon*, the world's first index of ideas, as a guide to the Great Books. Adler was convinced that the Great Books held the keys to wisdom and that these timeless works should be reread continuously. He found that the best way to discipline himself to keep rereading them was to conduct a Great Books course.

In 1951, Adler moved to San Francisco. Kelso became his lawyer and also a director of his Institute of Philosophical Research. When he heard that Adler would give his lectures in San Francisco, starting that year, he thought:

> There are plenty of chances to get great books, but this is something different. This fellow Adler has accumulated the sort of scholarship that I could accumulate in about two more lifetimes, so I'm not going to miss this chance to learn the Great Books through him.

Kelso stayed with the course for more than four years. Adler was something of a martinet as a lecturer; he expected total acceptance of his views and was in the habit of informally polling his students on key issues. In one of these polls early in 1955, all those attending the lecture agreed with Professor Adler's views on the theories of Adam Smith and Karl Marx— all, that is, except Louis Kelso. At the time, Adler did not challenge Kelso; he probably thought that Louis had simply misunderstood the question.

But Mortimer Adler was not one to forget that a mere student had disagreed with him. Later that year, it happened that he and Kelso were invited by Prentice Hale, chairman of Broadway Hale Stores, to a weekend party at Hale's ranch in Cloverdale, California. Kelso recalls the conversation they had as they strolled around the swimming pool.

> ADLER: Why the hell did you disagree with me at the seminar last winter?
>
> KELSO: Because your conclusion was inconsistent with the theory of universal capitalism.
>
> ADLER (*after giving Kelso a dirty look*): You'd better pick some other field if you want to do a snow job on me. This is a field I know as much about as any man alive or dead. *There isn't any theory of capitalism,* universal or otherwise—there just isn't a theory about it!
>
> KELSO: Sorry, Mortimer. You just haven't really surveyed the whole field.
>
> ADLER: I'm telling you, I know more about it than you do!
>
> KELSO: Yes, but you haven't been in my closet.

Kelso proceeded to explain that he had written the first theory of capitalism in the Canal Zone in 1945 and had put the manuscript away. Adler's initial response was:

> Oh, my God, don't go dragging me through a big, dog-eared pile of papers. I don't have time to read that kind of stuff. Just tell me—give me the five-minute version or the ten-minute version of what your so-called theory is all about.

Kelso started to give Adler the ten-minute version, but he got through only about two minutes. He had just covered the idea of using broad diffusion of capital ownership to solve the income distribution problem when Adler dropped his pipe to the pavement and began jumping up and down and shouting excitedly:

> Goddamn it, why the hell did *you* have to discover that! I've been looking for that for twenty-two years! Of course, this is the answer. I knew that robber baron capitalism wasn't the answer. I knew that robber bureaucrat socialism wasn't the answer. I know communism is not the answer. *Obviously, that is the answer!*

Did Professor Adler then retreat to the quiet of his room to contemplate this great discovery? Not according to Kelso.

> Then he began spraying me with questions. He was like a machine gun firing bullets. We ruined the dinner party, just converted it into a shambles. We went on until about three in the morning. Mortimer was staying with his wife in a house on the opposite side of the swimming pool, and he was still talking when I went to sleep. Then, of course, he began bugging me, charging me with being a coward, an intellectual coward—"How dare you not publish that ten years ago!"—giving me hell, and so forth.

Writing
The Capitalist Manifesto,
1955-1958

So began what Kelso describes as two of the most hectic years of his life. He was busy enough with his law practice, and he did an enormous amount of reading just to keep current on economics, philosophy, government, and his other interests. On top of this, the relentless Mortimer Adler finally convinced him that he must update, polish, and publish his closeted manuscript. He started in 1955, and by working many nights into the wee hours of the morning, as well as weekends and holidays, he finally completed the revised manuscript, which he renamed *Capitalism*, in 1957. He had been giving copies of each chapter to Adler as he went along, and now that it was finished, he looked forward eagerly to the professor's final appraisal. Here's how it went:

> ADLER: It won't do. Too scholarly. Only a few people would ever read it. Too damn long. Looks like it would make an eight- or nine-hundred-page book. It's got to be simpler; you've got to have a simplified version first, one that will be read by corporate management.

> KELSO: Listen, Mortimer, I'd like to wring your neck for what you put me through. It half killed me to get this job done, and now you say it won't do. I just don't have the time to go through this again. I'll do it someday, but I just can't do the simplified version right now.

> ADLER: Okay, supposing I join you, and we just take the highlights of your long manuscript, and we publish it under the title of *Capitalist Manifesto?*

> KELSO (*knowing Adler's crowded schedule and feeling relieved at getting out of another nasty job*): Great, Mortimer, we'll do that when you get around to it.

But here Kelso was fooled. Somehow, Adler put everything else aside and insisted that the two of them go at it right away. Adler worked during the day; Kelso, at night. In five weeks, they rewrote the manuscript three times and boiled the 900 pages down to less than 300. One morning near the end of this intensive rewriting, Kelso went to Adler's office to give him one of the last batches of manuscript and received another surprise.

> ADLER: Oh, Lou, one matter. I've changed the title.

> KELSO (*turning back from the door he had just opened to leave*): You did what?

> ADLER: Well, I changed the title.

> KELSO: To what?

> ADLER: I changed the first word from "The" to "A," "*A* Capitalist Manifesto" instead of "*The* Capitalist Manifesto."

> KELSO: What do you mean? Why should that be changed?

> ADLER: Well, it's pretty presumptuous, you know, to say "*The* Capitalist Manifesto." I mean, it ought to be a little more modest.

KELSO: Mortimer, this is the first approach to modesty that I have ever seen you even pretend to. Where did it come from? Modesty is something you ain't got at all!

ADLER: Well, I just thought that would be a little more delicate way to handle it.

KELSO: Well, now, do you know of any other theory of capitalism? You told me before that you didn't.

ADLER: No, there is no other theory.

KELSO: Do you think there is room for any other theory of capitalism?

ADLER: No. I guess I was wrong. We'll change it back to "*The* Capitalist Manifesto."

And that's the way they sent it to four publishers. All four accepted it immediately. Kelso and Adler decided to accept the offer made by Random House, and *The Capitalist Manifesto* was published in February 1958.

It quickly became a best seller, and there were many enthusiastic reviews. The two that impressed Kelso most were in *Time* and *Pravda*. The *Time* review, which appeared in the February 10, 1958, issue, was written by Ralph P. Davidson, who by 1976 had risen to the rank of publisher. He said:

> The overriding merit of this book is a reminder to the reader—a reminder that capitalism is a revolutionary force in human affairs offering still unplumbed promise for the future.

As might be expected, *Pravda* did not give the book rave notices. But to Kelso, the very fact that *Pravda* reviewed it was highly significant. He told me that

> it was really more of a diatribe than a review. They called our plan "cannibalistic." They said in essence that Adler and I were out to finish the total enslavement of the American worker, which told us that we had struck a nerve. In other words, we said something important, or they wouldn't have bothered to review it. In the first place, it isn't reviewed in *Pravda* unless it is damned important. This is a little tiny newspaper; usually, it is only four or six pages. They devoted two-thirds of a page to our book.

Although *Pravda* found the book significant enough to give it a long review, the American academic economics establishment practically ignored it. Nevertheless, Kelso and Adler were convinced that the capitalist revolution was under way. They received hundreds of enthusiastic letters from thoughtful readers. They assumed that the launching of the idea and the momentum of the book would generate a movement to install universal capitalism as the economic policy of the United States.

They were wrong. Although the book created a great deal of intellectual interest, nothing else really happened as an immediate result of its publication. Despite the sale of more than 50,000 copies in hard cover, it was never published in paperback. (In 1975, Greenwood Press, a reprint house, brought out a hard-cover reprint.)

The *Manifesto* is my favorite among Kelso's books. Maybe that's because it was the beginning. Kelso and Adler were stepping off into the darkness. There was no precedent (other than Marx) for this kind of a book. Neither man was a professional economist, and they had very little access to feedback from professional economists. To me, the *Manifesto* is a great creative work that some day may be mentioned in the same breath as *The Wealth of Nations, Das Kapital,* and *The General Theory of Employment, Interest and Money.* It has the timeless quality of a classic; in fact, it would need very little revision if it were issued as a new book today.

The foresight that Kelso and Adler showed in the *Manifesto* can be illustrated by this sentence: "Our mixed economy cannot solve its problems of inflation and full employment." And they devoted an entire section to "Mixed Capitalism's Insoluble Problem: Inflation." Remember that this was written in 1958, during the Eisenhower years, when unemployment and inflation were both at levels that seem unbelievably low to us today.

The *Manifesto* is divided into two parts: "The Idea of the Capitalist Revolution" and "The Program of the Capitalist Revolution." When Kelso and Adler started out, they intended to write only the first part, the theory of universal capitalism. They hoped that the mere statement of the theory would lead economists and politicians to see the light and develop a practical program for carrying out the revolution. They felt that it was not their job to work out the details, particularly because they expected that it would take at least fifty years to complete the revolution. But in discussing the project with friends, they learned that the theory would seem too utopian if they did not offer a practical plan of action. So they recognized the necessity of adding a second part, the blueprint for achieving universal capitalism.

They put forward their plan of action rather tentatively. In fact, they say that they do not believe it is the best plan that can be devised and that their proposals "call for the most intense study that can be given them by the best economic, political, legal, and scientific minds in our society." They call upon the leaders of politics and economics to undertake this study, and they insist that if their proposals are found unsuitable, the politicians and economists must go on from there to draft new plans to make capitalism universal.

Unfortunately, neither of these things happened. Political and economic leaders did not make a serious study of the *Manifesto,* nor did they try to come up with their own ideas about how capitalism could be made more nearly universal. Why did the book have so little impact? Probably because in 1958 it looked as if nonuniversal capitalism was working and because an idea of such breathtaking scope takes a long time to settle in before it makes any real impact.

If you don't have time to read the whole *Manifesto,* I urge you to read the ten-page preface written by Mortimer Adler alone. Adler modestly disclaims any credit for the "original and basic theory of capitalism on which this Manifesto is based. That theory is entirely Mr. Kelso's." He says that until he met Kelso, he had doubts that capitalism could establish "the kind of economic democracy which political democracy required as its counterpart." He had concluded that the economic injustices of nineteenth-century industrialization were intrinsic to capitalism, and so he was concerned with finding a substitute for it. It was only through discussions with Kelso that he learned how capitalism *could* be made universal. Kelso's vision filled out the full picture of democracy that Adler had been searching for.

Kelso and Adler included the Financed Capitalist Plan in their practical program for the revolution. They spelled out most of the details, including bank financing of stock purchased by the New Capitalists, CDIC guarantees of the bank loans, gradual elimination of the corporate income tax, and 100 percent payout of earnings as dividends. The only features not included are the rediscount of notes by the Federal Reserve Banks and the very low interest rates suggested for New Capitalist loans. These ideas came a little later. In the *Manifesto,* they made it clear that they wanted the New Capitalists to get stock in well-seasoned, successful corporations and that start-ups and speculative securities should be bought only by "those with already large capital holdings, who are therefore better able to afford the risk involved."

A considerable amount of space is devoted to the Financed Capitalist Plan and the idea of broad diffusion of capital ownership throughout the society without using the employment relationship as the channel of distribution. Kelso and Adler also mention modification of death and gift taxes to make it easier for the wealthy to spread their holdings to people who have no capital.

There is very little mention of the ESOP concept in the *Manifesto;* less than two pages are devoted to "equity-sharing plans." As we shall see, ESOP was a later addition to the program of universal capitalism that was developed as a practical way of opening the door to broader capital ownership.

From the *Manifesto* to *The New Capitalists,* 1958-1961

With the publication of *The Capitalist Manifesto,* Kelso found himself busier than ever answering correspondence from interested readers all over the world. One of them was a Canadian farmer named James L. O'Dell, who read the *Manifesto* and then, in February 1959, published his own twelve-page pamphlet called *My Theories Pertaining to our Canadian Enterprise Systems,* which was an explanation of universal capitalism. Since 1959, O'Dell has spent about half the year working his farm near Barrhead, Alberta, and the other half advancing the capitalist revolution. His business card reads, "James L. O'Dell, Farmer and Universal Capitalism Aspirant."

Another early reader was a young Mexican student named Abel Beltran-del-Rio, who had just earned his master's degree in business administration at the Monterrey Institute of Technology when the *Manifesto* was published. Beltran-Del-Rio had been reading the Great Books under the Adler program since 1952, and he had helped to organize a Great Books discussion group that met on Saturdays in his hometown, Chihuahua. Because he had been following Adler's activities for some time, he read the *Manifesto* and made it a topic for his discussion group. He also started corresponding with Kelso. We shall meet him again in Chapter 10.

In later years, Kelso was to meet hundreds of influential people who told him that they had been deeply moved by reading the *Manifesto* and were waiting for someone to organize the revolution so that they could join it.

In order to gain more freedom of action and more time to devote to the capitalist revolution, Kelso left Brobeck, Phleger & Harrison with their good wishes and launched his own San Francisco law firm in June 1959. It was called Kelso, Cotton and Ernst (later Kelso, Cotton, Seligman and Ray).

After the first year of feedback on the *Manifesto,* Kelso and Adler decided that the best hope of bringing about the capitalist revolution was to concentrate on winning the support of financiers and investment bankers. Kelso had many clients and friends in the financial community, and despite his humble beginnings, he was now a man of finance rather than labor. He believed that financiers could not fail to see the logic of his theory and that they had the power to reshape corporate finance in order to bring universal capitalism into being, particularly through the Financed Capitalist Plan.

Kelso was not optimistic about converting labor leaders to his cause in the 1950s because he felt then that universal capitalism would probably make drastic changes in the functions of labor unions. On the other hand, he was living and working among frightened capitalists who knew that they had a good thing but realized that it might not last forever. It was to this audience of frightened capitalists and financiers that Kelso and

Adler addressed their second book, *The New Capitalists,* which was published in March 1961.

Kelso had learned that there were quite a few financial people who were interested in the concept of universal capitalism but who would not take the time to read a philosophical work such as the *Manifesto. The New Capitalists* (which was only 109 pages long) was designed as a financial handbook for practical implementation of the Financed Capitalist Plan, which Kelso and Adler felt was the best means of bringing about universal capitalism.

The subtitle, *A Proposal to Free Economic Growth From the Slavery of Savings,* is the main theme of the book. The audience they were trying to reach was attuned to the principle that capital formation must be based on past savings; *The New Capitalists* was designed to convince them that capital formation could also be financed from future earnings. It demonstrates that most capital acquired by corporations is actually paid for out of future earnings and that directors of modern corporations usually will not approve capital acquisitions unless they are supported by projections showing that they will pay for themselves.

The New Capitalists deals only with the Financed Capitalist Plan; it contains no mention of ESOP or any other form of employee-benefit plan. The description of the Plan is just about the same as it is in the *Manifesto,* but it includes the new concept of rediscounting of the notes by Federal Reserve Banks. (There is no mention of special low interest rates for Financed Capitalist loans, which is introduced in Kelso's third book, *Two-Factor Theory.*)

The New Capitalists ends with a call for the free world to use the Financed Capitalist Plan as a weapon against communism:

> Of even greater importance for the American economy is the fact that, through the method of financing new capital formation which we have outlined, the economic race between the free world and the communist world can be placed in its proper perspective, and our chances of winning it can be increased immeasurably. No longer would the issue merely be one of whether socialist meth-

ods or traditional Western methods of bringing about economic growth can create the higher standard of living. Rather, the rivalry would be between a totalitarian technique of forcing industrialization by mandate upon a propertyless and freedomless people, and a capitalist system of simultaneously creating a high level of wealth production and consumption along with the conditions of maximum individual freedom and maximum personal incentive. We have no reservations in predicting that, on this basis, the West can win.

At first, Kelso and Adler thought they had a big winner in *The New Capitalists.* In October 1961, Leonard Spaceck, chairman of the board of Arthur Andersen & Co., one of the nation's largest public accounting firms, bought 4,250 copies and distributed them to members of his organization. But apart from more correspondence for Kelso to answer, nothing concrete came of this very promising gesture.

An early and important convert to Kelsoism through the *Manifesto* and *The New Capitalists* was William E. Chatlos, a partner in Georgeson & Co., Wall Street's oldest and largest proxy-fighting and stockholder-relations specialists. Chatlos reviewed *The New Capitalists* in the September 1961 edition of *Trends,* the Georgeson house organ: "There seems to be little question that the proposed changes are the most imaginative and provocative to appear on the economic scene in many years."

Despite this praise, nobody moved to put these imaginative changes into operation. Kelso and Adler were once again disappointed by the reaction of the financial community. As had been the case with the *Manifesto,* there was a lot of intellectual enthusiasm but no movement to start the capitalist revolution. The times were still working against Kelso and Adler, for as John Kenneth Galbraith noted, the twenty years from 1948 to 1967 may well be recorded as the high point of mixed capitalism. It seemed to be working like a charm, and ideas for radical change were bound to be put on the back burner no matter how beautiful the underlying philosophy might be.

The Revolution Sputters, 1962-1964

In 1962, Kelso received his first and only formal academic recognition, an honorary degree of Doctor of Science in economics from Araneta University in the Philippines. The award was based on his original contribution to economic thought as discussed and developed in "the epochal book *The Capitalist Manifesto* which in future generations . . . will be regarded as the answer to *The Communist Manifesto* and a good, complete and definitive answer thereto." Kelso's work had captured the imagination of Dr. Salvador Araneta, president of Republic Flour Mills and Araneta University and a member of the Philippine cabinet. But apart from this distant applause, the academic economics establishment officially ignored Kelso and Adler.

Through the early 1960s, Kelso struggled to keep up with his thriving law practice and continued to subsidize the universal capitalism movement out of his own pocket. There really was no thrust to the movement other than Kelso's writings, lectures, and correspondence. Kelso would make a speech or write an article at the drop of a hat and would often travel at his own expense. Even though he continued to get many enthusiastic letters, some of them from executives of large corporations, he realized that he wasn't making any real progress. No legislation had been drafted, and no academic or research organizations were making studies of his proposals. So in 1963, Kelso decided to seek formal academic recognition of his theories in the United States.

Kelso turned to the nearby Stanford Research Institute (SRI) for help. He proposed that SRI assign one of its economists to make a detailed study of his theories. SRI considered the proposal but found that no members of its staff felt particularly qualified or stimulated to do the research. In April 1963,

P. J. Lovewell, then general manager of economics and management research for SRI, suggested that Kelso should offer a doctoral fellowship for study of the major questions raised by his theories, questions such as "by what means can wider distribution of corporate ownership be achieved?" Lovewell felt that this kind of study could be done by doctoral candidates under the supervision of a prominent political economist. However, this suggestion was not very helpful to Kelso because he was looking for something faster than a doctoral thesis and because no prominent political economists had even opened their minds to universal capitalism.

After being rebuffed by SRI, Kelso decided that he would try to institutionalize the movement himself in a small way. He felt that his best bet to keep the movement going was to try to pierce the economics and political establishments through his own writings, and for this purpose, he needed more scholarly research than he had time to do on his own. So he started looking for a full-time assistant and collaborator, someone who could handle the heavy correspondence, help him write speeches and articles, and work on an updated version of the *Manifesto*.

In October 1963, he hired Patricia Hetter, paying her out of his own pocket. Patricia was a political scientist and writer who had gone to live in Sweden in her twenties; she had just returned to America after seven years abroad. She recalls her disillusionment with Sweden:

> If I'd lived in Sweden only one year, I would have gone back home a socialist. But I stayed there seven years, and I left absolutely opposed to socialism. On the other hand, I also understood that if there was no alternative that could allow ordinary people a chance for a decent standard of living, socialism would be inevitable. I love the Swedes, and I think they're too good for socialism. That's one of my themes.
>
> I saw that those who had the power to take property took it in Sweden, and they were the ones who had the best standard of living. At that time, the Swedes were very docile, and they wore the yoke of the socialist bureaucrats very meekly. They had no alternatives, you see; this is the problem. The alternative always involves unacceptable suffering.

Patricia Hetter had perceived the tyranny of Swedish socialism that was to drive film director Ingmar Bergman and actress Bibi Andersson out of the country in 1976, but she didn't know what to do about it. Like Mortimer Adler in the early 1950s, she had thought that the only choices were socialism or nineteenth-century robber-baron capitalism.

Although Kelso had been looking for someone with a doctorate in economics, he was impressed by Hetter's writing ability and her tremendous enthusiasm. Before meeting Kelso, she had checked *The Capitalist Manifesto* and *The New Capitalists* out of the San Francisco library and read them both in one night.

Her assignment was a heady one: to bring *The Capitalist Manifesto* to life and start the capitalist revolution. There was no handbook around Louis Kelso's office to tell her how to do this, so she had to improvise. One of her first steps was to wade into the stacks of unanswered letters that Kelso had received from all over the world. Although some of the letters were several years old, she managed to breathe life into relationships that were to become important when the capitalist revolution got under way.

In 1964, Kelso and Hetter began their writing collaboration with a brilliant article called "Uprooting World Poverty— A Job for Business." Twelve years later, this piece strikes me as a much wiser plan for Western relations with underdeveloped nations than anything that came out of the lengthy 1976 United Nations Conference on Trade and Development held in Nairobi. Louis and Patricia maintained that U.S. foreign policy played into the hands of the Russians by forcing poor nations to turn to socialism or communism for lack of any other choices. They showed how the West offered only three choices to the poor nations: foreign capital as loan or investment, foreign aid, or domestic capital owned by the local pinnacle class. None of these provided the great masses of people with an alternative that looked as good to them as those offered by socialism or communism. The few jobs created by these three forms of financing never did enough good, and the masses were attracted to state ownership of capital because they had no hope of ownership themselves.

Kelso and Hetter drew up a blueprint for a practical Western economic policy toward the poor nations; they proposed that the Financed Capitalist Plan be adapted for use abroad. They showed how the mythical poor nation of Xlandia could develop factories that would be owned by poor Xlandian families. The stock purchased on credit by the poor families would be paid for out of the factories' future earnings. American businesses would provide the elements needed for the industrialization of Xlandia, but not by government handout or American ownership that would later be expropriated. The Financed Capitalist Plan would enable Xlandian industries to pay American businesses for their goods and services. Thus, American business would have new customers (Xlandian industries owned by the poor masses of Xlandia), and American foreign policy would be promoting local private ownership by millions of Xlandian New Capitalists, instead of forcing Xlandians into socialism or communism.

The beautiful dream of Xlandia filled Patricia with enthusiasm, but Kelso had been burned so many times that he cautioned her not to expect immediate acceptance of the article. As she recalls,

> We sent it to practically every established business and economics journal in the United States, and everyone turned it down. I just about figured that I had run out of places to send it, but I did some more research and found one last hope, *Business Horizons,* published by the Graduate School of Business of the University of Indiana.
>
> We sent it off to Indiana, and to my surprise, they published it. On top of that, a few months later, we got a telegram, followed by a $1,000 check, saying that the article had won the 1964 McKinsey Foundation Award for significant business writing. When the telegram came, after all those disappointments, I thought that someone was playing a joke on us!

The McKinsey Foundation award is of more than academic significance because McKinsey & Company, for which the prize is named, is one of the world's leading management consultants. But in spite of this great start, Patricia Hetter was to learn to share the frustrations of trying to turn intellectual acceptance into real-world action. Twelve years after the award, there was still no movement toward making the Xlandia plan part of U.S. foreign policy.

Goldwater at the Bohemian Grove, 1964

While Patricia Hetter was beginning her search for the way to start the capitalist revolution, Kelso got his first chance to influence a presidential candidate. For that opportunity, he owed more to his membership in a club than to his years of writing and lecturing.

When Kelso was a partner in Brobeck, Phleger & Harrison, he had become a member of the exclusive Bohemian Club, an organization that is the epitome of what G. William Domhoff calls "ruling class cohesiveness." Domhoff, a professor of sociology at the University of California, Santa Cruz, wrote a book called *The Bohemian Grove and Other Retreats.* He describes the city clubhouse, a six-story building in downtown San Francisco. He explains that membership is limited to the upper crust of business, the professions, the arts, education, and politics. Most fascinating is his description of the Bohemian Grove, the summer retreat for club members and their carefully selected guests that *Time* called the "walled-in Walden for the well-to-do":

> Imagine an annual gathering of rich, white, mostly elderly men, the wealthiest and most influential in the country. Such gatherings exist, and one, set in 2700 acres of giant redwoods 65 miles north of San Francisco, the Bohemian Grove, dates back to 1880. At this encampment, an essential part of the ambience is the performance of rituals reminiscent of a college fraternity. A relaxed, distracting mood is carefully planned by a staff at great expense for the annual High Jinks and Low Jinks. There is the comaraderie of renewing old friendships and much drinking and singing. But unlike that at

ordinary social clubs, the casual chatter around the fire at the Bohemian Grove represents one of the most influential meetings of the powers-that-be from New York to Los Angeles.

After the opening banquet, the Hamadryad appears to lead all to the Cremation of Care, to implore the gathered Bohemians to cast their grief to the fires and be strong with the holy trees and the spirit of the Grove. And so, the ruling social class begins another two-week frolic, away from its responsibilities as captains of industry, as the decision makers and opinion molders of corporate America.

Domhoff names members and guests who have attended the two-week seminar encampments at the grove: Dwight Eisenhower, Richard Nixon, Ronald Reagan, John Kennedy, Lowell Thomas, Bing Crosby, Art Linkletter, Edgar Bergen, Herman Wouk, Neil Armstrong, David Sarnoff, Wernher von Braun, Lucius Clay, Earl Warren, Herbert Hoover, and Nelson Rockefeller.

Lou Kelso made it a point to get up to the grove for two weeks every summer, and he used these meetings to spread the gospel of universal capitalism to many influential people. That's how he came to meet Barry Goldwater in the summer of 1964, during Goldwater's campaign for the presidency.

Kelso got Goldwater's ear and pumped it full of universal capitalism. Goldwater listened politely, but like most presidential candidates, he was not strong on economics; he left that to experts such as Milton Friedman. As soon as Goldwater mentioned that he would have to consult Friedman, Kelso felt that there was no chance of convincing the senator. He was right.

But Kelso is not easy to discourage. He continued his breakneck schedule, heading one of San Francisco's busiest corporate law firms and fomenting the capitalist revolution on the side. He would write an article or deliver a speech whenever there was the slightest hint of interest. He spoke at such places as the Fort Dodge Senior High School in Iowa and the annual convention of the American Land Title Association in Philadelphia; he contributed articles to such publications as the North Dakota Law Review and The Cooperative Accountant. He also continued to move in more prominent circles. He still believed that frightened or enlightened capitalists were his most likely allies. He thought that his best chance lay with the Republican party, even though his meeting with Goldwater had failed to produce results. He tried the Republicans again in 1964 and in 1965. As usual, the nongrubby revolution convened at an exotic place: Aspen, Colorado.

FROM ASPEN TO THE MONTPELIER ROOM OF THE MADISON HOTEL: THE KELSO MOVEMENT, 1964-1973

The divine insanity of noble minds,
That never falters nor abates,
But labors, endures, and waits,
Till all that it foresees it finds,
Or what it cannot find, creates.
Henry Wadsworth Longfellow

Congressman Ford at Aspen, 1964

The beautiful ski resort town of Aspen, Colorado, forms the backdrop for one of our finest cultural centers, the Aspen Institute for Humanistic Studies. In summer months, the institute offers the Aspen Executive Seminars, which draw leaders of business, finance, government, and labor to two-week sessions at stiff fees (more than $1,000 per week). In a campuslike setting, the participating executives attend three hours of lectures and discussion in the morning; the afternoons are left free for reading.

Mortimer Adler has been on the faculty of the Aspen Executive Seminars since the 1950s, lecturing on philosophy and the Great Books. After he and Kelso wrote *The Capitalist*

Manifesto, Adler selected a series of readings from the Great
Books that raised questions about economics, questions that
were not answered by the Great Books or any standard economics textbooks; the final reading was the *Manifesto* itself.
The whole course was designed to lead into the *Manifesto,* to
show how universal capitalism supplies answers that are not
found anywhere else.

During the 1960s, Adler moderated several two-week
Aspen courses each summer, and Louis Kelso usually moderated
one. In addition to the executives, the institute always invited
three or four "resource people" to each session, people that the
seminar could draw upon to broaden the discussion. The resource people could be senators or congressmen or Supreme
Court justices or famous professors. In the summer of 1964, one
of the resource people at Aspen was Congressman Gerald Ford
of Michigan, and he happened to catch Louis Kelso's turn to
moderate the Adler-Kelso seminar.

Kelso led the course through the Great Books to the punch
line of universal capitalism, and Jerry Ford got the message. He
saw the great political possibilities of universal capitalism and
suggested to Kelso that his theories should be studied for possible inclusion in the Republican party platform. Kelso happily
agreed that this would be a splendid idea and that Ford should
try to arrange an invitation from the Republican party for a
Washington meeting as soon as possible. Kelso thought that this
might be the big break he and his associates had been looking
for. Even though it seemed unlikely at the time that Jerry
Ford's name would ever become a household word, Ford certainly had enough clout with Republican leaders to arrange the
Washington meeting.

When Congressman Ford returned to Washington, he did
not forget about the vision of universal capitalism he had seen
in Aspen. He continued to correspond with Kelso and finally
was able to set up the meeting for February 22, 1965.

Kelso Meets the Republican Task Force, 1965

By this time, the Kelso movement had attracted a valuable and energetic ally: Walter Lawrence, a very successful San Francisco advertising executive. Like a lot of other people, he had been excited by the Kelso-Adler books and felt that he could make a contribution as a practical marketing expert. He undertook the job of presenting universal capitalism in simple language and illustrations, so that it could be absorbed by a broader audience.

Lawrence did a fine job on the condensed popular version of Kelso, which he first prepared on flip charts and later transferred to a narrated filmstrip. He used the term *second income plan* (SIP) to describe all of Kelso's capital diffusion schemes. The first income came from wages; the second income plan would give everyone access to income from capital.

Lawrence's keen sense of marketing seemed particularly suitable for presenting Kelso's ideas to politicians, who are usually unwilling to concentrate on theoretical economics for very long. So Walter Lawrence and his flip charts accompanied Kelso to Washington for the meeting.

About thirty leading Republican senators and congressmen attended, and the meeting lasted about three hours. The Republican legislators seemed to share Jerry Ford's enthusiasm for the general idea but felt that the economic details were over their heads. They arranged for Kelso and Lawrence to meet with Bryce Harlow, a top adviser to leading Republicans during the Eisenhower and Nixon presidencies. Harlow listened to the presentation and then volunteered to arrange a meeting with the Republican party's Task Force on Fiscal and Monetary Policy, which was headed by Maurice Stans. Kelso and Lawrence agreed to come back to New York for the meeting with Stans's task force on October 21, 1965.

By that time, Lawrence's filmstrip was ready, and he and Kelso used it in their presentation. The meeting was held in the exotically furnished, lavishly decorated board room of the Chase Manhattan Bank in New York; the nongrubby revolution had now found its way inside New York's second-largest bank. Among those attending were Maurice Stans; George Champion and David Rockefeller, the top officers of Chase Manhattan; several other bank presidents; and four professional economists, headed by Dr. Raymond J. Saulnier of Barnard College, who had been chairman of President Eisenhower's Council of Economic Advisers.

The presentation, made by Kelso, Walter Lawrence, and Kelso's law partner, Aylett Cotton, was very enthusiastically received. As Maurice Stans said in an October 26, 1965, letter to Kelso,

> The members of the group, who as you know are all very practical financial experts, economists or politicians, expressed themselves unanimously that the slide film presentation was superbly done and that the goals and concept of the plan are extremely attractive. Your presentation has tremendous impact.

During the meeting, several participants stated that although the Republican task force agreed with the goals and aspirations of the second income plan, they had no way of determining its feasibility and its impact on the economy without some kind of an econometric study. In response, Kelso agreed to arrange for a "systems analysis of the plan by a professional organization." Kelso was delighted by the reception, and in his optimism, he felt that it would be easy to produce the systems analysis study. As Maurice Stans's letter goes on to say:

> We will be intensely interested in seeing the final plan when your research on its economic impact and feasibility is completed. If we can be satisfied on these points, we will proceed promptly with appropriate action to bring it before the parent Republican Coordinating Committee for policy considerations.
>
> We concur in your conclusion that a systems analysis study of the Plan by a professional organization is the next step, and it is the conclusion of our Task Force that it should withhold further consideration or any endorsement until the results of such a study are available and clearly demonstrate feasibility.
>
> The questions in the minds of the Task Force which

remain to be answered deal with the fiscal impact, expansion of credit, money supply, securities prices, government finances, and similar areas. Such matters should be expected to be covered by the survey, as would the measurement of inflationary or deflationary forces.

Kelso immediately began to search for a suitable organization to do the analysis. He had already been rebuffed by Stanford Research Institute, and he was unable to interest any other academic institutions in the project. Finally, Kelso was forced to take the proposal up with a private organization, Spindletop Research Corporation, of Lexington, Kentucky. The Spindletop people told Kelso that they could produce the kind of analysis requested but that it would cost between $350,000 and $500,000. This estimate was much higher than the cost of doing the analysis through an academic or nonprofit organization, but Kelso could not gain access to these existing facilities. Such groups have econometric models and computer programs already set up, whereas Spindletop would have to duplicate a lot of that spadework just to be in a position to make the analysis of Kelso's plan. The Spindletop fee was beyond Kelso's means, even if he had wanted to pay for it himself. He organized a nonprofit, tax-exempt foundation, the Institute for the Study of Economic Systems (ISES), to solicit donations for the research; but in the end, he was unable to raise the money. So he had to report back to Stans that he could not undertake the analysis at his own expense. He suggested that the task force produce the analysis by using its own funds and its access to existing research facilities. The Republican task force eventually advised Kelso that it could not assume responsibility for the cost of the study, and so the promising start at Aspen came to nothing.

Jerry Ford called Kelso after he heard about the turndown, and said:

> I'm sorry that it turned out this way, Lou. I just want to tell you not to be discouraged. In Congress, we run up against this sort of thing all the time. It takes a lot of time to get a new idea introduced. Just keep in there pitching, and don't get discouraged. I know you're on the right track.

Kelso remains bitter about the decision of Stans's task force.

If they call themselves the Republican Task Force on Fiscal and Monetary Policy and they admit that the current national policy was an error, it would seem that they had elected themselves to do a job. Then when they admitted that the concepts in my presentation were valid but they required checking out, it was ludicrous for them to tell me to take a half a million dollars out of my pocket to check this out for them.

The guys on that committee among them commanded access to a hundred billion dollars. Therefore, as I look back on the Stans committee, I regard it as an obvious brush-off. It is simply a case of the establishment saying, "Don't rock the boat. We like the way it is. Go away."

In 1965, when they were still intrigued with the prospect of making universal capitalism part of the Republican platform, Kelso and Lawrence arranged to see Richard Nixon. They met in Nixon's New York law offices, where he practiced with his future attorney general, John Mitchell. Nixon spent almost five hours with Kelso and Lawrence. Kelso recalls that Nixon listened intently and took a lot of notes on his yellow legal pad. At the end of the meeting, Nixon picked up a copy of *The Capitalist Manifesto*, thumbed through the pages, and said:

Well, I'm no economist, but I do think I understand politics, and I will say politically that I could sell this to the American people in six months.

But like Kelso's meetings with Goldwater and Stans, the meeting with Nixon produced no real progress. Kelso was beginning to realize that to make any dent in the establishment, he would have to organize some kind of continuing presence in Washington. The opportunity to do this was not far away, for in February 1966, Kelso met Norman Kurland.

Washington Outpost, 1966

Norman Kurland was planning director of the Citizens Crusade Against Poverty in Washington when he first heard of Kelso. In March 1965, Kurland met Mark Goldes, who began describing Kelso's theories. As Kurland puts it,

I had my mind blown within a few seconds. I already knew that income redistribution wasn't going to make it. But I had never thought of private property in political terms as the economic power diffuser and as a nongovernmental alternative for directly distributing incomes among citizens. Kelso's ideas opened up my mind to the notion that economics comes *first*, even before one-man, one-vote, for the purpose of decentralizing power and linking it to each member of society.

I was already a supporter of free markets and unimpeded technological advances. I knew we needed peaceful order and an economic level before we could overcome disorder in the political and social arenas. I knew we needed a more refined order of economic justice. I knew we needed a sounder logic for structuring our economic system. I knew we needed a moral component to economics. I could now see the means I was searching for to satisfy these needs and realize the Jeffersonian ideals to which I had already been committed.

I was ready to devote the rest of my life to the cause of universal capitalism.

That's the way Norm Kurland talks. He earned his law degree at the University of Chicago in 1959. He studied there under a full-tuition scholarship, taking his antitrust law course from Professor Edward Levi, later to become attorney general. He served in the air force as an electronic countermeasures officer stationed in Japan. He brought his law degree to Washington and held government legal jobs with the Department of Health, Education, and Welfare (1960–1962), the Commission on Civil Rights (1962–1964), and the Office of Economic Opportunity Poverty Program (1964–1965). His work with the Civil Rights Commission brought him into Mississippi during the early days of the Kennedy administration's civil rights campaign. There he worked closely with black civil rights leaders such as Medgar Evers and Aaron Henry of the NAACP and the student activists involved in the Mississippi one-man, one-vote campaigns. Then, in 1965, he joined Walter Reuther's Citizens Crusade Against Poverty, hoping that he could help the cause of economic justice.

In February 1966, Kurland had to fly to Oakland for a Poor Peoples' Conference, and he arranged to meet Kelso in San Francisco on that trip. This first meeting reinforced Kurland's conviction that he wanted to devote the rest of his life to universal capitalism. Kelso had no funds available for a Washington office at that time, but he and Kurland agreed that they would find a way to open one, with Kurland in charge, as soon as possible.

Kurland felt that he could help Kelso to develop contacts among liberal journalists and leaders of labor, black activist, and civil rights groups, and Kelso was eager to do this. Kurland went right to work on this even though he remained with the Reuther crusade; in fact, he hoped that the crusade would support Kelso's ideas. He arranged for Kelso to be invited to Washington to speak at the group's first annual meeting in April 1966.

Kelso made his speech and got favorable responses from many of the delegates, but the meeting itself turned into a fiasco. There were some revolutionaries from Students for Democratic Society and other radical groups in the audience, and they were determined to break up the meeting. Sargent Shriver, then head of the Office of Economic Opportunity, was in the middle of his speech when the revolutionaries went into action. They managed to drive him out of the hall and break up the convention. Kurland hoped that this experience would not dampen Kelso's enthusiasm for working so closely with the poorer beneficiaries of the capitalist revolution. But Kelso rather enjoyed himself, especially because he got a much better reception than Shriver did. This fortified his belief that promises of menial jobs and welfare, even by well-meaning people such as Walter Reuther, will not solve America's long-range economic problems.

Norm Kurland remained with the Citizens Crusade until late in 1968, but during those years, he donated much of his spare time to the Kelso movement. On September 1, 1968, he officially joined the Kelso movement full time.

Publication of
Two-Factor Theory, 1967

Meanwhile, Patricia Hetter kept things going at the San Francisco office. Adler had moved back to Chicago, so Patricia was working with Kelso to bring the *Manifesto* up to date and add some new ideas. They put it all together in a new book that was published in hard cover by Random House in November 1967; the book bore the title *How to Turn Eighty Million Workers Into Capitalists on Borrowed Money.* This title was thought up by Walter Lawrence. Kelso had submitted it to Random House as a courtesy to his hardworking marketing adviser, but he never thought that Random House would accept it. Much to his amazement, they did.

A paperback edition (also by Random House) followed in 1968, thanks mainly to Kelso ally Roger Sonnabend, chairman of the Sonesta Hotels and the Hotel Corporation of America, who placed a healthy order for paperbacks to stock the bookstores of his hotel chain.

The original title had not caught on too well, and Kelso had always been uncomfortable with it. The paperback edition gave him the chance to change it, and he renamed the book *Two-Factor Theory: The Economics of Reality.*

The 1967 book is somewhat shorter than *The Capitalist Manifesto,* and it is broken up into a larger number of shorter chapters for easier reading. Like the two books written with Adler, this one is full of beautiful philosophy. Here are some examples:

> Never in history has universal suffrage been built on a sound economic foundation; it is this defect, not the ordinary man's inability to cope with freedom, that accounts for the notorious fragility of democratic institutions.

> If the corporation wishes to produce on foreign soil, it must have constituents there whose power to consume is

commensurate with the power of their economies to produce.

We submit that Universal Capitalism is the rationale of a free industrial society, and that in understanding, applying and teaching that rationale the United States can again become a leader that truly leads by inspiring, as it once did, the minds and the hearts of men.

The *Two-Factor Theory* follows the basic theories laid down in the *Manifesto* and *The New Capitalists* and also introduces some new ideas. In their description of the Financed Capitalist Plan, Kelso and Hetter suggest for the first time that loans to New Capitalists for their stock purchases should be made at very low interest rates. The low interest rates in turn are based on the assumption that the participating commercial banks will be allowed to sell the notes to the Federal Reserve Banks so that the commercial banks do not have to use depositors' funds to make the loans.

The book suggests capital ownership for corporate employees through what Kelso then called the *second income plan trust*. This forerunner of ESOP receives only a few pages of discussion, and it is not put forward as the basic means of bringing capital ownership to the entire society.

The book closes with a draft of the first specific legislation proposed by Kelso to launch the capitalist revolution: the Full Production Act. (It is printed in small type as an appendix.) The act contains some ingenious ideas for bringing about universal capitalism, including use of existing elements such as the Joint Economic Committee of Congress and the annual *Economic Report of the President*. Unfortunately, it also contains a lot of two-factor language that combines capital diffusion with the alleged exploitation of capital and the need to cut wages. Also, I must say that I found the language of the Full Production Act a little complex and difficult to follow, unlike the beautiful philosophical writing of the main text. I suspect that that is the reason no one seems to have undertaken a written analysis of the act; most readers probably didn't make the effort to read it.

Sales of *Two-Factor Theory* were satisfactory, although not so strong as the hard-cover sales of the *Manifesto*. Once again, there was a very favorable reaction to the book—from those who read it. But its immediate effect was the same as the effects of the two earlier books: There was no sign that the capitalist revolution was about to start.

With his third book behind him and the revolution seemingly as far away as ever, Kelso decided to try to make things happen in Washington. And in 1968, he turned to Norman Kurland.

Institute for the Study of Economic Systems, 1968-1969

Together, Kelso and Kurland tried to breathe life into the Institute for the Study of Economic Systems, the nonprofit foundation Kelso had set up in 1965 to raise the money for the study requested by the Republican task force. A one-window attic in an Embassy Row building owned by the Union of American Hebrew Congregations became the Washington headquarters of ISES. The rent was $75 a month. Norm Kurland manned the telephone, the typewriter, and the entire operation, with occasional help from volunteers. He was given the title of executive director of ISES, but little else. At that point, Kelso was paying Kurland out of his own pocket, and he was barely able to help Norm secure the basic necessities of life. Fortunately, Norm's wife was working, which helped his family to survive the difficult early years of Kelso operations in Washington.

The office was launched in September 1968. For the rest of 1968 and most of 1969, Kelso and Kurland enthusiastically solicited contributions from foundations throughout the country. They were looking for $25,000 in 1968 as seed money and $250,000 for 1969, modest sums compared with the money that was being lavished by foundations on much less promising projects.

They put together a highly diversified board of directors. Some representative names will give you the flavor of the group: Mortimer Adler; Dr. Vernon R. Alden, chairman of the Boston Company and former associate dean of the Harvard Business School; Dr. Salvador Araneta, former Philippines cabinet minister; Charles A. Black and his wife, Shirley Temple Black; Winnett Boyd, president of Arthur D. Little of Canada, the famous management consultants; Harry Bridges, president, International Longshoremen's and Warehousemen's Union, San Francisco; Frank S. Capon, financial vice-president, Du Pont of Canada Ltd.; William E. Chatlos, partner, Georgeson & Co., New York; Theodore L. Cross, publisher and editor in chief of *The Bankers Magazine;* Ennis Francis, director of economic development, Central Harlem Council of Neighborhood Boards, New York; Hazel Henderson, writer and futurist, New York; Patricia Hetter; Rabbi Richard Hirsch, director, Religious Action Center, Union of American Hebrew Congregations, Washington; Walter Lawrence; the Honorable Maurice Macmillan, managing director, Macmillan and Co., Ltd., and member of Parliament, London; Floyd B. McKissick, founder of Soul City, North Carolina; James L. O'Dell, farmer and universal capitalism aspirant, Alberta; Fred Smith, Rockefeller Family and Associates, New York; Roger P. Sonnabend, president, Hotel Corporation of America, Boston; Leonard Spacek, chairman of Arthur Andersen & Co., Chicago; Dr. Franklin H. Williams, director of the Institute of Urban Affairs, Columbia University, New York; and Livingston L. Wingate, executive director, New York Urban League.

Most of the strength of ISES was in its board. At its peak, there were 63 directors and 160 other dues-paying members, a total membership of 223. But despite the high caliber of the board and Kelso's impressive credentials, an amazing thing happened. Kelso and Kurland were not able to raise so much as one dollar for ISES from any foundation, even though they spent a great deal of time and energy in the effort.

After this experience, it was not surprising that in 1970 Kelso decided to sidetrack the effort to bring about universal capitalism by do-good methods. But instead of giving up the fight, as most men would have done, he bounced back and decided that he would bring on the capitalist revolution by creating a profit-making business based on the concepts of universal capitalism. Because Kelso is not your average revolutionary, he was equal to the task of creating just such a business (and later a whole industry).

Putting the Revolution on a Paying Basis, 1970

Kelso decided to use his expertise in corporate finance to build an investment banking business, one that would be profitable enough to provide the money he needed to carry on the ISES Washington operation and the other crusading activities that he had been paying for out of his own pocket. It would also solve another pressing problem for Kelso. By 1970, he had reached the point where he could no longer impose on his law partners by spending so much of his time in the quest for universal capitalism. Unless the revolution was to come to a halt, he had to put it on a paying basis.

Kelso found that he could start one part of the capitalist revolution on his own, without any new legislation and without any help from economists, investment bankers, or union leaders. All he needed was something that he already had: law clients who had capital needs that could be satisfied by financing plans which included diffusion of capital ownership. In all three of his books, he had mentioned briefly the idea of "equity-sharing" or using existing tax provisions to distribute stock to employees in a way that would also serve the employer's capital formation needs. He had put this principle into practice himself in 1956 for one of his Brobeck clients, Peninsula Newspapers, Inc. (PNI).

PNI published the *Palo Alto Times,* the *Redwood City Tribune,* and half a dozen other small northern California newspapers. In 1956, 72 percent of PNI stock was owned by three principal stockholders, and the other 28 percent was owned by various PNI employees. The three principal stockholders were getting along in years and wanted to sell their stock. However, they had a continuing interest in the welfare of the newspapers. They could have sold their stock to outsiders, but they felt that the business would run better if it was owned by the newspapers' editors, reporters, salesmen, and production workers. The went to their lawyers (the Brobeck firm) to try to find a way to get their money out of PNI and still arrange for it to be owned by the employees, even though the employees did not have the money to pay for the stock. The Brobeck firm decided that this was a job right up Lou Kelso's alley.

The PNI project made Kelso's mouth water. Here he had the ideal situation: owners of capital who wanted to spread that ownership among the people most important to the business, the salaried employees of the newspapers, who owned little or no capital themselves. Kelso figured out a way to do this.

He set up seven separate profit-sharing trusts, one for each of the six unions involved and one for the nonunion employees, and arranged for them jointly to buy out the three principal stockholders of PNI. He drew up the agreement so that the profit-sharing trusts would have twenty years to pay for the stock. Because the profit-sharing trusts were going to receive most of PNI's profits, Kelso calculated that they would be able to pay for the stock comfortably out of the profits earned during that period. If Kelso's ideas worked, within twenty years, the seven profit-sharing trusts would own the 72 percent of the stock bought from the three retiring owners without any cash payments by the employees. The remaining 28 percent of PNI stock was still owned directly by various employees who had bought their stock for cash before Kelso was called into the picture. However, ownership of these floating shares was restricted to PNI employees.

Kelso's blueprint was a smashing success. The newspapers prospered and expanded under the ownership of the employees' profit-sharing trusts, and the trusts paid the entire purchase price to the retiring owners in only eight and a half years. The trusts' annual report for 1974 showed a net worth of more than $6.3 million after payment of more than $3 million to retiring and terminating employees and long after paying the entire purchase price to the three retiring owners.

The Peninsula Newspapers plan was not an ESOP, but it was the first Kelso plan to be put into operation. As we shall see in Chapter 8, an ESOP uses a stock bonus trust rather than a profit-sharing trust as the vehicle for diffusion of stock ownership. However, in 1956, Kelso was not thinking about ESOP or any particular form of organization as the vehicle for the capitalist revolution; he was thinking about spreading ownership to people who could not afford to pay for it by allowing them to buy it through the profits that the capital itself returned to its owners. Therefore, Peninsula Newspapers is in every sense the first Kelso model. It was not leveraged in the sense of using bank financing, but long-term financing was supplied by the three selling stockholders, who agreed to let the profit-sharing trusts have twenty years to pay them the purchase price.

Gene Bishop was vice-president of PNI back in 1956 when the Kelso plan was put into effect. When the three principal stockholders sold out, he became president and later chairman of the board, retiring in 1975. Bishop says that during his last few years with the company, he was approached by at least twenty-five major publishing firms who wanted to buy the PNI chain. He told them that most of the 500 employees of PNI who own the company through their profit-sharing trusts enjoy their work, are happy with their employee ownership, and are simply not interested in selling out to anybody.

The Peninsula deal gave Kelso added confidence that his capital diffusion schemes would work. One of the reasons that he had planned to keep his Canal Zone manuscript in mothballs for twenty-five years was to give him the opportunity to test some of his ideas in the real world.

With Peninsula Newspapers behind him in 1956, he had continued the strenuous work on *The Capitalist Manifesto* with Mortimer Adler. During this same period, Kelso was to get another chance to put his theories to the test. This time the vehicle was Valley Nitrogen Producers Inc., and it was to take him more than two years (from 1957 to 1959) to get the plan into operation.

Valley Nitrogen is one of the great business stories of our times—not just a story about business but also about farming, cooperatives, and reducing the cost of food for the American people. The important part of the Valley Nitrogen story for us is that it gave Kelso his first chance to use his theories to create widespread ownership of a large business using return on capital to pay for that ownership. Valley Nitrogen turned out to be a much bigger enterprise than Peninsula Newspapers, even though Kelso helped to start it from scratch in the face of roughhouse competition from five giant chemical manufacturers who were selling fertilizer in California at that time.

Valley Nitrogen was the brainchild of Carl H. Haas, an Austrian who emigrated to the United States in 1940. His family had been in the fertilizer business in Europe since 1892 and after an honorable discharge from the U.S. Army in 1943, Haas entered the fertilizer business in California. He established himself near Modesto as a seller of high-quality low-price fertilizers and developed a wide circle of farmer friends. In 1955, anhydrous ammonia fertilizer was being sold in California by major producers such as Standard Oil of California, Shell Oil, Hercules, and Monsanto at about $220 per ton; Haas knew that it could be produced for about $60 a ton. He felt that he could get a good number of California growers to join him in the construction of a new fertilizer plant that would be owned mostly by its customers.

Haas lived in Hillsborough, a fashionable suburb of San Francisco, and had played tennis with Louis Kelso there. He called on Kelso to help him organize a new producer of anhydrous ammonia, one that would have its major customers as stockholders and would bring down the price of fertilizer and the food that it helped to produce.

Kelso drew up an operating plan and formed a corporation called Valley Nitrogen Producers Inc. In 1957, Haas started signing up growers to a subscription form drafted by Kelso. The form provided that the grower-subscriber agreed to buy all the fertilizer he needed from Valley Nitrogen if the price was competitive and if services were equal to what they could get in the market. It also provided that the grower would have an option to buy stock in the corporation, which agreed to pay out all its profits to its shareholders as dividends. Haas spent two years rounding up subscriptions while Kelso worked on the bank financing needed to construct an ammonia plant.

Word of the new grower-owned operation began to spread, and the subscriptions started coming in. Then, within the space of one month, the three major producers dropped their prices from $220 to less than $80 a ton. If this move was designed to knock out Valley Nitrogen before it got started, it did not work.

By some rather upside-down reasoning, the farmers apparently decided that because they were saving so much money on fertilizer prices, they could now afford to subscribe to the stock of Valley Nitrogen, and subscriptions started coming in faster than ever. Perhaps the farmers realized that if they did *not* subscribe to Valley Nitrogen stock and the project consequently collapsed, they might be paying $220 a ton again very soon.

By 1958, Haas and Kelso had the Valley Nitrogen project ready to go as a stock corporation organized for profit, passing all the profits back to its customers in the form of dividends on stock. Then, at the last minute, their bank financing was pulled out from under them without warning. Kelso smelled foul play, and he was all for making a big antitrust case out of it. But Haas and the growers did not want to get into litigation with the major fertilizer producers because they were dependent on those producers for other items, such as gasoline and insecticides. So Kelso simply took another route. He quickly changed Valley Nitrogen from a California business corporation to a nonprofit agricultural cooperative corporation. This enabled him to arrange the necessary financing through the Berkeley Bank for Cooperatives. The function of Valley Nitrogen was just about the same as it would have been if it had been organized as a business corporation, but instead of paying out its profits to its customer-owners in the form of dividends on stock, it would now pay this money to the same people as its member-owners in the form of *patronage dividends*.

Valley Nitrogen's annual report for 1975 shows sales of more than $125 million, with net earnings of more than $22 million and a net worth of over $50 million. Thousands of California growers, as well as people all over the world who eat the produce of California's farms, can thank Valley Nitrogen for providing a source of high-quality low-cost fertilizers. In 1975, Valley Nitrogen had approximately 30 percent of the total fertilizer market in California and 35 percent of the Arizona market. It is owned by 5,000 farmer-customers, most of whom paid for their ownership shares solely from dividends.

Peninsula Newspapers and Valley Nitrogen convinced Kelso that he was on the right track, that ownership of large and small enterprises could be broken out of its old pattern and spread around to employees, to customers, to anyone so long as the business could take on new capital investment and make the new capital pay for itself over a reasonable period of years. These ventures and others that he was working on as a lawyer made him feel that he should be spending more time developing diffused-ownership financing plans for more businesses. But as a lawyer, even as head of his own firm, his scope was very limited. He could install these plans only for clients who came to him, and he could not solicit business. How could he spread the gospel beyond the limited circle of his own clients?

The answer was to form his own investment banking firm, which would specialize in Kelso-type innovative corporate finance. He asked Henry McIntyre to help him organize it. McIntyre, a very successful San Francisco financier, had helped to organize Hiller Helicopters and had gone into a variety of venture capital investments during the 1950s and 1960s. Having made his fortune, he devoted himself passionately to the cause of Planned Parenthood and became one of its leading fund raisers.

McIntyre had met Kelso and become interested in his work in the 1950s, but he told Kelso that he saw universal capitalism then as something that would not happen in Kelso's lifetime. They met again in 1970, and McIntyre recalls that Kelso was no longer talking about immediately changing the entire U.S. economic system. He now wanted to start boring from within the establishment by setting up an investment banking firm of his own because he had failed to attract other investment bankers (to whom *The New Capitalists* was dedicated) to universal capitalism.

By 1970, McIntyre had found a common purpose for Kelso's capitalist revolution and his own work with Planned Parenthood. He had seen that in many of the world's poorest countries, poor families deliberately had lots of children as a way of fighting poverty; the parents needed many hands to work at the primitive tasks that brought in the little money available. He knew that birth control would not succeed in those desperate countries unless the people had some other hope for survival. McIntyre also knew that limiting population growth was not the whole answer, that some new kind of economic system was needed to prevent starvation and chaos in many countries where his philanthropic work took him. And he had never found anyone but Kelso who held out any hope for income except from toil. Therefore, as a practical financier interested in the welfare of mankind, he decided to devote himself to two practical means of survival: birth control and greed control. The headquarters for greed control was Louis Kelso's office in San Francisco. McIntyre agreed to help organize Kelso's investment banking firm.

McIntyre took an inventory of Kelso's resources and contacts and decided to use one of Kelso's satisfied clients as the cornerstone of the investment banking operation. Harold W. Bangert was chairman of the Statesman Group Inc., a group of insurance companies based in Des Moines, Iowa, for whom Kelso had installed an ESOP in 1969. The Statesman Group's plan was one of the earliest models of an ESOP; bank financing was used to pay for $1.8 million worth of newly issued stock sold by the company to a trust set up for its employees. Because Harold Bangert wanted to participate in spreading Kelsoism throughout the world, he agreed to lend his name to the investment banking operation, and it was christened Bangert & Company, Inc.

With the help of McIntyre and other financiers, Bangert & Company tapped eighteen investors for $25,000 each, raising a total of $450,000 in 1970. The original stockholders included Donald Weeden, head of the well-known Wall Street brokerage firm that bears his name; William Ruder, chairman of a major public relations firm, Ruder & Finn; and David Mahoney, chairman of Norton Simon Inc.

At the time Bangert & Company was organized, Kelso felt that it was no longer fair to saddle his law partners with a worldwide crusade, and so he amicably parted company with them and formed his own law firm, Louis O. Kelso, Inc. The Bangert & Company offices were established in Kelso's law offices at 111 Pine Street, San Francisco. Kelso continued to run his law practice and was given the titles of economist and legal counsel of Bangert & Company, the first investment banking firm dedicated to bringing about a revolution.

Kelso was hopeful that these moves would solve the problems he had run into when he was trying to start a revolution while serving as a partner in a corporate law firm. Of course, he now had a little more to do in his spare time; he had to manage an investment banking company as well as a law firm and ISES. But he took on the extra work eagerly, hoping that Bangert & Company would be the key to the capitalist revolution.

Soul City
and the Black Leaders

As Bangert & Company was getting under way, Kelso kept on trying to find additional ways to start the revolution. Norman Kurland, working from the Washington attic office, button-holed legislators, government officials, labor leaders, educators—anyone who would listen. One of the people who listened was Floyd McKissick, former National Director of the Congress of Racial Equality and the prime mover in the creation of Soul City, a brand-new community in North Carolina.

Soul City was organized by McKissick to develop a rural tract of farmland fifty miles northeast of Durham. It was designed to give its residents a chance to work *and* to own. McKissick was one of the first black leaders to recognize that political equality without access to capital ownership can be almost meaningless. At a time when most of the other black leaders were talking about jobs and welfare, he was concentrating on creating a community built on broad capital ownership. He turned to Louis Kelso for advice, and Kelso gave it freely.

Largely through Kurland's work, Kelso was to find himself talking to audiences in Harlem, Watts, and other ghettos, trying to sell the capitalist revolution to some of its beneficiaries. But to people who were thinking about jobs and welfare, his talk of capital ownership seemed a too-far-distant dream. Although some black leaders, including McKissick, Ennis Francis, and Livingston Wingate, were enthusiastic, Kelso soon found that he could not get his revolution going among poor blacks.

Kelso's Man in Latin America

In 1968, shortly after Kurland set up the ISES Washington office, he advertised for a part-time office helper. The ad was answered by a Georgetown graduate student named Joseph Recinos, whose interest in the job was straightforward and in keeping with Washington tradition.

> I thought the Institute for the Study of Economic Systems must be some kind of government-funded outfit. I figured that the work would be easy and that I'd have plenty of time to read and study on the job.

He was a little taken aback to find that ISES was a one-man operation quartered in an attic. But within a few minutes, Norm Kurland had Recinos entranced with his description of what ISES was all about. Recinos says that

> it was like a light bulb went on in my mind. *Everything* suddenly made sense. After listening to Norm for an hour, I suddenly knew what I wanted to do for the rest of my life.

Joe Recinos was only twenty-three then, but he knew himself pretty well. In 1976, he was still working full time for ISES.

Joe Recinos is one of the most remarkable young men I've ever met, and yet he is typical of the people who have decided to devote their lives to universal capitalism. He was born in Guatemala, where his father was a dentist. The family moved to New York when Joe was very young, and he was brought up and educated there, graduating from City College of New York in 1966. He went on to graduate work in economics and Latin American affairs.

Today, Joe is engaged in a one-man capitalist revolution in Latin America as representative of ISES and Kelso. He operates on the tightest budget of any lobbyist or investment banker I know. He started at ISES at $150 per month total salary and expense allowance; in 1975, he was upgraded to $300 per month. That was all Kelso and ISES could afford to devote to Latin America.

Joe worked with Norm Kurland in Washington for a couple of years before returning to Latin America. He helped to organize the Washington Area Free University (WAFU), which he and Norm used as a platform to spread the Kelso gospel to young people. It was also a device for recruiting more help. One of the first and most diligent WAFU students was Larry Good, a red-bearded political science major who became a volunteer assistant to Norm Kurland in the attic office and who in 1976 was still contributing a lot of time to the movement.

In 1970, Recinos decided to return to Guatemala, where he could use his native Spanish and his family connections in the service of the Kelso cause. He has functioned there as a one-man army, traveling by bus to pop up in government and corporate offices all over Latin America, selling the idea of universal capitalism. He says that the bus fare for the 1,000 mile trip from Guatemala City to Mexico City is only $20, and he usually manages to convert at least one fellow passenger to Kelsoism on each trip.

Joe's first important accomplishment was the publication of a Spanish version of *Two-Factor Theory*. This took some doing in Guatemala. Joe recruited a friend who owned a pamphlet-publishing business. But the book job was beyond their regular capacity, so Joe went to work for them and practically got the book out by hand himself. It was published in 1972 and distributed to key government, business, and labor leaders throughout Latin America. In the Spanish version, it is called *Un Tercer Camino* (*A Third Way*). Kelso wanted it titled *El Tercer Camino* (*The Third Way*), but Recinos was advised by sympathetic Latin American officials that *The* would be interpreted by some as Yankee arrogance.

I wish I had the space in this book to tell you the whole story of Joe Recinos's bus rides through Latin America; his confrontations with giant multinationals such as United Fruit and International Nickel; and his adventures in the rural plantations, where the Marxists accused him of being a CIA man and the rightists called him a communist agitator. He has come remarkably close to getting capital diffusion projects started in Mexico and Guatemala, and he has gotten many influential government, corporate, and labor people to consider Kelso's ideas as an alternative to Yankee imperialism and Marxism. The economics minister of Guatemala (who is Joe's cousin) is now an outspoken Kelso advocate. And Joe has taught courses in universal capitalism at the University of Guatemala and the National University of Mexico.

But Recinos runs into the same roadblocks that confront the Kelso movement everywhere. A presentation of Kelso's theories gets into fairly complicated economics, at which point the listeners (whether government, corporate, or labor officials) send for their own traditional economists or, more likely, ship the written presentation to them. The presentation usually comes back marked "crackpot," and the decision makers are afraid to take any action based on a theory rejected by their own professional or academic advisers. So American multinationals continue to practice nineteenth-century capitalism in Latin America, and their businesses get expropriated sooner or later. But Recinos remains undeterred; he keeps on trying to convince them that they should build a constituency in the Latin American countries by making the native workers part owners.

Still Waiting for a Miracle, 1970-1973

Although Norm Kurland brought Kelso into closer contact with noncapitalists, Kelso did not stop preaching to the wealthy. In fact, he has never lost the conviction that universal capitalism has logical appeal for every group in our society and that therefore it must eventually succeed. In the early 1970s, William F. Buckley wrote favorably of Kelso in his syndicated column, and John D. Rockefeller III used Kelso's theories as examples of humanistic capitalism in his book *The Second American Revolution*. And in the early 1970s, Kelso also gained two valuable allies, both from the same family, George and Charles Pillsbury, of the Minneapolis flour-milling Pillsburys.

Charles Pillsbury had turned down a comfortable niche in

the milling dynasty founded by his great-grandfather and had become an anti–Vietnam War activist. By 1972, he was campaigning for George McGovern. His father also left the Pillsbury Company in 1969 to devote himself to private investments and good works in the public sector. George Pillsbury remained a conservative Republican and backed Richard Nixon in 1972. Father and son rarely agreed on anything relating to politics or economics—until both of them stumbled across Kelso.

Both Pillsburys were sold on universal capitalism by 1972, even though each came to it from a different direction. Charles decided to enroll in Yale Law School to prepare himself for an active role in the capitalist revolution. By the time of his graduation in 1975, he had published an outstanding article on Kelsoism in the *Boston University Law Review*. George Pillsbury became a state senator, and in 1974, he was able to push through a bill that made Minnesota the first state to adopt universal capitalism as its public policy.

The counterestablishment also took notice of Kelso. The *Whole Earth Catalog* published a favorable review of *Two-Factor Theory* in 1970, winding up with this plea to Kelso:

> Come on Lou, grow long hair, drop all that establishment costumery, immerse yourself in the now generation, and start to work with a constituency that wants you and needs you. If you don't some bright young radical economist certainly will.

After Kelso freed himself of obligations to law partners in 1970, he threw himself even harder into his backbreaking schedule. After a hectic day at law practice, investment banking, and ISES evangelizing, he would spend the evening meeting influential people from all walks of life, and he never missed a chance to give them the message of universal capitalism. Because of his amazing energy, his presentation at a dinner was almost as fresh as it was first thing in the morning. In this way, he got hundreds of people thinking about his theories; and in many cases, his listeners were sold. But once again, nothing happened. He seemed to be right logically, but he could not come up with a way of putting his revolution into action. Bangert & Company was spending a lot of its money on salaries, trying to design employee ownership plans and collect advisory fees. But as the end of 1973 approached, Bangert & Company could hardly be called a big success. It had put only a handful of ownership plans into action, and most of these were on the small side. Kelso began to wonder whether his investment banking creation would be able to bring off the revolution.

A circular, "Authors' Cautionary Note to Idealists," mailed to supporters by Kelso and Hetter in June 1973, summed up their frustration. It described the typical reaction of idealists to Kelso's theories. First, they are convinced by the logic. Then they are exhilarated at the broad ramifications, realizing that this is a weapon that can solve so many problems. Then they become converts and try to persuade others. Some others *are* persuaded, but *nothing happens*. Because nothing happens, they feel let down; eventually, they drop the whole idea as a daydream. Kelso and Hetter urged their followers to be patient and not to expect miracles so quickly.

But miracles started to come their way on November 28, 1973. On that day, a historic meeting took place in the Montpelier Room of the Madison Hotel in Washington. Present were Louis Kelso, Norman Kurland, Senate aide Wayne Thevenot, and Senator Russell B. Long (Democrat, Louisiana) , son of the late Huey P. Long and chairman of the Senate Finance Committee.

ESOP EXPLAINED

*The term "employee stock ownership plan" means a defined
contribution plan*

*(A) which is a stock bonus plan which is qualified or a
stock bonus and a money purchase plan both of which are
qualified under section 401 (a), and which are designed to
invest primarily in qualifying employer securities; and*

*(B) which is otherwise defined in regulations prescribed
by the Secretary or his delegate.*
        Internal Revenue Code, Section 4975 (e) (7)

I think it's about time I explained ESOP to you. I've been
avoiding this chore for seven chapters because I wanted you
to understand that ESOP is *not* Kelso's master plan for universal capitalism. But we've reached the point now where an
explanation of ESOP will help you to understand how it might
help bring about universal capitalism. So I'll break off the
story of the Kelso movement here to tackle ESOP, and then in
Chapter 9 we'll sit in on Kelso's historic 1973 meeting with
Senator Long.

The most important thing for you to know about ESOP is
that it has very limited application. It will *not* solve any major
economic problems. For most corporations, it is an expensive
and cumbersome way to raise money, because it involves repayment of a $1 loan plus issuance of $1 worth of stock for each
dollar raised. It is useful mainly to owners of successful closely
held corporations who are concerned about estate tax problems,
and to employees of subsidiaries of large corporations who want
to buy the subsidiary from the parent corporation.

The limitations of ESOP spring from the fact that it is a
tax-sheltered employee benefit plan, like pensions and profit-
sharing. Under the law, it is supposed to benefit employees exclusively. It was not designed to benefit corporations or to solve
basic economic problems. Kelso has used it for broader purposes, and this has caused thousands of people to take note of
Kelso's ideas for the first time. He is still working to expand and
improve ESOP, but its basic limitations would create lots of

inequities if we ever tried to use it broadly to diffuse capital ownership. It is based on the employment relationship, and because it creates stock ownership in proportion to wages, it brings the greatest benefits to the highest-paid officers and employees of successful corporations. And these benefits are paid for by other taxpayers.

The real importance of ESOP is that it focused attention on Kelso and universal capitalism and started a lot of people thinking about broadening capital ownership. I don't think that ESOP itself will ever be an important factor in the national economy as a whole. But please note that I'm talking now only about ESOP. There is another plan called TRASOP (Tax Reduction Act Stock Ownership Plan) which I think will become much more important than ESOP, and which we'll hear more about in Chapter 9.

Before I reached this not-so-enthusiastic conclusion about ESOP, however, I studied it for more than a year. Let me summarize the results of my studies in this chapter, giving you just enough detail to help you understand the role of ESOP in our story. Because some readers may want more details, I have added an Appendix that covers ESOP's functions and limitations in greater depth at the end of the book.

ESOP as an Employee Benefit

ESOP is one of four major types of employee benefit plans that are eligible for favorable tax treatment if their structures comply with the requirements of the Internal Revenue Code. (The other three are pensions, profit-sharing, and stock bonus plans.) Plans that comply are known as *qualified* plans, meaning that they qualify for special tax treatment.

In a qualified plan, there are tax advantages for both the corporation and the employees. The corporation gets an immediate tax deduction for the contributions (payments) that it makes to the plan, even though the employees do not receive the money immediately. The employees pay no taxes on the money contributed to the plan by the corporation until they actually receive the benefits, which is usually after retirement or upon leaving the company. There is a third important tax advantage: As long as the contributions remain in the plan and are not distributed to the employees, no taxes are paid on the income or capital gains realized by these funds. Thus the income can accumulate for many years without any tax bite. Even when the benefits are paid out to the employees, they may be taxable at lower rates than ordinary income.

All four plans use the same device to receive and hold the employer's contributions: a *trust*. Whether it's a pension trust, a profit-sharing trust, a stock bonus trust, or an employee stock ownership trust (ESOT), the functions are the same: to receive, hold, and invest the employer's contributions and eventually to pay out benefits to the employees. So don't get confused between ESOP and ESOT. ESOP (employee stock ownership *plan*) is the overall plan. It includes the trust, ESOT (employee stock ownership *trust*), as the device that receives and administers the contributions made to the plan.

Although some qualified plans are limited to salaried employees, most plans are open to all employees, and they receive benefits in proportion to their compensation. Thus, the $75,000 executive will usually receive ten times as much in benefits as the $7,500 clerk.

Because of the favorable tax treatment, there are limits on the contributions that can be made by corporations each year. These limits, and other features of the four types of plans, are discussed in detail in the Appendix and summarized in the chart on the following pages.

Comparison of Four Major Types of Qualified Employee Deferred Benefit Plans

Pension Plan
Stock Bonus Plan
Profit-Sharing Plan
Employee Stock Ownership Plan (ESOP)

1. Is the employer's annual contribution tax deductible by the corporation?

Yes, in all four types of plan.

2. What are the maximum tax-deductible contributions allowed each year?

For profit-sharing plans, stock bonus plans, and ESOPs, the maximum is 15 percent of annual payroll. This overall limit applies whether one, two, or all three plans are used by a corporation.

For pension plans, it's a little more complicated. In money purchase pension plans, the maximum is 25 percent of payroll, up to a maximum of $25,000 for each employee. In defined benefit plans there is no percentage limitation; the maximum is whatever amount that actuaries determine is needed to provide benefits for each employee. The benefits are limited to $75,000 per employee (plus cost-of-living adjustments).

In addition to all these limitations, when a pension plan is combined with any of the other three plans, the *overall limit* on contributions is 25 percent of payroll.

3. Do employees pay any income taxes on these annual contributions?

Not until they receive benefits.

4. When are benefits paid?

Benefits are generally paid when employees die, retire, or

leave the corporation. This applies to all four types of plan; that's why they're all called *deferred benefit* plans.

Because benefits are deferred until retirement, employees do not become stockholders in the employer corporation during their working years, even if benefits are distributed in employer stock.

5. What device is used to receive, hold, and invest the employer's contributions until benefits are paid to employees?

A trust: pension, profit-sharing, stock bonus, or employee stock ownership (ESOT).

6. Is the trust subject to income or capital gains taxes on the funds that it holds and invests?

No, not in any of the four types of plan.

7. What rules govern vesting of benefits?

Vesting must comply with 1974 Pension Reform Act (ERISA), which provides a choice of vesting schedules. One schedule often chosen is gradual progressive vesting, which starts after the fifth year of employment, with 100 percent vesting required after fifteen years. (Benefits become vested when employees obtain fixed and irrevocable rights to claim them.)

8. Can the trust invest in employer securities?

Under pension plans, investments in employer securities are limited to 10 percent of total assets. The "prudent man rule" requires conservative diversified investments.

Under profit-sharing plans, the trust may invest in employer securities. No percentage limit, but "prudent man rule" applies, so investments should be diversified, should bring a fair return, and should provide liquidity for distribution of benefits.

Stock bonus plans are intended to be used for investment in employer securities, without limitation. The trust must own enough employer securities to distribute benefits when they come due.

ESOPs are intended for investment in employer securities without limit. The trust *must* invest primarily in employer securities and must own enough employer securities to distribute benefits when they come due.

9. Can "leverage" be used; that is, can the trust borrow money to buy employer securities?

Only an ESOP can use leverage. A leveraged stock bonus plan is considered an ESOP. Pension plans and profit-sharing plans cannot use leverage.

10. Is the payment of benefits insured?

Payments of benefits of up to $750 per month (plus cost-of-living adjustments) under defined benefit pension plans are insured by a federal agency, the Pension Benefit Guarantee Corporation. No other types of plan are insured by this agency.

11. Are the employers' annual contributions limited by profits of the corporation?

Only in profit-sharing plans.

12. In what form are benefits distributed?

In pension and profit-sharing plans, benefits may be distributed in cash or any securities but are usually paid in the form of a monthly income for life (called an *annuity*). In stock bonus plans and ESOPs, benefits may be distributed only in the form of employer securities.

13. Do employees share in appreciation of value of stock held by the trust?

Pension plans: generally no. Most pension plans call for fixed benefits, and any appreciation in value of stock held by trust will further reduce contribution costs of the employer rather than increase benefits to the employees. However, in money purchase pension plans, appreciation of stock value does benefit the employees.

Profit-sharing plans: yes. Stock bonus plans: yes. ESOPs: yes.

14. Must the investments of the trust be diversified?

Pension plans: yes. Profit-sharing plans: usually. Stock bonus plans: there may be some diversification, although enough employer stock must be owned to pay benefits in that form when they come due.

ESOPs: practically no diversification. Most of the eggs are in the basket of the employer securities.

Because ESOP is tied to the employment relationship and requires all benefits to be paid in stock of the employer, it is structurally unsuitable as a tool for diffusing capital ownership throughout society. Each employee gets stock only in the corporation that he works for, and there simply aren't enough employers whose stocks are successful enough over the years to make ESOP work on a macroeconomic scale. In this respect, ESOP is similar to profit-sharing, which has been used successfully by thousands of corporations since the nineteenth century, but is not flexible enough to lead the way to universal capitalism. For example, Sears Roebuck installed a profit-sharing plan in 1916, investing most of the contributions in Sears stock. Over the years it has been very successful, and has brought substantial capital ownership to many retiring Sears employees. But if all American retailers had done the same thing in 1916, in most cases their employees would have received little or nothing on retirement. The fortunes of business are such that there aren't enough long-term winners around to enable employment-based capital diffusion to work on a large scale.

For reasons that we'll see in a moment, not many large corporations have installed ESOPs. But of those that have, a large percentage use them as a substitute for pension or profit-sharing plans. This concentrates the potential retirement benefits in the stock of the employer, when diversification would be more prudent in most cases. If the employer runs into financial difficulties, the worker can lose both his job and his retirement benefits.

Another big problem with ESOP is that it comes between the worker and his union, which accounts for the almost total silence of organized labor on the subject of ESOP. As workers become stockholders in the employer corporation, they may develop divided loyalties. They will always be interested in higher wages, but they are not as likely to depend entirely on their unions to fix wage demands, since they have a new interest in holding down costs to raise profits and stock values.

The first reaction of American labor leaders has been to ignore ESOP, hoping that it will go away. They have taken the same attitude toward *codetermination,* the European movement toward giving workers representation on boards of directors, with or without stock ownership. European labor leaders are moving in the opposite direction. First they negotiated for codetermination in the form of board representation, and now they are starting to push for union ownership of major businesses. Worker ownership based on a percentage of the payroll, such as the 15 percent of payroll that is the maximum under ESOP, would build up very rapidly. If ESOP were adopted by major American corporations, within ten to fifteen years ESOPs would hold enough stock to control many businesses, since this usually requires no more than 15–20 percent of the total stock outstanding. ESOP could then be used as an ideal device for unions to take control of business, as we'll see in Chapter 10.

Its proponents claim that ESOP increases productivity because of the strong motivation that goes with ownership of employer stock: the original piece of the action, a share of the business you are working in. It's probably true that employees of small corporations who receive significant percentages of stock will work harder to make their stock worth more. But in large corporations, where the effects of individual effort are hard to determine, motivation studies have produced mixed results. Anyway, the big hole in the motivation argument is that macroeconomic use of ESOP would cause millions of workers to become stockholders in losers. If there is motivation in such stock ownership, it is likely to be the reverse of what is needed to increase productivity.

Use of ESOP for Corporate Finance

The stock bonus plan was available as an employee benefit long before Louis Kelso started practicing law. One of his big accomplishments was to make the stock bonus plan do double duty, as both an employee benefit and a tool of corporate finance. He did this by adding leverage to the stock bonus plan. In fact, a simplified definition of ESOP is a leveraged stock bonus plan.

Thanks to Kelso, ESOPs can borrow money to buy large blocks of employer stock on the installment plan, something that can't be done under other employee benefit plans. This little wrinkle allows a corporation to get the benefits of tax deductions for both principal and interest payments on the money that the ESOP borrows to buy the corporation's stock. Normally only the interest would be tax deductible, but in a leveraged ESOP the corporation makes annual contributions which are used to pay the principal as well as the interest, and these annual contributions are tax deductible.

However, there is a price to pay for this tax advantage: for every dollar raised by selling stock to an ESOP, the corporation must issue $1 worth of its stock *and* repay the loan principal of $1 plus interest. Even though the $1 loan principal can be repaid with $1 worth of pretax profits, the $1 loan still costs the corporation at least 50¢ after taxes, plus interest. If the corporation can borrow $1 from a bank or if it can sell $1 worth of its stock at fair market value, it is better off doing one or the other, at a cost of about $1, than doing *both* through an ESOP at a cost of at least $1.50.

Obviously, ESOP is an expensive way for most corporations to raise money. There has to be a special reason to justify its use in place of a straight loan or a straight stock sale. Unfortunately, these special reasons seldom exist except in privately held corporations or publicly held parent corporations that want to get rid of subsidiaries or troubled operations. ESOP can be very useful in these cases, but taken together they would not produce enough capital diffusion to make a dent in the nation's economic problems.

Owners of privately held corporations can use ESOPs to reduce estate taxes and to retain control of the business while selling it to the employees over a period of years. Since the owners are usually high-salaried employees themselves, they can get back large blocks of stock after selling to the ESOP (see Appendix for further details) . Without getting into the merits of using the tax laws to create such benefits for owners of successful privately held businesses, we can dismiss them because they simply don't have enough total capital to help us in the quest for universal capitalism.

The only other transaction in which ESOP has proven

useful as a tool of corporate finance is the divestiture of a subsidiary, division, or troubled operation to its employees. Often the employees are the most eager buyers of a subsidiary that the parent corporation no longer wants, for their jobs (especially high executive positions) may disappear if the operation is sold to strangers. ESOP can enable the employees to buy the entire operation on long-term credit, repaying the loan principal and interest as tax-deductible expenses. This use of ESOP brought Kelso worldwide publicity in 1975, when he teamed up with an agency of the U.S. Department of Commerce, the Economic Development Administration (EDA), to design a plan that rescued a venerable machine tool manufacturer, South Bend Lathe, and saved 500 jobs in the process. The story of how Kelso and EDA arranged $10 million in loans to the South Bend Lathe ESOP, and then helped the employees to buy the operation from the parent corporation that was about to scrap it, is told in the Appendix.

While South Bend Lathe is a fine model for ESOP rescue of a failing operation, it's not what we're looking for as the foundation of universal capitalism. We've got to diffuse ownership of stock in the successful giant corporations, not their discards. Also, South Bend Lathe and a second ESOP rescue (Okonite Company) involved outright grants of federal funds by EDA, which would not be possible on a large scale.

As of mid-1976, less than 500 corporations had installed ESOPs, and most of them involved small or closely held businesses. The few large corporations that had installed ESOPs did not use them to raise money by issuing new stock; there were other special motives that would not apply to most large corporations.

ESOP and the Public Interest

Even if ESOP could be modified to make it more attractive to large corporations and their employees, it would not be an ideal method of capital diffusion. Broad use of ESOP would create many new inequities that could be avoided if instead we adopted a more universal and equitable scheme such as the

Financed Capitalist Plan. ESOPs, like other employee benefit plans, benefit mainly the people who are least in need of help—those who have good jobs with leading corporations. Since most ESOPs distribute stock to employees in proportion to their salaries, the biggest benefits go to those with the best jobs.

Of course, we could change this for ESOPs. If we found that ESOP was an ideal method of broadening capital ownership, we could make special rules that would eliminate the favoring of higher-salaried employees. But more basic inequities would remain.

ESOPs, more than any other benefit plans, would favor employees of the leading corporations in each industry. Leaders such as IBM and Xerox may already have the best personnel in their industries; maybe that's one reason why they are so successful. If they installed ESOPs, their employees would benefit greatly from stock ownership. Employees of their weaker competitors, on the other hand, might get practically no benefit from ESOP, since the prices of their stocks are less stable. This would tend to make the best people in every industry gravitate to the leading companies instead of sticking it out with less successful competitors. The result would be a widening of the gap between winners and losers, with serious injury to the most vulnerable part of the economy, the millions of jobs in the firms that are not leaders of their industries.

Of course, there are other incentives that attract the best people to work for the industry leader. That's part of the free enterprise system. But if you advocate broad use of ESOP, you're talking about using the tax system to *subsidize* the most successful corporations, to widen their competitive advantages by letting them use tax dollars to give their stock to their employees. Obviously, tax subsidies to the most successful corporations are among the least equitable and least sensible ways to lay the foundation for universal capitalism.

And even if these were just bugs that could be ironed out, ESOP would apply to only about 60 percent of the present work force. Approximately 40 percent of the work force is not employed by corporations, and probably never will be. These are the people in the armed forces, in government work, in agriculture, people who are self-employed, people who work for medical, educational, or other noncorporate employers. Then there is the mass of the unemployed. None of these people would get any benefit from ESOP or from any other stock ownership plan based on employment.

As we saw in Chapter 4, the Financed Capitalist Plan can use the same pumping mechanism that ESOP uses (the credit power of major corporations and their ability to make capital pay for itself) for the benefit of all Americans in equitable measure. It would not cause the new inequities that ESOP threatens to bring, or come between the worker and his labor union, or interfere with existing pension and retirement systems. Therefore, broad use of ESOP would not be in the public interest even if we could make it into a much bigger pump. Again, it would simply fill the wrong bathtubs.

The Overselling of ESOP

Louis Kelso's appearance on "60 Minutes" in April 1975 was followed by numerous interviews and articles in *Business Week, Barrons, Fortune, Wall Street Journal,* and many other publications. Then the professional seminars and conferences started, meetings of lawyers, accountants, financial executives, and employee benefit specialists addressed by experts like Kelso and other ESOP consultants. Books and pamphlets began to appear, describing the benefits of ESOPs and how to design and install them. Throughout this explosion of interest in Kelso's work, the topic was almost exclusively ESOP.

That's one of the big problems about ESOP and Kelso; practically everybody who has ever heard of Kelso thinks that the "Kelso plan" for universal capitalism *is* ESOP. Kelso is very impressive as a public and private speaker, and much of his writing on economics reaches a very high moral and philosophical level. When he uses ESOP as his punchline, as the vehicle that is going to bring the beautiful dream of universal capitalism to life, people take him seriously. They assume that ESOP is on a par with the very high standards that Kelso has set for himself in all his writings and activities.

Then comes the letdown. ESOP is a very limited device,

and it has been overpromoted and oversold. Kelso catches some of the blame for this because he has accepted all the ESOP publicity without saying much about its limitations. He continues to preach the golden gospel of universal capitalism, and then he talks about ESOP, and the listener assumes that one leads to the other. When the listener learns the limitations of ESOP, there is disillusionment and sometimes even resentment. So the overselling of ESOP can be harmful to the universal capitalist movement.

Yet, I don't think it is fair to blame Kelso for this. Remember that he tried for fifteen years to push the Financed Capitalist Plan, and nobody listened to him. He was not able to gain attention or get any legislation going in the direction of universal capitalism, until he seized on the *existing* tax advantages, however limited, that ESOP afforded. It is practically impossible to put a revolutionary idea such as the Financed Capitalist Plan into operation in one lifetime, especially with mixed capitalism working pretty well throughout much of the period.

So Louis Kelso took the only road open to him. He invented ESOP, created ESOP models with his own clients, and used it to capture the spotlight. When his big chance came with Senator Long, he was able to show that he was not an idle dreamer but a practical lawyer who had actually installed stock ownership plans that were working. ESOP is a capital diffusion scheme in being, and Kelso says that it can be improved with a few changes in the current tax laws.

Some people have the erroneous impression that Kelso has made a fortune by installing ESOPs. He gave up a prosperous law practice in which he was being well paid for advising clients like the Rockefellers and the Wells Fargo Bank, not about ESOPs but about the more lucrative legal and tax problems that come up in large corporations. It was this secure practice that brought him his personal fortune, and he put that fortune on the line by devoting himself exclusively to Kelso & Company, investment bankers (the new name for Bangert & Company, which Kelso adopted in 1976).

It is true that Kelso & Company is dependent on the fees it collects for installing ESOPs and that Louis Kelso has a commercial axe to grind when he talks about ESOP today, but he could probably make a lot more money in his comfortable old corporation law practice, without the headaches of supporting a revolution out of ESOP consulting fees.

Now I've explained ESOP to you—as it had become in late 1976. When Kelso started using ESOP on his own, however, it was a much cruder device, with very little solid basis for it in the tax laws. He knew that if he was going to use ESOP as an icebreaker, there would have to be some changes in the tax laws. That's why he tried so hard to meet Senator Russell Long. And that brings us back to Kelso's first meeting with Long in November 1973.

ENTER SENATOR LONG: THE KELSO MOVEMENT, 1973-1976

The very rich in this nation who right now might think that they should be against this so-called Kelso plan are very insecure in what they own. They are going to be less secure in the possession of the enormous concentrated wealth that they have until a great number of other people have some of the ownership of these great corporations themselves.

Senator Russell B. Long

W hen Kelso decided in the early 1970s to use ESOP as the icebreaker for universal capitalism, he realized that new tax legislation was essential to make ESOP more attractive to employers. To accomplish this, he had to develop some clout with either the House Ways and Means Committee or the Senate Finance Committee. Each committee was dominated by its chairman. Kelso was not able to make headway with Congressman Wilbur Mills, the Arkansas Democrat who ran Ways and Means. Perhaps Mills was preoccupied with the nocturnal adventures that later caused him to resign his important chair under fire. So in 1972, Kelso decided to concentrate on Russell Long.

How Kelso Met Long

Kelso turned to Henry McIntyre, the trusted financial adviser who had helped him to organize Bangert & Company. As one of the chief fund raisers for the Planned Parenthood movement, McIntyre had contacts all over the country, including Louisiana. It occurred to him that his friend Dr. Joe Beasley of New Orleans, chairman of National Planned Parenthood, might know Senator Long. In 1972, McIntyre called Dr. Beasley and found that the doctor did indeed know the senator and was willing to introduce Kelso to him. But Beasley recommended that the approach to Long be made through his Washington legislative assistant, Wayne Thevenot.

Wayne Thevenot, then thirty-eight years old, had been legislative assistant to Senator Long for nearly ten years. Wayne was born for the job. He has all the charm and cornball humor of the rural Southern politician, and yet he knows exactly what he is doing when it comes to getting legislation through Congress. He grew up poor in Cottonport, Louisiana, and worked his way through Louisiana State University, graduating with a degree in political science in 1961. Then he became campaign manager for Gillis Long, a cousin of Russell Long, when Gillis was running for Congress. Gillis Long was elected to Congress in 1962, and Wayne decided to move up to Washington. He joined Russell Long's staff in 1963 and earned a master's degree in government at American University in 1965.

Dr. Joe Beasley had worked closely with Thevenot on legislative problems. He felt that Kelso should try to sell his theories to Thevenot first and then let Thevenot carry the ball to Senator Long. So he called Thevenot in Washington and told him about the wonders of Kelso. Beasley also sent him a copy of *Two-Factor Theory*. He followed up with telephone calls, and every time he called, he would ask Thevenot if he had read the book. Each time, Thevenot said that he had been too busy but that he hoped to get to it very soon.

After months of fruitless effort, Beasley took the bull by the horns. He called Thevenot and said that he was going to San Francisco and wanted him to come along to meet Kelso. By this time, Thevenot realized that Dr. Beasley was not going to leave him alone until he had absorbed Kelso's theories, so he decided that he might as well get the word from Kelso himself. He agreed to fly to San Francisco, and he took along his copy of *Two-Factor Theory* to read on the plane. As Thevenot tells it, by the time the plane was over Chicago, he was both captivated and annoyed by the book:

> After reading the book, I realized either I was terribly naïve or the guy had something that had implications be-

yond anything I had ever run into. I'm not an economist
or a lawyer. I had cynicism built into me after ten years
of working in the United States Congress, and I was
frankly very skeptical about the book. There was obviously something wrong with it. It was too damned easy.
It spanked of snake oiling. I've heard so many save-the-
world ideas that I've become immune to them.

But after two days in San Francisco listening to Kelso,
Thevenot's attitude changed.

After asking Kelso every tough question I could think
of, I just became totally sold on the idea. But the question was, then, what do I do about it? Well, by myself
I could do absolutely nothing. But if I could convince
Russell Long that this idea had merit, then we were off
and running because, after all my years with him, I knew
that when he gets ahold of an idea, he's going to ride it,
it's going to go!

Back in Washington, Wayne Thevenot took the first opportunity to talk to Senator Long about Kelso:

I didn't have to go very far because Long started tracking
on it right quick. By that time, I had some limited knowledge of Kelso. It wasn't very easy to articulate, but I gave
him the basics of it, and he said, "I've got to meet this guy
Kelso."

That was in November 1973, and on the twenty-seventh of
that month, Kelso and Norman Kurland had dinner with Senator Long and Wayne Thevenot in the Montpelier Room of the
Madison Hotel. The Montpelier Room is one of the fanciest
restaurants in Washington: Brazilian rosewood paneling, Ital-
ian marble, impressionist paintings. Chef Claude Picard has a
worldwide reputation that helped the Montpelier Room to a
ranking as one of the world's grand restaurants. You can tell
that it has a lot of class; if you walk in without a reservation,
even if the place is empty, the maître d' will slowly scan his
seating chart and talk with his colleagues in French for four or
five minutes before he brusquely assigns you to an obscure
table.

Here is Wayne Thevenot's description of that dinner
meeting, which lasted more than four hours.

Kelso spent the first forty-five minutes going through his regular explanation. And Russell Long listened quieter than I have ever seen him listen—just listening. And then he started asking questions. And after a few minutes of asking questions, Long started expanding on it himself. Senator Long is an extremely quick study. You don't have to read the whole novel to him. Just give him the outline, and he'll fill in the rest of it. So he and Kelso had this great meeting, a meeting of the minds and a mutuality of goals that was just beautiful to behold.

By the end of the meeting, the groundwork had been laid for the first ESOP legislation:

> LONG: Okay, what's your plan? What can I do to get this thing moving?

> KELSO: Well, the Senate Commerce Committee is meeting in executive session tomorrow on the Rail Reorganization Act to reorganize the bankrupt northeast railroads. Since the federal government is going to put an awful lot of money into that program, why should the government bail out these failing railroads and then have the benefits of the taxpayers' money go to the present stockholders of the railroads? If you're going to use federal money, why shouldn't some of this money go to the workers? This is an ideal place for the workers to own a piece of the action. The increased motivation of the railroad workers will help to make the railroads profitable, and at the same time, you won't be using federal money just to benefit the present owners of these sick railroads.

> LONG: That sounds like a good place to start. Have you got any thing written up?

> KELSO: Yes. Here's a draft of an amendment to the Rail Reorganization Act which would help us to get started.

That was all Russell Long needed. The next morning, he sailed into the executive session of the Commerce Committee and told his fellow senators that they had better put an ESOP provision into the Rail Reorganization Act, a provision that would force the railroads to set up ESOPs so that some of the ownership of this new capital coming in through federal funding would go to the railroads' employees. None of his colleagues understood much of what he was talking about, but they went along with him and approved the amendment on the basis of Long's personal prestige and drive. The only exception was Senator Warren Magnuson, the committee chairman, who abstained from voting. He said that it sounded like a good idea but that he didn't know enough about it to vote one way or the other.

Anyone who knows Senator Russell Long would not have been surprised by his ability to grasp a new idea at dinner one night and get it into legislation the next morning. He has one of Washington's fastest and most incisive minds, and he knows how to use legislative power about as well as anyone who has ever sat in the Senate. Because he is the most important Kelso advocate and also one of the most powerful men in the government, let's trace the steps that led him to endorse Kelso.

Russell Long's Heritage: Huey Long

To understand Russell Long's interest in universal capitalism, it is necessary to go back to the colorful history of his father, the late "Kingfish," Huey P. Long. In his struggle against poverty, Huey became a traveling salesman for kerosene lamps, lard products, and laxatives. He educated himself by prodigious reading and managed to get enough formal schooling to pass the Louisiana bar exam in 1915, when he was twenty-two. He worked in the lower echelons of Louisiana politics for thirteen years, until he was able to put together enough antiestablishment votes from poor whites, struggling farmers, and a few blacks to become governor of Louisiana in 1928. His successful campaign was directed against the image of the capitalist fat cat.

Governor Huey Long hit Louisiana like a cyclone. His regime was best described by Marshall Frady in "The Longs of Louisiana," written for the London *Sunday Times* in 1975.

> His tenure was nothing less than seismic in its effect on the state. He abolished the poll tax. He provided free

text-books for all schoolchildren. He imposed a debt moratorium. He initiated free night-schools for adults, along with hugely expanding appropriations to schools. He amplified free hospital services. He accomplished a panoramic road and bridge system in a state whose interior up to then had been laced with little more than gullied goat-paths.

In all this, most importantly, he succeeded in delivering Louisiana for a time from the thrall that the corporate custodial estate had so long exerted over its affairs, ransacking their tax privileges to boot. Their desperation soon reached the point where they conducted a discreet state-wide collection of $1000 donations to compile a pot for bribing the legislature to impeach him. Scrambling furiously, Huey managed to confound that gambit too.

Despite his good works and genuine concern for the poor, Huey Long is best remembered as the dictator of Louisiana. He didn't think he could carry out his radical plans simply by being governor, even though he used patronage in ways that had never been seen before; so he also grabbed control of the Louisiana courts and legislature and held them tightly in his power even after he was elected to the U.S. Senate in 1932. In his 1967 book, *Huey P. Long*, T. Harry Williams said:

> On frequent occasions he would storm back to the state, order his governor to call a special session of the legislature, and take over personally the job of running the session. At these special sessions laws were passed at a breathtaking rate and without much regard for parliamentary niceties or deliberation. In seven sessions within the space of a year a total of 463 bills was turned out, and on one memorable occasion 44 bills were enacted in 22 minutes.

Although many people feared Huey and likened him to his contemporaries Mussolini and Hitler, nobody ever accused him of being vague on the issues. When he was told that an official of the Georgia Ku Klux Klan was coming to Louisiana to campaign against him, Huey called a press conference and announced to the reporters:

> Quote me as saying that the Imperial Bastard will never set foot in Louisiana, and that when I call him a son-of-a-bitch I am not using profanity but am referring to the circumstances of his birth!

After he got to Washington in 1932, Huey began to frighten people outside of Louisiana. As Williams describes it,

> Long broke with Roosevelt for personal and political reasons. He could not be second to anyone, just as Roosevelt could not be, and he thought that the President's New Deal did not go nearly far enough in coping with the problems of the depression or the maldistribution of wealth in America. Long had his own programme to deal with these problems, one that called for drastic increases in income and estate taxes, which he named, to the fright of conservatives: Share Our Wealth.

Huey's Share Our Wealth scheme included these features: a "homestead" of $5,000 for every family in the United States, a government guarantee that every family would receive an annual income of $2,000 to $3,000 (enough to live on in those days), old-age pensions, generous bonuses for World War I veterans, and a program that would limit work to thirty hours a week and eleven months a year in order to increase the demand for labor. According to Huey's calculations, there would be enough money to provide these benefits if the federal government imposed two new taxes: one that would prevent families from earning more than $1 million a year and a second that would prevent families from owning total wealth of more than $5 million.

Although his arithmetic was not very accurate, there was nothing wrong with Long's sense of mainstream politics. Huey was a hero to the poor, almost a messiah, even though it was not easy for them to get his message in those pretelevision days. By the time he was assassinated in 1935, there were more than 25,000 chapters of his Share Our Wealth movement, with a total membership of more than 4.5 million Americans spread through all forty-eight states. Their motto was Every Man a King. T. Harry Williams clearly states just how close Huey Long came to national power:

> The battle between Long and Roosevelt pitted against each other two great politicians. It was fought in the great arena of national politics—in the Senate and in presidential press conferences and over the radio and in the press. The whole nation watched it with rapt attention. In the fight Roosevelt had solid advantages. His

mastery of politics was fully equal to Long's and he operated from a stronger base, the presidency, with all its immense resources.

Still, Long managed to hold his own. It was his fulminations against the failure of the New Deal to attack the concentration of wealth, and the very evident mass following that he was arousing by his speeches, that forced Roosevelt to turn, finally, to the left in 1934. Indeed, some observers thought that Long was more than holding his own, that he might defeat his rival in the end. He had let it be known that he planned to run a third-party candidate against Roosevelt in 1936, in the hope of taking enough votes to throw the election to the Republicans. The Republicans, he thought, would be incapable of dealing with the depression, the economic system would collapse, and by 1940 the country would be crying for a strong man to save it. Then Huey Long would take over and put the pieces together—as he wanted to put them. . . .

Roosevelt and his advisers were acutely alarmed by Long's threat to intervene in the election of 1936, actually believing that he might be able to cause Roosevelt's defeat. It has recently been revealed that the President feared Long for a more fundamental reason. He thought that if the New Deal failed to meet the crisis of American Capitalism there would be some kind of revolution—one from the left led by Long or one from the right led by Douglas MacArthur. Long and MacArthur, Roosevelt once said, were the two most dangerous men in the country.

Russell Long's Rise to Power

Russell Long was just short of seventeen when his father was gunned down in a marble corridor of the Louisiana capitol at Baton Rouge. That was in 1935. The Share Our Wealth movement died with Huey. By 1973, Russell had become very wealthy himself and was best known as a defender of tax shelters for the rich. But he never forgot his father's central theme: that America could come apart, or perhaps could be taken apart, on the issue of maldistribution of wealth. So it was not strange that

Huey Long's son listened intently to Louis Kelso in the Montpelier Room in 1973.

Russell was an outstanding student and president of his class at Louisiana State University. He received a law degree from LSU in 1942 and then enlisted in the navy, serving as an officer on an amphibious ship in the Mediterranean theater. After the war, he returned to Baton Rouge and practiced law there until 1948. Then U.S. Senator Overton died in midterm, and Russell won a special election to fill Overton's seat. He was only twenty-nine when he was elected, but he reached the minimum Senate age of thirty in time to take his seat in December of 1948.

Although Russell looks a lot like Huey, his style is not nearly so flamboyant as his father's, and his first two terms in the Senate were rather quiet. But he was working his way up the seniority ladder, waiting for the chance to get some real power in his hands. History and the American political system were on his side, as Marshall Frady points out in "The Longs of Louisiana."

> Indeed, it is as if the South, having been confounded in the field, with an infinite resourcefulness gradually and inconspicuously proceeded to reverse that verdict—its senators and congressmen abiding on through the seasons through the old folk-loyalties of the tribal politics back home—by appropriating Washington in time simply through the congressional seniority system.

Russell became chairman of the Senate Finance Committee in January 1966. Up to that time, the Senate had been playing second fiddle to the House on taxes because the Constitution gives the House the sole right to initiate revenue bills. But Russell Long decided to change that, and he didn't let a little thing like Article I, Section 7, of the Constitution stand in his way. Nobody has written the full story of how he did it, but by 1975, Russell Long had made the Senate Finance Committee the main force in deciding what taxes Americans pay.

As nearly as I can determine, he used a combination of fancy moves. He began to amend House tax bills in such a way that he was really initiating his own new legislation, and in the final House-Senate conference committees that are always necessary to reconcile different versions of a bill passed by each house, he used parliamentary skills to outmaneuver his House colleagues.

In this way, Russell Long has become the most powerful Senate Finance Committee chairman in history; to some observers (such as the *Wall Street Journal*), he is *the* most powerful senator. The Internal Revenue Code is so complicated that only a handful of people on Capitol Hill actually understand what is in the existing tax law, to say nothing of new tax bills such as that 1,536-page monster, the Tax Reform Act of 1976. In 1947, one of the greatest federal judges in American history, Learned Hand, described the tax law in these words:

> The words of the income tax dance before my eyes in a meaningless procession: cross-reference to cross-reference, exception upon exception—couched in abstract terms that leave my mind only a confused sense of some vitally important, but successfully concealed, purport, which is within my power to extract, if at all, only after the most inordinate expenditure of time. I know that these monsters are the result of fabulous industry and ingenuity but one cannot help wondering whether they have any significance save that the words are strung together with syntactical correctness.

But Russell Long knows the existing tax law as no other senator does, and he knows how to get what he wants into new tax laws. So he combines power with nearly exclusive knowledge of what is going on in the game of tax legislation. As a result, changes in the U.S. tax laws in the mid-1970s are largely controlled by one man: Russell Long.

His great powers are constantly under challenge by senators who carry a liberal tag, particularly Edward Kennedy. Russell used his position to defend the oil depletion allowance for many years after other senators wanted to kill it, and he has been able to bottle up tax-reform legislation passed by the House and favored by many senators. There have been rumors that Senate liberals will make an all-out fight to strip Long of his committee chairmanship during the Ninety-fifth Congress (in 1977). But veteran Senate watchers are betting that Russell Long, in his prime at age fifty-six, after twenty-six years in the Senate and ten years as Finance Committee chairman, will continue to dominate tax legislation for years to come.

Why Long Endorsed Kelso

I have read all Senator Long's speeches and articles about Kelso, and I interviewed him in his Senate office in December 1975. From these sources, I think I have figured out why he became Kelso's strongest advocate.

Russell Long is a very smart man who is also very rich. (The two don't go together automatically.) He may also be very public-spirited, and he may share his father's concern for the plight of poor people, but I don't know him well enough to draw those conclusions. For purposes of this book, it is enough for us to know that he is very smart, very rich, and in a position of extraordinary power.

In speeches and interviews, Long has said that his father was right in wanting to correct maldistribution of wealth, but that Huey was wrong in going about it like Robin Hood. Russell wants the rich to stay rich while the poor get "a piece of the action," a phrase he uses in every speech. And he does not think that capitalism will last much longer unless there are a lot more capitalists.

His fears are based on his experience as a practical politician whose work makes him sensitive to changes in the American power structure. Business lobbyists pound away at his committee, seeking changes in the tax laws that they say are needed for the survival of free enterprise, but he knows that he can't get them through Congress unless they also benefit people who don't own businesses. Here are some of his thoughts:

> If you want free enterprise and capitalism to succeed, you've got to make it into a program which can win elections. If it can't win elections, sooner or later a government will come in that's hostile to it, and that government will do away with it.
>
> If you keep up the conflict between labor and the owners, labor in this country will win eventually because in the long run, while they own no property or plants or machines, they have the votes.
>
> So we need to get great masses of people into capital

ownership. This democracy will be safer, and the rich man will be safer in what he owns, if more people own some of what he owns.

His years on the Finance Committee have given him a clear insight into the immediate threat that the tax system poses to the wealthy.

You have a lot of old-fashioned capitalists who think that the success of capitalism depends on keeping it an exclusive club for just a few people. Now those people in my judgment are very misguided. They're going to wind up at a minimum having the eyeballs taxed off them.

If labor looks on the owners as their enemy, labor has the votes needed to tax the eyeballs off the owners, who now don't have many votes. So the owners would be well advised in the long run to see to it that capitalism is a good deal for everybody.

Wayne Thevenot worked for Senator Long for thirteen years, so his thoughts are worth noting here:

Working closely with Russell Long on a lot of these social issues that he's had some prime responsibility in—the welfare programs, the social security program—convinced me that none of these are going to work in the long run. I went through that period in the early sixties—the Kennedy administration, with their war on poverty and all their other well-motivated programs, through Lyndon Johnson's early years. And in retrospect, none of these have really worked.

We have succeeded in raising the abject poor to a little higher level; they're a *little* better off. But the government can't continue to do that. The government is going broke trying to redistribute the wealth a little bit. And it's not going to work because it's fundamentally the wrong way to approach the problem.

You can't continue to tax people to compensate for those people who can't make it on their own. You can't continue to increase welfare payments, subsidize housing, run up social security costs. We're running out of things to tax. There's a growing resentment about increased taxes that some day is going to create political havoc.

Russell Long has struggled with trying to do something for poor people, but there's a limit under the present makeshift type of solutions. There's a limit to what you can do. And we're getting perilously close to that limit.

Thevenot was on Senator Long's staff during the Nixon administration, when Long was largely responsible for killing Nixon's attempt to install the Family Assistance Plan. Long had his Finance Committee staff run the plan through a computer, and they came up with figures showing that under it over 50 percent of the people in Mississippi and over 30 percent of the people in Louisiana would be on the federal dole. Thevenot recalls:

> Russell Long started looking at those figures, and he said that the political implications were *devastating*. Once you get half of your voters, or a third of your voters, or even 20 percent of your voters dependent on federal checks, then a politician is faced with having to increase that constantly. You just can't do it; you can't continue to do it. You just run out of things to tax.

Russell Long has traveled all over the world and found the tides running against capitalism everywhere, with the governments of free-enterprise nations "running scared." He thinks that American capitalists should be running more scared than they are now, and he has told them so in his public speeches and in the privacy of his Senate office.

Louis Kelso brought Russell Long the weapon he was looking for, the tool to make capitalism a good deal for everybody without using Huey Long's soak-the-rich approach. So it's easy to see why Long has taken ESOP, an existing tool that can be improved through tax legislation, and tried to use it almost like Silly Putty, molding it into whatever shape is needed to broaden capital ownership. In one of his more exuberant speeches, Long used his down-home Louisiana style to sell ESOP:

> Just send us those tired, labor-plagued, competition-weary companies, and ESOP will breathe new life into them! ESOP is better than Geritol. It will revitalize capitalism. It will increase productivity. It will improve labor relations. It will promote economic justice. It will save our economic system. It will make our form of government and our concept of freedom prevail over those who don't agree with us!

In all Long's speeches and interviews, I didn't find mention of any Kelso idea other than ESOP. I wondered whether he really thought that ESOP, with its many limitations, would carry us all the way to universal capitalism. I put it to him this way:

> Do you think that you can bring capitalism to the point where it is a good deal for everybody just by broadening ESOP through tax legislation?

His answer was illuminating.

> No. To get what I'm talking about, you have to do a lot more than just changing tax laws, but ESOP starts people thinking about the idea. It moves them in the right direction, and when we have people thinking about it and working to make capitalism a good deal for everybody, then we have a chance for broader legislation. I think ESOP is important because it helps to sell the concept that unless you have broad-based ownership, the free-enterprise system is not going to survive. It's losing out all over the world where they've failed to realize that you need broad ownership, and that's a sad thing.

So Long, like Kelso, sees ESOP as a stepping-stone. He is not shooting in the dark when it comes to the macroeconomic effects of broadening capital ownership. He is one of the country's most astute practical economists, and since the early 1960s, he has been doing a lot of homework on the agonizing problem of inflation. He is convinced that capital diffusion, if properly handled, will not be inflationary.

> This is one way that you can improve the net worth of masses of our people without inflation. It is an ideal way to create additional capital that is not inflationary. It stimulates production, it increases productivity, and in all respects, it tends to work against inflation and to expand production and put more people on jobs.

Long added that he agrees fully with Kelso's idea that we must establish credit priorities favoring increased capital formation instead of concentrating on consumer credit.

> You're not going to build this enormous production plan from money that somebody's going to be taking out of his sock. There's not that much money in people's socks anymore. It's going to have to be done by new credit policies.

In Japan, for example, they're trying to allocate their credit in the areas where it's going to be needed most. That makes sense to me, but we have no national policy or planning in that direction at all. We're still hoping that somebody will come up with the savings out of his sock to finance this hugely expanding economy which we need to create jobs for everyone.

Even though Russell Long has been concentrating on pushing ESOP, he has his eye on the big picture. When I continued to probe for his ideas on how we were going to get all the way to universal capitalism, he told me:

> The American people now have a net worth of about $3 trillion. We expect to double that figure in the next twenty years, so that by 1995, the total net worth of the American people will be about $6 trillion.
>
> Right now, 15 percent of our people own about 85 percent of that $3 trillion net worth. It seems to me that we ought to start planning right now so that the second $3 trillion that we are adding to our net worth will be better distributed. Even if 30 percent of our people owned 85 percent of this second $3 trillion, that would be a lot better than having the present top 15 percent continue to own 85 percent of all our net worth.

How would he go about distributing this $3 trillion of added net worth during the next twenty years? He doesn't have the whole blueprint drawn up yet, but he's going to keep on writing ESOP into every tax law in which he can fit it. He's going to try to force corporations to broaden the ownership of new capital, even if he has to do it all by himself. This is clear from the four laws relating to ESOP that he pushed through the Ninety-third and Ninety-fourth Congresses between 1973 and 1975.

First Three ESOP Statutes

As we have seen, the morning after he met Louis Kelso, Russell Long took the Senate Commerce Committee by storm and got it to agree to write ESOP into the Rail Reorganization Act of

1973. The idea was that if the federal government was going to help bail out the bankrupt northeastern railroads, the railroads should be required to issue some stock to their employees through an ESOP. But because Long was new at the ESOP game and the Rail Reorganization Act was not really under his control, the final ESOP provision was watered down. It gave the new Conrail Corporation discretion on whether to use an ESOP. In the end, Conrail retained some consultants to study ESOP; and they decided against using it, saying they did not believe that it would increase productivity.

However, the 1973 act contained the first legal definition of ESOP, calling it "a technique of corporate finance that uses a stock bonus trust . . . in connection with the financing of . . . capital requirements of the corporation." This was the first direct statement in federal law or regulations that an ESOP or a stock bonus plan could be used to benefit a corporation as a financial device and also confer benefits on the employees of that corporation.

Senator Long's next shot at ESOP legislation was another bill that was not primarily in the bailiwick of his committee. The Employee Retirement Income Security Act of 1974 (ERISA), also called the Pension Reform Act, was a long and tremendously complicated piece of legislation designed to bring some badly needed regulation to private pension and profit-sharing plans. Most of the work on this bill was done by the Senate Committee on Labor and Public Welfare and the House Committee on Education and Labor because it had broad effects on labor laws. But quite a few of its provisions affected the tax laws, and this brought Senator Long's committee into the drafting process.

This time, Long was able to achieve another first; he succeeded in getting a definition of ESOP written into the Internal Revenue Code for the first time. Unfortunately, the ERISA provisions that define ESOP as a technique of corporate finance are not quite so clear as those in the 1973 rail act. In fact, ERISA was almost a disaster for ESOP and the entire Kelso movement. Few legislators knew exactly what they were voting on when the bill finally came to the floor. During one of the many hurried amending sessions, some provisions were inserted that would have knocked out the use of ESOPs in any way that could benefit corporations. At the last minute, thanks to Senator Long and to weeks of unofficial lobbying by Lou Kelso and Norm Kurland, the ESOP provision was salvaged. ESOPs are still covered by the provision that requires employee-benefit plans to be set up for the exclusive benefit of employees, but other sections of ERISA and the Internal Revenue Code recognize, at least by implication, that ESOPs can also be used as financing devices for corporations.

Senator Long was also able to get an ESOP provision written into the Trade Act of 1974, which provides federal guarantees for loans made to companies injured by foreign competition. It gives preferences on government loans to corporations that agree to use 25 percent of such loans for ESOPs. And once again, the act's definition of an ESOP includes the phrase "a technique of corporate finance."

These first three ESOP statutes were just warmups for Russell Long. He had been forced to reach out into the territory of other committees to push them through. But he was cooking up something special for his own committee, and he found the perfect vehicle for it in the Tax Reduction Act of 1975.

Senator Long's Secret Weapon: TRASOP

Senator Long's X ray vision of the tax laws enabled him to zero in on a sensitive spot that he could use to *force* corporations to broaden capital ownership: the *investment tax credit*. This provision has been in and out of the tax laws since 1962. It was designed to encourage business to make capital expenditures for new plants and equipment in order to stimulate production and reduce unemployment. It gives businesses a tax credit for capital outlays (and remember, a tax *credit* is about twice as valuable as a tax *deduction* because the credit is subtracted directly from taxes payable).

The investment tax credit has had a checkered history. It

has been turned on and off, depending on whether the government was more concerned about inflation or recession. Some critics say that it isn't a useful device because its effects lag behind the economy and that it gives business firms a bonanza for buying things that they need and would have to buy even if they could not get a tax credit. Some say that it actually increases unemployment because it encourages businesses to buy new machines that may decrease the number of workers needed. But one thing is clear: It is a free handout from the government to the stockholders of leading corporations, who benefit to the tune of between $5 and $9 billion a year. That's how much extra money remains in corporate treasuries after the investment tax credit is applied, and of course, the extra money is automatically owned by the present stockholders, who contribute nothing extra in order to obtain this additional ownership.

Senator Long knew that the investment tax credit handout was a sensitive area in which he could exercise considerable control. So when Congress was working on the Tax Reduction Act of 1975, and there was strong support for increasing the investment tax credit from 7 to 10 percent in order to spur the lagging economy, Long agreed to support the increase. But he added a little twist. He tacked on a provision that would allow businesses to take an extra 1 percent investment tax credit, making a total credit of 11 percent, if that extra 1 percent credit was put into a *Tax Reduction Act* [1975] *stock ownership plan* (*TRASOP*). Some people call this device an ITC-ESOP because it is a special form of ESOP arising out of the investment tax credit, but its official title in the federal regulations is TRASOP.

Here is an example of how TRASOP works. A corporation spent $10 million on new capital outlays in 1976. That corporation is entitled to a tax credit of $1 million under the regular 10 percent investment tax credit and another credit of 1 percent of the $10 million ($100,000) if it has set up a TRASOP and issued $100,000 worth of new stock to it, or bought $100,000 worth of stock for it in the market. The net effect of the TRASOP provision is that the federal government gives this particular corporation and its employees a free ride on $100,000 worth of stock. This is a gift of $100,000 from the government to the employees, just as the $1 million regular investment tax credit is a gift of $1 million from the government to the corporation's present stockholders. The $100,000 worth of stock contributed by the employer to the TRASOP is treated as an ESOP; that is, the stock is held in trust and later distributed to the employees as a deferred benefit in proportion to their salaries.

However, TRASOP does not seem to offer a strong incentive for the employer to take the extra 1 percent investment tax credit and give it to its employees because the corporation does not get any direct financial benefit. The corporation getting the extra $100,000 tax credit would have to issue $100,000 worth of new stock to its TRASOP, and the net effect is the same as if they had sold $100,000 worth of stock at market value. TRASOPs are a little tougher on employers than ESOPs are because the benefits must be vested immediately and the employees must be allowed to vote the stock allocated to their accounts immediately (rather than having to wait until they receive the stock, as they usually do under an ESOP). Furthermore, the TRASOP provision in the 1975 Tax Reduction Act was only temporary; it covered only 1975 and 1976. Therefore, corporations could be left with an expensive administration job if TRASOP was not renewed. But Kelso and Senator Long claimed that the corporation does get an important benefit: increased productivity from employees who have a piece of the action.

You would expect that in 1975–1976, employees of large corporations and their union representatives would have demanded their TRASOP stock; after all, it was sitting there, free for the asking. But there was practically no union demand for TRASOPs. As of late 1975, only a handful of corporations had established TRASOPs and taken the opportunity to pass along a government gift of stock to their employees. Obviously, the TRASOP message was not getting across. So Senator Long decided to do something, and he is not a man who thinks small. He decided to get his point across through the nation's biggest corporation, American Telephone and Telegraph.

In a speech at a Louisiana State University seminar on ESOPs in October 1975, he singled out AT&T for a very direct message. The corporation had scheduled capital outlays of over

$5 billion for 1976 that would qualify for the regular invest-
ment tax credit of 10 percent, a total credit of more than $500
million. Under the TRASOP provision, it would be entitled to
an additional credit of 1 percent, which comes to an additional
$50 million; that is, AT&T could give its employees ownership
of $50 million worth of its stock without any cost to the com-
pany because it would get a credit of the full $50 million on its
1976 tax bill.

Here is the way Long explained things to his LSU
audience:

> Now unfortunately in America there are really not
> enough people running scared. I see that there is a repre-
> sentative of AT&T here, and I would like to suggest to
> him that AT&T is a great company which ought to be
> running a lot more scared than they are, just to take an
> example.
>
> This great company is entitled at this very moment
> to claim $50 million tax-free from the U.S. Treasury in
> order to buy stock for its employees and to help finance
> expansion, to buy new equipment, or whatever they
> might need. Now if I were a union organizer, I would
> have something to say about a company that would turn
> down $50 million out of the U.S. Treasury rather than
> let their workers have it.
>
> I'd tell the workers that the AT&T management
> have so little regard for you that they'd throw that $50
> million down the *rathole* rather than see you have any
> of it.
>
> I might even be thinking about getting some of the
> employees together to bring a *lawsuit* if the company
> didn't take advantage of this government-financed stock
> for its employees.

A little later in his speech, Long said that he hoped he had
gotten the attention of AT&T. Apparently he had. John Bain,
AT&T's representative at the seminar, telephoned his superiors
in New York that same day and told them about Long's speech.
Soon after that, AT&T announced that it was going to take
advantage of the 1 percent TRASOP, provided that certain
technicalities of the tax law relating to utilities could be cleared
up. It turned out that Long had been rather easy on AT&T. He
had mentioned $50 million worth of TRASOP stock, but
AT&T actually spent about $9 billion on capital outlays in

1975, so the 1 percent TRASOP would involve about $90 million worth of free stock.

TRASOP moved slowly in 1975–1976, mainly because the 1975 Tax Reduction Act stipulated that the entire 11 percent investment tax credit would expire in 1976. Most large corporations were able to duck the issue by saying that it was uneconomical to set up a special stock ownership plan that would receive contributions for a mere two years. Only those directly in Russell Long's line of fire, namely AT&T and some of the major oil companies, agreed to establish TRASOPs. But Long knew that the investment tax credit would be coming up for reconsideration in the summer of 1976 as part of the Tax Reform Act of 1976. There was a big push on to make the 10 percent investment tax credit permanent, and Long would then have his shot at making TRASOP permanent.

When I interviewed Long in December 1975 and put together the pieces of his strategy for universal capitalism, I wasn't overly impressed with the prospects for TRASOP. True, it is a main-arena program, focusing on the successful giants who make most of the new capital expenditures. But it has many of the defects of ESOP. It distributes benefits to all employees of major successful corporations in proportion to their salaries—filling up the wrong bathtubs again. And it works at the expense of all taxpayers because the tax credits that pay for TRASOP reduce federal revenue and put the burden on taxpayers to make up the losses, either now or in the future. It is strictly a government subsidy, and it does not make use of Kelso's basic discovery that capital will pay for itself out of its own earnings. It does not require issuance of new stock; instead, it allows the corporation the alternative of contributing cash and having the TRASOP buy existing stock in the market.

When TRASOP was enacted in 1975, I didn't see how it could be of much use in the move toward universal capitalism. But I jumped to that conclusion without knowing all the aspects of Senator Long's strategy. In 1976, I learned that TRASOP is really a secret weapon to force business, labor, and Congress to come up with a better plan for broadening capital ownership. If they do not, they will choke on TRASOP because Senator Long will feed them bigger and bigger doses of it. (The full story of Long's strategy is the subject of Chapter 11.)

If you ask Senator Long why he uses TRASOP as a bludgeon even though he knows that it is not the ideal instrument for capital diffusion, he'll answer you something like this:

> Okay, give me a more equitable system, and I'll use it. But in the meantime, until we get a new economic policy which gives us better tools for broadening capital ownership, I'll continue to use the TRASOP and any other ESOP provision I can to put into any tax law to force management and labor and the rest of the country to face up to the need for broadening capital ownership.

The first four ESOP bills received wide coverage in the business press. Without this publicity, the overwhelming majority of business executives, financiers, and lawyers probably would never have heard of Kelso or ESOP. And as Wayne Thevenot says,

> Senator Long's constant pushing of ESOP forced other senators, business and labor leaders to ask, "What in the hell is this?" From then on, we were off and running!

Russell Long is well aware of the limitations of TRASOP and ESOP. He is also aware of the great potential of the Financed Capitalist Plan, but like the rest of us, he has no solid data on which he can base an opinion about its potential side effects on the economy. Furthermore, the Financed Capitalist Plan involves legislation outside the tax field, which means that other congressional committees will have to carry the ball. That is why he continues to concentrate his legislative efforts on TRASOP and ESOP; they already exist, and their future is in the hands of his Senate Finance Committee. But you can be sure that Russell Long will use his power to back any legislation that involves broadened capital ownership.

On the question of how universal capitalism will finally be achieved—in his words, how capitalism will be made a good deal for everybody—Long told me:

> I'm not ready to say precisely how we're finally going to get the whole job done. We're not going to get there from here in one jump. We'll continue to work on TRASOP and ESOP, and we'll concentrate on certain industries and try to get the idea across that everybody has to work on finding ways of broadening capital ownership. We've

just got to have more capitalists if capitalism is going to survive.

As we'll see in Chapter 11, Russell Long has a talent for getting people to work on finding ways of broadening capital ownership, including many people who never thought that they had any interest in the subject.

Long as a Hero

At first blush, there is a temptation to write off Senator Long's advocacy of Kelso as the self-protective reflex of a rich man who has a close-up view of the rich-poor gap and can visualize the rocks heading toward his picture window in the near future. But there are plenty of richer men in the Senate and outside it who will not stick their necks out to back a radical idea, especially one that has been condemned by academic economists. It's easy for such men to conclude that their fortunes are safe today and that they can probably pass millions of dollars along to their children and grandchildren. The overwhelming defeat of George McGovern in 1972 by a man with the limited personal appeal of Richard Nixon says a lot about the staying power of the private-property system as long as it appears to have any chance of curing its own major illnesses.

So on a closer look, Senator Long has to be regarded as a hero. His constituents in Louisiana do not demand heroic innovations. Apparently, he doesn't need anything more than his last name to get reelected and retain his tremendous power. His father was succeeded in the Senate by his mother; his Uncle Earl hung on to the governorship of Louisiana while he was spending most of his time wooing Blaze Starr, a famous stripper; and his cousins Gillis Long and Speedy Long have served as congressmen from Louisiana. Clearly, Russell Long doesn't have any need to rock the boat.

He could use his power as chairman of the Senate Finance Committee to benefit much narrower interests than those of the people who will be the New Capitalists. Yet he subjects himself to controversy and uses up some of his precious trading power, not for the wealthy oil barons, but for those very same New Capitalists, people who don't even know their own identity and who have no voting power in Louisiana and no lobbying power in Congress. Therefore, if universal capitalism comes to America in the twentieth century, we're going to have to build a monument to Russell Long, maybe one even bigger than the twelve-foot bronze statue of Huey Long in Baton Rouge (which Russell himself posed for after his father's death, by the way) .

If we look back on America's heritage, it doesn't seem all that strange that a rich man who wants to hang onto his wealth should become the champion of the poor. George Washington was one of the wealthiest men in the colonies, and most of the men who signed the Declaration of Independence were rich. They had amassed their wealth under the protection of the British crown, and they had a great deal to lose by sticking their necks out in 1776. The Magna Charta, which is considered the cornerstone of Anglo-American liberty, was not the work of a band of downtrodden peasants. It was wrung from an unwilling King John in 1215 by the wealthiest noblemen in England (its official title is The Articles of the Barons at Runymede) . So it is not really surprising that the Kelso movement includes the names of Russell Long, John D. Rockefeller III, and the Pillsburys.

In my view, a man is not disqualified from becoming a hero just because he is running scared. Some of our most reliable heroes were running scared. Ask any combat pilot whether he'd rather fly with the man who *wants* to be a hero or with the man who is a little afraid and just wants to do his job and come home alive.

I first met Senator Long when I went to Washington in December 1975 to attend the public hearings on ESOP held by the Joint Economic Committee of Congress (JEC) . Those hearings and Senator Long's use of TRASOP during debate on the Tax Reform Act of 1976 gave me an excellent chance to see him in action.

ESOP GOES TO WASHINGTON

These plans [ESOPs] have been heralded as the basic solution for many of our economic ills. Specifically one of our chief proponents who will be testifying today, has said the widespread adoption of ESOPs will accomplish the following objectives: the restoration and acceleration of economic growth to unprecedented levels; create legitimate full employment for two or three decades; and lay the foundation for arresting inflation.

I must confess that these are some *claims. Certainly no one since I have been chairing this committee has come before us with any program that promises that much.*

Senator Hubert H. Humphrey, Chairman, Joint Economic Committee, ESOP Hearings, December 11, 1975

I started to write this book in December 1975. By then I had spent a lot of time with Kelso, and I had read all his books and speeches. I was convinced that he was on the path toward universal capitalism, but I had pretty well decided that ESOP was not the tool that would achieve it. The theme of this book was to be the need for extensive study of Kelso's Financed Capitalist Plan and any other ideas that might lead to universal capitalism. I hoped to stimulate discussion of universal capitalism in academic, government, and business circles. I dared to hope that this discussion might lead to serious congressional activity, perhaps even a declaration of national economic policy in favor of making capitalism universal, and then a congressional search for the best way to do it.

I talked to a few knowledgeable people about the chances for such action, and they told me that this would be very difficult because it meant taking on the academic economists, whose minds were not open to such a radical idea, and that the chances of getting any serious consideration were probably three to six years away.

These predictions have turned out to be inaccurate. Even

before this book was published, the Joint Economic Committee of Congress declared itself in favor of a new national policy of broadening stock ownership, and various congressional committees had begun an intensive search for the best way to carry out this policy.

All this took place in 1976, after I had decided that my fact-gathering was done and it was time to finish my writing. But the facts would not stand still for me; they kept right on happening as this book went to press. This chapter is the story of how the pieces fell into place and how Congress wrote the punch lines for me.

How I Decided ESOP Was Not the Answer

I decided that the best way to investigate ESOP was to discuss it with business executives and union officials, who are, after all, the people who are supposed to benefit from it. I started with businessmen and tried to concentrate on executives of fairly large publicly held corporations. Very quickly, I learned that ESOP was too expensive for them to use for financing; they could do much better by simply borrowing or selling their stock to the public. They could see no point in creating $1 worth of debt *and* issuing $1 worth of stock for each dollar raised, even if part of the debt could be repaid with tax dollars.

Next I talked with executives of smaller publicly held corporations. Their reaction was the same. It took them about five minutes to figure out that ESOP financing would cost much more than straight debt or stock sales. In the case of one small publicly held corporation whose stock price was depressed below its book (liquidation) value, the chief executive officer said that they needed working capital but that they had borrowed up to their banking limits and didn't want to sell stock at such a low price because that would dilute the holdings of existing stockholders. Would ESOP solve any of his problems? He didn't see how it could, since it would involve selling stock to the

ESOP at market value (below book value) and would require taking another loan, which he didn't think any bank would give them. On top of all that, he ridiculed the idea of using an employee benefit plan to raise money. I countered with the Kelso argument: Wouldn't his company get all the extra cost back through increased motivation and productivity?

His answer was that none of his employees were very much impressed with deferred compensation; they all looked in their pay envelopes to see how much their take-home pay was. And he was not speaking only of the lowest-echelon employees. He said that even his executive vice-president (who happened to be his son-in-law) spoke only of his take-home pay and did not figure in his fringe benefits. He said that if he wanted to increase motivation and productivity, he would not try to do it by giving his employees a stock that had a history of ups and downs; rather, he would try something more direct, something the employees could get their hands on immediately, such as a cash bonus plan. Furthermore, he would probably confine the cash bonuses to a small number of supervisory employees who would be in a position to increase the productivity of the lower echelons.

I've had some personal experience that bears out how limited the appeal of fringe benefits is. Our law firm has had a pension plan and a profit-sharing plan ever since lawyers were permitted to incorporate. Each year, we contribute a total of 25 percent of the payroll to these two plans so that each employee receives the equivalent of a nontaxable 25 percent bonus, which then accumulates tax-free until the benefits are paid (when the employee retires or leaves the firm). This is unusual in law practice; most of the medium- and large-size law firms are not incorporated and cannot offer such benefits. But I can't say that these extra benefits have helped us in recruiting or keeping employees over the years. Mostly, they're interested in take-home pay, the type of work they'll be doing, and the chances for advancement. Very few have shown any real interest in the benefit plans.

I didn't bother checking with businessmen who controlled closely held corporations because I knew that many of them would be interested in the possibilities of ESOP. I also knew that if all of them installed ESOPs, the result would simply be a large tax subsidy for wealthy people, without diffusing enough capital ownership to mean anything.

Then I attempted to talk to labor union officials about ESOP, but I couldn't find anyone willing to discuss the subject. A few said they were studying ESOP, but most said they considered it harmful to their members because it would inevitably be used as a substitute for a sound pension plan and would leave the workers without retirement benefits. One union official called it "socialism for the rich and capitalism for the poor."

In November 1975, I attended an ESOP educational seminar sponsored by the Association for Corporate Growth and held at the plush Pierre Hotel in New York. The program included speeches by lawyers, accountants, government officials, politicians, and ESOP consultants, all discussing the latest techniques for use of ESOPs. In the audience were well-dressed lawyers, accountants, bankers, and business executives—but nobody from labor. As I gazed at the elegant French doors in the seminar room, I pictured a horde of angry workers breaking through the glass and storming the meeting, demanding their piece of the pie. But there were no workers in sight, angry or otherwise. The whole seminar was devoted to perfecting methods of giving away stock to workers, yet the beneficiaries were not even interested enough to send an observer. That summed up for me the immediate prospects of interesting organized labor in ESOP.

On the basis of these reactions from labor and management, I began to question the whole concept of moving toward universal capitalism through the employment relationship. At first glance, it looks like the best approach. There are well-established, tax-favored devices for passing stock from employers to workers, and it makes a lot of sense to give workers that extra incentive. Kelso was able to design ownership plans under existing laws way back in the 1950s, long before the term ESOP was invented. But after closer study, I began to realize that the obstacles to bringing about universal capitalism through employee benefits were staggering.

First of all, there is the problem of the worker's relationship with his union. Labor union leaders shy away from any plan that dilutes their position as advocates for the workers, and they naturally look upon worker stock ownership as a threat to the union's main function, which is collective bargaining.

There are enough obstacles to universal capitalism without trying to come between the worker and his union. Kelso seems
willing to take this battle on, but I don't think it's practical to
try to pull off a revolution of capital diffusion over the opposition of organized labor. And as we'll see later in this chapter,
there is the possibility that after union leaders find that capital
diffusion is here to stay, they'll try to turn it to their advantage
by taking control of major corporations, something they could
do rather easily if we followed the ESOP method of giving
workers stock in their own employers' corporations, based on a
percentage of the payroll.

Then there is the problem pointed out by Peter Drucker
and discussed in Chapter 8: Only a handful of corporations
continue to be successful operations for periods of forty to fifty
years, so in the end millions of workers would be stockholders
in losers. Universal capitalism has to plug everyone into the
winners and diversify against the drain caused by the losers.

Not just ESOP but all qualified employee benefit plans are
deferred payments, and to many workers that means they are
promises payable in the hereafter. Kelso ran into this feeling
when he addressed a labor group in 1975. He told them the
story of a black warehouse laborer who never earned more than
$125 a week during his working career but was fortunate
enough to get in on a stock ownership plan that made him
wealthy when he retired, largely because the corporation he
worked for had distributed stock to a profit-sharing plan at low
prices before it went public. Kelso thought this story would
electrify his audience. He was amazed to learn that most of
them saw only the tragic side of the story: The worker had
struggled through most of his life trying to support his family
on $125 a week, and then when his ship finally came in, he was
too old to enjoy it.

On another occasion I listened to Kelso addressing a Washington lucheon meeting of vice-presidents of major corporations. His audience seemed only mildly interested until he
started talking about "flattening out the wage rise curve" in
exchange for ESOP benefits; then they really perked up. This
helped me to realize how difficult it would be to achieve universal capitalism if ESOP were the only tool available.

Before turning away from ESOP and the employment relationship, I struggled with the productivity question. There again, I found ESOP more of an obstacle than a bridge to universal capitalism. "Productivity" is a term that is used very loosely, and there are no really scientific methods of measuring it. Usually it is expressed in terms of dollar output per hour of labor. But economists differ sharply on how to increase productivity, and they cannot really break down the contributions of capital and labor, even though all agree that investment in new machinery will usually increase labor productivity as it is now measured. In a 1976 study of productivity for the Joint Economic Committee, Professor Edward F. Renshaw of the State University of New York said: "Our knowledge with regard to how to promote productivity is rather meager and, in terms of certainty, about on a par with our knowledge of how to control inflation."

Historically, American productivity (as measured by dollar output per hour of labor) has increased by an average of about 3 percent a year since 1900. However, many observers feel that we will not be able to maintain that rate in the future. It has already fallen off to about 2 percent since 1966. When most jobs were done by manual labor, it was easier to increase productivity by mechanization; but it doesn't work that well in service-type jobs, which are fast overtaking production jobs. And a lot of capital that might have been used to increase output will have to be diverted to pollution control.

It seems impossible to prove that turning millions of workers into part owners will motivate them to increase productivity. Studies made by experts go both ways. AT&T, for example, found that they could temporarily increase productivity by almost anything they did to indicate that they were interested in their employees. They actually got some productivity increases by turning the same program on and off, because both steps showed the employees that their management was interested in them.

Peter Drucker, one of our leading experts on management, in his 1976 book *The Unseen Revolution,* takes a very dim view of the productivity potential of worker ownership:

> For well over a century, if not for longer, there has been
> a persistent belief that a change in the "system" which

> made the workers the "owners" would automatically take care of the problems of industrial society, whether the disease be diagnosed as "alienation," as "subordination of man to the machine," as "the assembly line," "exploitation," or simply the boredom and drudgery of work. But for well over 100 years we have also known that this belief is a delusion. For worker ownership has a much longer history than most people realize. It has been tried many times, and has never had any but the most transitory impact on the work, the worker, or the relationships at work. Even total ownership of a business and full worker control seem to have little effect on industrial and human relations at work.

Drucker goes on to give examples, based on his broad knowledge of American and European business. He also points out that during the average human working life of forty years, the great majority of workers will be employees of corporations whose stocks perform erratically, and many will see their employers' securities become practically worthless. If there is any motivation involved in that kind of ownership, it is likely to be the reverse of what we are looking for.

Because productivity is so hard to measure and will vary so much from job to job, I don't see how we can base the case for universal capitalism on its ability to increase productivity. I think we'd just get bogged down in a side issue which would take decades to settle. So that is just one more reason to avoid the employment relationship as the channel for broadening capital ownership.

If productivity can be increased by worker ownership of stock or by any other employee benefit, then I am all for it. If we put into effect the Financed Capitalist Plan or any similar plan which brings the whole populace into stock ownership, there is still room for employee benefit plans that increase productivity. ESOP and the Financed Capitalist Plan need not clash or even overlap; both plans can be developed side by side if they have merit.

Please understand that I fully appreciate the importance of increasing productivity. Most leading economists agree that productivity must be increased if we are to maintain our standard of living. Peter Drucker states that the economy's number-one need for the rest of this century is "greater productivity of all wealth-producing resources." But attempting to tie increased productivity to broad programs of worker stock ownership such as ESOP is not practical. Productivity is too slippery to form a base for universal capitalism. The case for universal capitalism must be built on clear and simple concepts such as capital outlays, profits, dividends, and return on investment, all of which can be measured precisely.

These obstacles to use of the employment relationship drove me back to the drawing board. If we couldn't get to universal capitalism through ESOP, the plan being pushed by Kelso himself, how could we do it?

Then I remembered there were two plans that had been put together for serious legislative consideration but were *not* based on the employment relationship. One was the Puerto Rican plan devised by Governor Ferre, Kelso, and Joe Novak in 1972 and described in Chapter 5. Under this broad program the government would help people earning between $800 and $7,800 a year to obtain stock ownership in a diversified fund, not stock in the companies they worked for.

The second plan was devised by Canadian businessman–politician Winnett Boyd, a Kelso disciple whom we'll meet in Chapter 13. In 1975 Boyd published a book called *The National Dilemma,* in which he proposed a broad stock ownership plan for Canada. It was similar to Kelso's Financed Capitalist Plan, and it was not channeled through the employment relationship. It proposed giving all Canadians of working age the opportunity to acquire stock through the use of long-term nonrecourse credit. I asked Winn Boyd why he had chosen this type of program rather than ESOP. His reasons coincided with my own conclusions about the obstacles to employee programs, and he also gave me one I hadn't thought of:

> To get a program like this through, you're going to need the approval of government officials, and you have to get broad support from the whole population. There's only one way to do that. You've got to make stock ownership available to everyone, regardless of whether they work for a corporation.

So here were two plans put together by practical politicians after very careful consideration of the public interest, and both were patterned after the Financed Capitalist Plan rather than ESOP. That sent me back to Kelso's writings, particularly his first two books, which concentrated on the Financed Capitalist Plan and said practically nothing about employment-based plans. Then the whole picture became clear to me. Kelso had not merged all his plans for universal capitalism into ESOP. He was simply using ESOP as a door opener because it was in existence, whereas the Financed Capitalist Plan was a wispy dream that had been ignored for nearly twenty years.

So I had to start thinking about concentrating the book on the Financed Capitalist Plan. This was not a decision to be taken lightly because nearly everyone who had heard of Kelso assumed that ESOP was the embodiment of all his wisdom. The Joint Economic Committee of Congress had scheduled two days of hearings in December 1975 on ESOP and nothing but ESOP. Jeff Gates had already spent a lot of time interviewing officials of corporations that had installed ESOPs, and a lot of this travel and research would go to waste if I changed the focus of my book.

But in the end I decided that there was no other choice. I could see no way to universal capitalism through ESOP; I did see such a hope in the Financed Capitalist Plan. But how could Congress be convinced of this, when its only interest seemed to be in ESOP?

Before answering that question, I have to fill in an important part of the story by taking you on a little detour through the world of econometric models.

WEFA and the Arithmetic of Kelso

As we saw in Chapter 6, Abel Beltran-del-Rio read *The Capitalist Manifesto* and started corresponding with Kelso just after he got his master's degree in business administration at Mexico's Monterrey Institute of Technology in 1959. Concerned about the economic problems of his native Mexico, Abel became intrigued with the possibility that Kelso's theories might help to solve them. But he didn't know enough about economics to investigate this possibility, and there was no school in Mexico that he felt offered the proper training. So in 1964 he enrolled in the graduate program of the University of Pennsylvania's Wharton School.

Abel left a well-established business position in Mexico and went to Philadelphia with the goal of becoming an economist mainly so that he could understand and contribute to the Kelso movement. In the process, he decided to become an econometrician, and he developed the idea of testing Kelso's theories by simulating their effects on econometric models.

He received a master's degree in 1966 and then started on his Ph.D. In 1968, Professor Lawrence Klein, father of econometric model building, became Abel's Ph.D. advisor. Then in 1969, Klein organized Wharton Econometric Forecasting Associates (WEFA), a nonprofit corporation owned by the University of Pennsylvania. WEFA's purpose was to furnish econometric forecasting services to industry and government subscribers, using Klein's models of the U.S. economy as a basis.

These econometric models are not like construction models or graphs or charts. They are complicated sets of mathematical equations published in book form and programmed into high-speed computers. The equations are developed from historical data, and they are put into a system that enables econometricians to forecast future variables.

There are small models confined to a single subject, such as the relationship between prices and sales volume in a particular industry. Then there are the giant macroeconomic models, such as those designed by Klein, that can be used to forecast the bottom line of the entire economy years in advance. The models are flexible enough to make a lot of different assumptions about the future and to forecast the effects of these varying assumptions in terms of GNP, inflation, unemployment, and other large aggregate statistics. Computers are used to make thousands of calculations that simulate the workings of the entire economy.

These big models are relatively new. Klein pioneered them in the 1950s, and they really gained acceptance in the 1960s. In 1976, there were about half a dozen large models capable of forecasting America's GNP, all of them based on Klein's techniques.

Abel was one of the group of econometricians who started WEFA in 1969. His mission was to perfect the model of the Mexican economy that he had developed in 1968 under the direction of Klein. Abel's model was the largest one built for a developing country for regular forecasting purposes, and it was the subject of his doctoral dissertation. The model was still being used in 1976, supported by forty-three large Mexican companies and government agencies. It has been studied by officials of other Latin American countries who hope to use it as a prototype for models of their own economies.

While making his living as an econometrician at WEFA, Abel kept up his studies of Kelso, and he began to form ideas on how Kelso's theories could be checked. Furthermore, he now had the chance to discuss Kelso with a leading Keynesian economist, for Professor Klein was not only the pioneer of econometric modeling but also the author of *The Keynesian Revolution*. Abel found that unlike a lot of other academicians, Klein had an open mind on the usefulness of capital diffusion, although he spotted flaws in Kelso's theories and noted the complete lack of statistical backup.

In May 1975, Kelso told me about his correspondence with Abel, and I decided to meet him. We got together in Washington that June. He turned out to be a handsome Latin type, with a charming smile and Mexican accent that made me think of Warner Baxter playing the Cisco Kid. His first words to me were "I am Abel," so I'll keep calling him Abel.

One of the first things I asked Abel was why leading economists did not try to analyze the function of capital ownership and its effect on income distribution. His answer was revealing.

> The economists would say that they don't need to meddle with the distribution of wealth because that belongs in the area of the sociologists or the lawyers—we don't go into that area because that involves social value judgments, and we frown on that. We are very scientific, you see, and we are above that. We don't discuss those things that belong to the priests, that belong to other scientists or to people in other areas of life, and we say that we are strictly involved with the science of economics.

Through Abel, I met Lawrence Klein and the other WEFA econometricians. They were kind enough to invite me to sit in on one of their quarterly forecasting meetings, which was attended by representatives of most of their 120 subscribers —organizations such as General Motors, Bethlehem Steel, the U.S. Treasury Department, and the Congressional Budget Office, whose top economists and modelers come to these meetings. But the subscribers don't just sit there; they are called upon by Professor Klein to give forecasts of what they see ahead in their own bailiwicks. They even participate in seminars designed to improve the model. When I was there, they discussed inclusion of the wholesale price index in the next version (Mark V) of the WEFA quarterly model, which forecasts eight quarters into the future. The present model, Mark IV, includes the consumer price index, but wholesale prices usually change before retail prices do. Professor Klein told the seminar that the wholesale price index probably would be included in the new Mark V model.

My aim in meeting Abel and the WEFA people was to try to interest them in making an econometric analysis of Kelso's theories. I had concluded that it was impossible to determine from purely theoretical reasoning whether capital diffusion can produce adequate income for all without serious side effects. I was hoping that econometric analysis would produce the answers. Abel was already sold on the idea, of course, and had been suggesting it to Kelso for a long time, but Kelso was busy with his own projects and quite properly felt that he should not be called upon to devote time and money to investigating his own theories.

At first, we talked about checking out ESOP because we had assumed in 1975 that ESOP was the embodiment of all Kelso's workable theories. I decided to try a small experiment at my own expense. I asked WEFA to determine the effects of ESOP on a major U.S. airline over a twenty-five-year period. But I couldn't afford the cost of simulating the ESOP twenty-five years into the future because that would involve a lot of assumptions about the performance of the airline and the economy during those years. So I cheated a little; I asked WEFA to go *back* twenty-five years and assume that in 1950 the airline had installed an ESOP. It would be easier to go back than to project forward because all the statistics about the airline and the economy as a whole for the last twenty-five years were available.

Abel arranged for WEFA to undertake this little experiment. They made a lot of different assumptions about how the ESOP would be set up, and their report included fifty-four pages of computer printout figures. The experiment revealed a grave problem of ESOP from the standpoint of management: the very rapid buildup of worker ownership.

As a part of the study, WEFA went back to the cash wage raises that were actually given between 1950 and 1974 and simulated them as 50 percent in cash and 50 percent in stock at market value contributed to an ESOP. If the airline had used this 50–50 formula for twenty-five years, the ESOP would have owned more than 35 percent of the outstanding stock, more than enough to elect the board of directors and control the business, although the value of the stock contributed to the ESOP never exceeded 3 percent of the payroll in any year. Remember that corporations can contribute stock worth as much as 15 percent of the payroll each year to an ESOP. If this airline (or almost any major corporation) actually used the maximum 15 percent ESOP, the workers would own a majority of the stock within ten to fifteen years.

Let's use General Motors as an example. In 1976, GM had about 287 million shares outstanding, selling at about $70 per share, making the total market value of their stock about $20 billion. Their annual payroll was about $10 billion. If GM set up an ESOP and contributed to it the full 15 percent permitted by tax law, they would be giving their employees about $1.5 billion worth of stock (15 percent of the $10 billion payroll) each year. Assuming, for the sake of simplicity, that the payroll stayed at $10 billion and that GM did not issue any new stock other than to the ESOP, you can see that the ESOP would control GM in a short time. After three years, the ESOP would own 18 percent of GM stock; after five years, 27 percent; after ten years, 42 percent; and after fourteen years, more than 51 percent. Of course, it doesn't take 51 percent of the stock to control a major public corporation, but you get to 51 percent ownership pretty quickly anyway.

Soon after WEFA completed the airline experiment, I decided to concentrate on the Financed Capitalist Plan. The experiment had taught us that it would be a very complicated task to check out the effects of widespread use of ESOP because of the many variables within each separate corporation as well as the broader variables that apply to the whole economy. But I had the feeling that the Financed Capitalist Plan would be easier to check out because it deals mainly with the bottom-line figures of the entire economy. When I asked Professor Klein about this, he answered, "Of course it would be easier to check than ESOP. All we have to do is push around a few large aggregates."

After a lot of discussion within WEFA, Abel finally got clearance from Klein to commit WEFA to check out Kelso's capital diffusion theories. WEFA estimated the cost of a one-year study at about $150,000. This study would not necessarily give us a final answer on feasibility, but it would certainly produce a lot more hard information than anyone has now on the effects of introducing Kelso's theories into the present economy. The econometric models are not foolproof, but they can serve the same functions as the flight simulators used by airlines to train pilots on the ground. Simulators won't produce a pilot who is ready to captain an airliner, but they will allow him to make his mistakes and learn by trial and error in the safety of a hangar. Obviously, we need to absorb all the information that the econometric modelers can give us before we take off and use real money on capital diffusion schemes.

Now the problem was down to where to get the $150,000. Fortunately, about the time that Abel and I were working on this project, it came to the attention of Eli March, an economist in the Washington office of the Economic Development Administration who supervises EDA's research on ESOP and capital diffusion schemes. (You'll recall that EDA was the agency that used ESOPs to save the workers' jobs at South Bend Lathe and Okonite.) After several meetings with March, I learned that he had received a commitment from his superiors that EDA would award a research contract to WEFA in the fiscal year beginning October 1, 1976. So as I write this, I am hopeful that we are finally on the way toward producing the first econometric analysis—the first economic measurement—of Kelso's theories.

Another happy side effect of my interest in WEFA was that Jacob Sheinin, an Israeli graduate student at Wharton, became interested in doing a Ph.D. dissertation on capital diffusion. Jacob had worked on WEFA's twenty-five-year airline simulation, and that had whetted his appetite to learn more about the subject. In 1976 Professor Klein agreed to be his Ph.D. advisor, and so was launched the first ongoing academic study of capital diffusion.

Of course, I'm happy that we can look forward to the EDA–WEFA project, but I think that it's an awfully small stab at the kind of analysis we will need eventually. And we won't get the final report until long after this book is off press. I'm hoping that somebody who reads this book will help us find a way to accelerate WEFA's econometric research, especially since so many congressional committees will need this information (as we'll see in Chapter 11).

WEFA is not the only organization that can do this job. I also corresponded with Harvard economist Otto Eckstein, a member of Lyndon Johnson's Council of Economic Advisers, who is the head of Data Resources, Inc., of Lexington, Massachusetts. DRI has even more subscribers than WEFA. I asked Professor Eckstein whether his organization would be able to make a meaningful econometric analysis of Kelso's Financed Capitalist Plan. His reply is a marvelous example of an econometrician's way of saying yes.

> It is the kind of proposal for which econometric models are a useful evaluation technique. For example, the Data Resources model of the U.S. economy, for which I have responsibility, includes the financial flow-of-funds of the corporate sector, the total financing needs and how they are met, and the resultant balance sheets. The model automatically calculates, based on the historical structure, what the impact of changing these financial flows (and the flows of households) would be on the major macroeconomic dimensions of the economy, such as real economic growth, capital formation, employment, prices, interest rates and so on.

Professor Eckstein went on to say that the analysis would require conversion of the Kelso theories into the variables that are built into the DRI model and a lot of other development work that would bring the cost to about the same as the WEFA figure, about $125,000 to $150,000, with the final report taking six months to a year to produce.

In agreeing to make the WEFA and DRI models available for this analysis, Professors Klein and Eckstein are not endorsing Kelso in any way. They are simply willing to use scientific methods to try to find out if his theories or any other methods of capital diffusion may be useful in solving any of the nation's economic problems. Nevertheless, their willingness to analyze Kelso takes some courage in the face of other academicians' charges that Kelso's theories are crackpot. Professor Klein is in an especially sensitive position because he was elected president of the American Economic Association in 1976 and became chief economic adviser to Jimmy Carter for the 1976 campaign. But Klein and Eckstein now have a perfect answer to criticism from any of their colleagues. It is no longer a matter of looking at Kelso's theories as abstractions that can be ignored by economists. As we'll see in Chapter 11, billions of dollars of federal tax revenue are about to be spent on *one* of Kelso's capital diffusion schemes. Isn't it about time that econometric models were used to see if these billions are being spent on the best possible plan?

If we finally do get WEFA or DRI to push around the large aggregates and come up with a scientific measurement of the effects of capital diffusion, much of the credit will belong to the Mexican econometrician with the musical name who first began to dream about universal capitalism in Chihuahua nearly twenty years ago.

Joint Economic Committee Hearings on ESOP

The public interest in ESOP that Kelso had generated throughout 1975 came to a climax with the announcement that the Joint Economic Committee of Congress was going to hold public hearings on ESOP on December 11 and 12, 1975.

The committee, which was established by the Employment Act of 1946, has a total of twenty members, ten each from the House and the Senate. Its main function is to report to Congress its evaluation of the annual *Economic Report of the President.* This boils down to a broad assessment of the entire economy in the form of the annual *Joint Economic Report.* In addition, the JEC in recent years has been conducting detailed studies of the American economic system and has been exploring new ideas for improving it.

The chairmanship of the JEC rotates every two years between the House and the Senate. During 1975 and 1976, the chairman was the energetic Senator Hubert Humphrey of Minnesota. In January 1977, Representative Richard Bolling (Democrat, Missouri) took over for a two-year term.

The JEC poked into many uncharted areas of economic thinking during Senator Humphrey's term, holding hearings in all parts of the country, reviewing the Employment Act of 1946 and its effectiveness, studying such questions as comprehensive economic planning and job guarantee programs, and publishing a series of economic studies with contributions from leading economic thinkers around the world. Therefore, it was not surprising that Senator Humphrey scheduled hearings on a populist measure such as employee stock ownership. Because of Senator Russell Long's strong interest in ESOP, he was invited to participate in the JEC hearings even though he was not a member of the committee.

The hearings provided me with a great opportunity to pull together my thoughts about ESOP and universal capitalism and to hear the first public high-level discussion of these subjects in Washington. I arranged to attend, along with Jeff Gates and Abel Beltran-del-Rio.

As the hearings approached, I began to get the feeling that they might develop into a lynch party for the Kelso movement, with Kelso himself supplying the rope. The subject of the hearings was "Employee Stock Ownership Plans (ESOPs)." From Kelso's office I received an advance copy of his very detailed written presentation. Although Kelso described ESOP as merely the tip of the iceberg, most of his prepared statement dealt with ESOP. Buried deep in the paper were a few sentences mentioning the Financed Capitalist Plan, but there was no explanation of the plan, and it was not mentioned in the list of fifteen recommendations that Kelso made for new federal legislation. All through his JEC testimony, Kelso used "two-factor theory" and "two-factor economics" as overall descriptions of his plans.

Senator Humphrey called the hearings to order, and his opening statement increased my queasiness:

> As I said in the press release announcing these hearings, these plans have been heralded as the basic solution for many of our economic ills. Specifically, one of our chief proponents who will be testifying today has said the widespread adoption of ESOPs will accomplish the following objectives: the restoration and acceleration of economic growth to unprecedented levels; create legitimate full employment for two or three decades; and lay the foundation for arresting inflation.
>
> I must confess that these are *some* claims. Certainly no one since I have been chairing this committee has come before us with any program that promises that much.

The audience was packed with lawyers, economists, and journalists eager to hear this wonderful plan that would cure all our ills. As the flashbulbs popped and the TV cameras turned, I wondered what the audience reaction would be when they learned what ESOP was all about.

Before the testimony started, Senator Jacob Javits of New York made an opening statement confirming his long-standing interest in the diffusion of capital ownership. But he expressed reservations about ESOP, particularly about the use of ESOP as a tradeoff for other fringe benefits and the risks of putting all the workers' eggs in one basket.

Senator Charles Percy of Illinois also made an opening statement in which he told of his very successful experience with profit-sharing when he was chief executive officer of Bell & Howell in Chicago. He said that when he took over management of the company in 1949, he installed a profit-sharing plan that improved productivity and made the employees feel that Bell & Howell was "our company." Percy said that he has never forgotten that lesson and has been a booster of profit-sharing ever since. But he didn't express any views on ESOPs, other than his concern about how few companies seemed to be interested in installing them voluntarily.

The first witness was Assistant Secretary of the Treasury for Tax Policy Charles M. Walker. Speaking for the Ford administration, Walker said that they believe it is desirable to diffuse stock ownership but that this must be done through a broad-based program that would take care of the many millions of people who are not in a position to benefit from ESOP.

Then Louis Kelso took the witness chair and gave a rapid-fire lecture on two-factor economics for about twenty minutes. He didn't have time to describe any plan other than ESOP, although he told the committee that it was only one of many financing techniques built on two-factor economics. Since these were ESOP hearings, that's what he had to push, and he wouldn't have had time to explain anything else. He described ESOP as a macroeconomic tool that could solve many major economic problems, if it was backed up by the Capital Diffusion Insurance Corporation and by *pure credit* (the rediscounting of ESOP loans by Federal Reserve Banks at 3 percent interest).

Most of the witnesses were opposed to the concept of ESOP. Their testimony and their hefty written presentations, which swelled the hearing record to a total of 949 pages, concentrated on the shortcomings of ESOP and the dangers of expanding its use.

One exception was Harry L. Thurmon, vice-president and treasurer of E-Systems Inc., of Dallas, Texas, a corporation that had engaged Louis Kelso to install an ESOP in 1973. Thurmon testified that the ESOP had worked out very well and that in his opinion it had increased employee productivity. However, he did not mention that when E-Systems installed the ESOP, its stock was selling well below book (liquidation) value, making it a tempting target for an unfriendly takeover. The E-Systems ESOP did not involve the issuance of new stock and therefore was not a classic Kelso ESOP designed to raise capital for the company. Instead, it made a tender offer for 25 percent of the company's outstanding stock, which was enough to block a takeover attempt. This brought the 25 percent block of stock under the control of ESOP trustees who were appointed by the E-Systems management. It was a neat way of keeping that large block of stock from being voted against the incumbent management.

Another important witness was Robert N. Flint, vice-president and comptroller of AT&T. He took a lukewarm position on ESOP. Remembering the lessons of Senator Russell Long's Baton Rouge speech, Flint testified that if certain technical changes were made in the law, AT&T would take advantage of the extra 1 percent investment tax credit and install a TRASOP. But Flint went on to say that although ESOP clearly had some utility for smaller corporations and privately owned businesses, AT&T had some grave misgivings about its use on a broad scale. He echoed the feelings of many people about Kelso and ESOP:

> In summary, the Bell System finds itself in broad agreement with Mr. Kelso's objective of encouraging expanded employee stock ownership. The vehicles he has developed for achieving these objectives give us some grounds for some serious questions.

Flint's testimony reflected the widely held notion that Kelso equals ESOP. In his written presentation, he referred to "the ultimate Kelso plan" as being a very broad use of ESOP, with CDIC and low-interest, long-term financing being applied only to ESOPs. So the hearings rolled on, with everybody concentrating on how to turn ESOP into universal capitalism.

One of the most interesting witnesses was Dr. Hans Brems, professor of economics at the University of Illinois. He was born in Denmark, got his Ph.D. at the University of Copenhagen, and has been teaching at Illinois since 1954. He has written hundreds of papers and articles and several important books, the best known being *Output, Employment, Capital and Growth,* published by Harper in 1959.

Before the JEC hearings, I learned that Professor Brems was the leading American authority on European workers' stock ownership and that he had written several articles on this subject. He sent me copies of his most recent papers, and I arranged to meet him in Washington the night before the hearings began.

Hans Brems, Abel Beltran-del-Rio, Jeff Gates, and I went to dinner that night in Georgetown. Carrying on the tradition of the nongrubby revolution, we dined at La Niçoise, a French restaurant equally famous for its great food and for the fact that its waiters move around on roller skates.

Hans Brems turned out to be a white-haired, jovial movie version of a European economics professor. Abel, Jeff, and I were encouraged by an academic economist of Brems's stature coming into the picture, and we tried to find out the reason for his interest in the broadening of stock ownership. I tried to draw him out with searching, lawyerlike questions, such as:

> Surely you don't have any time to waste on schemes that aren't going anywhere? Your research and writing on wage earners' investment funds and other types of capital diffusion seems to indicate that you feel that they have an important role to play in the economy. Therefore, you must agree with some of Kelso's conclusions. Is that right?

This interrogation drew nothing but polite laughter from Brems. Yet, throughout our dinner and other discussions, I got the impression that he, too, saw an important role to be played by capital diffusion. Being a careful scholar, he was not about to line himself up with Kelso, especially with the two-factor label hovering over everything that Kelso put out. Still, I felt that universal capitalism had an important ally in Professor Hans Brems. His knowledge of European plans and his ability to relate their lessons to the American economy are important resources that he willingly shared with the JEC.

He testified on the first day of the hearings, shortly after Kelso. He made a great contribution by summarizing European wage earners' investment funds (WEIFs), various versions of which are being studied or used in West Germany, Holland, France, Sweden, and Denmark. WEIFs came about through initiatives of unions or labor governments rather than employers, and do not offer employers any special incentives other than the hope of greater productivity and harmonious labor relations. Most of them involve employer contributions of some fraction of either the payroll or profits. The funds that hold these contributions usually can diversify their investments. Unlike American deferred employee benefits, most of the WEIFs allow workers to turn their shares into cash before retirement, usually after about seven years.

None of the WEIFs have used Kelso's leveraging ideas; they are all based on contributions of stock or cash by employers or tax-favored cash contributions by workers, without using credit to speed up capital diffusion. Some WEIFs are single-employer plans; others would establish joint funds for employees of entire industries, areas, or even nations. There is a wealth of experience available to us in these European plans, but few Americans apart from Professor Brems have bothered to study them.

The JEC asked Brems to give his assessment of ESOP. Although he disassociated himself from Kelso's economic theories and claims for ESOP, he said that ESOP could very well improve labor productivity by giving workers a financial interest in their employers. He also put his finger on one of ESOP's great weaknesses:

> ESOP asks the employee to own corporate wealth in a form so risky that no stockholder, individual or institutional, that I have ever known, voluntarily chooses to do it that way. For that reason, U.S. labor—presumably the beneficiary of the whole thing—has shown not much, if any, interest in ESOP.

He went on to say that more diversified funds, which would be more acceptable to the beneficiaries, might do less "for labor productivity at the plant floor than ESOP does, but might do more for capital and labor mobility in the economy at large, and thereby ultimately do more for labor productivity at large."

Brems then revealed to the JEC why he was interested in capital diffusion:

> Although wealth distribution is not as unequal as Mr. Kelso believes it to be, I personally should like to see it becoming more equal. I should like to see that, not because of any belief that the economy would otherwise "grind to a halt," but simply because I happen to believe that a more equal wealth distribution would make our democracy a healthier and more smooth-working one.

Hans Brems deserves credit for making an important contribution to the JEC hearings—and special credit for coming forward to testify at all, when other distinguished scholars simply turned their backs on the whole subject.

Throughout the hearings I listened carefully for any hint

of Senator Humphrey's attitude toward ESOP. I was impressed by his knowledge of the subject. He has a well-deserved reputation for doing his homework. Although he tries to portray himself as an unpretentious pharmacist, he holds a Phi Beta Kappa key and has taught political science and economics. Humphrey said nothing during the hearings to indicate his feelings about ESOP, but I learned from people close to him that he was concerned about labor union hostility. Humphrey then was in the midst of his final bid for the Democratic presidential nomination. He has always enjoyed strong labor support, and it would not have been logical for him to take a stand in favor of anything that was not favored by organized labor.

The questions and comments of Senator Javits indicated the same concern. The lack of labor support made him feel that the benefits of ESOPs went mainly to the corporations and that ESOP might even be dangerous to the workers if its use was broadened. But he always made it clear that he was dedicated to the principle of broadening stock ownership. It was only the ESOP method that he was questioning.

I learned a long time ago that most congressional hearings are shaped by the full-time committee staffs. Senators and congressmen don't have the time to get into such details as preparing agendas, selecting witnesses, and writing reports. All they can do is lay down broad policy guidelines that are then carried out by the staff.

In this case, the JEC staff was represented by Robert Hamrin, a young Ph.D. who had taught economics at the University of Idaho and Hong Kong Baptist College, and who joined the committee as an economist in 1974. JEC staff positions are highly prized. The committee has the power and prestige to command participation of the world's leading economists. The work is all the more interesting because it flows immediately into the annual *Joint Economic Report* and other JEC publications that influence the formulation of national economic policy. Hamrin's main assignment was to compile a series of publications titled "U.S. Economic Growth from 1976 to 1986: Prospects, Problems, and Patterns." As an extra project, indirectly related to these studies, he was assigned to organize the JEC hearings on ESOP and write the staff report based on those hearings.

The way the hearings were going, I felt they were bound to result in the disillusionment of those who were expecting a panacea in ESOP. I was concerned that the Kelso-equals-ESOP feeling might drown all the prospects for universal capitalism, so I decided that I had better get to know Bob Hamrin and see what I could do to convince him that there was more to Kelso, and that ESOP was not the only road to universal capitalism.

I found Hamrin very receptive to other methods of capital diffusion. He said that one of his concerns about ESOP was that it did not benefit enough people. When I told him that I was writing a book on this subject, he invited me and Jeff Gates to lunch in the Senate dining room, where the famous Senate bean soup would take its place on the menu of the nongrubby revolution.

I was all set to convince Hamrin that there was a lot more to Kelso than ESOP and that Kelso's ideas were too important to dismiss on account of ESOP's shortcomings. But I found that Hamrin already knew this. He had focused the hearings on ESOP only because Senator Humphrey was specifically interested in examining it. Hamrin was most receptive to any non-ESOP contributions, and he agreed to publish in the hearing record a four-page statement that I submitted.

In my statement I called attention to the need for serious consideration of capital diffusion as a new national policy. I suggested that the JEC should not limit its study to the known limitations of ESOP but should address these broader questions: What can the United States accomplish by adopting as national policies the broadening of employee share ownership and the diffusion of newly created capital? What are the best instruments for achieving such national policy?

I also suggested that because of the paucity of other ideas for beneficial structural changes in the national economic policy, the JEC should give highest priority to further detailed studies of the proposals of Kelso and others in an effort to find tools that are capable of achieving much broader diffusion of newly created capital—and that "the nation's best minds and strongest fact-finding resources should be brought into the search for workable methods of achieving such a national economic policy."

The hearings ended on December 12, 1975. The 949-page

record of testimony and exhibits compiled by the JEC is easily the best collection of materials on ESOP. But it deals only with ESOP. I knew then, of course, that very few people would read the complete hearing record. Many important decision makers *would,* however, read the JEC staff study summarizing the hearing record and reaching firm conclusions. It was going to take Bob Hamrin five or six months to write that study because he had to compile a lot more data and wait for answers to the detailed follow-up questions sent to Kelso, Brems, and other witnesses who testified at the hearings. In those early months of 1976, I could only keep my fingers crossed and hope that Bob Hamrin and his colleagues would not limit their study to ESOP. If they did, I felt that universal capitalism would be dealt a staggering blow.

Kelso Meets Ralph Nader

When the nongrubby revolution descended on Washington for the JEC hearings, Kelso asked me to try to arrange a meeting with Ralph Nader. Kelso knew that I had represented Nader in his invasion-of-privacy suit against General Motors back in the 1960s. Kelso felt that there were many points of convergence between his theories and Nader's work, and he was anxious to get Nader's support.

As usual, Ralph's schedule was tight, but he told me that at least fifteen other people had given him copies of Kelso's books and had suggested that the two had objectives in common. Therefore, he agreed to meet us at 10 o'clock on the night before the JEC hearings, 10 P.M. being a routine appointment time for both Nader and Kelso. Ralph arrived at my hotel room along with two associates who were very knowledgeable on corporate organization and financing. Ralph seems to grow a few inches every time I see him, and he looked particularly tall when Kelso walked into the room, since he towers over Lou by nearly a foot.

Nader and his associates listened intently as Kelso began his basic speech. By then I had heard it about a dozen times, but

Lou always makes it so exciting that you can't be bored. Ralph was particularly fascinated by Kelso's stories about the Bohemian Grove and the history of Valley Nitrogen, a consumer cooperative project right up Nader's alley.

Nader and Kelso got along famously. Both are lawyers who are trying to make American capitalism work by forcing it to respond to the requirements of true democracy. Their styles are very different, of course: Kelso the epicure, Nader the ascetic; Kelso's Bohemian Grove and Nader's famous boardinghouse. And their ideas for making capitalism democratic were very different, too. But I could see why many people thought they should meet. Each was the leader of a one-man revolution that challenged most of the established concepts of what corporations were supposed to be like in the twentieth century.

When the meeting ended, Ralph stayed on and gave me his impressions. Obviously he liked Kelso personally, but he was appalled at the potential abuses of ESOP, which he saw as a plaything for corporate manipulators and hardly a blessing for the workers. And he was afraid that if employees became heavy stockholders in the companies they worked for, they would be much less concerned about product safety and environmental dangers, which are two of Nader's main interests. He said that it was hard enough for him to fight manufacturers' lawyers and lobbyists on safety and environmental issues. If the workers and their unions joined the battle on the corporation side because they had big stock interests, Ralph felt that his efforts to protect the consumer would be obstructed.

Personally, I think Ralph Nader is underestimating the power of the consumer movement that he started. Largely because of Ralph's crusading, there are enough legal safeguards against product and environmental hazards to overcome the combined forces of labor, management, and stockholders. Of course, it's a constant struggle to enforce these safeguards. So it's natural for him to look upon the worker–stockholder as still another threat to product and environmental safety.

Nader's attitude toward the worker–stockholder is one more argument against approaching universal capitalism through the employment relationship. But I have the feeling that Ralph can be sold on universal capitalism if a scheme such as the Financed Capitalist Plan is shown to be practical. Ralph has his hands full fighting the consumer's battles, but he has an open mind for any idea that can make capitalism truly democratic. And he knows that under the present system of mixed capitalism, those who seek to enforce product and environmental regulations are often confronted with the argument that enforcement will cause unemployment, inflation, or both. As Kelso has often said, only a truly affluent society can afford to put the public interest ahead of jobs, and only through universal capitalism can the capital and the broad affluence needed for environmental protection be developed.

Who Will Control the Corporations?

The Kelso–Nader meeting helped me to reach some conclusions. I know that Ralph is honestly and selflessly dedicated to what's best for the consumer (meaning every person in the United States). He is opposed to the excesses of big business, big government, and big labor. His idea for preventing abuses by all three is to diffuse power by spreading it to individuals whom he sees as consumers. But consumer power is difficult to mobilize and sustain, except in rare emergencies. Therefore, I see a need for Ralph to start thinking about a more promising way of using the individual as a bulwark against the overconcentration of power, and I believe that way is capital ownership by individuals. Capital ownership, unlike consumerism, will automatically give individuals economic power; and it can be exercised very easily, by simply signing proxy forms that control the elections of corporate directors. If Nader doesn't move into this vacuum, others will.

I am convinced that within a few years, American labor leaders will realize that they can't make capital diffusion go away by ignoring it. And when they do, their next step will be to try to take control of it. Such an attempt is already under way in Europe, where the labor unions are moving from codetermination (labor representation on corporate boards without stock ownership) toward *union stock control*. In Sweden, a plan designed by union economist Dr. Rudolf Meidner proposed that every Swedish corporation employing over fifty workers be forced to transfer 20 percent of annual before-tax profits to a *collective employee fund,* in the form of a special issue of stock. The collective employee funds would be controlled by the Swedish labor unions, *not* by the individual workers. Within ten to twenty years, the unions would achieve majority or voting control of every significant business in Sweden.

The Meidner plan was staved off by the defeat of the Social Democrats in the 1976 Swedish election, but as we'll see in Chapter 13, it is not dead by any means. With capital diffusion on the way toward becoming a national policy of the United States, it is only a matter of time before American labor leaders latch on to the Meidner plan and try to take control of major American corporations.

When labor leaders turn their attention to the power they can grab through capital diffusion plans such as ESOP, they will find another sleeping giant waiting to be exploited. In *The Unseen Revolution,* Peter Drucker gives some startling statistics:

> Through their pension funds, employees of American business today own at least 25 percent of its equity capital, which is more than enough for control. The pension funds of the self-employed, of the public employees, and of school and college teachers own at least another 10 percent, giving the workers of America ownership of more than one-third of the equity capital of American business. Within another ten years the pension funds will inevitably increase their holdings, and by 1985 (probably sooner), they will own at least 50—if not 60—percent of equity capital. Ten years later, or well before the turn of the century, their holding should exceed around two-thirds of the equity capital (that is, the common shares) plus a major portion—perhaps 40 percent—of the debt capital (bonds, debentures, and notes) of the American economy. Inflation can only speed up this process.
>
> Even more important, especially for Socialist theory, the largest employee pension funds, those of the 1,000–1,300 biggest companies plus the 35 industry-wide funds (those of the college teachers and the teamsters for instance) already own control of practically every single

one of the 1,000 largest industrial corporations in America. This includes control of companies with sales well below $100 million, by today's standards at best fair-sized companies, if not actually small; the pension funds also control the fifty largest companies in each of the "non-industrial" groups, that is, in banking, insurance, retail, communications, and transportation. These are what Socialist theory calls the "command positions" of the economy; whoever controls them is in command of the rest.

Drucker calls this development the "revolution no one noticed" because the pension fund trustees have not tried to exercise all their rights of ownership. They are concerned mainly with getting a good return on investment so that they can pay workers' retirement benefits in cash when they come due. (The workers themselves don't become stockholders through their pension funds.) Also, because pension funds must diversify their investments, no single fund actually controls the stock of its employer corporation. For example, the General Motors pension fund does not have stock control of General Motors and probably never will own more than a small percentage of the total GM shares. But *collectively,* the American pension funds have become the largest owners of corporate stock. And if American labor leaders ever get a notion to take control of major corporations, the giant pension ownership position is a juicy target, just waiting to be added to the stock that unions could control through ESOP or any other capital diffusion scheme that works through the employment relationship.

Therefore, if the New Capitalists are workers who get stock in their own employer corporations, the stage will be set for an overconcentration of power in big labor. The only solution I can see is to make sure that the New Capitalists are individuals who get stock interests in many different corporations and to make sure that they exercise their voting power individually or through groups that do not pose the threat of overconcentration of power.

Senator Helms's
Stock Gift Proposal

Between the time when the JEC hearings ended and Bob Hamrin completed his staff study (in June 1976), three new bills to broaden capital ownership were introduced in Congress. The first came just before the 1975 Christmas recess, when conservative Republican Senator Jesse Helms of North Carolina got into the act. He introduced in the Senate the Employee Business Ownership and Capital Formation Act of 1975.

In his press statement, Senator Helms acknowledged his debt to Kelso and ESOP. His bill proposed that corporations be permitted to give stock to their employees in an amount equal to 25 percent of the employee's annual salary, up to a maximum of $25,000 a year, with a lifetime maximum of $500,000 per employee. This plan was similar to ESOP in that the corporation would get a tax deduction for the gift of stock and the employees would not realize any taxable income when receiving the stock. But there was one very big difference: The stock would not be held in trust; it would become the outright property of the employees as soon as it was given to them by the corporation. The employees would thus be free to sell the stock or hold onto it and collect dividends immediately.

Senator Helms's bill tried to remedy one of the shortcomings of ESOP: the fact that employees do not receive their stock until they retire or leave the corporation. But most experts would probably say that it is dangerous to hand out stock that can be sold immediately by the workers. Apart from the possible squandering of these benefits by the workers, there would be lots of problems for corporations whose stock is not heavily traded or not publicly traded at all.

The Helms bill offers no particular incentive for large corporations to make the gifts of stock. True, they get a tax deduction for the gift, but they also get tax deductions under the present law for raising wages or making any other payments to employees.

Even though the Helms bill itself will probably not receive serious consideration as a major means of broadening capital ownership, it is encouraging that one of the leading conservative senators came forward with such a plan. It showed that the JEC hearings had stimulated wide interest and that there is a deep reservoir of bipartisan support for a workable capital diffusion plan.

Jerry Ford's BSOP

Early in 1976, it began to look as though Louis Kelso's teaching of Jerry Ford at Aspen was going to bear fruit. The Ford administration began to show signs of interest in Kelso's theories, and Treasury Secretary William Simon seemed to buy Kelso's basic idea that capital ownership should be diffused, though he would not endorse ESOP as a specific way of doing it. He continued to search for a better plan.

Then on January 19, 1976, President Ford said in his State of the Union message:

> I propose tax changes to encourage people to invest in America's future, and their own, through a plan that gives moderate-income families income tax benefits if they make long-term investments in common stock in American companies.

This seed ripened into the broadened stock ownership plan (BSOP). The general idea was to allow every person a tax deduction of up to 15 percent of his earned income, with a maximum deduction of $1,500, for buying corporate stock that would be held for a minimum of seven years. The maximum deduction of $1,500 would be available only to those with earned income below $20,000. For those with income of $20,000 to $40,000, the benefits would gradually reduce, reaching zero at $40,000. If the stocks were held for seven years or more and then sold, the proceeds would be taxed as capital gains. But if any stocks were sold before seven years, gains would be taxed as ordinary income.

Kelso did not think this bill would bring much benefit to anybody other than stock brokers. In fact, he dubbed it the "Stock Broker's Relief Act of 1976." It would bring the little man back into the stock market, and despite the tax advantage, he would still be gambling some of his own money, with encouragement from the government. Since there is nothing in BSOP that encourages or forces corporations to issue new stock, the plan would simply cause more people to bid against each other for the existing public supply of stock, thereby forcing stock prices up artificially. So BSOP was a device that would accelerate the so-called casino activity of the stock market, the kind that was condemned by Keynes and later by Kelso.

Other critics of BSOP said that it probably would not result in new savings, that it would merely shift savings from bank accounts into the stock market. There was no evidence that BSOP would increase purchasing power. In fact, the forced-savings aspect might have just the opposite effect. This type of tax-sheltered saving is already available through the Individual Retirement Account Plan (IRA) and the Keogh (H.R. 10) Self-Employed Retirement Plan. And like all stock ownership plans based on savings, it would be used mostly by people who are fairly well off to begin with.

BSOP did not capture the imagination of Congress. It was voted down in the Senate Finance Committee and finally killed on the floor of the Senate on August 4, 1976, despite the support of Senators Long, Javits, and Percy. But with all its shortcomings, I think it was very significant. It was the first legislation proposed by an American president to broaden stock ownership, and in making tax-favored stock ownership available to all Americans regardless of their employment, it took a stab at overcoming one of the drawbacks of ESOP. Certainly, BSOP is one more idea that should be studied in depth to see if it has useful features that can be incorporated in the ideal plan of universal capitalism.

The Javits–Humphrey Bill: Getting Organized Labor into the Act

On April 13, 1976, New York Republican Senator Jacob Javits held a press conference to announce the introduction of the Employee Stock Ownership Fund Act of 1976, which he sponsored jointly with Senator Hubert Humphrey. Both Javits and Humphrey have shown keen interest in broadening stock ownership, but both were concerned about the coolness of organized labor toward ESOP. They designed their Employee Stock Ownership Fund Act (now called the Javits–Humphrey Act) to make employee stock ownership an element of collective bargaining, thus bringing unions into the act and getting them interested in bargaining for employee stock ownership.

Their proposal would apply to only one form of stock ownership plan: the type that provides for joint trusteeship by the employer and the union under Section 302 of the Taft–Hartley Act. This may seem like a narrow channel, but it actually involves a great many of the largest corporations whose pension and health plans are managed by trustees selected jointly by employer and union. As the laws are written now, it would not be possible to have a jointly trusteed ESOP; the union officials would be prohibited from serving as trustees. Javits and Humphrey used this barrier as a springboard for public hearings that would bring labor leaders into a discussion of employee stock ownership for the first time.

The Javits–Humphrey bill would permit ESOPs to be jointly managed by labor and management trustees and would make these ESOPs the subject of collective bargaining. But there would be some special provisions in these ESOPs, designed to meet some of the principal objections to ESOP. First, a pension plan would have to be in effect before the ESOP was adopted. Second, no more than 30 percent of the ESOP assets could be invested in employer stock (as against 100 percent in an ordinary ESOP). And lastly, the benefits would become fully vested after three years; that is, employees could start withdrawing stock after three years instead of having to wait for retirement.

Senator Javits said in his press conference that the 30 percent figure for employer stock was put into the bill merely to start discussion. The final percentage might be higher or lower, but they had to start somewhere to deal with the problem of putting all the workers' eggs in the one ESOP basket.

Javits and Humphrey think that labor unions must be brought into the process of creating ESOPs if they are to become an equitable means of broadening stock ownership. They also want to use their bill as a way of getting the Senate Committee on Labor and Public Welfare into the process of drafting ESOP legislation, instead of leaving it all up to Senator Long's Finance Committee. The Javits–Humphrey bill was referred to the Labor Committee, and Senator Javits was hopeful that its chairman, Senator Harrison Williams of New Jersey, would agree to hold public hearings on it during 1977.

The bill is consistent with Senator Javits's position on capital diffusion, which goes back more than thirty years. His older brother, the late Benjamin A. Javits, was a New York lawyer who spent much of his career working for broadened stock ownership. Benjamin Javits wrote a book in 1969 called *Ownerism,* in which he drew the broad outlines of "people's capitalism" and "consumer capitalism." Like Kelso, Ben Javits tried to get financiers and investment bankers to see the need for broadened capital ownership, although he did not attempt to develop a specific tool such as ESOP for this purpose.

Way back in January 1973, nearly a year before Kelso met Russell Long, Senator Javits addressed the New York State Bar Association on tax reform for expanded employee stock ownership. Even at that early date, he foresaw the problems of ESOP (a term that had not yet been invented). But these problems did not diminish his interest in finding an ideal plan for universal capitalism.

Jacob Javits has brought universal capitalism into the political spotlight. He made broadened stock ownership a part of his successful campaign for reelection in 1974. He was re-

sponsible for the statement in the 1976 Republican party platform "supporting proposals to enhance the ability of our
working and other citizens to own 'a piece of the action'
through stock ownership." And he used his televised speech at
the 1976 Kansas City Republican Convention to bring this message to the whole country.

Javits agrees with Kelso and Long that capitalism is in
trouble unless a way is found to create more capitalists. After
thirty years, he is still searching for the ideal way of creating
more capitalists. His prestige and his reputation for thorough
homework make him one of universal capitalism's most important supporters. And as we shall see in the next chapter, he
played an important role in the Senate debate on the TRASOP
provisions of the 1976 Tax Reform Act.

THE GOVERNMENT COMES THROUGH

Men and nations will act rationally when all other possibilities have been exhausted.
Katz's Law

Whatever the means used, a basic objective should be to distribute newly created capital broadly among the population. Such a policy would redress a major imbalance in our society and has the potential for strengthening future business growth.

To provide a realistic opportunity for more U.S. citizens to become owners of capital, and to provide an expanded source of equity financing for corporations, it should be made national policy to pursue the goal of broadened capital ownership.
The 1976 *Joint Economic Report*, Joint Economic Committee of Congress, March 10, 1976

The 1976 Joint Economic Report

Since Bob Hamrin had told me that his JEC staff study report on the ESOP hearings would not be published until June 1976, I did not expect to hear anything from the JEC about how to broaden capital ownership until then. But on March 10, 1976, I got a pleasant surprise: the 1976 *Joint Economic Report*, which included a three-page section entitled "Broadening the Ownership of New Capital."

The *Joint Economic Report* is the main business of the JEC, since the Employment Act of 1946 requires the JEC to issue this report each year as the congressional reaction to the president's annual *Economic Report*. It is usually the most important economic report issued by any committee of Congress.

The 1976 report recited statistics about the overconcentration of wealth, pointing out that the last comprehensive effort by the federal government to measure wealth concentration was made by the Federal Reserve Board in 1962. That 1962 study estimated that more than three-quarters of the country's total wealth was owned by less than one-fifth of the people, and more than one-quarter of the total was owned by the top ½ percent.

The 1976 *Joint Economic Report* said that the ownership of corporate stock was particularly overconcentrated, even more so than total wealth, with the top 1 percent of the people owning 51 percent of individually owned corporate stock. It also described the present system of corporate capital expansion in these terms:

> Meanwhile, the new capital assets generated by business, which in recent years have averaged well over $100 billion annually, redound largely to the benefit of these persons who already have great wealth.

Then came the punchlines, words that I had never expected to see in the 1976 *Joint Economic Report:*

> To begin to diffuse the ownership of capital and to provide an opportunity for citizens of moderate incomes to become owners of capital rather than relying solely on their labor as a source of income and security, *the Committee recommends the adoption of a national policy to foster the goal of broadened ownership.* The spirit of the goal and what it purports to accomplish was endorsed by many of the witnesses at our regional hearings. [Italics added.]

The report did not recommend any particular method of broadening capital ownership. It concluded:

> Whatever the means used, a basic objective should be to distribute newly created capital broadly among the population. Such a policy would redress a major imbalance in our society and has the potential for strengthening future business growth.
>
> To provide a realistic opportunity for more U.S. citizens to become owners of capital, and to provide an expanded source of equity financing for corporations, it should be made national policy to pursue the goal of broadened capital ownership. Congress also should request from the Administration a quadrennial report on

the ownership of wealth in this country which would assist in evaluating how successfully the base of wealth was being broadened over time.

Coming within three months of the nearly disastrous ESOP hearings, here was a declaration of the Joint Economic Committee that broadened capital ownership should be made a national goal and a new economic policy of the United States. I learned that Bob Hamrin had done most of the drafting of that statement. Now I had some hope that his report on the ESOP hearings would not be fatal to universal capitalism.

The Hamrin Report
on the ESOP Hearings

The 1976 *Joint Economic Report* was an unexpected windfall for the principle of universal capitalism, but it did not mention any plan for achieving capital diffusion. So we still had to look ahead to Bob Hamrin's staff study for the first JEC statement on specific plans. I kept in touch with Hamrin, and in the spring of 1976, I learned that he was not planning to comment on the Financed Capitalist Plan, or any Kelso plan other than ESOP for a sound reason: Kelso's JEC presentation concentrated on ESOP and did not suggest any legislation relating to the Financed Capitalist Plan. Indeed, most of the JEC staff had never heard of the Financed Capitalist Plan and assumed that *the* Kelso plan was ESOP.

I decided to poke my nose in at this point. I sent Bob Hamrin a summary of the Financed Capitalist Plan, along with the page numbers in Kelso's books where the plan was described. I had the feeling that Hamrin and his colleagues were anxious to find a broader and more equitable plan than ESOP, and the Financed Capitalist Plan certainly fitted that description.

After Hamrin considered the plan, he became enthusiastic about its possibilities. However, he was concerned about inflationary effects if it was started up full blast—that is, if we attempted to start with the entire $120 billion of 1976 new capital formation and force it into equity ownership for the New Capitalists. The banks would need help from the Federal Reserve System to finance $120 billion in loans. This would cause an increase in the money supply, which Hamrin thought might be inflationary. So Hamrin suggested a modification of the Financed Capitalist Plan: if we started diffusing ownership of about 10 or 15 percent of the total corporate capital outlay to New Capitalists, we would not put much strain on the banking system. Gradual implementation would make unnecessary the most difficult step in the Financed Capitalist Plan: rediscounting by the Federal Reserve System, which in Hamrin's view might expand the money supply too rapidly and thus fuel inflation. If the plan proved to be practical, Congress could gradually scale it up to higher percentages of the total corporate capital outlay. It wasn't necessary to take the risks of starting with 100 percent.

With that important modification, Hamrin told me he was going to cover the Financed Capitalist Plan in his report. It was issued on June 17, 1976. Its official title was "Broadening the Ownership of New Capital: ESOPs and Other Alternatives—A Staff Study Prepared for the Use of the Joint Economic Committee, Congress of the United States." Since Senator Humphrey's letter of transmittal states that the study was prepared by Dr. Robert Hamrin, I am going to shorten that mouthful of title and simply call it the Hamrin report.

The title was very significant to me. The December 1975 hearings were labeled "Employee Stock Ownership Plans (ESOPs)," and one might have expected that the JEC report covering those hearings would bear the same title. However, ESOPs were put into a secondary position, along with "other alternatives." The spotlight was put on the new national economic policy of broadening the ownership of new capital.

The Hamrin report covered sixty-two printed pages, thirty-three pages of which were devoted to the pros and cons of ESOP. The major points of the Hamrin report's ESOP discussion are covered in Chapter 8 of this book.

To me, the section devoted to the Financed Capitalist Plan was more significant than the ESOP discussion. After listing Kelso's claims for the plan, the report concluded that "the full

Financed Capitalist Plan is not feasible as it stands, primarily because of its scope rather than its substance." Inflation was seen as the main problem, inflation caused by the rediscounting of notes by the Federal Reserve System. The report also pointed out some possible effects on financial markets. Since corporations would be forced to issue stock instead of bonds for new capital additions, the value of outstanding bonds would probably increase, and this would provide a windfall to present bond holders, who are mostly wealthy people. At the same time, the value of shares held by present equity stockholders might be diluted.

Hamrin also foresaw difficulties in establishing criteria for the selection of New Capitalists. And under immediate 100 percent implementation of the Financed Capitalist Plan, a major outlet for American investors, the new stock issued by corporations each year, would be shut off. But then he proposed a solution:

> One change would alleviate most of [these] problems . . . to initiate the plan at a much more modest level. For example, the plan could require that only 15, not 100, percent of all new capital expenditures be financed out of stock that is made available to the plan. Further, corporations could be required to pay out a certain percentage of their earnings as dividends rather than the full payout specified in the plan. Over time, these percentages could be increased if the plan works well. In a scaled-down version, the rediscounting provision, which is the most objectionable part of the plan, could be eliminated. This phased-in system would not break completely with all traditional corporate financing practices and would allow for the plan to be evaluated over time. If successful, the scope of the plan could be increased so that more households could benefit.

The Hamrin report explained why pension funds cannot be relied on to achieve the goal of broadened capital ownership, even if you assume that pensions represent indirect ownership of stock rather than just the right to receive cash income during retirement. It said that pension funds are now devoted partly to making transfer payments to retired workers rather than to capital formation and that by the late 1980s they are likely to become "pure transfer mechanisms." That is, because of increased longevity of the working population, pension funds will reach a point where they will have to pay out more in retirement benefits than they will be receiving in contributions from employers. When that happens, pensions will be a form of "dissaving" rather than capital formation.

The Hamrin report discussed another plan which had not been mentioned at the December 1975 ESOP hearings: the "capital formation plan," which was first suggested in a 1972 publication, *Expanded Ownership*, by the Sabre Foundation. *Expanded Ownership* acknowledged that "it will be recognized that the Capital Formation Plan owes a clear debt to principles first enunciated in Kelso's works, particularly *The Capitalist Manifesto*."

Basically, the capital formation plan is a method of encouraging stock purchases by people who would be in a position to buy stock with a little help from the government. Here is how it would work, as proposed by the Sabre Foundation in 1972 and modified by the Hamrin report:

- All persons with taxable incomes below $20,000 would be eligible investors, regardless of employment.
- Eligible investors would be allowed a tax deduction or a tax credit of up to $3,000 per year for their purchase of shares of capital formation funds (CFFs).
- Capital formation funds (CFFs) would be organized like mutual funds, but would be more flexible. They might be set up by life insurance companies, savings banks, unions, or other institutions. But they would have the single purpose of receiving the savings of eligible investors and using them to buy a *diversified* portfolio of corporate stock. This plan does not involve the employment relationship; it simply helps people to buy a diversified portfolio of stock with their own savings.
- To encourage corporations to sell stock to CFFs, the tax laws would be changed to make the dividends paid on shares held by CFFs tax deductible by the corporation for ten years.
- To encourage corporations to issue new common stock rather than to continue financing mainly through retained earnings and debt, we would change to a split-rate corporate income tax, a system now used in Germany, Japan, and Austria. Hamrin's report suggested a 20 percent corporate income tax

on earnings that are distributed, and a 50 percent tax on retained earnings. This would give corporations a strong incentive to use much more equity financing than they do under the present system, which taxes all corporate earnings at the same rate regardless of whether they are retained or paid out as dividends.

The capital formation plan's debt to Kelso is clear from the tax treatment of dividends and retained earnings. But as the Sabre Foundation said of the plan:

> This plan makes no pretense of serving the very poorest group in society. One must be able to amass some savings in order to take advantage of the investment deduction. One must be liable to pay a fairly significant amount of taxes. . . . This is not a plan aimed at helping the poor acquire capital on credit. . . .

Although the capital formation plan is not so ambitious as Kelso's Financed Capitalist Plan, it would be easier to put into operation because it is much less radical. It certainly would create a lot of new stockholders, and for that reason alone, it deserves careful study as part of a new national policy of broadening capital ownership.

If the capital formation plan is enacted, it will owe a double debt to Kelso. First, there is the acknowledged use of Kelso's ideas. Second, the 1972 study *Expanded Ownership* had been gathering dust for nearly four years until Kelso's promotion of ESOP brought on the JEC hearings and resurrected the capital formation plan.

After discussing the capital formation plan and the Financed Capitalist Plan, the Hamrin report concluded:

> There are numerous ways to achieve the goal of broadened ownership of new capital. Since this is a goal for all Americans and not just employees of corporations, serious consideration should be given to plans that are open to all individuals so that anyone desiring to purchase stock under special beneficial provisions may do so up to a specified ceiling. The plan should also provide incentives for firms to finance their future capital formation through issuance of new shares of stock as this would serve two purposes: (1) it would enhance economywide efficiency since funds channeled through the capital mar-

kets would be allocated to the areas with the highest rates
of return and (2) it would help ensure that a significant
amount of new stock would be continually available for
purchase by individuals.

The Capital Formation Plan and the Financed
Capitalist Plan are comprehensive programs containing
specific provisions to help each of the above objectives.
These plans in particular, and others of a similar scope
and nature, should be subject to detailed debate within
the Federal Government beginning this year so that the
people of this country may soon benefit from such programs, both directly through their stock ownership and
indirectly through the more efficient economy that would
result.

Since I had undertaken to call the Financed Capitalist
Plan to the attention of the JEC and had suggested in my written statement the need for an urgent federal search for the best
means of achieving a national economic policy of broad capital
diffusion, I felt personal satisfaction with the Hamrin report's
conclusions. I don't want to exaggerate my limited role, however. Hamrin and the JEC staff didn't need any help from me
to decide that we needed a broader plan than ESOP. But the
Hamrin report demonstrated to me that anyone who has re-
searched the existing plans for capital diffusion can make a contribution to the important federal studies and debates that lie
ahead, because there has been so little study and discussion of
this subject.

When the Hamrin report was published I had completed
most of the writing of this book, and I thought the report was
the last government action I would cover. But the Senate debate
of August 4, 1976 on the Tax Reform Act changed all that.

Senator Long Uses
His Secret Weapon

The Tax Reform Act of 1976 was one of the most complicated
pieces of legislation ever devised by man. The first printed version presented to the Senate was 1,536 pages long. By the time

that dozens of amendments were added during the twenty-five days of Senate debate, it was more than 2,000 pages long—each page full of almost unreadable paragraphs, subparagraphs, clauses, and subclauses.

One of the least controversial provisions of the act was the fixing of the investment tax credit at a permanent level of 10 percent. The amount of this credit had been changed many times since its introduction in 1962, and now there was broad support for making it permanent at 10 percent. But as we noted in Chapter 9, when Senator Russell Long helped to raise the investment tax credit from 7 to 10 percent for two years in the 1975 Tax Reduction Act, he also managed to slip in a temporary two-year extra 1 percent investment tax credit ESOP provision, known as TRASOP.

As Long guided the 1976 Tax Reform Act through his Senate Finance Committee, he went along with fixing the investment tax credit at a permanent level of 10 percent. But this time he also held out for making TRASOP permanent at a level of 2 percent. In other words, corporations could get a total investment tax credit of 12 percent by taking the regular 10 percent of capital outlays as a credit against federal taxes and contributing the equivalent of 2 percent of capital outlays (in the form of employers' stock) to a TRASOP. Senator Long had no difficulty getting this provision approved by his committee. But when the 1976 Tax Reform Act came to the floor of the Senate, there was an ambush party waiting for him.

It may seem surprising that such big names as Senators Humphrey, Javits, Muskie, Kennedy, Proxmire, and Percy would gang up to back an amendment that would knock out the permanent 2 percent TRASOP and replace it with a temporary 1 percent TRASOP, which would continue for only two years. Only a handful of corporations had put in TRASOPs, and there was practically no public discussion of TRASOP by either corporate or labor officials. Why, then, should Senator Long's new TRASOP provision kick up such a ruckus?

The answer lies in Long's strategy for the use of TRASOP. Once there was a permanent 2 percent TRASOP, Senator Long, Louis Kelso, and other ESOP supporters could use this provision to force many large corporations to take advantage of the opportunity to give their employees free stock at government expense. Senator Long had not hesitated to warn AT&T that they might face a lawsuit by their employees if they did not use the TRASOP gift provisions. As long as TRASOP was temporary, corporations had a good excuse for ignoring it. But if it was made permanent, especially at 2 percent, corporations like AT&T could hardly pass up the chance to give more than $100 million worth of stock each year to their employees, when the government was offering to pay for it.

Opponents of TRASOP also felt that Senator Long eventually would try to make the entire investment tax credit contingent on use of the TRASOP provision. In other words, even with a permanent 12 percent investment tax credit, corporations were still free to use the 10 percent provision and to pass up the 2 percent TRASOP. But what if Senator Long later pushed through a provision that the corporation could have its regular 10 percent investment tax credit *only* if it also used the 2 percent TRASOP provision? And further down the road, wouldn't he try to make it a 50–50 deal; that is, the corporation would get a 6 percent regular investment tax credit provided that it also contributed the equivalent of another 6 percent to a TRASOP? There seemed no end to what Long could do with TRASOP once it was made a permanent part of the tax law.

Ironically, most of the senators who backed the amendment aimed at sidetracking TRASOP are also devoted to the concept of broadening stock ownership. But Senators Javits, Humphrey, and Percy were opposed to TRASOP and very doubtful about ESOP. They saw TRASOP as a benefit mainly to the well-paid employees of our most successful corporations. They simply did not regard TRASOP as the kind of broad and equitable plan that could justify huge tax subsidies, subsidies that Senator Muskie calculated would cost the federal government $3.2 billion in lost tax revenue over the first five years of the 2 percent TRASOP provision.

The battle was joined on the Senate floor on August 4, 1976, when Senators Javits and Humphrey introduced an amendment aimed at reducing the permanent 2 percent TRASOP to a 1 percent TRASOP with a life limited to two years. Senator Javits spoke first, saying that he was heartily in favor of broadened stock ownership but that the TRASOP provisions benefited only a minority of the American people. The predicament of the attacking group was summed up by Javits:

> It would be easy to picture myself and my associates in this impending amendment as being against workers' plans. We simply have to run the risk that people have more sense than that. We are on the same side, Senator Long, I and my associates. We have some very grave differences as to what is the best way to attain that result, but certainly as to motivation and purpose there is no question whatsoever.

Javits went on to argue that TRASOP and ESOP discriminate against lower-paid employees in favor of the higher paid, that the entire investment is at risk because of lack of diversification, and that tying the government gift of stock to the investment tax credit discriminates in favor of people who work for corporations that make large outlays for capital expansion. (By far the majority of Americans are *not* employed by capital-intensive industrial corporations.)

Then Senator Hubert Humphrey took the floor and put himself in the same position as Javits:

> First of all, Mr. President, I think it should be clear that, speaking for myself and I know this is the case of the main sponsor, Senator Javits, that we speak from, and stand for, a position of full and complete support for the goal of broadening stock ownership in the nation's enterprises.

Humphrey dramatized the unfairness of using the investment tax credit as the basis of capital diffusion by quoting some statistics. He said that 72 percent of the entire labor force would receive no benefit from TRASOP; that the average salaries of those who would receive the benefits were already 20 to 100 percent higher than those who would be shut out; and that among the few who did receive benefits, the employees in capital-intensive industries like electric, gas, and sanitary services would receive an annual average of $256, while those working in retail and service industries would get only $3 to $5 each.

Humphrey went on to describe the JEC hearings, and he quoted the statement from the 1976 *Joint Economic Report* urging adoption of a new national policy of broadening capital ownership. He mentioned the Hamrin report, which "analyzes

in considerable detail many of the methods, other than the so-
called ESOP, that would broaden capital ownership in the
United States." He concluded:

> That is the point, Mr. President. We are at the early
> stages of a very important national dialogue and debate
> as to how best we can move toward broadening capital
> ownership, particularly by workers in industries.
>
> What Congress needs now is the time to conduct suf-
> ficient investigation of the numerous means available to
> achieve this rather important goal.
>
> Particularly, there are plans much more comprehen-
> sive than ESOP which should be subject to debate by
> Congress and the appropriate executive departments, as
> they have two distinct advantages over what we know as
> ESOPs.
>
> First, they stimulate both the issuance of stock and
> its distribution to new stockholders, and secondly, the
> new stockholders could, if it was desired, consist entirely
> of low and middle income Americans, who currently own
> a very small share of this country's outstanding stock.
>
> It is my intention that the Joint Economic Com-
> mittee, along with other committees of Congress, continue
> their efforts in this area by examining these types of plans
> over the coming years. I urge other committees to ex-
> amine the goal of broadening capital ownership and the
> means to achieve it.

These ideas were echoed by Senator Percy, and then it was
time for Russell Long to take the floor.

Long defended ESOP and TRASOP, not on the grounds
that they were the ideal methods of diffusing capital ownership,
but because they were available for use now, and something had
to be done now to start diffusion of capital ownership. Warming
up to the debate, Long pounded away on this theme:

> With all the oratory I have heard, these people are talk-
> ing about continuing the status quo. They do not have a
> pension program to offer today. They do not have a
> profit-sharing plan. They are just talking about continu-
> ing the system under which the great majority of Ameri-
> cans get nothing. . . .
>
> But you have to get it started somewhere. Some way
> you have to start moving in terms of getting employee
> stock ownership going, if you want it to exist in America.
> And if we get it going, the American Telephone and

Telegraph Company will put it into effect for their company provided it does not have to come out of the equity interest of their existing shareholders. That will stimulate thought and interest by other companies about employee stock ownership. . . .

That will cause other companies that are less capital-intensive to be thinking in terms of the ways they can participate. The question is, do you want to move ahead with employee stock ownership, or do what we have been doing for the last 28 years that I have been here and Senator Humphrey has been here, just leave it where it is, where nothing ever seems to happen? Where we have great talk about what we want to do for people, but all we ever do is put up charts showing that one fourth of our people own less than zero, which is about where it was 20 years ago.

That pretty well summed up the case for TRASOP. Then Senator Muskie took the floor in a last-ditch effort to overcome Long's arguments. He reminded the Senate of the billions of tax dollars that TRASOP would cost, and he pointed out that TRASOP did not require corporations to issue new stock. He said that most major corporations would probably choose to contribute cash to the TRASOP and let it buy the corporation's stock in the market. This would avoid the dilution of present stock holdings and consequent reduction of earnings per share. But it would not result in any new capital formation; it would merely be a handout of tax money to the employees of favored corporations.

Senator Long moved to table the proposed amendment aimed at crippling TRASOP. His motion was brought to a vote, and the score was 62 in favor of Long and TRASOP, and 28 opposed. So by a margin of better than 2 to 1 Russell Long had carried through the Senate the provision making TRASOP permanent at 2 percent, a measure that would virtually force major corporations to distribute billions of dollars worth of stock to their employees at the expense of the federal government. And let's not forget that the debate made it clear that even the senators who voted against TRASOP were in favor of conducting an intensive search for a more equitable method of broadening stock ownership.

If I had ever questioned the wizardry of Russell Long, I could no longer doubt it after that performance. In a "Dear

Colleague" letter to his fellow senators, he had let it be known that TRASOP was the most important provision in the whole massive tax bill. He had even sent the same kind of letter to the wife of each senator—apparently the first time this tactic had ever been used.

He had convinced two-thirds of the Senate to back this handout of billions of dollars to employees of leading corporations, including their presidents and executive officers. And even those who opposed TRASOP were saying that they supported capital diffusion in principle, though they hoped to find a better way of bringing it about. Thus, by putting all his weight behind TRASOP, which seemed like only a minor addition to the investment tax credit, Long had succeeded in lining up practically the entire U.S. Senate on the side of universal capitalism. True, not many senators realized what was happening, but those who did had been propelled into an urgent search for the ideal capital diffusion plan, for fear of choking on TRASOP.

The Final Version of the 1976 Tax Reform Act

Following the debate of August 4, 1976, and the overwhelming vote in favor of the 2 percent TRASOP, Senators Humphrey and Javits got together to plan some concrete steps toward finding a better plan. They came up with the idea of appointing a special commission to make a detailed study of the various plans for broadening stock ownership.

This idea ripened into an amendment that was presented on the Senate floor by Senator Javits on August 6, 1976. It was accepted by Senator Long and tacked onto the Senate version of the Tax Reform Act. It provided for a commission on expanded stock ownership with fifteen members, five appointed by the President, five by the Senate, and five by the House. The commission would "conduct a comprehensive inquiry with respect to broadening stock ownership," particularly with regard to

ESOPs "and all other alternative methods for broadening stock ownership to the American labor force and others," and would present its report to the president and Congress by March 30, 1978.

The Senate finally passed the entire 1976 Tax Reform Act on August 6, the day that the Javits study commission amendment was added on. Then the Senate version had to face a House–Senate conference committee to iron out the differences between it and the House version. The Senate version did not comply with the guidelines set by Senator Muskie and his Budget Committee, which had charged Congress with the task of producing $2 billion additional revenue through the 1976 Tax Reform Act. Therefore, the conference committee was under great pressure to eliminate provisions that decreased revenue.

Senator Long went into the conference determined to dig in his heels and hold onto all the yardage he could for TRASOP. However, he knew he would have to make some compromise. In the final bill he had to give up the 2 percent permanent TRASOP, but managed to keep a 1 percent TRASOP provision extended for four years (to 1980). There was also a provision for an extra ½ percent TRASOP, provided that the extra ½ percent was matched by employee contributions. The ½ percent provision was rather complicated, but large corporations that already have employee thrift plans (as many of the major oil producers do) might be able to comply, thus giving Russell Long his 2 percent TRASOP after all. The investment tax credit itself was extended for the same four years at 10 percent, instead of being made permanent as in the Senate bill.

The conference committee also decided to drop Javits's commission on expanded stock ownership. Instead, it was agreed that broadened stock ownership would be referred to the Joint Pension Task Force, a group of Senate and House committee staff members who were already studying pensions and other aspects of the Pension Reform Act of 1974.

At first I was disappointed that the commission had been dropped. It seemed like a golden opportunity to put the spotlight on capital diffusion, particularly the plans that were not based on the employment relationship. However, I recalled that other federal study commissions often developed inertia and tended to slow down legislation. It is always easy to put aside legislation while awaiting the report of a study group.

I learned from Bob Hamrin that the Joint Economic Committee was hoping to hold more hearings on capital diffusion in 1977, particularly on plans other than ESOP. Senator Javits had announced his intention to seek 1977 hearings on the Javits–Humphrey bill before the Senate Labor Committee. And during the August 4 TRASOP debate, Senator Humphrey had urged all his colleagues to get into the act and start fashioning capital diffusion legislation as quickly as possible. So we didn't really need a study commission; we needed research and hearings by congressional committees that would lay the groundwork for legislation.

The passage of the 1976 Tax Reform Act was another triumph for Russell Long. The *New York Times* called him "the single most influential legislator" in the entire Congress, and on September 20, 1976, *Time* said: "Russell Long, the wily chairman of the Senate Finance Committee, was the dominant figure in the conference."

He was able to put enough tax reform into the act to justify a broad interpretation of its title, but he kept alive a lot of tax shelters that the House bill would have knocked out. And he kept his secret weapon, the 1 percent TRASOP, intact for four more years. Along the way, he also slipped in a provision designed to put the brakes on restrictive ESOP regulations that had been proposed by the Internal Revenue Service on July 30, 1976. The conference committee adopted a strong statement setting out liberal guidelines which the IRS would have to consider before issuing any final ESOP regulations.

Even though the conference committee on the Tax Reform Act held its sessions in public for the first time, there were still very few people who actually understood the provisions being discussed. The conferees themselves were described by the press as exhausted and bleary-eyed. And the *Wall Street Journal* made history by admitting in its editorial of September 14, 1976:

> The reason we have delayed in commenting on the compromise legislation agreed upon by House–Senate con-

ferees last Thursday was the vain hope that with a little time we could make some sense out of the legislation. But even after enlisting the aid of a number of eminent private economists and financiers, who spent the weekend slogging through those 1,500 pages, the *Wall Street Journal* is forced to announce its despair.

As the curtain fell on the 94th Congress, Russell Long was not the only hero of the universal capitalism movement. His tremendous leverage as chairman of the Senate Finance Committee had set loose forces that caused other senators and congressmen to react. But it was Senator Hubert Humphrey's action in calling for the JEC hearings on ESOP in December of 1975 that focused the spotlight on the need for a broader plan of capital diffusion. Humphrey then joined with Jacob Javits to alert the Senate to this pressing need. Javits and Humphrey drew important support from Senator Charles Percy of Illinois, a long-time champion of broadened ownership.

Then there were two conservative Republican senators: Paul Fannin of Arizona, one of the earliest Kelso adherents, who consistently supported Russell Long's ESOP legislation; and Jesse Helms of North Carolina, who represents the Ronald Reagan wing of the Republican party and who came forward in 1975 with his own legislative plan for broadening capital ownership.

On the House side, there were Representatives Gillis Long of Louisiana, cousin of Russell Long and member of the Joint Economic Committee, who played an important role in the JEC deliberations; Jack Kemp of New York, former pro quarterback for the Buffalo Bills and now a staunch advocate of expanded ownership; and William Frenzel of Minnesota, who has sponsored many proposed ESOP improvements.

We should also recall some of the early Kelso supporters who helped him to gain recognition and momentum on Capitol Hill: Senator Mark Hatfield, Republican of Oregon, and former Senator Vance Hartke, Democrat of Indiana, who helped to enact the first ESOP provision in the Regional Rail Reorganization Act of 1973; and former Senator Fred Harris of Oklahoma, who called the attention of Congress to the Kelso–Samuelson confrontation in Puerto Rico way back in 1972.

When I started to write this book, I didn't have much

hope that universal capitalism would get serious legislative consideration until professional economists got interested in it. Legislators usually are afraid to consider radical economic changes without approval of professional economists. But I was wrong. This time the legislators had moved ahead of the economists, thanks to the courage of men like Long, Humphrey, and Javits.

There was at least one professional economist helping them—Bob Hamrin of the JEC. Hamrin has not had the time to pile up teaching and writing credits, but his work on the 1976 Joint Economic Report and his staff study of the ESOP hearings are important milestones on the road to universal capitalism. It took considerable courage for him to suggest the broadening of capital ownership as a national goal in 1976, on the skimpy record presented by its proponents and in the face of the ostrich act performed by almost all other professional economists.

This brings us to another multiple-choice question. This one is open to all readers, but it is especially addressed to economists, professors of economics, and their students.

Given the facts that

1. The 1976 Joint Economic Report unanimously recommended a national policy of broadening capital ownership and suggested that the means of reaching this goal should be the subject of intensive federal study and debate immediately.

2. The United States has already adopted a policy of broadening capital ownership through TRASOP, under which tax revenue will be used to subsidize the gift of billions of dollars worth of stock to officers and other employees of our most successful capital-intensive corporations, in proportion to their salaries.

3. The Joint Economic Committee and other committees of Congress are searching for a more equitable way to broaden capital ownership.

4. TRASOP will continue at least through 1980 and will probably get bigger each year.

__ (a) Professional economists should continue to *ignore* capital diffusion because it is not part of Keynesian economics and because traditonal economists have never made any studies of the use of broadened capital ownership as a means of improving income distribution.

__ (b) Even though they have never studied the subject, professional economists should *condemn* capital diffusion, and should work against its adoption as national policy, because it was first suggested by Louis Kelso, a lawyer whose writings on economics have not been published or reviewed in professional economists' journals.

__ (c) Professional economists should immediately begin a crash program to study the potential uses of capital diffusion and the effects of such a policy on the economy. They should start cooperating with the Joint Economic Committee and other congressional committees studying this subject so that the billions of tax dollars that would otherwise go to TRASOP may be used to broaden capital ownership more equitably.

The Kelso Movement, 1976

Throughout the climactic developments in Congress during the summer of 1976, Louis Kelso was right there in Washington with his bow tie and pixieish smile. He would fly in from San Francisco at the drop of a hat to talk to anybody in Washington who could help the movement, and he told his story with as much enthusiasm as if he had thought up his ideas the night before.

The man who had started the revolution naturally was pleased with all the attention it was getting in 1976, particularly when things came to a head with Senator Long's TRASOP victory. At age sixty-three, he was still operating on a schedule that would make nervous wrecks of most men. He was the key figure in a law firm, a lobbying organization, a social revolution, and the world's most unlikely investment banking firm, Kelso & Company.

Patricia Hetter was still holding forth in the world headquarters of the nongrubby revolution, which are located on the penthouse floor of a San Francisco skyscraper. The offices of Kelso & Company were formerly occupied by the executive headquarters of Foremost-McKesson, Inc. Kelso himself has the office that was custom built for the chief executive officer of

Foremost. It features expensive paneling, executive shower and washroom, adjoining board-of-directors meeting room, and private bar well stocked with chilled wines.

Also aboard in San Francisco was Ron Ludwig, one of the solid men of the Kelso movement. Ron is a lawyer who served in Washington as tax law specialist for the National Office Pension Trust Branch of the Internal Revenue Service before he joined Kelso in 1973. He was also an adjunct professor at Georgetown Law School, teaching pensions and deferred compensation. When it comes to explaining ESOP to businessmen or lawyers, or drafting an ESOP plan, or working with Congress and the IRS on ESOP legislation and regulations, Ron Ludwig has no peer.

In keeping with the increased Washington activity, Kelso set up new Washington headquarters in 1976, located in a plush new office building. Early in 1976, Wayne Thevenot left the job he had held with Senator Russell Long for thirteen years, and joined Kelso & Company. He became their chief Washington representative after Norman Kurland decided to continue working for universal capitalism on his own. Norm kept the old attic office on Massachusetts Avenue where the Washington phase of the revolution had begun.

As the 1976 election approached, Kelso was busy making his case to both parties. He had meetings with Treasury Secretary Simon as the Ford administration's interest in broadening capital ownership increased—perhaps through prodding from the Ronald Reagan forces, since Reagan was a long-time supporter of Kelso's basic ideas. Louis also met with Jimmy Carter's advisers, hoping that Carter would be impressed by the fact that Kelso's writings draw on the theological works of Reinhold Niebuhr, who also had a strong influence on Carter.

The results of these political thrusts were the same, regardless of the party. The listeners always showed great respect for Kelso and strong interest in the basic idea of broadening capital ownership. But after analysis of ESOP, the tool that Kelso put forward as the means of accomplishing capital diffusion, both candidates decided not to make Kelso a campaign issue because his plan did not measure up to the great promise of Kelso's theories. And in both parties, the politicians who decided the campaign issues had to refer Kelso's presentation to economic advisers, mostly professors who were stopped short either by Kelso's two-factor theory or by the assumption that ESOP was his total plan for universal capitalism.

As Kelso headed into 1977 and the twentieth anniversary of *The Capitalist Manifesto,* he was still trying to make it on his own, without support from professional economists and without any econometric analysis of his theories. Of course, he never quite felt alone as long as he had Russell Long in his corner. But apart from the work of Brems and Hamrin, there were very few economists willing to analyze his theories. I was able to find only professors James L. Green of the University of Georgia, Howard D. Segool of the University of Massachusetts, Glen W. Atkinson of the University of Nevada, and James A. Buss of Fairfield University who had done any serious research on this subject. Green, Segool, and Atkinson are long-standing admirers of Kelso, while Buss is uncommitted but thinks Kelso's theories should be checked out econometrically and has started to do so with his own limited facilities.

I got some idea of the professional economists' indifference to Kelso when I attended the September 1975 Atlantic Economic Conference in Washington, D.C. The program included a session titled "Louis Kelso's Economic System." Out of more than 800 economists registered at the conference, not a single one attended the Kelso session. The audience consisted of two guests of Norman Kurland, three college students, Dr. Abel Beltran-del-Rio, Jeff Gates, and me.

I hope this book will open the minds of more economists to the need for studying capital diffusion. And I hope that Kelso will be encouraged to make his theories more accessible to traditional economists by refraining from wrapping all of them in his two-factor theory.

While Kelso still insists that his two-factor theory is valid and is an important part of universal capitalism, I noticed some hopeful signs in 1976. In July, the name of his organization's newsletter, which up to that time had been called *Two-Factor News,* was changed to *The New Capitalist;* and Kelso was using the term "universal capitalism" in places where he would have said "two-factor economics" in the past. These steps will certainly help to open the way for dialogue with traditional economists. Maybe then Louis Kelso will not have to complete his revolution alone.

Where Do We Go from Here?

The JEC reports and the 1976 Tax Reform Act put capital diffusion squarely before Congress. It is no longer possible to ignore or be neutral about capital diffusion. You are either in favor of finding a broad, equitable plan that would benefit most of our citizens or you are in favor of the narrow TRASOP variety, which would bring billions of dollars worth of free stock to officers and other employees of major successful corporations at taxpayer expense.

The complexities of tax legislation have obscured the significance of these events, but it's all there for anyone to read, in the statute books, the *Congressional Record,* and the financial reports of major corporations. It seems clear to me that something definitive has to happen during the 95th Congress (1977–1978). Either we will get well along toward finding a broad, equitable plan, or we'll have to sit back and let TRASOP diffuse billions of dollars worth of stock into the wrong bathtubs. By late 1976, TRASOP was beginning to make headway with major capital-intensive corporations. Thirteen of the fifteen major American oil producers were in the process of establishing TRASOPs, and so were such giant corporations as Consolidated Edison Co. of New York, International Paper Co., Westvaco, Weyerhaeuser Co., and Union Camp Corp.

Obviously Russell Long will continue to push TRASOP, and this will disturb those who want to distribute capital ownership more equitably. But if he relaxes the pressure, we might go back to the kind of do-nothing attitude which he so colorfully described in his Senate TRASOP speech. So Long will hold Congress's feet to the fire until they come up with something better than TRASOP. Long and Kelso have shifted the burden of proof, as lawyers say. They no longer have to prove that we should use capital diffusion. They have kicked the ball into the court of those who oppose capital diffusion through TRASOP, and they can sit back and wait for proof that there is a better method.

If you're satisfied with TRASOP as a national policy of capital diffusion, then you don't have to read any further. But if you would prefer a more equitable plan, you may be able to help. The only way we're going to find a better plan is to get our best brains and resources working on the problem immediately—and almost everyone can do something. Just make a list of all the people you know who could help to shape the ideal capital diffusion scheme: economists, teachers, students, business executives, labor union officials, legislators, bureaucrats, financiers, social workers, and just plain workers, for a start. Then tell them the story of TRASOP and what will be happening in the 95th Congress.

The Joint Economic Committee is planning to study and hold hearings on all types of schemes for broadening capital ownership in 1977. The Senate Labor and Public Welfare Committee will probably hold hearings and conduct studies on the Javits–Humphrey Bill in 1977. The Joint Pension Task Force has a statutory mandate to study and report on broadening capital ownership by March 31, 1978. The Department of Commerce's Economic Development Administration is planning to commission Wharton Econometric Forecasting Associates to make an econometric analysis of Kelso's theories in 1977. And the new Carter team in the White House will be watching for signs that there is a way of making capitalism work for all Americans.

All these momentous projects have gotten underway with practically no support from economists, business, labor, or the general public. But the subject is far too important to be left out of the mainstream of public interest. The stakes are very high. Let's take a final look at them.

UNIVERSAL CAPITALISM: WHAT'S IN IT FOR AMERICANS?

This land is your land
This land is my land
From California to the New York island
From the Redwood forest
To the Gulfstream waters
This land was made for you and me!
© Woody Guthrie, *This Land is Your Land*

What's at Stake?

The best way to evaluate what's at stake for Americans in universal capitalism is to review briefly some of the important points we covered in the preceding chapters.

As we saw in Chapter 2, the 1976 American economy is in a continual crisis, a crisis both of performance and of confidence. Schumpeter described it all too accurately as "capitalism in an oxygen tent." Our system of mixed capitalism is being kept alive by redistribution of income. Productive people are being taxed heavily for transfer payments to keep a lot of Americans from starving or revolting or both. As a result, unemployment and inflation have zoomed: rates of 6–8 percent for both are now accepted, though this is two or three times the levels of the 1960s. The near-bankruptcies of New York City and New York State have shown that redistribution is bringing our system to the breaking point.

We know that the breakdown of the free enterprise system poses threats to national defense, democracy, and freedom in America. Despite the clear evidence of this crisis, and the yearning of many informed people for structural changes in the economic system, traditional economists haven't come up with any new ideas. Even the 1976 presidential campaign produced no new concepts. Both parties offered versions of the same old theme: redistribution based on transfer payments.

We are also facing a shortage of capital. The capital needs of industry are estimated at $4.5 trillion for the decade 1975–1984, yet America lags behind all other major industrialized nations in the percentage of gross national product devoted to capital outlays.

As we start our third century, it looks like our economic system of mixed capitalism is headed inevitably toward evolution or revolution into socialism or communism unless we can find a new wrinkle to make capitalism work. Why should the great majority of Americans, who are noncapitalists, continue to vote for a system that denies them any real chance for capital ownership? It seems likely that eventually they will vote for a system of collective ownership.

Kelso and Adler have shown that there are four forms of capitalism: primitive, state, mixed, and universal. The primitive capitalism of Adam Smith, based on laissez-faire, always concentrated ownership in very few hands. Without government intervention, it doesn't satisfy our 1976 standards of morality or income distribution. It depends on trickledown, the belief that what's good for businessmen will eventually result in good for the rest of the country.

The examples of state capitalism provided by Russia and China have convinced most of us that we'd lose our democracy, liberty, and freedom if we concentrated economic and political power in the hands of bureaucrats. Not many of us, therefore, are ready to go that route.

Mixed capitalism looked like it would work until the 1970s. But now we know how it feels to live in an oxygen tent.

So we're left with universal capitalism. It's the only form that has never been tried, and Kelso makes some strong claims for it. He portrays it as the economic counterpart of political democracy: It would avoid totalitarian concentration of power, give us a classless society with the high living standards that can be produced only by free enterprise, and eliminate both the robber baron and the entrenched bureaucrat. It would combine the emotional appeal of Marxism with the self-betterment drive of Adam Smith's laissez-faire and harness the moral forces of socialism within the free environment of capitalism. And it is the only system built upon economic freedom and economic justice for all.

There is no other proposal for change in our economic system that even begins to promise as much as universal capitalism does, and traditional economists have offered no scientific evidence that the promise is empty. Thus, if we didn't try to find a way to make universal capitalism work, we'd be losing an opportunity to transform America into an ideal society.

As we saw in Chapter 4, ours is *not* an affluent society. Wealth in the United States remains highly concentrated. Corporate stock is especially so: the richest 1 percent of the people own more than half of all individually owned shares. The present system of taxation and corporate finance perpetuates this overconcentration by rigging the plumbing so that the ownership of newly created capital is piped into the overflowing bathtubs of the people who are already wealthy, while those who own no capital get none.

Kelso zeroed in on this phase of our economy and came up with the following theses:

• Productive capital can be made to pay for itself over a period of years, regardless of who owns it (Kelso's "wooden Indian" theory).

• The key to capital ownership is long-term credit.

• We can diffuse capital ownership without invading present wealth. The annual pool of newly formed business capital ($120 billion in 1976) is an ideal basis for capital diffusion, since it is not owned by anyone now and is going to pay for itself in the future regardless of who owns it.

• We can rerig the taxation and corporate finance systems so as to pipe capital ownership to anyone—a wooden Indian, an already-rich capitalist, or a New Capitalist who owns no capital now. We can use the credit power of major corporations to build capital ownership and purchasing power into New Capitalists.

• This rerigging will make capitalism a moral and equitable system. It will also solve one of our great problems: lack of mass purchasing power to consume the huge productive capacity of the capitalist economy.

• Diffusion of capital ownership can distribute income more equitably, leading to increased production and consumption and the creation of more jobs without the inflationary pressures that accompany nonproductive income distribution by transfer payments.

• This rerigged system can also help to solve the capital shortage by creating a new source of capital for our corporations.

• Our national economic system is supposed to be free enterprise capitalism, but our national economic policy is to distribute income through employment and government handouts. The main benefit of capitalism is capital ownership, but it has never been the subject of any national economic policy.

• Until we have a truly affluent society, with capital ownership diffused throughout the population, we will not be able to take care of our environmental problems, devote sufficient money to the public sector, or provide adequate funds for research and development.

• Capital diffusion can bring into our economic system democracy, freedom, justice, and logic. It faces up to economic reality and it accepts the basic drives of human nature. Unlike Marxism, it does not try to destroy man's natural acquisitive drive or thirst for freedom; and unlike the primitive capitalism of Adam Smith, it does not depend on an invisible hand to overcome human nature.

• Capital diffusion would give America a decisive weapon in the global struggle against communism: a foreign policy based on exporting economic justice and human dignity to underdeveloped countries.

• Capital diffusion is consistent with all of our great liberal and conservative traditions. It leads to the independence of individuals and families. It reduces taxes, transfer payments, and government bureaucracy. It has strong appeal for all of our major political factions.

With all of these claimed advantages, it is clear that nobody in his right mind could oppose Kelso's goals. But Kelso has not laid out a plan for achieving universal capitalism that has been tested in practice or backed up by econometric analysis. He has put into practice employee stock ownership plans (ESOPs) which can be highly beneficial in special circumstances, but there is no evidence that ESOPs can be made broad or equitable enough to bring us truly universal capitalism. Therefore, we must begin the search for the ideal plan of capital diffusion—a plan that would bring us as close as possible to universal capitalism, first in the United States and then in the rest of the world.

Traditional economists have recognized both capital and labor as factors in production, but they have never studied capital diffusion as a means of making income distribution equitable. Traditional economic theory has no instrument for capital diffusion.

Ownership of corporate stock by pension funds has increased dramatically, so that in 1976 pension funds collectively owned over 25 percent of all of the outstanding stock of American corporations. They are predicted to own over 50 percent by 1985. However, for reasons which we will discuss later in this chapter, pension funds will not lead us to universal capitalism. They are simply a device for providing retirement benefits, and they don't produce ownership or current income. In fact, they produce nothing for most Americans who now own little or no productive capital.

Even though traditional economists have not formulated any strategy for capital diffusion, it is well on the way toward becoming a new national economic policy. Thanks to the work of Kelso and the support of Senator Russell Long, the Joint Economic Committee in 1976 set the United States on the road toward a new goal of broadening capital ownership, and recommended immediate debate within the federal government to develop the ideal plan of capital diffusion. In the meantime, we *have* adopted as our national policy of capital diffusion the TRASOP mechanism that Senator Long wrote into our tax laws.

TRASOP gives us a start toward capital diffusion, but it is far from an ideal plan because its benefits go mainly to officers and other employees of our most successful capital-intensive corporations, in proportion to salaries. It involves the use of billions of dollars of tax subsidies, and its benefits flow to less than 30 percent of the national labor force—to people whose incomes are already much higher than those of the great majority of workers. This majority would receive no benefits from TRASOP at all.

TRASOP also lays the groundwork for takeover of major businesses by labor unions. Labor union officials have opposed ESOP and TRASOP, just as they usually oppose profit-sharing plans. But once they accept the fact that such plans are here to stay, their next move may be an attempt to use them to gain stock control of major corporations. This move is already under way in Europe, and will not take long to get started in America.

Because TRASOP has been written into the law through 1980, and because Senator Long will probably try to expand it, the pressure is now on Congress and the rest of the country to come up with the ideal plan of capital diffusion. Otherwise, we will follow a new national policy of capital diffusion through TRASOP. That may alleviate the maldistribution of capital ownership to a small degree, but it will deprive us of a golden opportunity to win much higher stakes by finding the way to universal capitalism.

Those who continue to ignore or condemn capital diffusion are simply casting their votes in favor of TRASOP as our national economic policy of capital diffusion. Therefore, it is clear that we need a crash program to bring our best minds and strongest resources into the search for the ideal plan of capital diffusion.

Before we discuss details of the ideal plan, let's look at some of the very big stakes that are involved for *all* Americans.

At Stake for All Americans

You had only to read the 1976 newspaper headlines to learn that our "détente" with Russia was breaking down, if indeed it ever had any real substance. The International Institute for Strategic Studies in 1976 reached the conclusion that the political–military system that has kept some semblance of global order since World War II was deteriorating, with nothing in sight to replace it. A group of atomic and political scientists from Harvard and MIT concluded at a 1975 meeting that a nuclear war would occur before the year 2000, unless all major nations surrendered their sovereignty to a world government. The Stockholm International Peace Research Institute reported in 1976 that about thirty-five countries were within ten years of being able to make atomic weapons, and predicted that when that happens, nuclear war will have become inevitable. The world energy crisis that spurred expanded use of atomic reactors will probably accelerate this process.

Every major weapon devised by mankind is used eventually in combat. Don't forget that it was the good old United States that used the atomic bomb in the first place—we, the most benevolent major power that ever existed. Tomorrow, people like Idi Amin will have access to nuclear weapons—unless we can come up with a new idea to prevent it.

I feel that only one thing can give us adequate security against a nuclear holocaust: a real *entente* between the world's major nuclear powers, Russia and the United States. Together we might be able to control nuclear proliferation and terrorism, but it will take entente rather than détente. In 1976, entente with Russia seemed like a wild dream, since the ideological warfare between capitalism and communism continued unabated throughout the world. If we allow this battle of economic systems to continue, I don't see how it can end up any differently from the major economic wars of the past—in military conflict. As Dryden said, "War seldom enters but where wealth allures."

In universal capitalism, I see a glimmer of hope that we can unite with Russia in an economic entente that would combine the best features of capitalism and communism. First we would have to make universal capitalism work in America, by spreading capital ownership throughout our society while maintaining the advantages of the free enterprise system. If we can do that, we will have achieved one of Marx's main goals, the ownership of the means of production by all the people.

This might not make the people in the Kremlin very happy, because it would demonstrate that the main benefits of socialism can be obtained without giving up democracy, liberty, and freedom. No doubt they would want to hang on to their power and special privileges. But could they do that for very long if we made universal capitalism work in America and then started exporting it, first to industrial democracies, then to developing nations, and then to communist countries like Yugoslavia, Hungary, and Poland?

There would be a risk that the Soviet leaders might start a war rather than change their system, but that's about the same risk as we're courting now with our global economic warfare against communism. The Soviet leaders were, after all, smart enough to gain total power over their huge nation, so I think they'd come out pretty well if shares of stock in Soviet corporations were parceled out by the government. And if we did spread universal capitalism to the rest of the world but failed to penetrate Russia, we'd still be in a pretty strong position. The Soviets would have no ideological basis on which to oppose American economic policy and very little to offer other nations as incentive for carrying on a cold war against us.

By 1976, the communist movement in Western Europe was trying to adapt Marxism to the parliamentary democracy and traditional personal liberty that most Western European nations enjoy. Many socialist countries were being forced to adopt capitalistic measures to solve economic crises. And in an article titled "Communism's Crisis of Authority" (*Fortune,* February 1976), Daniel Seligman listed 121 communist parties throughout the world, of which only 65 were considered pro-Soviet; the others were independent or pro-Chinese. Many of these parties, whether pro-Soviet or not, were questioning or opposing one-party rule. Thus the Kremlin was being forced toward the center by communists rather than capitalists.

Against this background, I don't think Russia's ruling clique could deny their own citizens direct ownership of capital indefinitely, if we made universal capitalism work and spread it around the world. Certainly they would have no ideological basis for claiming that Russians must own capital through the state mechanism, if diffused individual ownership were bringing a better life to both "capitalists" and "communists" elsewhere. These terms start to lose their meaning when capital ownership is spread throughout society.

We could even let the Russians claim that the whole thing

was their idea, or Marx's idea, since it's hard to tell from his writings whether he wanted the state or the workers ultimately to own the means of production. Peter Drucker claims that the real thrust of Marxism was ownership by the workers themselves rather than the state, and he says that this view was taken by Engels, Bebel, Kautsky, Victor Adler, and Rosa Luxemburg. Since the state is supposed to wither away under Marxism anyway, it would be difficult for Marxists to justify perpetuation of state ownership of capital if diffused ownership by individuals were shown to be practical.

Why do you suppose that *Pravda* extensively reviewed Kelso and Adler's *The Capitalist Manifesto* in 1959, when all the American economics journals ignored the book? And why did *Pravda* distort the *Manifesto* so grotesquely, by telling their readers that Kelso and Adler advocated extermination of workers who were replaced by machines? Obviously the Russians were afraid of this book. They must have thought that its logical and attractive reasoning would sweep through the West and then threaten the foundations of the Kremlin. The *Manifesto* was an attack on American capitalism, but the Russians reacted to it more defensively than if it had been an attack on Marxism. Why? Because it contained a simple idea that could make the Russian brand of communism redundant.

Maybe this stuff sounds naive to you, especially the idea that the people of Russia could force their rulers to give them back their country, and that much of the world could unite behind a system which would bring us peace, justice, and sharing of wealth. Maybe it is naive. Some experts say that Marxist ideology is irrelevant today, that it's just an excuse for keeping the Soviet rulers in power. But what better hope do we have than one based on ideology?

If you think our 1976 détente policy is practical, consider that our all-time record high defense budget of $112 billion for the 1977 fiscal year will not even keep us on a par with the Russians. Even the Brookings Institution, which is not known as a haven for hawks, concluded that we will have to spend a greater percentage of our gross national product on defense in future years. In a 1976 publication, *Setting National Priorities*, Brookings found that the defense budget will have to go up to about $140 billion by the fiscal year 1980. And as we go on developing new generations of missiles and sophisticated weapons, the pressure increases for spending a greater portion of GNP on the defense budget, which means that we must neglect social programs and risk further inflation. It is becoming apparent that there is no rational policy to cope with the problems of ruinous defense budgets, other than to look for a way of ending the need for them.

Then there is the joint need of America and Russia to protect themselves and the rest of the world against terrorists who will soon be equipped with nuclear weapons. Before we get to the point where a gang no larger than Jessie James's can hold mighty nations to ransom with nuclear weapons, isn't it time to make a major effort to remove the basic cause of Soviet–American confrontation, the worldwide power struggle between our two economic systems? This competition is pretty silly when you consider that neither American capitalism nor Russian communism has any logical policy on the ownership of capital, and that most of the citizens of both countries are denied the benefits of capital ownership.

Expanded capital ownership is accepted as a way of decreasing the strife between labor and management. The best way to create unity and avoid friction is to get people on the same side and give them common interests. It is a rare bird who will foul his own nest. But Kelso and Adler have given us a much broader view of the potential of expanded ownership for decreasing strife. They have shown us that it can be a way of decreasing *all* human strife—not just American against American, but American against Russian, and even Arab against Jew. Norman Kurland has started work on a plan to diffuse ownership of important production units of the Middle East, to bring the people of Israel and the Arab countries together economically, as a stepping stone to permanent peace.

The same principle applies to the spreading cancer of crime. I am not one of those who would suspend criminal laws until we have created a utopia with equal opportunity and wealth for all. If we let crime proliferate because criminals are poor—or for any other reason—we'll never survive. But there is no doubt that the alienation of people at the bottom 20 percent of the economic ladder, which tops any other segment of the population for crime, is aggravated by poverty and lack of economic hope. No way has been found to control the crime rate under mixed capitalism. Our jails are already overflowing. We are drifting dangerously toward acceptance of unemployment rates of 20–40 percent among the people who commit most of our violent crimes. And we know that giving them welfare handouts, without making them part of the capitalist system through ownership, does not make them any more respectful of the law. So universal capitalism is one of the few ideas that could help to control crime, especially if participation in capital ownership were limited to people with no criminal convictions.

Then there's the prickly subject of wage and price controls, which have worked in America only when we were a people united in a war effort. Universal capitalism might produce the same kind of community of interest as a war effort, and unite us to the point where we could use wage and price controls to fight inflation, as Galbraith proposes.

These arguments for universal capitalism may seem somewhat emotional. But the giants of structural economic change were keenly aware of the importance of emotion in making an economic system work. Marx's appeal was largely to the feelings: he dramatized the injustices of capitalism and relied on the emotional force of his arguments, without laying out a detailed blueprint of how a substitute economic system would work. Nor did John Maynard Keynes overlook the emotional factor. In his classic *General Theory,* he said:

> There is the instability due to the characteristic of human nature that a large proportion of our positive activities depend on spontaneous optimism rather than on a mathematical expectation, whether moral or hedonistic or economic. . . . Thus if the animal spirits are dimmed and the spontaneous optimism falters, leaving us to depend on nothing but a mathematical expectation, enterprise will fade and die—though fears of loss may have a basis no more reasonable than hopes of profit had before.

Our economic and military problems are so great that the only structural change worth considering is one that can unite people emotionally—our people and most of the people of the world. Now that we have reached the point of being able to blow ourselves up overnight, there is only one way we can avoid the explosion: we must get everybody on the same side. Those with religious faith hope that God will take care of the problem. But if that miracle doesn't happen, then *we* must find a way, through a new idea that has universal appeal, emotionally and economically.

We don't know whether universal capitalism can be made to work, but we do know that it is the only structural change in the American economic system that promises to solve so many basic problems. So we can't afford to pass up any reasonable chance of making it work. That's how high the stakes are for all Americans.

At Stake for Special Groups of Americans

We've discussed the broad mainstream appeal of universal capitalism. We've seen that such diverse people as black poverty leader Floyd McKissick and economic royalist John D. Rockefeller III have embraced Kelso's ideas. It's obvious that *every* American would benefit from a truly democratic capitalism that made our economic system operate more equitably and removed many of the sources of social unrest. But there are some groups of Americans who should take a special interest in universal capitalism.

Bankers, stockbrokers, and *financiers* have special reasons for looking into universal capitalism. Kelso's theories present great challenges and opportunities for our best financial minds, including the chance to develop new forms of capital ownership with the potential to save the free enterprise system. Universal capitalism will not mean the end of the stock market. In fact, it could mean a new beginning—a real capital market based on performance rather than speculation. But if Wall Street ignores universal capitalism, new forms of capital ownership (like TRASOP) will be fashioned by the government without participation of the private financial sector.

Economists, economics professors, and *students* also have special reasons for studying universal capitalism. This may seem obvious, but so far these groups have acted as if Kelso simply did not exist. We need college and graduate level courses on capital diffusion; we need seminars, books, articles, and debates. At this writing, the only known academic program relating to capital diffusion is the Ph.D. dissertation that Jacob Sheinin is starting under the supervision of Professor Lawrence Klein at the University of Pennsylvania's Wharton School. This paucity of academic activity is amazing when you consider that Congress has already made TRASOP a national policy of capital diffusion, to the tune of billions of dollars of tax funds. How long are our economists, professors, and students going to keep themselves out of the mainstream of this developing national economic policy?

Clergymen and *religious groups* have an important role to play in universal capitalism because its principles are in harmony with almost every organized religion. Many clergymen and religious organizations are in positions to initiate studies of universal capitalism at affiliated schools. What more worthwhile project could be assigned to the economics departments of such institutions, than an effort to help Congress in its search for an equitable means of broadening capital ownership?

Some religious groups have been working on capital diffusion for a long time. In his 1891 encyclical, *The Condition of Labor (Rerum Novarum)*, Pope Leo XIII proclaimed:

> The law, therefore, should favor ownership, and its policy should be to induce as many people as possible to become owners.
> Many excellent results will follow from this; and first of all, property will certainly become more equitably divided.

These principles were reaffirmed by succeeding Popes, and they were brought right down to the language of Kelso's Financed Capitalist Plan by the encyclical of Pope John XXIII, *Peace on Earth (Pacem in Terris)*, in 1961:

> It is not enough, then, to assert that man has from nature the right of privately possessing goods as his own, including those of productive character, unless at the same time, a continuing effort is made to spread the use of this right through all ranks of the citizenry.

In 1968, the U.S. National Catholic Rural Life Conference unanimously adopted a policy statement called "Ownership and Income." The conference is primarily concerned with farming areas, and the first two points of their policy statement dealt with the need for helping young couples and small farmers to purchase farm land and equipment. But their third recommendation went much further: it adopted Kelso's Financed Capitalist Plan, asserting that it should be made the economic policy of the United States, and should be promoted as a policy for developing countries and even for communist countries. Their report said:

> We make these recommendations in very general terms, presuming that those who are seriously concerned will fill in details after study and debate. Doubtless, other proposals will result from such a study.

As we have seen throughout this book, it is not safe to presume that those who are seriously concerned will fill in details. All of us are going to have to get together to *force* the study and debate which will develop detailed plans for spreading capital ownership. Clergymen and religious groups can help a lot.

The Campaign for Human Development of the United States Catholic Conference has continued the Catholic work in this field. In 1974 they published *Poverty In American Democracy: A Study Of Social Power,* which highlighted the maldistribution of wealth and the concentration of capital ownership in the United States. Although they are not a policy-making group, they have continued to provide funds for studies and special projects aimed at broadening ownership in the United States.

The time is ripe for other religious organizations to get into the act. Nothing could be more ecumenical than the spreading of capital ownership "through all ranks of the citizenry" as envisioned by Pope John XXIII.

Businessmen and *businesswomen* should become intensely interested in universal capitalism, unless they are satisfied with TRASOP as a national policy of capital diffusion, and unless they are willing to take the risk that American labor union officials will grab control of major corporations as their European counterparts are trying to do now.

Consumer activists have special reasons for becoming involved in universal capitalism. The ownership of capital by millions of individuals would give them economic power which is almost impossible to muster through the consumer movement. This economic power would be a safeguard against the excesses of big business, big labor, and big government—the three superpowers that consumer activists are constantly fighting.

Environmentalists have learned in the 1970s that concern about pollution is quickly put aside when we run into inflation, unemployment, and capital shortages. Universal capitalism holds the promise that we can develop the economic base necessary to make an effective fight against pollution. As Louis Kelso said:

> The real destroyer of our environment is poverty. We already have the technology to solve most pollution problems—if we could only afford to use it. . . . People already short of purchasing power cannot pay the cost environmental protection invariably must add to prices they cannot afford now.
>
> Only the truly affluent can afford to safeguard the environment. . . .

Old capitalists, those few Americans who now enjoy substantial income from capital holdings, have special stakes in universal capitalism. As Senator Russell Long pointed out, people who are already wealthy will be much more secure in their wealth when capitalism becomes a good deal for everyone. Otherwise, as tax expert Long puts it, "They're going to wind up at a minimum having their eyeballs taxed off them." There is also the prospect that they will be able to use the word "capitalist" without whispering. Receiving income from capital ownership can become acceptable behavior in a capitalistic society, if we can arrange to get enough people to participate.

Journalists should take a special interest in universal capitalism. In 1975–1976, there was extensive press coverage of Kelso, but very little of it dug any deeper than ESOP. There is a much bigger story in universal capitalism. In fact, I can't think of any subject that is more important for journalists to write about, since the average reader knows practically nothing about it.

Lawyers should get involved in universal capitalism because it represents the only real chance for America to achieve economic justice. Lawyers can help to create understanding of universal capitalism, particularly in business and labor circles. Lawyer Daniel Webster said:

> The freest government cannot long endure when the tendency of the law is to create a rapid accumulation of property in the hands of a few and to render the masses poor and dependent.

Lawyers were largely responsible for having made the corporation an efficient tool of capitalism in the past. But now the corporation is in danger of obsolescence because the corporate finance plumbing system (designed by lawyers) perpetuates the overconcentration of capital ownership and doesn't distribute purchasing power equitably enough. Prominent corporation lawyer Louis Kelso and a doughty band of followers, mostly lawyers, have been trying to change the plumbing system before Webster's prophecy is fulfilled. We need the expertise of a lot more lawyers in the search for the ideal plan of capital diffusion.

Foundations could not find a more appropriate project to spend their money on than the study of universal capitalism. For a measly $150,000, a foundation could sponsor econometric analysis of capital diffusion plans under the direction of Professor Lawrence Klein of Wharton Econometric Forecasting Associates. And there are many other useful studies that could be made for small amounts of money, considering that the possible return on the investment is nothing less than survival of capitalism, democracy, and freedom in the United States.

The Ideal Plan of Capital Diffusion

If you expected to find a blueprint for the ideal plan of capital diffusion in this book, you're going to be disappointed. It would be presumptuous of me to suggest that I have discovered or formulated such a plan when professional economists have hardly begun to study the feasibility of capital diffusion. The real purpose of this book is to explain the importance of finding such a plan, and to suggest some elements that should be considered for inclusion. But as I have said many times, the ideal plan must be the product of our best economic minds and resources.

Let's start out by agreeing that the ideal plan will have to be a lot better than our present system of alleviating poverty by redistributing income through the tax system. We know that redistribution has a lot of defects, but at least it has kept the rocks from coming through most of our windows. The main purpose of any plan of capital diffusion is to provide more equitable distribution of income. Therefore, it won't pay us to make a radical change like installation of a complicated system of capital diffusion if we're only going to wind up with an income distribution that's not much better than our present tax-transfer system. We have a lot of experience with tax-transfer redistribution, and for many years our best minds have been working on ways of improving it. But when we start playing around with capital ownership as a means of bringing about equitable income distribution, we're sailing into uncharted waters.

It's true that by diffusing capital ownership, we're trying to do more than merely improve income distribution. We're also enabling millions of nonwealthy people to participate in our economic system as capitalists, and we're creating new capital formation techniques. However, in the final analysis, the most important effect we hope to achieve by capital diffusion is equitable income distribution.

But requiring the ideal plan to improve income distribution greatly doesn't mean that the plan has to be perfect. Quite often, valuable innovations are put aside because their opponents are able to show that they are not perfect. They compare the new idea with a standard of nonexistent perfection, whereas the existing system is usually far from perfect and may even be completely ineffective.

What we're looking for is a plan that will give us a decent chance to improve income distribution substantially, without causing unacceptable side effects. If we can make capital diffusion do that, we already know that it will have at least two favorable consequences: the emotional impact of bringing millions of New Capitalists into the mainstream of our economic system, and the economic benefits of creating a new mechanism for capital formation.

I'm going to make some suggestions about how we should start constructing the ideal plan, but I hope that more definitive proposals will eventually come from our best economic thinkers.

I think we should use Kelso's Financed Capitalist Plan as a starting point for research and analysis. I suggest this use of the Financed Capitalist Plan (FCP) because it is the type of broad and equitable plan we're looking for: its beneficiaries can be anybody that Congress designates, and it is not tied to the employment relationship or any other fixed channel that forces us to favor any particular group. It plugs into what I consider to be Kelso's most important discovery: that productive capital will pay for itself over a period of years no matter who owns it (the wooden Indian theory). I don't know of any other plan that actually takes full advantage of this discovery. Some ESOPs do, but they can also be used in ways that are not related to the ability of productive capital to pay for itself.

The details of the FCP are laid out in Chapter 4 and illustrated in Figures 1–5. To summarize, new FCP legislation would require major corporations to pay for their capital outlays by issuing stock instead of by the present method (issuance of debt and use of retained earnings). This stock would be made available to the FCP, and would be issued to New Capitalists selected according to standards established in the new legislation. Commercial banks would lend the money to pay for the stock. These loans could be rediscounted by the Federal Reserve System and guaranteed by a new government corporation, the Capital Diffusion Insurance Corporation (CDIC). The loans would be nonrecouse and self-liquidating. The banks would hold the stock until dividends had repaid the loans in full with interest; then the stock would be turned over to the New Capitalists. Corporations would be required to pay out nearly all their earnings as dividends, and dividend payments would be tax deductible by corporations, in order to provide dividends high enough to repay the loans. With a return on investment of about 20 percent before taxes, the stock would pay for itself out of dividends in about seven years.

Clearly, the FCP avoids many of the problems of ESOP. It does not come between the worker and his union, since it is not based on the employment relationship. It does not create the opportunity for union leaders to take over control of corporations, since there is no employer stock channeled to workers or unions as such. It does not favor corporate officers or executives, or people who are fortunate enough to be working for our most successful corporations, as ESOP does. It can be tailored to favor anybody we want to help. It is not built on tax subsidies, tax benefits, or the loss of tax revenues, except to the extent that dividend payments by corporations are made tax deductible—a change that is probably coming anyway, even without the adoption of capital diffusion plans.

The FCP ties all of our people into the capital formation of our most successful corporations. In this way, the credit power of these corporations and their ability to make capital pay for itself can benefit the entire country. The FCP can also create the mass purchasing power needed to consume the huge productive potential of our capitalist economy.

An important reason for starting with the FCP is that it draws on a reservoir of capital that is not owned now, does not have to be taken away from anybody, and yet is large enough to provide substantial capital ownership for every American. We have often referred to the figure of $4.5 trillion as the estimated amount of new capital outlays by American corporations for the decade ending in 1984. While there is some dispute about this figure, there is no doubt that a figure approaching that size would be correct for some period of ten to twenty years immediately following 1976. We now have about 55 million families and about 70 million households in the United States. If we established a goal of average capital ownership of $100,000 per family, it appears that we could accomplish this through the FCP during the next fifteen to twenty years, depending upon the percentage of the corporate capital outlay that we brought into the plan each year. In other words, there will be enough water in the reservoir to fill every bathtub in the United States to a reasonable level of capital ownership, if we can just develop a plumbing system that will do the job.

There are some interesting statistics in Bob Hamrin's JEC report that support this conclusion. The latest figures available, for the year 1972, showed that the American people had total personal wealth of $4.3 trillion, and total net worth (after deducting debts and liabilities from personal wealth) of $3.5 trillion. This meant that if the wealth were evenly distributed, the average size family would have total wealth of about $73,000, and net worth of close to $60,000. Of course, only one American family in eight actually had a net worth of $60,000 in 1972.

The Hamrin report went on to estimate that personal wealth during the next ten years (1976–1985) would increase by $3 trillion to $4 trillion. This is very close to the amount of new capital ownership that would be available through the FCP during that decade, through the $4.5 trillion total corporate capital outlays. FCP gives us the opportunity to use that $4.5 trillion of unowned capital to diffuse its ownership so that it doesn't get concentrated like the present $3.5 trillion of net worth.

Hamrin's JEC report pointed out a number of problems of the FCP, as we saw in Chapter 11. He thought that starting the FCP with the entire $120 billion pool of new capital might cause a rapid increase in money supply, disruption of financial markets, and other side effects. But then he suggested that *gradual implementation*—starting out with about 15 percent of the $120 billion new capital reservoir—could eliminate these hazards. As his report said, "since the basic thrust of the plan has much merit, it should not be dismissed but simply scaled down."

Hamrin's recommendations constitute the first effort by

the United States to use the great potential of the FCP. Hamrin has made an excellent start all by himself. He can do a lot more if he gets help from our leading economists.

There are many other modifications that are worth looking into. Inasmuch as we now have forty-year mortgages for house buyers, for example, I think we should consider a longer payout period than the seven years that Kelso has suggested for the FCP. If we spread the payments for the New Capitalists' stock over ten or twenty years, there would be enough dividends left over each year so that the New Capitalists could immediately start to receive some income on their stock. We could apply half of the dividends to the principal and the loan interest, and pay the other half to the New Capitalists in cash right from the very first year. The effects of this modification could be determined by econometric analysis.

We should also decide whether we actually need the CDIC to guarantee the bank loans or whether direct government financing should be used, either by having the federal government make the loans directly to the New Capitalists, or by having the government directly guarantee repayment of the loans. Perhaps there are good reasons to create the CDIC, but it is another layer of bureaucracy, which should be avoided if possible. The credit of the United States government would be behind the CDIC anyway, even though the CDIC is envisioned as a self-sustaining unit that would pay its own expenses and make good its own guarantees through loan insurance fees charged to the participating banks. Econometric analysis should be able to tell us whether it would be more efficient for the government to make or guarantee these loans directly, rather than using the structure suggested by Kelso: the commercial banks, the Federal Reserve System, and the CDIC.

If you think it far-fetched or revolutionary to provide federal government loan guarantees, consider this provision of the Federal Aviation Act:

> It is hereby declared to be the policy of Congress, in the interest of the commerce of the United States, the postal service, and the national defense to promote the development of local, feeder and short-haul air transportation. In furtherance of this policy it is deemed necessary and desirable that provision be made to assist certain air car-

riers engaged in such air transportation by providing government guarantees of loans to enable them to purchase aircraft suitable for such transportation on reasonable terms.

This is one of many federal loan guarantee programs, and it certainly is worthwhile to help local airlines acquire suitable airplanes. But is that nearly as important as enabling the New Capitalists to participate in our economic system?

Another suggestion: in setting up the FCP, we should not automatically follow the present system of corporate finance. I don't think we should be bound forever by the present forms of stock and other securities, many of which trace back to seventeenth-century corporations like Hudson's Bay Company and the East India Company. The early English corporations were formed to finance risky overseas expeditions. Only those who shared the financial risks could become owners. The man we know as Clive of India was really Clive of the East India Company. In 1757 he led his corporation's armed expedition of 3,200 men against an army of 50,000 natives at Plassey and won India for the East India Company. Later, control of India was taken over by the British government.

The role of corporations has changed somewhat, but the rights of ownership in our 1976 corporations are about the same as those in the East India Company. The purpose of the FCP is to create a new method of participation in capital ownership for people who would never become owners under our present corporate finance system. The New Capitalists are not buying shares with their own money or taking the entrepreneurial risks of corporate ventures. They are being brought into capital ownership to give them more income and to allow them to participate in capitalism by owning capital. But there is no reason why their participation must be in the form of common stock, preferred stock, bonds, or debentures, all of which were designed for purposes different from those involved in the FCP.

I think we should consider creating a new form of capital ownership. We could call it the *Capital Ownership Certificate,* and it would be a special class of securities for use only in the FCP. Its main function would be to give the New Capitalists ownership of the right to receive the return earned on capital investment. As far as I'm concerned, the Capital Ownership

Certificate need not have voting power. I don't think that change of voting control is a primary objective of capital diffusion. It doesn't necessarily follow that the people who need more income are the ones who should have the votes to select and control corporate management. I think we should concentrate on one revolution at a time, and capital diffusion is revolutionary enough without adding to it the burden of proving the case for a revolution in voting control of corporations.

Remember that the New Capitalists are not workers receiving employer stock as compensation for services. I don't think that the New Capitalists have the right to demand voting power simply because they are being allowed to participate in capital ownership through long-term financing arranged by the government. And I think that giving them nonvoting securities would lessen corporate opposition to the FCP. If the New Capitalists need representation on corporate boards of directors to protect their interests, this can be accomplished by giving their shares limited voting power, such as the right to elect one or two directors of each corporation.

If nonvoting securities were used, the return on the New Capitalists' investment would not have to take the form of a dividend, but could be paid in a way that would give the corporations a tax deduction. For example, it could be put in the same category as interest payments on debentures or bonds, which are tax deductible now. Or there could be special tax provisions for the Capital Ownership Certificate, which would not have any effect on the tax deductibility of dividend payments on the ordinary shares of stock issued by corporations. This would make it easier to put through the tax legislation needed for the FCP.

Use of a Capital Ownership Certificate would eliminate another obstacle to the FCP: the prospect that earnings per share might be reduced because of the issuance of a larger number of common shares than corporations normally wish to have outstanding.

I don't claim that nonvoting securities are indispensable to the FCP. I merely suggest that there is no reason for us to be bound by the ancient forms of stock certificates and corporate organizations. While many people will insist that capital diffusion must be accompanied by diffusion of voting power, I don't know of any evidence that our corporations would be better run if voting control were in the hands of either workers or New Capitalists. If we want to make sure that we're giving the New Capitalists something valuable—securities that will yield them about 20 percent annual return on invested capital—I don't think we should start out by tinkering around with the existing corporate management which makes such a return possible.

This may seem contrary to the concept of democratic capitalism, but let's be more precise in defining "democratic." As we use it here, we're talking about democratic *ownership* of capital. We haven't reached the point of allowing the whole nation to vote in the election of directors of every corporation. That's another revolution, and we don't want to add it to the revolution we'll need to bring about universal capitalism. Also, by starting with nonvoting securities, we're protecting against a takeover of corporate power by unforeseen forces, such as a group trying to exploit the New Capitalists' shares.

If we didn't use common stock, then we'd have to establish separate markets for the nonvoting Capital Ownership Certificates. This wouldn't be any problem, since our stockbrokers are always looking for new products and are ingenious enough to set up markets for new securities almost overnight. If we can trade in pork bellies, potato futures, and stock options, we can certainly have adequate trading markets for the billions of dollars worth of Capital Ownership Certificates held by the New Capitalists.

Synthesis with Pensions, Social Security, and Other Plans

I think it would be a miracle if the FCP proved to be the ideal plan all by itself. Remember that it was put together hastily by Kelso and Adler in response to the suggestions of early readers of their first manuscript that they propose some practical plan rather than just a bare theory. Not only has it never been tried out, it hasn't even been discussed extensively. Kelso himself hasn't talked about it since he started concentrating on ESOP.

We ought to think of the ideal plan as a *synthesis* of several forms of ownership, income, and security. For example, the whole area of pensions is related to capital ownership, even though the rights held by workers in pension plans do not actually make them owners of corporate stock. But as Drucker pointed out in *The Unseen Revolution,* pension funds now own over 25 percent of all the outstanding stock of publicly held American corporations, and will own more than 50 percent by 1985. As we have seen, this does not lead us to universal capitalism because pension funds are designed to produce cash retirement income in most cases, and are not a source of income during the years before retirement. But there is an obvious relationship between pension funds and the FCP.

Fortunately, the Tax Reform Act of 1976 requires the Joint Pension Task Force to make a study of stock ownership plans, and this could be the basis for some valuable research on the relationship between pensions and capital diffusion schemes. This should not be limited to the private pension plans of corporations. It should include study of government pensions and the two forms of tax-sheltered retirement plans for individuals: the Individual Retirement Account which allows annual contributions up to $1,500, and the Keogh Plan which allows annual contributions up to $7,500 by self-employed people.

Another potential subject of synthesis is the Social Security system. This is one of the really sick areas of our economy, and it is related at least indirectly to capital ownership and income distribution. In *The Unseen Revolution,* Drucker suggests synthesis of Social Security and the pension funds. It would probably make sense to consider all existing government benefit programs when we start drafting the ideal plan of capital diffusion.

Then there are the existing capital ownership schemes based on employment, such as profit-sharing plans, ESOPs, TRASOPS, and the European Wage Earner Investment Funds (WEIFs). Although I do not believe that the employment relationship is the ideal channel for broad diffusion of capital, there is a wealth of operating experience with these schemes which must be taken into account. Since there are many successful

profit-sharing plans and some successful ESOPs already established, we should try to harness whatever momentum these
plans can add to the drive toward universal capitalism. The
employment-based schemes should be synthesized with the
broader ideal plan to avoid any overlap and to retain incentives
for increased productivity.

Other broad schemes have been proposed, such as the
Capital Formation Plan discussed in the Hamrin report, and
the BSOP (Broadened Stock Ownership Plan) suggested by the
Ford administration in 1976. Several broad plans were suggested by the Sabre Foundation in its 1972 report, *Expanded
Ownership*. Some excellent research went into that report, but
nothing had ever been done with it until Bob Hamrin included
the Capital Formation Plan in his 1976 staff study of the ESOP
hearings. All of these proposals should be reviewed for possible
integration into the ideal plan.

Another related subject is taxation. The Tax Reform Act
of 1976 reminded us of how cumbersome our tax system is and
added momentum to the push for extensive tax reform. There
are bound to be more changes in personal and corporate income
taxes, and the ideal plan of capital diffusion will have to be
synthesized with whatever changes are made in the tax system.
For example, the 95th Congress is scheduled to consider eliminating double taxation of corporate dividends—a key provision
of the FCP. Much of our present corporate finance system is
based upon adaptation to the tax laws, and capital diffusion
schemes must be designed to fit into our overall tax structure.

Finally, the insurance industry should try to synthesize
capital diffusion schemes with present and future forms of insurance. Kelso has tried on his own to bring commercial insurance
companies into the long-term financing of capital ownership. So
far he hasn't had any luck, but perhaps our insurance companies can figure out their own way to participate in capital
diffusion, once they learn that it has become a national economic policy. Their vast research capabilities should be used to
help us to find the ideal plan.

I don't know exactly what roles these synthesizing forces
would play, but I think that it would be silly to launch a major
structural change like capital diffusion without studying its relationship to pensions, profit-sharing plans, ESOPs, TRASOPs,

WEIFs, taxation, insurance, and government benefit payments. All of these elements are growing rapidly in different directions. They are all related, but for the most part they are not integrated.

Perhaps the attempt to synthesize all these elements would slow down the development of the ideal plan. But I don't think it makes any sense to try to develop such a plan in a vacuum. It has to be enacted by Congress, which has dozens of committees dealing with the other elements—and Congressional committee chairmen are not likely to let such a sweeping change slip by them without sticking an oar in. The Joint Economic Committee has a mandate broad enough to study all of the elements which need to be synthesized into the final plan, but it can't finish the job because it isn't a bill-writing committee.

This big job of synthesis will have to overcome the resistance of Congress to broad macroeconomic solutions. Congressmen are naturally skeptical about making big changes, since they often get burned when they try to do too much in one bill. Probably that's why Russell Long sticks to a simpler tool like TRASOP. It doesn't make any big structural changes, and it may achieve part of Long's immediate objective: ownership of the next $3 trillion of our net worth by 30 percent of Americans instead of the 15 percent who own our present $3 trillion net worth. But I think that we need to do much better than TRASOP.

In the 95th Congress, Bob Hamrin of the Joint Economic Committee is taking on the job of finding the ideal plan almost alone. He needs help from all of us. This job is too important and too complicated to be left to anything short of our best national effort.

What we're really talking about is construction of a theory and a working model of American capitalism—something which has never been undertaken. We've accepted "capitalism" as an epithet from the lips of Marx, and we've tried to make it work defensively, without ever designing a system of capitalism that responds to the demands of American democracy.

Until somebody comes up with a better idea, I think that we should go all out to make Kelso's Financed Capitalist Plan the starting point for the ideal plan; that we should crank in Bob Hamrin's idea of gradual implementation; and that we should get this model working as soon as possible, so that it can start the job of saving American capitalism by making it democratic and universal.

Who Will the New Capitalists Be?

We come back to the question left unanswered in Chapter 4. Assuming that we can develop an ideal plan of capital diffusion, how do we decide who gets new capital ownership each year, and how much they get, annually and during their lifetimes?

I'm assuming that the ideal plan will not be based on the employment relationship. If wages were the basis, as with ESOP, pensions, and profit sharing, then we wouldn't have this problem: the amount of annual benefits would be calculated automatically as a percentage of the payroll. But if we try to make the ideal plan universal, we have to start out with a blank slate of beneficiaries.

There are arbitrary ways of picking the New Capitalists. For example, the National Dividend Plan, formulated by Florida industrialist John H. Perry Jr. and publicized through his generous financial support, takes a simple approach. It would benefit all registered voters in the United States equally, whether they were millionaires or on welfare. It would take the present federal corporate income tax payments of about $50 billion per year and distribute them equally to all of our 100 million registered voters, giving each voter about $500 per year. The voters would pay no taxes on this income. Perry would also impose a moratorium on new federal spending programs so that the revenue from the corporate income tax wouldn't be needed. He would fix a ceiling of 50 percent on corporate income taxes to avoid pressure from voters to jack up the corporate tax in order to increase their annual payments; and he would end federal income taxes on dividends received by investors.

Perry feels that the National Dividend Plan would make millions of voters probusiness, since they would be benefitting directly from corporate profits. Of course, at least $50 billion is already being handed out to Americans through government benefit programs, and it is distributed more equitably than a flat $500 to each voter. But government transfer payments do not necessarily make their recipients feel they are participating in the success of American business.

Perry thinks of his plan as a national profit-sharing scheme, which will give all Americans a stake in the success of American business and a share of the fruits of capitalism. At first glance, the National Dividend Plan doesn't look like it can accomplish very much. But it has attracted some support, mainly from frightened capitalists. Since we have so few ideas on how to broaden the benefits of capitalism, we can't afford to dismiss any plan that has this objective.

Not having come up with the ideal plan yet, I'm not in a position to lay down a list of its beneficiaries. This is a subject of even broader significance than the form of the plan. It is as broad as the question of what kind of society we want, and I'm not about to try answering that one in a few paragraphs.

I do have a few suggestions. As we saw in Figure 5, we can provide $100,000 in new capital ownership to 45 million of our 55 million families during the next ten to twenty years if we use most of our corporate capital outlays as the reservoir for the FCP. This could provide each of 45 million families with capitalist income of $20,000 a year before any family member brings home a paycheck. But we must preserve the work incentive. If $20,000 annual income puts families far above the poverty level in the 1980s and 1990s, then I'd be in favor of limiting this income or finding some other way to make it attractive for members of these families to work as long as they are able to.

I'd also favor special priorities for groups like servicemen, policemen, firemen, nurses, and others who perform dangerous or demanding public services at low pay. Perhaps politicians should be included. The idea is to make participation in capitalism more attractive to public servants than graft or featherbedding or early retirement under onerous tax-supported pension plans.

Perhaps we could allow each citizen to set a goal of capital ownership up to a limit like $100,000. The ideal plan could set up machinery to enable each citizen to acquire $100,000 in capital ownership, preferably on nonrecourse self-liquidating credit, as in Kelso's FCP. Maybe each citizen should be required to *earn* his annual new capital ownership, within the limits of his abilities. For the least fortunate, the requirement might be something as basic as avoiding criminal behavior. For those starting out in better circumstances, the requirements could be higher. The idea is to provide incentives for the kind of economic performance and social behavior that our nation needs.

Working out a system of property ownership for people who have no savings, while preserving the work incentive, is a tricky problem. But it's well worth the effort, considering the stakes. The New Capitalists could be offered greater stock ownership if they work, so that it would be worthwhile for them to stay off the welfare rolls. There are also important advantages in having low-income families own property. They become part of the mainstream community and thus have more to lose than to gain from violence. If they are convicted of crimes, they can be fined and they can be sued by their victims and thus lose their property. These remedies exist today but are rarely used, since most criminals do not have publicly recorded assets which can be reached by courts levying fines or by victims seeking damages. And the present system is rapidly pushing millions of low-income Americans into the position where they feel that they have little to lose by attacking private property and breaking the law.

The ideal plan would have to include those who have the lowest incomes and the least capital ownership now. One of its basic objectives is to increase purchasing power, so that we can begin to consume our great productive capacity. The lower the present income of the New Capitalists, the more capitalist income they will spend, and thereby strengthen our economy by increasing gross national product. The 1972 Ferre plan, which passed one house of the Puerto Rican legislature, was open to all residents of Puerto Rico who were *earning* between $800 and $7,800 per year. It included the lowest-income workers, but it left out the jobless. Joe Novak wanted to include nonworkers from the start, and Kelso announced that the plan would be broadened to include them later. But Governor Ferre thought these ideas too ambitious, and he chose to leave the problems of the unemployed to direct government assistance.

Ferre thought that the unemployed might not be able to handle capital ownership without some education. To discourage New Capitalists from selling their stock, Ferre's plan made sellers ineligible to get any more stock for three years after each sale. His ideas are worth considering. The final decision on inclusion of the unemployed depends on synthesis of the ideal plan with other government benefit programs.

We don't have much more to guide us than our sense of the kind of nation we want. Senator Hubert Humphrey made a stab at defining the New Capitalists in his 1976 floor speech opposing TRASOP and supporting a broader plan:

> . . . The new stockholders could, if it was desired, consist entirely of low- and middle-income Americans, who currently own a very small share of this country's outstanding stock.

In Kelso's first book, he suggested that the FCP start out with workers who had shown themselves best qualified to be Financed Capitalists; but in his latest book (1967), he describes the New Capitalists simply as low-income families. Nobody wants to get any more definite than that. The question is too big and complicated. There are lots of tough decisions for Congress to make in defining the New Capitalists, but they're not nearly as tough as trying to make mixed capitalism work in a democracy whose people have high expectations and in a world in which two-thirds of mankind lives on an income of less than 30 cents a day.

Congress could establish some priorities, and then have its Joint Economic Committee or other committees review them regularly. The priorities could be changed before any great damage was done, since capital diffusion has to be a long-term plan. But I suggest that Congress hang on to capital diffusion and not delegate selection of the New Capitalists to an administrative agency. It's too important for that. It should remain under direct control of our most sensitive instrument of democracy.

Apologists for capitalism like to claim that the institution of private property is the economic basis for democracy. But Kelso and Adler remind us that in the days of primitive capitalism, the small group of capitalists who owned most of the private property were vigorously opposed to letting nonpropertied workers vote. It is *diffused* ownership, not merely private ownership, that creates the economic equivalent of political democracy.

Political power is pretty well diffused in America now, but we haven't gotten around to diffusing economic power. As the noncapitalist majority becomes conscious of its power to redesign America's economic system through legislation, it becomes less likely that they will continue to vote for a system which excludes them from capital ownership. They've got the votes to bring in a government that would drop capitalism, as Russell Long told us. When a program of socialism or communism comes along that seems to appeal to their self-interest, some day they'll vote it in, even if it means concentration of economic and political power in the state and the end of democracy.

If we're going to keep democracy, we must diffuse economic power. For this we need the New Capitalists, and Congress will have to select them, just as an earlier Congress selected the beneficiaries of the Homestead Act when land was the principal form of productive capital.

UNIVERSAL CAPITALISM: WHAT'S IN IT FOR OTHER NATIONS?

I want people to be happy and live better, so what else can I be but a communist?
René Andrieu, editor of *L'humanité,* Paris, May 31, 1976

I cannot imagine anybody in India much believes in socialism anymore. They just can't think of anything else.
Ambassador Daniel Patrick Moynihan, *Nation's Business,* February 1976

It is time for America to move and to speak, not with boasting and belligerence, but with a quiet strength, to depend in world affairs not merely on the size of an arsenal but on the nobility of ideas.
Jimmy Carter, acceptance speech, Democratic National Convention, July 15, 1976

We submit that universal capitalism is the rationale of a free industrial society, and that in understanding, applying and teaching that rationale the United States can again become a leader that truly leads by inspiring, as it once did, the minds and the hearts of men.
Louis O. Kelso and Patricia Hetter, *Two-Factor Theory: The Economics of Reality*

A Plan for All Nations

If Kelso's Financed Capitalist Plan (FCP) can be made to work in the United States, there seems to be no reason why it would not work in other industrial nations. The FCP is based on the self-liquidating nature of productive capital when used by major successful businesses (see Figure 1), and the existence of a significant reservoir of unowned capital in the form of annual capital outlays of business (Figure 3). As we saw, the United States is at the very bottom of the major industrial nations in terms of the percentage of its gross national product devoted to capital investment—only 13 percent, compared with Britain's 18 percent, Italy's 20 percent, France's 24 percent, West Germany's 25 percent, and Japan's 35 percent.

The chances of making the FCP work should be about the same in all industrial nations, whether they are classified as communist, socialist, capitalist, or any blend thereof. They all use capital in production, whether the capital is owned by the state or by private citizens. The form of government is immaterial. In fact, since communist governments already restrict current consumption in order to increase capital formation, they should have an easier job of making the FCP work than capitalist or socialist democracies. Citizens of communist nations are accustomed to lower consumption and are aware of the need for emphasis on capital investment. They should be even more receptive to these restrictions if they become direct beneficiaries through individual capital ownership.

All industrial nations should take a close look at America's efforts to diffuse capital ownership. They should monitor the studies of the Joint Economic Committee, the Pension Task Force, and any other government efforts to broaden capital ownership. And they should put their own economists to work on a formula for making the self-liquidating nature of productive capital bring universal capitalism to their nations. Many industrial nations might be able to do this quicker than the United States, for their economies are easier to control and their legislative processes are faster than are those of the United States.

It seems clear enough that if the FCP works in the United States, it should work in other industrial nations. What is not clear is whether it would also work in developing nations. Louis Kelso says it would. Let's take a look at his arguments.

Developing Nations

The United Nations classifies most of the world's states, containing most of the world's population, as developing nations. They are also called nonindustrialized, underdeveloped, third world, or just plain poor. What they are trying to develop is a higher standard of living, and almost invariably they see industrialization as the quickest way to do it.

As we saw in Chapter 6, Kelso and Hetter laid out a blueprint for industrialization of developing nations in their prizewinning 1964 article, "Uprooting World Poverty." They said that the Financed Capitalist Plan could be adapted for use in developing nations, and that the basic principle of productive capital paying for itself regardless of ownership (Kelso's wooden Indian theory) would enable these nations to build capital ownership into their masses of poor people while the process of industrialization was going on.

Here we have to back up a minute and recall that in Figure 1 we specified that "productive capital *used by our major successful corporations* will pay for itself out of its own earnings no matter who owns it." This doesn't mean that all productive capital will pay for itself. The same factory and equipment used by two different corporations may produce profits for one and bankruptcy for the other. So we can't automatically transplant the FCP to a developing nation and assume that all capital items will pay for themselves there.

What we have to do, it seems, is to keep a major successful corporation in the picture as the user of the capital items. This is often the pattern anyway: a major multinational corporation puts capital items to work in a developing nation, perhaps in cooperation with the local government or local businessmen. If the managers of the multinational corporation apply the same feasibility tests to the project as they would use for a similar investment in their home country, then the chances that the capital items will pay for themselves out of earnings will be pretty good. But there are so many basic differences involved in operating abroad, particularly in developing nations, that the foreign projects must still be considered more risky. On the other hand, lower costs of raw materials and labor in developing nations may result in much higher profits and much quicker repayment of capital investments. That has always been one of the big attractions for the multinationals.

Despite the compelling arguments in "Uprooting World Poverty," I don't think we can assume that the FCP will work as well in developing nations as in industrial countries. But there is an offsetting advantage: the FCP could be installed in developing nations with much less difficulty and risk. It would be much easier to experiment with the FCP in developing nations, and even moderate success might be very beneficial to the local economy.

There may be a role for governments of industrial countries in Financed Capitalist Plans of developing nations. The credit resources of developing nations might not be strong enough to establish a Capital Diffusion Insurance Corporation capable of guaranteeing repayment of New Capitalist loans. In such cases, the American CDIC could be used to insure the loans, or the World Bank could be brought into the plan, as suggested by Kelso and Hetter in "Uprooting World Poverty."

Industrial countries are deeply involved now in helping developing nations to industrialize. But these efforts involve only three forms of financing: foreign capital in the form of loans or equity investments, foreign-aid handouts, and capital investment by a few wealthy local residents or businesses. In all three cases, there is little or no new capital ownership among residents of developing nations, who were poor before this financing and stay poor afterwards. Therefore, none of these three types of financing, not even the free foreign-aid handouts, are appreciated by the great majority of local residents. Often, in fact, they are so resented that eventually they are expropriated. The few jobs created by these efforts usually do not raise the purchasing power of developing nations very much. Only diffusion of capital ownership combined with industrialization would do that, according to Kelso.

For the United States and other industrial countries, there would be great benefits in successful use of the FCP in developing nations. The FCP would be a new source of funds for foreign operations. The increased purchasing power of the developing nations would create new markets for the industrial countries. And the industrialization of developing nations would make them good paying customers for services like engineering, science, and management.

Without the FCP or any other form of capital diffusion, it's easy to see why most developing nations are attracted to socialism or communism, and why democracy is becoming an endangered species among them. As Kelso and Hetter said in "Uprooting World Poverty":

> The totalitarian approach, after all, has its advantages. By fusing ownership of land and other capital with political power, it creates a central authority strong enough to force raw materials, land, and manpower into the priorities of industrialization. Totalitarian power can enforce austerity on the affluent few and hinder them from exporting their money; it provides a deceptive ideology around which energies can mobilize, and it may convince a desperate nation that it is able to bring about industrialization faster than could insufficient or irresponsible private savings.
>
> But these short-term advantages are bought at the price of freedom; the totalitarian approach forecloses any hope of democratic institutions.

Western capitalism offers nothing more attractive to residents of developing nations. We demand that they have accumulated past savings before they are allowed to own any capital; so, having none, they are willing to take their chances with state ownership of capital. Only by offering them a piece of the action can we overcome their natural tendency to accept socialism or communism.

Daniel Patrick Moynihan, former U.S. ambassador to India and then to the United Nations, and now senator from New York, has been on the firing line for the Western democracies in the ideological warfare over the developing nations. He summarized the situation in February 1976 for *Nation's Business:*

> It is most disappointing to me that so many of the new nations which were established as democracies after the

second world war, during the decolonization process, have now changed their system to state socialism. Small elites run them, and they aren't sharing societies. They aren't even socialist. The power of the state has been merged with business, and you have the greatest concentration of power that's possible.

Look across the avenue there at the United Nations. There are 144 member countries, and only about two dozen could be described as democracies. . . .

State socialism—or state capitalism, they come to the same thing—has proved a convenient excuse for concentrating power in the hands of those at the head of the government.

Kelso's efforts to bring universal capitalism to developing countries have not been confined to his writing. He and Norman Kurland and Joe Recinos have spent years trying to convince governments of developing nations and managers of American multinational corporations to try out Kelso's theories. As of this writing, however, not one had either tried them or organized any scientific study of them.

Kelso has concentrated his efforts in Latin America, which is the most logical place to export a new brand of American capitalism. Certainly the old brand has worn out its welcome. I learned this firsthand in 1946 when I led a group of American ex-Air Force pilots on a business mission: attempting to establish an aerial crop-dusting business in Cuba. We thought we would be welcomed as heroes who had come to eradicate the bugs that were eating up Cuban crops before they could get to market. Instead, Cuban soldiers had to guard our $500 military surplus biplanes against attacks by agricultural workers who were being put out of jobs by our highly advanced technology. During most of our stay, we were surrounded by the outstretched palms of agents seeking bribes for various officials who had the power to let us operate profitably or not. I am proud to say that we wrote one of the brightest chapters in the history of American multinational business operations: we didn't pay one penny in bribes. The fact that we had no money is irrelevant. Incidentally, we did practically no business, and in a few weeks we were happy to fly our old biplanes back to Florida. After Castro came into power, the work that we had started was taken over by Russian Antonov-22 biplanes flown by Russian Aeroflot pilots.

Latin America is a danger zone for American security, as the 1962 Cuban missile crisis demonstrated. By 1976, the Cuban brand of communism was threatening to spread to other Caribbean nations such as Guyana and Jamaica. Most of South America was controlled by military dictatorships, as Cuba had been when Fidel Castro brought in communism.

But there were also great opportunities in Latin America. By 1976, it was costing the Russians $2 million a day to keep communism going in Cuba, and they were not about to pick up the tab for other candidates such as Chile and Peru. Latin American nations anxious to industrialize (including left-wing Peru) were forced to turn to hated Western industrial nations for funds. On August 9, 1976, *Business Week* published a special report, "Latin America Opens the Door to Foreign Investment Again." Once again American capitalism had a chance to build a constituency in Latin America. But can it lead to anything better than expropriation, if the worn-out system of over-concentrated capital ownership is used again?

Writing from Havana in December 1976, Carl Rowan ended his syndicated column with an unanswered question: "What alternative other than the Cuban solution is the U.S. offering Latin Americans who are hungry and sick and miserable and feeling exploited and abused?"

All over the world, the developing nations are starting to take up the cry of redistribution. They want the so-called wealthy industrial nations to redistribute some of their wealth to the poorer nations. During 1976 there were many international conferences on this problem, but none of them considered what may well be the most promising solution: working out a system whereby the industrial nations can help the developing nations to improve living standards and increase purchasing power through universal capitalism.

Edward Korry served as U.S. ambassador to Chile from 1967 to 1971, and was on hand when the Marxist Allende regime took over. He told me that Eduardo Frei, the president who preceded Allende, was a dedicated liberal democrat who tried desperately to keep Chile from turning toward dictatorship, whether Marxist or military style. In 1968, Frei drew up a plan that would have given all Chilean workers ownership in leading Chilean corporations, in lieu of inflationary wage raises. The fate of the Frei plan is very revealing. As Ed Korry tells it,

> Frei's plan was a threat to the Marxist–Leninist leaders, who saw that it would deprive them of their most important talking point: the exploitation of the working class. So they promptly killed the plan by threatening a sabotage campaign of massive strikes for higher cash wages.

Korry is one of the American diplomats most experienced in dealing with Communist officials, from Russia to Eastern Europe to Latin America. He believes that a free-market economy is the surest way to preserve democracy:

> Giving the people a piece of the action is the best way to make sure that the economic system will work for *them,* and not just for the benefit of avaricious owners or despotic governments. It's the best way to pull the rug out from under totalitarians, whether they're Marxist–Leninists or military fascists.

Kelso Abroad

Since Kelso has been preoccupied with efforts to get universal capitalism under way in the United States, he hasn't had much chance to start movements in other nations. He and Joe Recinos keep trying to generate interest in Latin America, and he has disciples at work in Canada and Great Britain. In 1975, Kelso and Patricia Hetter introduced universal capitalism to Australia in a fortnight of intensive meetings, lectures, and interviews arranged by the Company Directors Association of Australia. The Liberal government of Prime Minister Malcolm Fraser followed up in 1976 by undertaking a study of Kelso's proposals.

While there is considerable interest in Kelso's writings in other nations, there is no movement comparable to the legislation that Russell Long has sponsored in the United States. But there is some history in Canada, Great Britain, and other nations which is worthy of study by those interested in universal capitalism.

Canada

The first Kelsonian in Canada was James O'Dell, the Alberta farmer who since 1959 has devoted his winters to publishing pamphlets about universal capitalism. In 1964 Frank Capon, then a vice-president of Du Pont of Canada, read Kelso and Adler's *The Capitalist Manifesto,* and became a convert. It was through Frank Capon that Winnett Boyd became interested in the work of Kelso.

Winn Boyd is truly a renaissance man. Trained as an engineer, he designed Canada's first two jet engines. The second, called the Avro Orenda, was rated among the world's most powerful and reliable jets. During the 1960s, he was chief designer of the NRU nuclear reactor at Chalk River, Ontario—the most powerful research reactor in the world. Since 1960 he has been president of Arthur D. Little of Canada, Ltd., Canadian subsidiary of the international management consultant firm. He has devoted himself to world peace and the betterment of mankind, as Canada's delegate to two of the Pugwash Conferences on Science and World Affairs and as one of the leaders of the Canadian Association for the Club of Rome.

Winn Boyd was a member of the Liberal party until Pierre Trudeau became its leader. Then, disillusioned with Trudeau's policies, which he considered socialistic, Boyd shifted to the Progressive Conservative party. After becoming a Kelso disciple himself, Boyd has been trying to persuade the Progressive Conservative party to offer universal capitalism as its platform against the "redistributive welfare state" offered by the Liberal Party. In 1972, he ran for Parliament in York-Scarborough, a district that had been won by the Liberals in the preceding election by 22,000 votes. Boyd campaigned vigorously on the platform of universal capitalism and lost out by only 1,847 votes.

In 1975, Boyd wrote a 105-page book with Kenneth Mc-Donald, *The National Dilemma and the Way Out*. It describes Boyd's version of universal capitalism in very clear language, and is illustrated by some delightfully homey cartoons. It quickly sold out two printings and has been read by thousands of Canadians. After acknowledging his debt to Kelso, Boyd lays out a practical plan for bringing universal capitalism to Canada. Here's how the Boyd plan would work:

- All Canadians between twenty-one and sixty-five years of age would be eligible to buy stock on nonrecourse government-insured credit, as in the Financed Capitalist Plan.
- A Canadian government corporation called the Investment Diffusion Corporation (IDC) would be formed. In the alternative, it could be a privately owned company.
- The IDC would review all publicly held Canadian companies and receive applications from those wishing to participate in the Boyd plan by issuing new common stock. The IDC would approve or disapprove the applications of Canadian companies to participate in the program based on their financial strength and the feasibility of their plans for the use of new capital.
- The IDC would receive applications from eligible Canadians to purchase shares up to the maximum allowable, which would change from year to year. These new stockholders would be able to choose shares of any participating companies, subject to availability. Employees would be given first preference to buy stock of the corporations they work for.
- IDC would arrange for the financing of stock purchases by Canadian banks. IDC would insure each loan by guaranteeing its repayment to the lending bank.
- IDC would then purchase the stock directly from the companies concerned and hold the certificates as collateral until the IDC purchase fee, the loan principal, the interest, and the annual loan insurance premium were repaid from dividends. When the loan was fully repaid, IDC would deliver the stock certificate to the purchaser, who would then own it outright.
- The interest rate would be in line with the Bank of Canada lending rate. Boyd estimates the annual loan insurance

rate at about 1/2 percent of the loan principal, as in Kelso's Financed Capitalist Plan.

Boyd's book describes his plan in considerable detail. He suggests that IDC could establish sales offices throughout Canada, making it as easy to acquire stock as it is to buy an airline ticket. He thinks the system should be computerized, so that IDC could match up the availability of stock and credit with the desires of each participating stockholder. But because the shares would have to be allocated on a first come, first served basis, with employees getting the first crack at their employers' stock, Boyd's plan would probably run into some serious priority problems. I think that in practice he would come around to using the mutual fund format, so that each participating stockholder would get the same opportunity to acquire shares in the winning corporations.

Boyd estimates that it would take about nine years for stock to be paid for and delivered to the participants. Like Kelso's FCP, the Boyd plan includes provisions for eliminating corporate income taxes and for payout of all earnings as dividends. Boyd believes that his plan would increase Canada's growth rate, drastically reduce welfare payments, and bring the majority of Canadians much larger capital ownership and dividend income than they have now.

So Winn Boyd, the practical engineer–businessman–management consultant–politician, chose the broad Financed Capitalist Plan instead of the ESOP format. Why did he jump over the employment relationship and start right off with a more radical plan which would be open to everyone of working age in Canada? Because Canadian tax laws are not hospitable to ESOP, and because Boyd thinks that the necessary legislation will be much easier to get through if the plan benefits all Canadians, not just those who happen to be working for successful corporations.

In 1976, Boyd became a candidate for the leadership of the Progressive Conservative party, running on a platform of universal capitalism. He didn't win, but he feels that the campaign was worth the trouble because he forced the other candidates to give serious consideration to capital diffusion. In fact, seven of

the twelve accredited candidates supported the broadening of
capital ownership. The new PCP leader, Joseph C. Clark of
Alberta, was not one of those who supported capital diffusion,
but he did promise to study it carefully. He is not likely to
forget this promise, since two of the strongest supporters of
Boyd's plan are members of Clark's policy advisory committee.

Boyd was also cheered by the action taken in 1976 by his
Liberal party opponents who control the government. The
Ministry of Industry, Trade, and Commerce set up a team to
study the broadening of capital ownership. Boyd met with the
team in 1976 and gave them his full presentation. You can bet
that he will keep the Canadian team posted on the progress of
the American Joint Economic Committee in the 95th Congress.

Winn Boyd has been trying to start the Canadian capitalist
revolution for more than ten years now. As of 1976 he seemed
to have made little real progress. But Boyd, at age sixty, thinks
he'll see some version of his plan adopted in Canada during his
lifetime. Here's the way he looks at it:

> It was just ten years ago [1966] that Louis Kelso made
> an excellent presentation to Canadian Liberal cabinet
> ministers and MPs, only to have his message roll off them
> like water off a duck's back.
>
> In comparison with the average time it takes to gain
> acceptance of a major invention in the material world,
> the relatively short period of time (eighteen years) it has
> taken to gain the present degree of acceptance of Kelso's
> philosophic idea is extremely encouraging. After all, it
> took twenty-two years and World War II to achieve the
> commercial acceptance of Whittle's jet engine. It has
> subsequently transformed the passenger transportation
> business. We still have four years to go to equal this. With
> the present desperate economic and political situation in
> Canada to help us, I am sure we will do so.
>
> It can therefore confidently be expected that by
> 1980, Kelso's ideas will be well established as the Western
> world's economic alternative to the socialism that appears
> to be about to engulf us.

Boyd's reference to Canada's "desperate economic and
political situation" can't be written off as a politician's rhetoric.
In his successful 1974 election campaign, Liberal Prime Minister Pierre Trudeau came out strongly against wage and price

controls—and then proceeded to install them soon after his re-election. Some observers saw this as courageous statesmanship, using an unpopular but necessary method of imposing restraint on labor and business. But Trudeau found that wage and price controls were not enough. As Canada settled into steady 6 percent inflation and 7 percent unemployment in 1976, the prime minister announced that the free-market system in Canada was dead, and that government would have to take an even stronger and more permanent position in regulating the economy.

Trudeau's program caused business investment in Canada to practically come to a stop in 1976. In fact, it started investment capital flowing south, so that Canadian companies became the largest foreign investors in U.S. manufacturing during 1976. Winn Boyd thinks this erosion will continue until Canada replaces redistribution with universal capitalism.

Great Britain

In 1958 Dr. George H. Copeman, an engineer who had earned his Ph.D. at the London School of Economics, published in England a book called *The Challenge of Employee Shareholding*. Copeman's book contained many of the principles that Kelso and Adler put forward in their 1958 book, *The Capitalist Manifesto*. Yet Copeman had not read or heard about the work of Kelso and Adler, and vice versa.

Copeman's 1958 book didn't have much of an impact in Britain, but it attracted enough interest to enable him to organize the Wider Share Ownership Council (WSOC). Copeman couldn't muster enough support for his new theories to devote WSOC entirely to universal capitalism, so the purposes of WSOC were made more general: encouragement of share ownership by more people. Most of the major British banks and business companies belong to WSOC, and their financial support has given Copeman a working platform.

But WSOC has not made much progress in the broadening of capital ownership, for several reasons. The British tax laws are not receptive to schemes like ESOP and profit-sharing, so

Copeman did not have the opportunity to install working models that would benefit the companies as well as the workers. The Labour governments that have ruled Britain during much of the life of the WSOC are very hostile toward the idea of capital diffusion, unless it results in trade union control of companies. The left wing of the Labour party has insisted on using nationalization as the means of capital diffusion. And there is the traditional reserve that makes the British resist change even when the whole world is telling them that their economic system is a monstrosity leading them to disaster.

In some ways, Copeman is a British counterpart of Kelso. He worked his way up from financial journalist to financial editor to managing director of a publishing company. While earning his living in publishing, he continued to contribute much of his time to WSOC, writing more books and articles and buttonholing industrialists and government officials whenever the chance arose. In the early 1970s he left publishing to set up shop as a consultant on profit-sharing and employee share ownership plans, scarce as they are in Britain. He remains chairman of the Industrial Committee of WSOC. Like Kelso, he is a writer–crusader for broadened capital ownership, with a consulting business practice in the same field.

As a first step toward capital diffusion, Copeman has been working on legislation that would make profit-sharing plans attractive in England for the first time. He holds little hope that this will ever happen under a Labour government. But if the Conservatives get back into power, Copeman believes there is a good chance that they will put through some enabling legislation for profit-sharing plans. He is responsible for a statement in the 1976 platform of the Conservative party supporting tax law changes that would encourage voluntary profit-sharing schemes.

Kelso made a trip to Britain in 1970, trying to plant the seeds of the capitalist revolution in the home territory of Adam Smith. He had scheduled several meetings with leaders of British trade unions, but found them mysteriously cancelled at the last moment. He did get to meet with Maurice Macmillan, son of former Prime Minister Harold Macmillan and a member of Parliament and cabinet minister himself. Maurice Macmillan helped George Copeman to organize WSOC in 1958, and kept up his interest in capital diffusion, but had not found any way of putting it into a concrete legislative plan. Macmillan was skeptical when he went into the meeting with Kelso, but after grilling Kelso for nearly five hours in a small room in the House of Commons, he came out with high respect for Kelso and his ideas.

With his usual bubbly enthusiasm, Kelso expected that a strong movement toward universal capitalism would develop in the wake of his brief stay in England. He arranged for an ex-RAF pilot, Harry Ball-Wilson, to act as his British representative. But apparently all the British officials who were approached on behalf of Kelso wanted to wait for some definitive development in the United States, and Kelso's visit resulted in little more than stirring up curiosity.

I interviewed Maurice Macmillan at his London office in November 1975, and found that he had an excellent grasp of Kelso's writings. Macmillan held out no hope of convincing the Labour government of then Prime Minister Harold Wilson to seriously consider Kelsoism as a cure for Great Britain's economic diseases. I thought there should have been some chance, because the chief financial advisor to Wilson was Harold Lever, a wealthy Manchester financier–lawyer who held the Cabinet title of Chancellor of the Duchy of Lancaster. Lever was an active member of WSOC for many years, and is sympathetic to the idea of capital diffusion. However, Macmillan felt that Lever did not have enough influence to overcome the prejudices of labor leaders against share ownership schemes. In the 1970s, the British Labour party was torn between the hard-core Marxists on the left, who were determined to nationalize practically all major British businesses, and the moderates like Harold Wilson and James Callaghan, who tried desperately to keep their party, their government, and their nation from splitting apart over economic problems.

Macmillan was eager to learn of American progress toward universal capitalism, but in the end he seemed certain that the idea would never get off the ground before the Conservative party returns to power. I got the feeling that many Conservative party leaders believe that the powerful left wing of the Labour party is more interested in wrecking capitalism than in finding a way to make it work. This seems a pity, because a capital diffusion scheme like the Financed Capitalist Plan might be the ideal solution to Britain's problems. Ideology still counts for something in Great Britain, and I don't think the Marxists could sell the British on state capitalism if their arguments against overconcentration of wealth were defused by the broadening of individual capital ownership.

British statesmen seem to be groping all around the problem of overconcentration, without facing the need for study of a radical but promising change like the Financed Capitalist Plan. For example, Sir Keith Joseph, one of the Conservative party's leaders, wrote in the London *Times* in November 1976:

> Yet to say that state ownership is equivalent to ownership by the community or public is to misuse words. The community or public cannot exercise ownership, which can be exercised only by individuals or organized groups. The stewardship of socialist states and party apparatuses which exercise ownership, ostensibly on behalf of the community, must be judged by reference to what they actually do. Almost invariably, they turn out to have blatantly abused their power for their own personal and caste ends in a manner which would be inconceivable in a democracy. As Djilas said in his *New Class* . . . "They squander the nation's wealth as though it were someone else's, and dip into it as though it were their own."

Well said. But what is the Conservatives' solution? A tepid provision in the 1976 platform for encouragement of voluntary profit-sharing plans, which have been operating in other nations since the nineteenth century.

The 1976 British economy was a nightmare scenario, with the pound plummeting, the balance-of-payments deficit increasing, inflation almost out of control, unemployment rising, productivity low, and taxation approaching confiscation. Yet there didn't seem to be any traditional remedy that either a Labour or Conservative government could use to solve these problems. Ultimately the strike weapon manipulated by a few left-wing labor leaders in key industries could shut down much of the economy and throw any government into chaos. Yet, the pay scales sought by these labor unions seemed moderate by American standards, especially when one considers the higher British rates of taxation and inflation during the 1970s. Perhaps their situation will get so desperate that leaders of both major parties will agree to take a look at the only form of capitalism that has never been tried: universal capitalism.

Britain is such an admirable country in so many ways that it is painful to watch this process of disintegration. It made me wonder what John Maynard Keynes would have done if he were alive today. During trips to London in 1975 and 1976, I tried to find an answer to this question. I was lucky enough to have several meetings with Nicholas Davenport, once a close associate of Keynes, who proved to be a gold mine of information.

Nicholas Davenport is a balding, twinkly eyed financier–journalist who worked closely with Keynes for many years. Davenport went into the City (London's equivalent of Wall Street) in the late 1920s, and held a variety of important jobs, becoming a director and then deputy chairman of the National Mutual Life Assurance Society, which Keynes served as chairman until 1938. At the National Mutual, he participated in important financial decisions with Keynes. He became financial correspondent of *The Nation* and its successor *The New Statesman,* both of which were owned by Keynes and his associates. Besides these professional collaborations, he was a personal friend of Keynes.

When I met Davenport in 1975 he was still active in financial advisory work, and he continued to write a sparkling weekly financial column in *The Spectator.* He had just finished writing a chapter for a book entitled *Essays on John Maynard Keynes,* which was published by Cambridge University Press in 1975. There were contributors such as Joan Robinson on the status of the Keynesian revolution and John Kenneth Galbraith on Keynes in America. Davenport was asked to write an essay on Keynes in the City.

It was a treat for me to sit and listen to Nicholas Davenport, who was at once a fascinating conversationalist, a former close associate of Keynes, and a distinguished author who had decided that universal capitalism was the only way to rescue the British economy. He reached this conclusion without having read any of Kelso's works. The idea came to him during the 1950s when he started to anticipate the problems of the British economy and searched his mind for a logical solution.

In his 1964 book, *The Split Society,* Davenport showed the need for capital diffusion:

How to make people who possess no capital feel that they
have a stake in the country is an awkward political problem. As long as they suspect that the nation is being run
in the interests of the finance-capitalists—the 2 percent of
the population who own half the wealth of the nation—
they will always feel alienated and at times incensed.

The Labour attempt to bring about a wider distribution of capital through nationalisation was futile.
Their whole socialisation programme tended to make the
rich richer. And it brought no uplift in the worker's
status. It was merely a change, as I have said, in management—and that of a peculiarly bureaucratic type. The
railway workers, for example, must feel, if Dr. Beeching
has his way, that far from having a stake in the country,
they do not even have a stake in the railways.

Labour should realise that a wider distribution of
capital cannot be secured by nationalisation (which
makes the rich more liquid) or by heavy discriminating
taxation (which would merely drive the rich abroad) or
by confiscation (which is rightly impossible in a democratic state). It can only be done by making poor people
less poor and giving the mass of wage and salary earners a
better chance to acquire some capital.

Davenport did not spell out a detailed plan of capital
diffusion. He felt that this was a very complicated question
which should be studied carefully by a high-level government
commission. But in *The Split Society* he did suggest a giant
mutual fund (called a "unit trust" in Britain) which would
make it possible for all British workers to become owners of
capital. He came out against any form of profit-sharing or employee ownership of employer stock. He saw the need for diversification, and felt that the inequities of employment-based
plans would create "a new privileged clique within the working
class at a time when we are all anxious to abolish privilege." He
was in favor of a broad-based plan that would benefit all British
workers, regardless of where they were employed.

Davenport started writing about this idea in *The Spectator*
in 1958, but had not been able to arouse any great interest in
it. Then in 1964 he talked to Harold Wilson about it, on the
eve of the election which was to bring Wilson to power as head
of the Labour government. He told Wilson that his aim was to
make the working class feel involved in the business of wealth

creation by sharing in capital ownership. He suggested that this was the only way to relieve labor's growing sense of alienation from capitalist society, and thus surely the only way to make a mixed economy work in harmony. He got the impression that Wilson agreed with him, and in a subsequent meeting with James Callaghan, soon to become chancellor of the exchequer and later to succeed Wilson as prime minister, he repeated his ideas. But in the end, according to Davenport, both Wilson and Callaghan were so compromised by the left wing of the Labour party, which Davenport feels is intent upon destroying capitalism, that neither man dared to act on his suggestions.

Davenport has not stopped trying to interest the Labour government in this scheme. When I visited him again in 1976 and met his charming wife Olga (a former actress and now a successful painter), he was about to have lunch with Harold Lever. He planned to urge Lever to seriously consider using capital diffusion as a means of healing the split society.

Nicholas Davenport sums up the British situation in his 1974 autobiography, *Memoirs of a City Radical:*

> When one party is financed by big business and the other party is financed by the trade unions, now increasingly dominated by militant Marxists, we have set ourselves on a collision course. It is the more regrettable seeing that the silent majority now has the means and desire to pursue a more comfortable and interesting life. . . .
>
> In the economic debate I was conducting in my weekly column, first in the *New Statesman* and then, after the war, in the *Spectator,* I was never diverted from my main purpose, which was to show how a dangerously split society could be unified in a mixed economy if the workers were brought into the game of capital growth on the lines I put to Harold Wilson in 1964. I cannot see why free enterprise and public enterprise cannot combine and flourish if the rival politicians would only learn from the past mistakes of capitalism and socialism and exercise some creative imagination. But Lord, O Lord, how long?

I was anxious to find out what Davenport thought Keynes would do today, if he hadn't died in 1946. It went like this:

SPEISER: Do you think that when Keynes wrote the *General Theory,* he was handing down a permanent structure, carved in stone? Or do you think that he was just improvising something to get out of the Depression as quickly as possible?

DAVENPORT: Of course he wasn't setting up a permanent structure. We had a frightful world Depression and millions of unemployed. He tried to find a way in which we could employ people with deficit spending. He wrote under that awful condition. If he had lived on into the boom years, you can be sure that he would have shifted quickly to concentrate on the need for spreading the benefits of capital growth.

SPEISER: Was Keynes's mind open to new ideas like capital diffusion, or did he tend to think in one groove?

DAVENPORT: I knew Keynes's mind so well. His mind flashed around quickly to invent some entirely new system whenever it was needed. He never stayed in the same groove for very long. I never knew a mind that could flash so quickly and reverse itself in no time. He was always interested in new ideas. Keynes had the most open mind of anybody I ever knew.

SPEISER: Do you think that if he were alive today, he would be in favor of a broad-based plan to make capital ownership available to everyone?

DAVENPORT: Of course he would. In fact, he started working on such a plan during the war.

Davenport's certainty about what Keynes would have done made me appreciate what a terrible loss the world suffered on Easter Sunday, 1946, when Keynes died at age sixty-two. He had ignored medical advice and continued to carry heavy international responsibilities after a serious heart attack. The economic problems of Britain and the rest of the world in the 1970s were so complicated and intractable that it would take a giant like Keynes to lead us to new solutions, as he did in the 1930s.

Keynes first gained international prominence in 1919, when he resigned his post as chief British treasury representative at Versailles, in protest against the economic provisions of the World War I peace treaty. He foresaw that the treaty would mean economic chaos for Germany, which in turn would embroil all of Europe. He wrote this in his 1919 book, *Economic Consequences of the Peace,* and the accuracy of his devastating analysis established his world reputation.

During the 1920s and early 1930s Keynes continued his great scholarship while indulging his renaissance tastes. He taught at Cambridge and wrote books, essays, and papers that require 22 pages to list. He was a member of the famous Bloomsbury group of leading British intellectuals, which included Bertrand Russell, Aldous Huxley, T. S. Eliot, Lytton Strachey, and Leonard and Virginia Woolf. He was a successful City financier; a leading art and book collector and patron of ballet, becoming chairman of Britain's Arts Council; and a widely quoted journalist who never hesitated to ridicule the antiquated economic policies (including those of Winston Churchill) that he felt were leading Britain and the West to disaster. But it was the worldwide Depression of the 1930s that inspired his greatest works. They were still the basis for the most important economic policies of the free world in the 1970s.

His 1936 masterpiece, *The General Theory of Employment, Interest and Money,* was one of the most important books ever written on economics, ranking with Adam Smith's *Wealth of Nations* and Marx's *Das Kapital.* Keynes was the source of economic theory supporting government deficit spending to stimulate the economy, to reduce unemployment, and to increase consumption and aggregate demand. He laid the foundations for today's macroeconomic analysis and planning, government management of the economy, and redistribution of income—the major elements of 1970s mixed capitalism. By the 1960s even conservative laissez faire capitalists like Milton Friedman and Richard Nixon were saying "We're all Keynesians now."

Despite his advocacy of government intervention, Keynes never wavered from dedication to capitalism. He simply recognized that in democratic nations capitalism had to be modified, sometimes drastically, to keep it working; and he had the foresight, the courage, and the stature to invent the necessary modifications.

Would Keynes stand by in 1976 and watch Britain's economy disintegrate, without opening his mind to new modifications of capitalism, however radical they might seem? There is clear evidence in the later writings of Keynes that he had started thinking in the direction of universal capitalism. In 1940,

Keynes published *How to Pay for the War,* in which he proposed a radical plan of forced savings which would bring about the broadening of capital ownership. It was based on conditions of wartime Britain, and it had limited purposes, like many of Keynes's quick fixes. But it contains the following prophetic language:

> In the last war we achieved the miracle of maintaining aggregate working-class consumption at, or near, its prewar level—the fall in real wage-rates being offset by increased employment and hours worked. I am not yet convinced that we may not achieve the same result this time. Until the full economic demands of the war have been disclosed, one cannot tell. But if aggregate earnings at the existing wage-rates increase because of overtime and full employment, a rise in basic wage-rates sufficient to compensate for higher prices would set our national economy the impossible task of raising consumption *above* the pre-war level. We cannot reward the worker in this way, and an attempt to do so will merely set in motion the inflationary process. But we can reward him by giving him a share in the claims on the future which would belong otherwise to the entrepreneurs.

Thus, in a time when income distribution through labor alone was threatening to cause inflation, Keynes's mind flashed to a new solution: income distribution through worker ownership of capital, or as he called it, "the accumulation of working-class wealth under working-class control." In the same 1940 book, Keynes said that this plan would bring "an advance towards economic equality greater than any which we have made in recent times."

By 1940, Keynes had moved beyond his 1936 *General Theory* statement that distribution of wealth had to be taken as fixed by the permanent social structure. Unfortunately he did not live long enough to carve this change in stone for the disciples who now rule economics in his name and who are still scratching away at the monumental problems of the 1970s with the primitive tools he designed to escape from the 1930s Depression.

Today, Keynes's memory is slandered by critics who blame his theories for inflation. These critics assume that his theories of the Depression years were static. They ignore the evidence that Keynes was aware of the inflation problem, and that he would not have hesitated to abandon his Depression theories in favor of more advanced tools. Can anyone doubt that if Keynes were alive today, at the very least he would have analyzed and tested Kelso's theories by every means available?

European Nations

Although no European nations have adopted anything similar to the Financed Capitalist Plan, most of them have some type of voluntary profit-sharing plans, which are the subject of negotiation between employers and unions. The amounts involved are not usually as great as they are in the United States and the tax laws usually are not as favorable.

The only country that has a compulsory plan is France. In 1967, Charles de Gaulle put through a profit-sharing scheme that requires all corporations with more than 100 employees to contribute part of their excess profits (defined as profits after allowing a 5 percent after-tax return on stockholders' equity) to an employees' investment fund. This contribution is tax deductible by the corporation.

In each corporation, a committee representing the employees decides how the fund will be invested. In most cases, these committees have decided to invest in diversified portfolios, rather than in stock of the employer corporation. Employees participate in proportion to their wages, with an upper limit of 6,840 francs (about $1,350) per year on the contribution to any employee's account. At the end of five years the employee may request that his investment be liquidated and paid out to him tax free.

The French government owns businesses that account for 35 percent of France's gross national product. These nationalized firms ordinarily do not issue stock, but because their workers complained about being shut out of de Gaulle's 1967 profit-sharing scheme, a law was passed in 1970 providing for issuance of shares to these employees. Initially 5 percent of the stock of nationalized companies was distributed to employees, under a formula based on salary and length of service. Eventually the employees will own a maximum of 25 percent of the shares, with the French government retaining 75 percent ownership.

These two schemes have broadened capital ownership in France, but they suffer from the basic inequities of profit-sharing that we discussed in Chapter 8. They completely exclude farmers, civil servants, employees of firms with less than 100 workers, and the unemployed. Nevertheless, they represent the only attempt by a major nation (apart from the United States) to broaden capital ownership by law, and they should be studied carefully. As of this writing, I was not able to find any report on the macroeconomic effects of these plans.

France is an important testing ground for capital diffusion. A 1976 study by the Organization for Economic Cooperation and Development (OECD) reported that France had the least equitable income distribution of any Western nation, with the poorest 10 percent of French households receiving only 1.4 percent of national income, and the richest 10 percent getting 30.5 percent of the income. The threat of a socialist–communist coalition gaining control of the French legislature in the 1978 elections was causing large movements of corporate assets to other nations, particularly from the major companies that are likely prospects for nationalization.

During the 1970s, socialist and labor parties in Europe became more interested in compulsory capital diffusion schemes. As of 1976, none of these schemes had been enacted into law, but there were significant attempts in Denmark and Sweden, both of them involving plans that would turn over voting control of major corporations to trade unions.

In 1973, the Danish Federation of Trade Unions proposed legislation to set up a large mutual fund, controlled by the trade unions, that eventually would take over voting control of most large Danish corporations. All Danish employers, including corporations both large and small, individual proprietorships, and government-owned firms, would have to contribute to the fund each year a percentage of payroll, starting at ½ percent and rising annually until it leveled off at 5 percent per year after eight years. This is what Professor Hans Brems calls an investment wage, as distinguished from profit-sharing. The fund would be free to invest its money in any Danish business enterprises.

The plan called for a diversified fund, and did not involve issuance of employers' stock to their own employees. However, the stock held by the fund would normally be voted by employees of each stock-issuing corporation. Each employee would own an equal share of the fund, regardless of his salary, his place of employment, or any other factors. The plan specified a holding period of seven years, after which any employee could withdraw his entitlement tax free.

Even though the Social Democratic party (Denmark's labor party) was in power, this proposal was considered too radical, and it failed to gain the necessary support for enactment in 1973. When the government resigned in December of that year, the bill lapsed, and as of this writing it had not been resubmitted to parliament. Danish Prime Minister Anker Jorgensen, a former trade union leader, was following the European trend away from starting new socialistic programs. Like other social welfare states, Denmark has very high taxation, with rates well over 50 percent for workers holding good jobs. Nobody was talking about dismantling the Danish welfare state, but there was a lot of grumbling about the high cost of social welfare programs. In that atmosphere, there was no sign that the trade union ownership scheme would be revived very soon. But it was sitting in the background, waiting to be activated if such a plan were installed elsewhere. The most likely place for that to happen is Sweden.

In August 1975 Dr. Rudolf Meidner headed a task force of the LO (the Swedish Trade Union Confederation) that drafted a proposal for a compulsory profit-sharing system. The Meidner plan was revised in March 1976, and the executive board and the 1976 Congress of the LO voted to support the revised plan.

The Meidner plan would require all private companies in Sweden with more than fifty employees to pay 20 percent of before-tax profits into a nationwide union-controlled fund. Companies would make these tax-deductible payments in the form of a compulsory issue of common stock to the fund. Individual workers would not receive any share ownership or dividend payments. The stock would remain in collective form in the fund, which would always be controlled by the trade unions. Under this plan, the Swedish trade unions would achieve majority or voting control of every significant business in Sweden in less than twenty years.

In 1976 Erland Waldenström, chairman of Gränges Corporation, a large Swedish metals producer, gave his opinion of the Meidner Plan:

> The Meidner plan would result in confiscatory losses in the assets of today's shareholders, difficulties in attracting capital to companies and the eventual disappearance of the Swedish stock market. It would have very serious effects on business transactions between Sweden and other countries. Foreign companies would not wish to expand or perhaps even maintain their operations in Sweden, while Swedish companies would be increasingly inclined to move their activities overseas.
>
> The Meidner proposals would have especially serious effects on small companies, which are already experiencing economic difficulties. They would gradually transform our current mixed economy into a mixed-socialistic system where power over economic policy would be shared according to unclear principles between trade unions owning most companies and the State. This double role for the trade unions, as representatives of both employees and owners, must seem extremely dubious even from the standpoint of the labor movement itself.

Waldenström suggested an alternative to the Meidner plan based on voluntary savings by employees, which would be subsidized by tax concessions. His plan was similar to the Broadened Stock Ownership Plan (BSOP) proposed by the Ford administration in 1976. It would result in ownership by individual workers rather than by trade unions.

In 1976 the Social Democratic party, which had been in power for forty-four years, faced a tough election. Prime Minister Olof Palme tried to avoid controversy about the Meidner plan by stating that a government commission on Employees and the Growth of Company Capital, known as the Mehr commission, would be studying the Meidner plan and would not make its recommendations before 1979. However, the plan did become an issue in the election, which resulted in defeat for Palme and the Social Democratic party. There were several key issues in the election, including the very high taxes needed to support Sweden's social welfare payments. As in Denmark, the average Swedish worker was in a tax bracket above 50 percent. The threat posed by the Meidner plan played an important part in the campaign, as reported by the *New York Times* on September 26, 1976, just after the election:

> The opposition won votes by attacking a labor-sponsored profit-sharing plan that would give the workers effective control over major corporations within five or six years and over all business within 20 years. "This frightened people," said a Swedish editor. "We're well paid, we all have cars, we have country places. We don't want radical steps."

Although Sweden has been labeled a socialist state and the party in power for forty-four years called itself the Social Democratic party, Sweden's economy is largely privately owned. Companies owned by the Swedish government produce only about 5 percent of Sweden's gross national product. About 10 percent of Swedes own common stock, which is roughly the same percentage as in the United States. The Social Democratic party took great pains to preserve this thriving privately owned industrial economy. While the taxation of individuals has been climbing toward the point of killing the incentive to work, the corporate tax structure has kept Swedish industry at a high level of capital formation. Even the Swedish social security system has been used to supply funds for capital investment in private business. It is likely that Swedish businessmen would have been happy to continue the Social Democratic party in power, so long as they were not threatened by loss of ownership through the Meidner plan.

Socialists often point to Sweden as an example of the success of their theories, but Sweden is more a managed capitalist welfare state than it is socialist. Remember that industrialist Erland Waldenström was afraid that the Meidner plan "would gradually transform our current mixed economy into a mixed-socialistic system."

Gunnar Myrdal, the Swedish Nobel laureate in economics, has long been a champion of Sweden's broad social benefit programs, but he acknowledges that some unique conditions have helped the welfare state to work there. In an interview with

Bernard Weinraub of the *New York Times* shortly after the 1976 Swedish elections, Myrdal said:

> We have not had a war since Napoleon's time. We have no religious differences, no racial problems. We have plenty of raw materials. We have iron ore, we have wood, and when we were hit by the oil crisis there was a raw material boom. My opinion about the Swedes is that with our history and our raw materials we should be doing even better.

The 1976 defeat of the Social Democratic party was another sign that there are limits to what the welfare state can accomplish, as taxation passes the 50 percent mark and people realize that they can live pretty well without working. During 1975 and 1976, Swedish labor costs, climbing at an annual rate of about 25 percent, were beginning to price Swedish products out of international markets.

Holland is another democratic social welfare state where most of the businesses are privately owned. The situation there was summarized by Michael Getler in the *Washington Post* on December 1, 1976:

> Nobody wants to destroy the welfare net or even take away the benefits already built up. But even among the country's socialist leaders, there is a feeling that the system is being abused and must be leveled off, that the incentive of people to work is becoming dangerously low. . . .
>
> Holland already has the world's highest minimum wage—$540 a month—and a 6-fold increase in welfare spending over the past decade has pushed the overall portion of gross national product used for public expenditures to some 55 percent here.
>
> Over the same period, the net profits made by Dutch businessmen on their invested capital has dropped from about 8 percent to what the Federation of Employers claims was zero last year. The businessmen claim this is largely due to the staggering costs of welfare contributions and taxes.

Against this background, the Dutch government of Prime Minister Joop M. den Uyl submitted to Parliament in September 1976 a compulsory profit-sharing bill that combined various features of the French law, the Meidner plan, and the 1973

Danish scheme. Like the French law, it called for contribution of excess profits, although the definition of excess profits was more complicated. Like the Meidner plan, it would result in trade union control of major corporations. And as in the Danish plan, each worker would receive an equal share of the fund.

The Dutch Vermogensaanwasdeling scheme, mercifully known as VAD, was proposed by the trade unions, and the prime minister was committed to supporting it as part of a deal with labor to keep wage increases down to 5 percent in 1976. It was denounced by Dutch business spokesmen, and it seemed doubtful that the bill would come to a vote before the general election scheduled for May 1977, an election that involves issues similar to those of the Swedish campaign of 1976.

The high costs of social welfare programs and the heavy taxation needed to pay these costs stemmed the tide toward union control of European business in 1976. But it seems inevitable that one of the many European nations controlled by labor parties will adopt a Meidner plan or a VAD eventually, unless the United States shows that the Financed Capitalist Plan or some other plan based on individual ownership can do a better job of capital diffusion while maintaining democratic safeguards.

It also seems inevitable that some major European democracies will elect communist governments soon, unless universal capitalism steps into the breach. Italy, France, and Portugal are headed in that direction. The communists in those nations say they don't take orders from Moscow. They pledge support of democracy and promise that if defeated in an election after taking power, they will step down peacefully. This remains to be seen. Luigi Barzini, author of *The Italians,* said in a December 1976 television interview:

> Once the Italian communists get into office, they don't intend to leave. Unless democracy succeeds—and quickly —totalitarianism is inevitable.

How can democratic capitalism succeed in Europe today? As a sign of hope, Professor Hans Brems points out the success of West Germany's voluntary investment wage scheme. Started in 1961, it allows employers to take a tax deduction for annual payments of up to 624 DM (about $250) per worker for saving and investment. The money may be invested in securities or savings accounts, or may even be used to finance home construction. The workers may withdraw the funds tax free after seven years. In 1976 the newly elected Social–Liberal coalition government proposed raising the annual contribution to about $375. Brems finds it significant that in West Germany, Europe's strongest capitalist economy, this voluntary plan is so appealing that two-thirds of the entire labor force is participating. He thinks that the two-thirds fraction demonstrates the great potential of capital diffusion in modern Western society.

Iran

Until 1975, most Iranian corporations had very few stockholders. Most businesses were owned by the government, multinational corporations, or wealthy families. But that picture was changed drastically by the shah's proclamation of May 1975, which announced a plan to spread capital ownership throughout Iranian society.

Under the plan, which is now known as the Law for Expansion of Ownership of Productive Enterprises, all major privately owned companies were required to offer to the public 49 percent of their common stock, and all government-owned companies with the exception of key basic industries were required to offer 99 percent of their stock. Each participating company had to offer these shares first to its own employees, and then to farmers and the general public.

The Iranian government set up two organizations to provide loans to stock purchasers. They offered three loans of $500 a year to each eligible worker over a three-year period, making a total credit of $1,500 per worker. The same terms were offered to the general public except for farmers, who were limited to three annual loans totaling about $600. The loans are for ten years and carry a 4 percent interest rate. While these terms would make it possible for the stock to pay for itself out of dividends, it does not appear that the loans are made "without recourse." Therefore, the purchasers run the risk that if the stock does not pay for itself, or if a particular company goes out of business, they will be personally responsible for repayment of their loans.

There is some protection against participation by shaky corporations, since the Iranian Council for the Expansion of Industrial Ownership evaluates the stock of each eligible company. To be eligible, companies must have capital of at least $1.5 million, or fixed assets of at least $3 million, or sales of at least $3.75 million, and all must have a production record of five years or more. In the first wave, the Iranian government selected a total of 320 companies, with total capital of over $1.5 billion. They included names like General Motors of Iran, B. F. Goodrich of Iran, and Esso Oil of Iran. The plan exempts some government-owned corporations such as oil producers and other basic industrial firms, which the shah says "must remain in government hands in view of their special significance."

This plan involves three revolutions at once: the start of serious public trading on the Teheran stock exchange, which was microscopic before 1975; the start of stock ownership by the Iranian public; and a program of enforced capital diffusion financed by the Iranian government. In addition, the corporate tax law has a sliding scale of rates that favors companies with broad equity ownership, and there is no tax on dividends paid to the new stockholders.

While the shah's plan lacks the nonrecourse feature of the Financed Capitalist Plan, it comes closer to the FCP than any scheme that was in effect anywhere in 1976. Although it is limited to $1,500 stock ownership per New Capitalist, this is a significant amount of capital ownership for a country like Iran. Obviously the program is experimental and can be expanded if it is successful. Because the average Iranian is not familiar with the nature of stock ownership, the government has been conducting an educational program through television, radio, and pamphlets to explain capital ownership.

You can bet the shah of Iran will be keeping his eye on the results. As he said at the time of his coronation in 1967:

> In spite of all the measures taken to protect the worker, the basic problem had not been overcome. He could still not be confident that his labor would not be exploited and that he would not be treated simply as a hireling. He

could only be sure that such was not the case if he knew that he had a share in the work that he did. Such participation would not only be important to him in material terms, but, and this was of special importance, it would make him really feel that his personality and his labor were being, and would continue to be, respected.

When the shah announced his revolutionary capital participation plan in May 1975, he said:

> The sale of industrial and mining shares to workers, other employees of the firms going public, and the general public, is as important as, if not more so than, the abolition of landed feudalism.

In December 1975 the shah announced that 95 percent of Iran's workers had applied for the maximum number of shares available to them under the plan. And in August 1976 the minister of Economic Affairs and Finance reported to the shah that the plan had helped to increase capital formation by 95 percent over the preceding year.

Israel

According to legend, the Jewish people would never be very good soldiers or farmers, but if they were given their own state, their natural ability to handle money and business affairs would create for Israel a model economy that would be the envy of the world. Since the establishment of Israel in 1948, the Israelis have performed feats of arms to rival any in history, and they have turned an arid sandlot into an agricultural miracle. At the same time, they have managed to construct an economic system so monstrous that it makes Great Britain look like an economist's paradise. Yet there are reasons for those interested in universal capitalism to study Israel's economy.

Israel operates a working model of the Swedish Meidner plan because its federation of trade unions, known as the Histadrut ("the organization"), is also Israel's largest private employer and capital owner. But unlike the scenario of the Meidner plan, the Histadrut did not latch on to its huge capital ownership by decree of a labor government. In typical Israeli fashion, they found a harder way to do it.

The Histadrut was founded in 1920, in what was then the British mandate territory of Palestine. The 100,000 Jews in Palestine were better equipped for shopkeeping and the professions than for industry or agriculture, so the Histadrut, with a nucleus of 5,000 workers, decided to build a new economy from scratch. They did everything that the most ardent laissez faire entrepreneurs would have done. They started up industries and agricultural organizations, obtained the financing, arranged for immigration and training of workers, provided their own business management, and then branched out into banking, insurance, transportation, and cultural and social services.

The Histadrut actually created a Jewish working class during the Palestine mandate. After Israel became a nation in 1948 the Histadrut continued to expand its operations, often in partnership with the government and private firms. By 1976, Histadrut business enterprises (known in Israel as the labor economy) employed nearly a quarter of the labor force; nearly 60 percent of the nation's population held Histadrut membership; and the Histadrut's agricultural cooperative handled the marketing of more than two-thirds of Israel's farm produce. This one organization represented practically all of labor and was the nation's largest private owner of capital. Its leaders were always major figures in the Labor party, which held power through various coalitions since 1948.

Given this history, it would be logical to assume that labor relations would be ideal, and that the stern measures needed to control inflation would be easier to enforce than in countries where labor representation, capital ownership, and government power are in two or three different hands. But again the perverse Israeli economy comes up TILT. Israel has one of the world's worst strike records, even though the Histadrut would seem to be striking against itself. During 1975 and 1976, Israel's inflation was careening out of control at a rate of 30–40 percent, and the Israeli pound was being devalued at the rate of 2 percent a month.

In the 1950s, Israel seemed to have the best chance of any nation to achieve a classless society. The Histadrut leaders and the other people who built the nation were mostly idealists.

The idyllic kibbutz life, one of the few successful forms of completely collective communal society, seemed to typify Israel's spirit of sharing. They didn't have overconcentrated private wealth or an entrenched capitalist class like Britain or the United States. They were united in religion and in their zeal to build a national homeland after centuries of Diaspora, and in times of doubt they were held together by the need to defend against hostile neighbors who outnumbered them by more than thirty to one.

In 1976 Israel was getting its first taste of big-time government corruption. Asher Yadlin, an important Labor party official, was about to become governor of the Bank of Israel (a post similar to America's chairman of the Federal Reserve Board) , when he was arrested and charged with receiving bribes and defrauding the government. This scandal led to the suicide of housing minister Avraham Ofer, a close friend and associate of Yadlin. Meanwhile on the labor front, first the airline pilots and then the doctors threatened to form their own corporations to sell their services at higher rates than they could command under existing wage scales. The dream of a classless society seemed to be going up in smoke, and it was every man for himself in the day-to-day battle for personal financial solvency.

Israel's economy and its whole society seemed to be in deep trouble. There were external causes, including the disproportionate cost of defense and the need to import oil at quadrupled prices. But there was massive aid from the United States government and from Jews living outside Israel. There are many knowledgeable people in Israel who feel that the economic system needs structural change, but as in other nations, nobody seems to have any promising new ideas. Yet the Israelis have one advantage over the Swedes, the Danes, and the Dutch. They know that trade union ownership of business is not the answer, because they have tried it and found it incapable of solving the economic problems of the 1970s. And it doesn't seem to instill any feeling of real ownership in the Histadrut members, because the profits are used mainly to expand the labor economy rather than to benefit the individual workers.

The government of Israel has never proposed any plans for broadening the individual ownership of capital. In 1975, I tried to stir up some interest by introducing Louis Kelso to Wim van

Leer. Wim is a member of a wealthy Dutch family that helped to build Israel, and he's been living there since statehood. In 1948 he came to New York looking for help in finding airplanes, pilots, and chemicals to establish the first aerial crop-dusting operation in Israel. I was probably the only lawyer around who had been foolhardy enough to dust crops, and somehow he found me. He's been a client and close friend ever since.

Wim built a very successful crop-dusting business, doing a lot of the flying himself, and later sold it to the Histadrut. Then in partnership with Matzuba, a kibbutz, he tackled beef cattle raising, which many people thought was impossible in Israel. He successfully pioneered that too, and after a few years as Israel's leading kosher cowboy he sold that business to the kibbutz and started the nation's first plastic sheet plant. In his spare time he wrote, produced, and directed plays and films, some of which won international awards.

I thought that if anyone could introduce universal capitalism to Israel, it would be Wim van Leer. I got him to read Kelso's books and he had a long discussion with Kelso in my office. He believes that the Israeli economy needs a new approach, and he's willing to take on the job of trying to get Israelis interested in universal capitalism. He's waiting for me to finish this book so that he can distribute copies to economists and government officials.

Universal capitalism won't come easily to Israel, because of the Histadrut and other unique factors in the Israeli economy. But with Wim van Leer on the scene, at least we can be sure that the case won't be lost by default.

EPILOGUE

We started with a television image: the "60 Minutes" show that brought together our main characters, Louis Kelso and Senator Russell Long, with Professor Paul Samuelson as the symbol of the economics establishment they were trying to buck. Then we went on to the 1975 economic summit meeting at Chateau de Rambouillet, France, where Henry Kissinger tried to assure the world that statesmen rather than witch doctors were making economic decisions for the Western nations. Let's finish up with a print image: the press coverage of the June 1976 follow-up economic summit meeting. It was held in Puerto Rico, and it involved some of our other principal characters.

Leonard Silk, the distinguished economic analyst of the *New York Times,* described the Puerto Rican summit meeting in these words:

> SAN JUAN, P. R.—When Rafael Hernandez Colon, Governor of Puerto Rico, was rushing to the airport to meet President Ford last month, his limousine blew a tire.
>
> By the time the tire was fixed, traffic was congested and a crowd demonstrating for Puerto Rican independence was blocking the airport's entrance.
>
> When Governor Hernandez Colon ordered his police escort to knock a locked gate down, the Puerto Rican police car couldn't do it. Finally, the Governor jumped over the fence, cutting his hand and muddying his shoes, had to explain his way past Secret Service agents, and made the runway with less than a minute before the President descended from Air Force One. For all that trouble he got to shake Mr. Ford's hand and hear his airport statement, aimed at Fidel Castro, warning outsiders not to "meddle in Puerto Rican or United States affairs."
>
> In its way, the Governor's run to the airport symbolizes Puerto Rico's troubles today: The problem of making the industrializing society work, the small but disturbing effect of the independence movement, the determination of Puerto Rico's leadership to leap over all obstacles, and the quick brush from Washington.

According to *Business Week's* Economic Diary for June 29th, Governor Hernandez Colon should have saved himself the trouble:

> The two-day economic summit meeting of the seven largest industrial democracies, held in Puerto Rico, ended yesterday. Judging by its results, the conference will rank as one of the greatest non-events in recent history. In a vague and hedged joint statement, the heads of state agreed to pursue the goal of sustained growth without reviving inflation (the policymaker's equivalent of being in favor of God and motherhood.)

The fruitless Puerto Rican summit seemed to sum up the frustration of 1976 economic policy, which perpetuates outmoded theories and ignores the possibility that a fresh idea like capital diffusion might change the picture. Both of our summit characters knew of this possibility. Jerry Ford learned about it from Kelso at Aspen in 1964, and he made a valiant effort to get his Republican colleagues to do something about it. But in the end he got nowhere, and when he became president he was surrounded by economic advisers whose minds were not open enough to investigate it. Instead they committed Ford to the old tools. He used them about as well as anyone else could, but they simply couldn't cope with simultaneous unemployment and inflation.

Governor Hernandez Colon also learned about capital diffusion from Kelso. In 1972 he managed to kill the Ferre plan by bringing in Professor Samuelson to alert the Puerto Rican legislature to the grave dangers of letting thousands of poor Puerto Ricans own $20 million worth of stock in successful Puerto Rican businesses.

Both Ford and Hernandez Colon sought reelection in November 1976. A few weeks before election day, *Newsweek* asked six leading economists to rate Ford's performance on economic issues. This brought Paul Samuelson back into our story. He gave Ford a grade of C, and under "comments" he said:

> That's a gentleman's C. He simply listens to his advisers, and he's the kind of President advisers like. An open mind is an empty mind.

An open mind is an empty mind. Yes, it's right there in print, in *Newsweek,* October 18, 1976, page 56. Samuelson's comments rang a bell. Somewhere among all the notes and quotes I pulled together while writing this book, somebody else had mentioned this subject. Ah, yes—it was Nicholas Davenport, sitting near the fireplace in his London home, telling me about Keynes: "Keynes had the most open mind of anyone I ever knew."

Then came election day, and both Ford and Hernandez Colon went down to defeat. Hernandez Colon's loss was more surprising, because his Popular Democratic party had lost only one other election since it was founded in 1940. Clearly, he lost because Puerto Rico's economic problems became a lot worse in the four years after he took over from Ferre.

As I watched the final election returns, I wondered how Professor Samuelson would grade Jimmy Carter. It seemed to me that Carter's mind was even more open than Jerry Ford's. Would Samuelson flunk him?

While I was pondering that question, I started to read *The Economists,* an important book by Leonard Silk, published in 1976. Silk uses fascinating sketches of the careers of five prominent economists as a backdrop for his own incisive analysis of America's economic and social problems. The five are Paul Samuelson, Milton Friedman, John Kenneth Galbraith, Wassily Leontief, and Kenneth Boulding. Silk sums up their positions:

> Of our five economists, only Samuelson is in the very center of the mainstream. Friedman is on the right; Galbraith and Leontief have shifted to the left and are fairly close to the radical or new left economists. Boulding, with his religious belief in love and the perfectibility of man, is distant from the radicals and their dialectics (he rejects conflict as a creative force). But Boulding, though a lover of freedom, is a long way from Friedman's intense concentration on the market as the source of all virtue or from Samuelson's agnosticism, willingness to live within the boundaries of traditional economics, and lack of interdisciplinary zeal or hope.

Silk included Boulding to emphasize his own conviction that leading American economists must outgrow the tools of the 1930s. As Silk puts it:

> Conventional economists, through most of the past century, have concentrated too narrowly on increasing the

efficiency and growth of production, while paying too little attention to the distribution of wealth and income, or to the still wider issue of social justice. . . .

To redeem their reputation throughout the industrial world in the years ahead, economists must move on beyond the economics of Smith and Keynes. Yet many of the leaders of the economics profession are reluctant to move.

Silk says that "economic policy needs to focus on structural economic problems," and he adopts the conclusions of Northwestern University Professor Robert J. Gordon:

A good argument can be made that the day of stabilization policy is past and that the real progress in the next ten to twenty years will be in the area of dealing with the allocation of resources and the distribution of wealth and income.

Silk is an outstanding journalist who puts his reputation on the line every week. He is a member of the editorial board of the *New York Times,* and formerly was a senior fellow at the Brookings Institution and Ford Foundation Distinguished Professor at Carnegie–Mellon University. So it was encouraging to read his strong views about the need for structural changes and for consideration of wealth distribution and social justice, even though his book did not endorse any specific plan of action.

The day after the 1976 elections I was enjoying Leonard Silk's book when Joe Novak telephoned. He told me that former governor Ferre had been elected to the Puerto Rican Senate, and that the landslide which swept Hernandez Colon out of office also gave Ferre's New Progressive party control of both houses of the Puerto Rican legislature. Joe was going back to Puerto Rico to help Ferre put together a 1977 version of his capital diffusion plan. "This time," said Joe, "things will be different."

Now it was Inauguration Day, January 20, 1977, and Jimmy Carter was calling for a New Spirit:

Let our recent mistakes bring a resurgent commitment to the basic principles of our nation, for we know that if we despise our own government we have no future.

We recall special times when we have stood briefly, but magnificently, united; in those times no prize was beyond our grasp.

For we cannot dwell upon remembered glory. We cannot afford to drift. We reject the prospect of failure or mediocrity or an inferior quality of life for any person.

I hoped that he would discover the new idea that was needed to sustain the New Spirit.

APPENDIX:
THE FUNCTIONS AND
LIMITATIONS OF ESOP

The explanation of ESOP in Chapter 8 includes no more detail than is necessary to show ESOP's role in the story of universal capitalism. This Appendix gives a fuller account of the functions and limitations of ESOP. Like the itemized summary in Chapter 8 comparing four major types of employee benefit plans, however, the following explanations are based on plans that apply to the average employee of the average large American corporation. Plans of the same general type do, of course, vary from corporation to corporation, but we cannot cover all the variations here.

Common Features of Employee Benefit Plans

Pensions, profit-sharing, stock bonus plans, and ESOPs are the four major types of *employee benefit plans* that are eligible for favorable tax treatment if their structures comply with the requirements of the Internal Revenue Code. Those that comply are known as *qualified* plans, meaning that they qualify for special tax treatment. This tax treatment is one of the common elements of all four plans. In a qualified plan, there are tax advantages for both the corporation and the employees. The corporation gets an immeditae tax deduction for the contributions (payments) that it makes to the plan, even though the employees do not receive the money immediately. The employees pay no taxes on the money contributed to the plan by the corporation until they actually receive the benefits, which is usually after retirement or upon leaving the company. There is a third important tax advantage: As long as the contributions remain in the plan and are not distributed to the employees, no taxes are paid on the income or capital gains realized by these funds; thus, the income can accumulate for many years without any tax bite. Even when the benefits are paid out to the employees, they may be taxable at lower rates than ordinary income.

The tax-free accumulation of income produces dramatic results. Money invested at 6 percent interest compounded annually will double in twelve years, triple in nineteen years, and quadruple in twenty-four years, provided that there are no taxes.

The same device is used in all four plans to receive and hold the employer's contributions: a *trust*. Whether it's a pension trust, a profit-sharing trust, a stock bonus trust, or an employee stock ownership trust (ESOT), the functions are the same: to receive, hold, and invest the employer's contributions and eventually to pay out benefits to the employees. This accounts for the two terms, ESOP and ESOT. ESOP (employee stock ownership *plan*) is the overall plan, which includes the trust, ESOT (employee stock ownership *trust*), as the device used to receive and administer the contributions made to the plan.

Lots of people, even some economics professors, confuse ESOPs with *stock options,* but ESOPs have nothing to do with options. There are qualified and unqualified stock option plans, but they usually are open only to key executives, and they simply give employees the right to buy stock with their own money. We're concerned here only with the four types of plans in which the corporation pays out its money for the benefit of its employees.

Another common feature of all four plans is that usually the contributions must be held in the trust until the employee leaves the company (through death, retirement, or for any other reason). The favorable tax treatment of employee benefit plans was put into the Internal Revenue Code because Congress realized that most Americans cannot save enough after taxes to help very much in old age and cannot live decently in retirement on social security alone. Congress made it possible for millions of Americans to build retirement estates through these employee benefit plans, the only tax shelters most Americans ever get to use. To ensure that these nest eggs will be available for the retirement years, most qualified plans are *deferred,* meaning that payment of benefits is deferred until retirement.

Because of the favorable tax treatment, there are limits on the contributions that can be made by corporations each year. The limit on ESOP, profit-sharing, and stock bonus plans is 15 percent of each employee's total compensation, and the total limit of 15 percent applies even if all three are used. If a pension plan is added, there can be an additional 10 percent contribution, making the total 25 percent of payroll. Any contributions above 25 percent would not qualify for the tax advantages. Also, since the Pension Reform Act of 1974 (ERISA) went into effect, there are limits on contributions made for very high-salaried employees that can bring them down below the general 25 percent maximum, but they only affect employees making six-figure incomes.

In all four types of plan, the trusts are managed by trustees, who are usually selected by the corporation that establishes the plan. Some pension plans are *jointly trusted*; that is, the trustees consist of an equal number of representatives of the employer and the employees. This gets union officials into the picture as representatives of the employees. The Teamsters pension plans are examples.

All four plans have similar requirements as to the employees who must be allowed to participate and the vesting of plan benefits. In order to qualify for tax benefits, a plan must avoid discriminating in favor of officers, shareholders, and highly compensated employees, but union members can be excluded if the union has its own benefit plan or if there has been "good faith bargaining" with the union about benefits. Benefits must become vested (become fixed legal rights that the employee can take with him even if he is fired or quits the company) according to rules laid down in the Internal Revenue Code. Progressive vesting usually must start after five years of employment, although there are alternatives that can start the vesting even earlier.

All these plans are based on contributions made by the employer. Many plans also provide for contributions by employees. There are some tax advantages, even though the employee must save up the money after taxes to make his contribution. After the employee contribution has been made, it becomes part of the fund held by the trustees, and the income on it is not taxed until it is finally distributed to the employee. There are also thrift and savings plans, under which the employee must make a contribution in order to qualify for a matching contribution by the employer. We have concentrated on the employer contribution plans, since that's where ESOP fits in.

Now let's see how the four plans differ from each other. The principal differences are in the kinds of investments that each plan can make and the duties of the trustees who select and manage these investments.

Pensions

Trustees of pension plans are quite restricted in their choice of investments because Congress was anxious to make sure that pension benefits would be available to help employees through their old age. Many pension plans provide "defined benefits," which means that they are designed to pay out a specified amount to each employee upon retirement or death. The defined benefit pension plans may use a portion of the employers' contributions to buy life insurance coverage for the employees. Their remaining funds can be put into stocks, bonds, and other types of investments, but no more than 10 percent of the total assets of a pension plan can be invested in securities of the employer.

Trustees of pension trusts are subject to the "prudent man" rule; that is, they must diversify investments to minimize risk of large losses, and they must handle funds as a prudent man would under the circumstances. They are also prohibited from lending money to themselves, to the employer, and to other "disqualified persons" who have a close relationship with the employer.

Annual contributions to defined benefit pension plans are calculated to provide enough money to cover the specified retirement and death benefits. This amount varies from year to year, depending on the number, age, and status of employees and the return on investment that the plans' actuaries assume the pension funds will earn. There is another form of pension known as the "money purchase" plan, which provides for a fixed percentage of the payroll to be contributed to each employee's account each year, regardless of how much future income or benefits this sum will buy.

Because of the high degree of security desired for pension plans, the 1974 Pension Reform Act (ERISA) established a new government entity, the Pension Benefit Guaranty Corporation (PBGC) to insure employees against loss of defined pension benefits. This is a distinctive feature of defined benefit pension plans; the PBGC does not insure profit-sharing, stock bonus, or ESOP benefits, or benefits under money purchase pension plans.

Profit-Sharing Plans

Profit-sharing plans have more flexibility than pensions because they are more like a special bonus than a regular retirement benefit that can be counted on as part of the employee's nest egg. Unlike pension plans, they are only payable out of profits; so if the company does not make a profit, it cannot make any contributions to its profit-sharing plan.

Trustees of profit-sharing plans are not subject to the 10 percent limitation on investment in employer securities, as are trustees of pension plans. However, profit-sharing trustees *are* subject to the "prudent man" rule, and there are three other requirements they must satisfy if they invest in stock of the employer: They cannot pay more than fair market value for the stock; they must get a return commensurate with the prevailing rate; and they must maintain enough liquidity to distribute benefits to retiring employees when they come due. This puts a heavy burden on profit-sharing trustees who want to invest in stock of the employer. It pretty much limits them to situations in which the employer is a large and profitable publicly held company whose stock can enable the trustees to get a good return on their money with safety and liquidity.

Other types of profit-sharing plans are not qualified because they distribute the funds to the employee each year instead of paying them into the trust to be accumulated for payment when the employee leaves the corporation. These profit-sharing contributions do not qualify for the favored treatment Congress intended for funds that are being accumulated for retirement. They are taxable to the employee as soon as he receives them, because they are just like additional wages or bonuses. Here we are interested only in the qualified profit-sharing plans which are deferred employee benefits.

Stock Bonus Plans and ESOPs

Unlike pension and profit-sharing plans, the trustees of stock bonus plans and ESOPs are permitted to invest heavily in stock of the employer; in fact, they are *required* to. They are also required to distribute their retirement benefits in stock of the employer, whereas pension and profit-sharing plans can make distributions in cash or any securities.

The differences between stock bonus plans and ESOPs are more difficult to spot, mainly because the four laws establishing ESOP are rather recent (1973 to 1975) and ESOP is defined differently in each of them. One apparent difference is that ESOPs are required to invest *primarily* in stock of the employer, whereas stock bonus plans have a little more flexibility to make other investments as long as they are able to distribute retirement benefits in the form of employer stock. Lawyers and other ESOP experts disagree on whether certain stock bonus plans are actually ESOPs. But this legal hair-splitting needn't concern us. We can look on ESOP as a special kind of stock bonus plan: one that permits the use of leverage.

The Leveraged ESOP

Thanks to the pioneering of Kelso and the provisions of the Pension Reform Act, ESOPs are permitted to be leveraged; that is, their trusts (ESOTs) can borrow money to buy stock and pay it back over a period of years. This enables ESOTs to buy large blocks of stock on the installment plan—something that trustees of other employee benefit plans cannot do. Also, it provides the biggest advantage of ESOPs, from the corporate standpoint: It enables the employer to take a tax deduction for payment of both the principal and the interest on the money borrowed by the ESOT to buy the corporation's stock. Interest is always a tax-deductible expense for corporations, just as it is on your personal income tax return. But repayment of the loan principal is never a tax-deductible expense, for individuals or corporations, unless a corporation has a leveraged ESOP.

The ESOP doesn't actually give the corporation a tax deduction for principal payments, but it has the same effect. The corporation makes tax-deductible contributions to the ESOT, and the ESOT uses these contributions to pay off the loan principal and interest. Therefore, the expenditure that is usually called "nondeductible repayment of loan principal" is changed to "deductible contribution to ESOT."

The leveraged ESOP is a pretty complicated device, so let's break it down step by step, for a corporation that wants to raise $1 million:

1. The corporation adopts an ESOP, gets it approved by the Internal Revenue Service as a qualified employee benefit plan, and sets up an ESOT as part of the plan.

2. The corporation requests a loan of $1 million from its bank. If the bank agrees, the loan is made to the ESOT rather than to the corporation, but the corporation guarantees that the loan will be repaid. The employees are *not* responsible for repaying the loans; only the ESOT and the corporation sign the note. Now the ESOT is holding $1 million loaned by the bank. Let's assume that it has to repay the bank loan in five annual installments of $200,000 each, with interest.

3. The ESOT then uses the $1 million bank loan to buy

$1 million worth of newly issued stock from the corporation at fair market value. The ESOT holds the stock in trust for the employees of the corporation, who will receive shares of this stock in proportion to their salaries when they retire or leave the company.

4. The corporation makes an annual contribution to the ESOT equal to 15 percent of its payroll. Let's say that the corporation's annual payroll is $2 million. Its maximum tax-deductible contribution to the ESOT would be 15 percent of $2 million, which is $300,000. The $300,000 contribution received from the corporation is used by the ESOT to pay the annual installments of principal and interest on the $1 million loan. The corporation makes a contribution every year, up to 15 percent of its annual payroll, until the ESOT has paid back the $1 million bank loan with interest. And the corporation has received a tax deduction for its entire contribution each year.

If we assume that the corporation is in the 50 percent tax bracket (although the average corporate tax is less than 40 percent), this means that it has to earn only $1 million to pay back the $1 million principal of the bank loan made to the ESOT. If the corporation borrowed the money itself and did not set up an ESOP, it would have to earn about $2 million to pay back $1 million of loan principal because it would have to pay about $1 million in federal and state taxes on the $2 million income before any of it could be used to pay off the loan. But because the loan was made to the ESOT and repaid indirectly by the corporation through tax-deductible contributions to the ESOT, the 50 percent tax is avoided and the entire principal and interest are repaid in before-tax dollars.

There's another version of ESOP in which the corporation itself borrows the money from the bank and then makes an annual contribution to its ESOT in stock rather than cash. The corporation gets a tax deduction for the fair market value of the stock. If it has a $2 million payroll, it can take the same $300,000 deduction (15 percent of payroll) for contributing $300,000 worth of its stock to the ESOT. The corporation can then use the tax savings to repay the bank loan, and again it has received the equivalent of a tax deduction for repayment of principal. This can be cheaper for the corporation if its stock goes up in value during the years that the loan is outstanding because it will have to contribute fewer shares each year to pay the loan installments. Under the first method, where the ESOT borrows the $1 million from the bank, the corporation has to issue $1 million worth of stock to the ESOT right away, and it loses the advantage of any future stock price rise.

Cost of ESOP Financing

There is a price to pay for this unique tax advantage: the corporation must repay a $1 million loan *and* issue $1 million worth of its stock, just to get $1 million in cash. Even though the $1 million loan principal can be paid back with $1 million worth of before-tax profits, the principal still costs the corporation at least $500,000, plus interest—and on top of that, they must issue $1 million worth of stock at fair market value. Therefore, if the corporation can borrow $1 million or can sell $1 million worth of its stock at fair market value, it is much better off doing one or the other, instead of doing *both* just to raise $1 million through an ESOP. So ESOP is really an expensive way for a corporation to raise money. There has to be a special reason for using an ESOP instead of a straight loan or a straight stock sale.

Special Reasons for Using ESOP

Special reasons abound, but after more than a year of study, I'm convinced that practically all of them concern only privately held corporations or publicly held parent corporations that want to get rid of subsidiaries or troubled operations. ESOPs can be very useful in those cases, but if you add them all up they will not broaden capital ownership enough to be of any macroeconomic significance.

From the standpoint of corporate finance, the main attraction of ESOP is the tax saving. ESOP is of no use to a corporation that is not profitable enough to pay heavy income taxes. And in order to take advantage of ESOP's leverage, the corporation has to have a strong line of credit so that it can borrow large sums to buy its own stock. Some ESOP proponents claim that banks will lend money to ESOPs in cases where they wouldn't make the same loan to the employer corporation, because the ESOP makes it twice as easy for the employer to pay back the loan. But I haven't found this to be true. All the bankers I've talked to say that they look to the employer for repayment of the loan and that they make the loan decision the same way as they would if it were straight corporate borrowing without an ESOP.

So, what kind of corporation can really use ESOP as an advantageous way of raising money? We've ruled out practically all of our large successful publicly held corporations, since they can use straight loans or stock sales to better advantage than ESOPs. We've ruled out unprofitable corporations, and ones that don't have strong borrowing power. What's left? Mainly successful privately held corporations whose owners can get some special advantages from ESOPs.

ESOPs in Closely Held Corporations

The use of ESOPs can put a lot of extra money into the pockets of owners of successful privately held businesses whose stock has never been sold to the public. "Closely held" corporations (those with only a few stockholders) are the best vehicles for the tax advantages of ESOPs.

Neil Wassner, a New York accountant, probably knows as much about the use of ESOPs in closely held corporations as anybody in the game. He is a partner in the national accounting firm of Main Lafrentz & Co. and is in charge of their merger and acquisition department. He's also their ESOP specialist. I met Neil soon after I became interested in Kelso and found him to be one of the few accountants who can give you a simple explanation of a financial transaction. Here is his description of the advantages of ESOPs for closely held corporations:

> The typical owner of a closely held corporation is interested in getting money out of his corporation at the lowest possible tax cost to himself and in a way that is deductible to the corporation. He wants to do this for personal estate liquidity reasons; he recognizes that it's very difficult to pass on a closely held corporation to his heirs because of the heavy estate taxes. Very often the threat of estate taxes drives the owner of a closely held company to sell his business.
>
> Now, ESOP has provided new alternatives to these people. They have the possibility of selling the business, in effect, to their own employees, rather than selling it to strangers or to a conglomerate. Most of my clients would prefer to sell their businesses to their own employees if the tax and financial effects are as favorable as in the conglomerate deal.

If you're interested in the mechanics of ESOP use in closely held corporations, you should read the ESOP references I've listed in the Bibliography. Most of the advantages revolve around the use of ESOP in place of "redemption" of stock by the corporation. In the past, owners of closely held corporate stock have tried to sell their interests gradually by having the corporation buy stock from them, hoping to pay moderate capital gains taxes. But the IRS has turned redemption into a minefield, and in many cases, redemptions have been treated as dividends instead of capital gains. ESOP brings into the picture a new legal person—the trust (ESOT)—and the IRS has ruled that since the sale of stock to an ESOT is like sale to an unrelated third person, the redemption rules do not apply and the owners can get capital gains tax treatment.

Remember, too, that the stock sold to the ESOT is going to be distributed eventually to the employees, which can include the officers who are usually the main stockholders of closely held corporations. In a small company, the owners can have their cake and eat it too because their salaries dominate the payroll that is the basis for distribution of ESOP benefits. And by naming themselves trustees of the ESOT, they can continue to exercise voting control even after they have sold their stock.

This bonanza for the owners is not necessarily harmful to the ordinary workers. Without ESOP, they probably would never own any of their employer's stock. If they are given stock through an ESOP, they lose nothing and may even gain a lot, if the corporation continues to be profitable. If the corporation does poorly, they don't necessarily lose any money because they are not responsible for repayment of loans made to an ESOT. But it's obvious that this use of ESOP isn't going to add up to any significant diffusion of American capital ownership. The closely held corporations are the sideshow of American business; the main arena is where the publicly held giant corporations appear, and that is where universal capitalism must operate.

ESOP Divestitures

A little closer to the main arena, there is one use of ESOP that can lead to more significant capital diffusion. That is in the field of *divestitures,* the selling off of subsidiaries or divisions, usually by conglomerates. Many large corporations went on acquisition sprees in the 1960s, only to find that they could not profitably operate all the businesses that they could acquire. In the 1970s, many large corporations decided to pare down their operations by getting rid of those divisions and subsidiaries that they had difficulty managing profitably. So began the reversal of the acquisition binge. But it is not always easy to find buyers for unprofitable operations.

ESOP stepped into this gap by making it possible for the employees of the unwanted subsidiary to buy it from the parent corporation. Often the employees are the ideal buyers of subsidiaries, and usually they are willing to pay a higher price than other buyers because they are anxious to hang on to their jobs. This is particularly true of the high-salaried officers, who might have difficulty getting new jobs at the same salary level. The ESOP structure makes it possible for the employees to buy the subsidiary on long-term credit, paying off the loan principal and interest as tax-deductible expenses. If bank financing is not available, often the parent corporation itself will extend credit to the new ESOP. Remember that this was the plan Kelso used in his first project, Peninsula Newspapers, where the old owners sold out to the employees on long-term credit.

The most dramatic ESOP divestiture was the South Bend Lathe deal in 1975. It is important because it saved 500 jobs and brought the Economic Development Administration (EDA) into the quest for universal capitalism.

EDA was established in the U.S. Department of Commerce in 1965 as a sort of economic trouble-shooting operation, designed mainly to fight pockets of unemployment in urban areas. South Bend, Indiana, meets the specifications of the EDA as an industrial disaster area. It has been a pocket of severe unemployment since 1964, when the 22,000-worker Studebaker plant closed down.

One of the troubled businesses left in the wake of Studebaker was South Bend Lathe, a division of Amsted Industries, Inc., of Chicago. South Bend Lathe (SBL) had been limping along as a losing proposition for years, and in 1975, the Amsted management decided that it was worth more dead than alive. South Bend Lathe was seventy years old, and its products were still highly regarded in the machine tool business; but the industry itself was in a slump because of low demand for machine tools. This, in turn, was a result of the shortage of capital for modernization of America's industrial plant. Amsted announced that it was going to liquidate the division, sell off its assets, and in the process eliminate 500 jobs.

Dick Boulis was the chief executive of South Bend Lathe when it was a division of Amsted. When he got the word that Amsted was going to fold up his division, he decided to try to save it by finding a way for the employees to buy it. He still had faith in SBL's products, which were selling at the rate of about $18 million a year, and he felt that SBL could be run successfully as a separate company by the employees even though it was not profitable as a division of Amsted.

While Boulis was struggling with this problem, he happened to have lunch with a friend of his in South Bend who knew some-

thing about ESOPs. When Boulis mentioned his desire to buy SBL
for the employees, his friend suggested that he look into ESOP,
and he sent Boulis a file full of articles on the subject.

Boulis went to see Robert F. McGinty, an officer of the First
Bank and Trust Company of South Bend, to seek his advice on the
use of ESOP. McGinty in turn went to Chicago to talk to James
Peterson, regional director of EDA, and John Gibson, an EDA
project specialist.

Things moved very rapidly from that point on. Peterson and
Gibson got very interested. They had been looking for a model
that would demonstrate that ESOP could be used to eliminate
pockets of unemployment in troubled areas such as South Bend.
They were also anxious to show what could be done with long-term,
low-cost financing, the kind of financing that Louis Kelso had been
touting for nearly twenty years as the best means for spreading
capital ownership and creating enough capital formation to keep
the U.S. economy growing.

When Boulis got encouragement from Peterson and Gibson,
he called in Louis Kelso as a consultant to do a feasibility study
on the divestiture of SBL to its employees. Kelso took on the job
at a reduced fee because he was being paid by the city of South Bend
out of emergency funds.

Within just a few weeks, Kelso, Boulis, Peterson, Gibson, and
the rest of the South Bend salvage team came up with a divestiture
plan. Amsted agreed to sell the SBL division to a new corporation,
South Bend Lathe Corporation, for $10 million. The corporation
set up an ESOP that would own 100 percent of its stock. That left
the ESOP with only one problem: Where would they get $10
million?

Half the problem was solved when EDA made a grant of $5
million to the city of South Bend, which used it to set up an ESOP
development bank. In turn, the South Bend ESOP development
bank loaned the $5 million to the ESOP established by South Bend
Lathe at 3 percent interest for twenty-five years. As the loan is
repaid, it will be used by the South Bend ESOP development bank
to fund similar projects, enabling ESOPs to buy out ownership of
business operations that will preserve or create jobs in South Bend.

The second half of the $10 million was obtained by Robert
McGinty of the First Bank and Trust Company of South Bend,
from his own bank, the Indiana National Bank, and Walter E.
Heller International Corporation. The second $5 million loan from
the banks is at a much higher rate of interest, about 4 percent above
the prime rate. But Boulis feels that the new South Bend Lathe

Corporation will be able to meet the payments on both loans, based on projections that he and Kelso drew up.

It was only a few months between the time that Dick Boulis learned about ESOP from his friend at lunch, and the completion of the purchase of the division from Amsted for $10 million. It went through with extraordinary speed largely because of the enthusiasm of Peterson and Gibson and their ability to sell their boss in Washington, Assistant Secretary of Commerce for Economic Development Wilmer D. Mizell, better known during his major league baseball career as "Vinegar Bend" Mizell, left-handed pitcher for the Pittsburgh Pirates and the St. Louis Cardinals. Indiana Senators Birch Bayh and Vance Hartke and Congressman John Brademas also helped to expedite the project, and Senator Russell Long let it be known that he was keenly interested in it.

On July 18, 1975, there was a big press conference at the SBL offices. Louis Kelso held forth triumphantly, along with Dick Boulis, Peterson, Gibson, and the various bankers involved in the deal. It was a great moment for Kelso because he saw his philosophy being applied to an emergency situation and saving 500 jobs in an area that was already terribly depressed. It also created a model for twenty-five-year financing at 3 percent interest, which is at the heart of Kelso's Financed Capitalist Plan as well as of ESOP.

The project received extensive press coverage throughout the world, and one of the articles about SBL resulted in a second ESOP divestiture financed by EDA. This time it was a successful operation, the Okonite Company, which happened to have the misfortune of being owned by a loser. Okonite was a wholly owned subsidiary of Omega-Alpha Corporation, which went into bankruptcy in 1975. Poor Okonite had earned over $7 million in that year, but the Okonite Company was put up for sale by Omega-Alpha's trustee in bankruptcy, and it looked like the best offer was coming from an Italian group that had plans to cut employment and move some of their plants, particularly the New Jersey plant, which was located in a depressed area.

Victor Viggiano, chairman and chief executive officer of Okonite, read about the South Bend Lathe deal in the *Wall Street Journal* and immediately started to work on doing the same thing for Okonite. Viggiano put in a bid of $44 million for 100 percent of the stock of Okonite. He then arranged for $13 million in financing from the EDA, in the form of an EDA grant to the State of New Jersey's Economic Development Authority. The New Jersey Authority loaned this $13 million to an ESOP established by Okonite, repayable over a period of twenty-five years at 3 percent interest. The rest of the financing came from the Bank of America and several New Jersey banks. In this way, the Okonite Company, manufacturers of electric cable since 1878 and suppliers of cable to Samuel Morse for his first telegraph lines, came to be owned 100 percent by its employees.

The saving of so many jobs at South Bend Lathe and Okonite can be credited largely to one man, Louis Kelso. That would be a sufficient lifetime accomplishment for most of us, but it is only a part of what Kelso has achieved in the face of great odds. No doubt there will be many more jobs saved by Kelso, ESOP, EDA, and the kind of salvage operation that EDA was established for. And this is all to the good, of course.

However, let's be realistic about it. We can't build universal capitalism on a foundation of marginal operations like South Bend Lathe. We've got to plug into the big winners, the successful giant corporations that use most of the capital, employ most of the labor, and make most of the profits. Rescues such as South Bend Lathe and Okonite are dramatic, but they will not solve macroeconomic problems. They involved *outright grants* by EDA, which had a total 1976 budget of only $77 million for all its rescue operations, including ESOP divestitures. Obviously, macroeconomic problems cannot be solved by handing out money this way; we would run out of money before we scratched the surface.

Kelso himself has always preached the doctrine of plugging the little guy into the credit and profits of the big winners, leaving rescue operations and startups to emergency government funds or venture capital funds of the very wealthy. He was forced into salvage operations because they gave him an opportunity to attract attention to ESOP as a means of solving some tough problems. His dramatic solution of the South Bend Lathe problem should not blind us to the limitations of ESOP.

Nevertheless, a lot of people are watching South Bend Lathe very closely to see how employee ownership works out. In the first few months after the ESOP was installed, Boulis announced that expenses resulting from waste and poor workmanship decreased by 70 percent. Absenteeism went down and productivity went up. According to Boulis, SBL earned a before-tax profit of 10 percent on its sales during the first year under ESOP. However, a good chunk of the profits came from one item: the old Amsted pension plan was terminated, and with it, a large annual contribution that had been partly responsible for Amsted's past losses was eliminated.

Termination of the old pension plan is a sore point among

the older SBL employees, who will not have time to make up lost pension benefits through ESOP. This is an issue that comes up often in ESOP divestitures. The employee group that takes control usually includes middle-aged and younger people who see elimination of pension costs as a way of turning around unprofitable operations.

The ESOP committee of South Bend Lathe, which now elects the board of directors, is composed of Dick Boulis and two other officers of SBL, plus John Deak and Gerry Vogel, president and vice-president of Local 1722 of the United Steelworkers Union. Most of the SBL employees belong to the United Steelworkers. Naturally, the local chapter of the United Steelworkers supported the ESOP divestiture because the 500 jobs and all the local union functions would have been wiped out if Amsted had liquidated SBL. However, the local chapter had plenty of trouble with United Steelworkers International because the higher echelon of the labor movement still takes a dim view of the idea of workers owning the company, especially 100 percent ownership. It creates a lot of questions about the functions of the union. Can they still push for higher wages, if higher wages will drive up the cost of SBL products and cut profits, thereby reducing the value of the stock held by all SBL employees? This is one of the great riddles of ESOP, and you can bet that if there was any alternative to the ESOP, even the local union would have opposed it.

Bob Baker is an assembler at SBL. He was interviewed on the day of the ESOP installation.

> The way I look at it now, if our bargaining committee spends $10,000 defending a man who is just a freeloader and is definitely in the wrong, we're just pouring money down a rathole. Any time we see a man who is in the wrong now, we ought to either straighten him out or get somebody else to take his place who's willing to work.
>
> Our outlook has changed already. You can see it in the men on the assembly line. Now we'll tell the freeloaders to get off their butts because they're chipping into our piece of the rock and they're also throwing their own money away.
>
> You can see the difference already, especially in the younger guys. Some of them used to lolligag around, but now they realize that every time they put out a dime's worth of work, a piece of it comes back to them. Profit definitely is not a dirty word when you're getting some of it.

But remember that SBL is not a typical example of ESOP's effects on motivation and productivity. It is a rare case, where the ESOP resulted in 100 percent ownership by the workers, and it is also a rescue from disaster. Under those circumstances, you can expect the employees to work their tails off to save their jobs and to make their stock worth something because they have the feeling of direct and substantial ownership of the entire operation. But in the successful giant corporations, we're not going to have this emergency rescue of jobs. And the workers are not going to get substantial percentage ownership of the winners. Usually, only the losers are ripe for 100 percent employee ownership.

The rescue of South Bend Lathe and Okonite brought worldwide attention to Kelso. They also generated great interest in ESOP and Kelso within the EDA, and this interest may prove important in the universal capitalism movement (see Chaper 11). Some of the reasons for EDA's interest were stated by the two officials who worked on the South Bend Lathe deal. John Gibson, EDA's poverty troubleshooter, said:

> In the past, it was always part of the American dream to work your way up into that high bracket of the 5 percent of our people who are really capitalists. But today, we have found that five capitalists can't carry ninety-five socialists on their back without some day coming down in a crash.
>
> Today, we have about 36 million people at the poverty level in the United States, and a lot of them aren't very calm about it, as you may know if you go down a dark city street at night.

Gibson's boss, James E. Peterson, director of EDA's midwest office, has also become a believer.

> At EDA, we are looking very closely at ESOP. Personally, I think that it is the vehicle to solve the problems of our cities. We are concerned with major dislocations in the economy and pools of unemployed people in specific cities.
>
> South Bend Lathe is a beautiful example of saving 500 jobs in an area of great economic dislocation. It is also an example of the use of 3 percent capital formation money, which I think is essential for this country to renew its productive capacity. The South Bend Lathe model is also intended as a message for the Federal Reserve System. The crying need now is for capital formation. But how are you going to have capital formation

with interest rates of 10 percent or 14 percent? In 1947, the prime rate was 1½ percent. The South Bend Lathe deal will show that it is possible to create capital formation at 3 percent cost, as Kelso has claimed for years.

ESOPs Compared with Profit-Sharing Plans

Both profit-sharing and ESOP have features that can motivate employees to do a better job. Advocates of profit-sharing plans claim that they produce more direct motivation than ESOPs because the employees do not receive any new benefits unless the corporation makes a profit. Under ESOP, the corporation continues to make contributions to the ESOT each year even if profits fall off, although the stock becomes much more valuable, of course, if profits increase.

ESOP fans say that ESOP creates more incentive because the contributions are invested almost entirely in stock of the employer, whereas most profit-sharing plans diversify their investments. But there are some very successful profit-sharing plans that have invested most of their funds in employer's stock.

If you're looking for safety of principal and diversification of risk, a profit-sharing plan is usually better for the employees than an ESOP. But if you're looking for a device to provide financing for the corporation, using leverage, then ESOP is your game because leveraging cannot be used with profit-sharing plans.

The concept of profit-sharing goes back more than 100 years, and the histories of some plans support the claim that it can improve motivation and productivity. There are some very old and successful American plans, such as those at Procter & Gamble (whose plan originated in 1887), Eastman Kodak (1912), and Sears Roebuck (1916). These plans have created quite a few millionaires and many comfortable retirees. Some of the most successful profit-sharing plans, such as the Sears plan, invested most of their funds in employer stock. But Peter Drucker pointed out the fallacy of trying to make this a universal practice: Fewer than half of all businesses remain profitable or even survive over the average working lifetime. In *The Unseen Revolution* (1976), Drucker described a chart that shows how employees of other leading retailers would have fared if their employers had adopted the Sears plan in 1916:

> More than half of the leading retailers of 1916 had disappeared by 1950, thirty-five years later—a good many of

them even before the depression. And the surviving companies, including such well-known names as Montgomery Ward, J. C. Penney, or the A&P, had done so poorly on average that employees dependent for their pensions on funds invested in these companies would, in 1950, have had to retire with little or no retirement income.

Kelso has a potential answer. He has been working on a scheme to provide insurance against decreases in the value of employers' stock contributed to ESOPs. However, no commercial insurer has ever been willing to cover the "entrepreneurial risk" or the hazards of the stock market. If the federal government were called upon to insure this risk, it would be subsidizing our shakiest and least efficient businesses. I think that the idea of government insurance against business failure creates more problems than it solves.

Despite many successful examples of profit-sharing plans over the past 100 years, most large American companies have not gone for it. And those that do use profit-sharing often substitute it for a pension plan. Many profit-sharing companies are not unionized, or they exclude union members from the plan, and so they limit the benefits to the managerial group. Like other qualified employee benefits, profit-sharing plans may be integrated with social security, which means that high-salaried employees benefit most because social security takes care of benefits based on the first $15,300 of wages. And some of the most successful plans require after-tax savings by the employees. The Sears Roebuck plan requires employees to contribute 5 percent of their salaries each year, which will be matched by contributions from the corporation.

If profit-sharing will substantially increase productivity, that is sufficient incentive for most corporations to use it. More than 300,000 profit-sharing plans were in effect in 1976, covering about 9 million workers. It is obvious that the managers of over 300,000 businesses think profit-sharing is good for them, since there is no government requirement and very little union pressure to install such plans. On the other side of the coin, the managers of most of our large businesses, which employ the great majority of our workers, feel that profit-sharing does not increase productivity enough to pay for itself. Otherwise they would have installed plans by now.

I happen to be a great fan of profit-sharing. We've had a profit-sharing plan in our law firm ever since lawyers were allowed to incorporate. But I don't think profit-sharing is going to solve macroeconomic problems, any more than ESOP will. I don't see any way to make the distribution of profits to employees (or any other employee benefits) accomplish the difficult task of diffusing capital ownership broadly enough to do the job we want. And it is possible that ESOPs and profit-sharing plans which invest in employer stock may actually increase concentration of wealth because they increase the possibility of runaway bonanzas for the relatively small segment of the population that is already in much better shape than the rest. Profit-sharing can broaden ownership somewhat and create a bigger group of owners than we now have, but there is no way in which it can be made broad enough to bring about universal capitalism.

What Can ESOP Do for Corporations?

As we have seen, a corporation can use a leveraged ESOP to get a tax deduction for repayment of loan principal. But usually this is interesting only to stockholders of closely held corporations, who are willing to accept some stock dilution and some decrease in earnings per share in order to improve their personal tax positions. The management of large publicly held corporations would not voluntarily use any financing device that decreases earnings per share. The performance of corporate management is judged by earnings per share, and the market price of stock is usually determined as a multiple of earnings per share. And, as we have seen, ESOP makes the corporation pay twice for its financing (once by repaying a loan and once by issuing new stock), which is unnecessary and unacceptable to most large corporations.

Proponents of ESOP claim a number of advantages to the corporation besides the direct tax savings: creating a private market for the corporation's stock without going public, financing acquisitions, refinancing debt on favorable terms, and creating operating losses that can be turned into tax refunds. But none of these devices are useful to large publicly held corporations.

Indeed, the use of ESOP to benefit *any* kind of corporation became doubtful in 1976 because of very tight ESOP regulations proposed by the IRS, which Senator Russell Long headed off at the last minute. This squeeze arises from the fact that ESOPs are basically employee benefit plans that receive special tax treatment if they are designed for the "exclusive benefit" of the participating employees, as required by the Internal Revenue Code. Kelso has ingeniously gotten around this requirement for years by getting IRS approval for plans that give the employees a free ride and at the same time provide some advantages to the corporation. But the spotlight thrown on ESOP in 1975 and 1976 caused the IRS to read the law literally, and it took the parliamentary skills of Russell Long to rescue ESOP (see Chapter 11).

This is one of the basic weaknesses of ESOP as a macroeconomic tool. When you try to use an employee benefit plan as a device to solve such huge problems as overconcentration of wealth and shortage of corporate capital, it's really like mixing apples and oranges. Also, ESOP is built on tax advantages that may be quite temporary. Sooner or later, we'll get some basic tax reforms that might eliminate these advantages and destroy the foundation of ESOP.

A feature of ESOP that is unattractive to management of large corporations is the possibility that it can lead to workers taking over voting control within a few years. Most large publicly held corporations are controlled by votes representing as little as 15–20 percent of the stock. It wouldn't take many years for an ESOT to acquire that much stock if the full ESOP contribution of 15 percent of the payroll were used each year. Initially, the corporate management might be able to control the voting of the ESOP stock by making themselves or their friends trustees of the ESOT, but there is a lot of pressure toward a requirement that the voting rights on stock held by an ESOT be passed through to the employees. In fact, two of the four early ESOP tax laws required this, and so did the regulations proposed by the IRS for all ESOPs in 1976.

You can be sure that there will be terrific pressure to make the voting pass-through requirement apply to any broad use of ESOP by large publicly held corporations. This would make corporate management uneasy on at least two counts: They would worry about keeping their top jobs and salaries, and they would be afraid that worker control might mean running the corporation to profit the workers more than the stockholders, even though the workers would also be stockholders.

The only real macroeconomic advantage claimed for ESOPs is that they can increase employee productivity because of the strong motivation brought about by stock ownership. This is a very tough one to evaluate. The motivation is obvious in situations like South Bend Lathe, where the workers not only owe their jobs to ESOP but also own 100 percent of the stock. It is highly probable that most employees of small corporations who receive significant percentages of stock through ESOP will also be motivated to work harder and make their stock worth more. But when you get down to the main arena (the giant corporations such as General Motors,

AT&T, and U.S. Steel), the picture is not so clear. Some studies seem to show that lower-echelon workers in large corporations, who receive few shares, simply do not make the connection between stock ownership and working harder.

Indeed, we must remember that we are not really talking about stock *ownership* through ESOP, since the ownership doesn't come until retirement. Many employees look upon all forms of deferred benefits as promises payable in the hereafter, and this includes executives as well as blue-collar workers. They concentrate on their take-home pay, and you can't take home your ESOP shares until you retire.

Also, if you're talking about ESOP as a macroeconomic device to solve big problems, then you're talking about making millions of workers stockholders in losers. About 10,000 U.S. businesses close their doors each year. Many workers are not attuned to riding the rollercoaster of the stock market, and there can be reverse motivation leading to decreased productivity if the workers are panicky or disillusioned about the performance of the employer's stock.

Motivation is probably the strongest argument that can be made for ESOP, but it is not strong enough to make ESOP an ideal instrument of capital diffusion because its benefits cannot be spread equitably. It is impossible to make every worker an employee of a winning corporation for his whole career.

The roster of corporations that have installed ESOPs makes it clear that most large corporations see more losses than gains in such a move. As of mid-1976, somewhere between 250 and 500 corporations had installed ESOPs. Nobody has a complete record because most of the ESOP users are small corporations that do not report their finances publicly. As part of the research for this book, Jeff Gates and I spent a lot of time talking to officers of corporations with ESOPs. We were not able to come up with a single corporation with sales of over $100 million that installed an ESOP for purposes of raising money for the corporation. The handful of large corporations that had installed ESOPs had special reasons for doing so, such as the desire to ward off a hostile takeover attempt by using the ESOP to buy existing stock in the market.

The staffs of large corporations are loaded with lawyers, accountants, financial executives, and benefits specialists. The dozens of seminars and conferences about ESOP held throughout the country during 1975 and 1976 were well attended by these sophisticated specialists. You can bet that if they saw advantages in using ESOPs, they would jump right in. Corporations don't hesitate to use other forms of employee benefit plans. In 1976, there were more than

420,000 corporate pension plans in effect, covering over 27 million employees, and 310,000 profit-sharing plans, covering 9 million employees, whereas there were only 250 to 500 ESOPs, most of them in small or closely held corporations.

Louis Kelso says that this limited use of ESOP is due to the newness of the idea and the very foggy position of the IRS, which makes executives of big corporations hesitate. He has suggested a number of tax amendments that would make ESOPs more attractive to large corporations. But in my opinion, ESOP cannot overcome the disadvantages of dilution, reduction of earnings per share, and the extra cost involved in having to issue stock as well as repay a loan in order to raise money. It can be a useful device for solving some special problems (as it was in the case of South Bend Lathe), and no doubt Kelso and others will increase its effectiveness. But employee retirement benefits were not designed to solve the basic problems of the economy, and I don't see how ESOP can be modified to accomplish that monumental job.

What Can ESOP Do for Employees?

The advantages of ESOP to employees are obvious: They receive stock ownership in the employer corporation without any cash outlay or financial liability (since they are not responsible for repayment of loans to ESOTs) and without any income tax liability until the stock is distributed to them, usually at retirement. If they happen to be working for a successful company, the stock in their ESOP accounts can become very valuable.

However, there are some potential drawbacks for the employees. If they work for a closely held corporation, they may run into difficulties associated with valuation of the corporation's stock. It is always a tricky problem to try to evaluate the stock of a corporation that is not publicly traded. This affects the amount of stock that is contributed by the employer, and it can also affect the employee when he retires and receives the stock. The tax he pays will be based on an appraisal or private valuation of the stock that is distributed to him by the ESOT. He will probably have to sell a good part of that stock to pay the taxes, and he may want to sell all of it if he is concerned about income during retirement and the corporation is not paying any dividends. Finding a buyer for a small block of stock in a closely held corporation can be very difficult.

The regulations proposed by the IRS in 1976 tried to solve

this problem by requiring the employer to agree to buy the stock back from retiring employees at any time within two years after the stock is distributed to them. However, even under those regulations, the determination of fair market value of the stock will not be easy. Some ESOP specialists say this requirement will be expensive enough to discourage quite a few corporations from using ESOPs.

The employees of large publicly held companies would not have any problems in disposing of their stock. However, history tells us that whenever large publicly held corporations give their employees a benefit such as ESOP, they are likely to think in terms of decreasing contributions that they might make to other types of employee benefit plans. An article by Charles G. Burck in the March 1976 *Fortune,* "There's More to ESOP Than Meets the Eye," shows that many ESOPs established by corporations with sales between $6 and $83 million were designed to replace pension or profit-sharing plans. This can be dangerous for the employees because ESOP puts all their eggs in one basket. If the employer corporation has financial difficulties, the employee can suffer a double loss: He can lose both his job and his retirement benefits. Because most pension and profit-sharing plans diversify their investments, the worker whose employer provided a pension or profit-sharing plan has a chance of salvaging his retirement benefits even if he loses his job or his employer gets into financial difficulty.

On the whole, employees of successful corporations have little or nothing to lose through ESOP, and they might make a considerable gain. Unfortunately, these benefits cannot be extended widely or equitably enough to make ESOP a means of bringing about universal capitalism.

What Can ESOP Do for Unions?

Organized labor has been very cool to the ESOP movement. Union leaders seem to be afraid that ESOP might cause workers to identify more closely with the ownership of the company than with their own union. If the workers have more to gain by a rise in stock prices than they do from a rise in their own wages, the main function of unions, collective bargaining, may be undermined or even eliminated.

ESOP raises the specter of *codetermination,* the European term for union participation in management. The European brand of codetermination does not necessarily involve worker ownership of stock, but it does put union representatives on the board of directors, sometimes giving labor as many as half the board seats. American labor leaders have shied away from codetermination; they have been willing to leave management to the managers and to stick to their own basic job of being partisan advocates for the workers.

Union leaders usually give other reasons for opposing ESOP. For example, they say that in the nature of collective bargaining, employers will always try to cut back on wage rises or other fringe benefits if they can point to substantial employee benefits from ESOP. And as we have seen, there is some data to back up this argument. In fact, Kelso and other ESOP proponents have talked about "flattening out the wage rise curve" by making the workers stockholders. In the long run, this might be beneficial for the workers. But the unions do not see it that way, and they are generally able to convince their membership that anything that cuts into their take-home pay has to be bad for them. The unions also point out that even in large publicly held corporations, ESOPs benefit the high-salaried executives most of all because the allocation of stock is based on the payroll.

Labor leaders in some European countries have become interested in taking control of major businesses through stock issued to workers but voted by unions (see Chapter 13). If American labor leaders ever develop similar appetites, ESOP would be an ideal device for such a takeover. As we have seen, worker stock ownership builds up very rapidly under ESOP, and there is already great pressure for passing the voting rights through to the workers as soon as the stock is acquired by the ESOP. It wouldn't take much effort by union leaders to convince the workers to give their proxies to union representatives.

GLOSSARY

BSOP. Broadened stock ownership plan. Proposed by the Ford administration in 1976 to encourage savings by individuals for purchase of stock.

Capital formation plan. A plan suggested in 1972 by the Sabre Foundation. It would encourage individual savings for purchase of stock in a manner similar to BSOP.

CDIC. Capital Diffusion Insurance Corporation. A proposed new government agency that would insure banks against losses on loans made for purchase of stock under the Financed Capitalist Plan (see Figure 4).

CSOP. Consumer stock ownership plan. Designed to help utilities raise capital and build stock ownership into their customers in proportion to their consumption.

Econometrics. Use of mathematical measurements and statistical methods for verification of economic theories.

ERISA. Employee Retirement Income Security Act of 1974, also known as the Pension Reform Act. This act extensively revised the government regulation of private pension, profit-sharing, stock bonus, and employee stock ownership plans.

ESOP. Employee stock ownership plan.

ESOT. Employee stock ownership trust. A trust established as part of an employee stock ownership plan to acquire, hold, and eventually to distribute stock to employees.

Financed Capitalist Plan (FCP). A plan devised by Louis Kelso to enable New Capitalists to acquire stock ownership on nonrecourse, self-liquidating credit (see Figure 4). In early Kelso literature, also called SIP (second income plan).

GNP. Gross national product. The value of a nation's total output of goods and services.

Investment tax credit. A credit that may be deducted from federal income taxes payable by businesses. The credit is based on their expenditures for capital items.

IRA. Individual retirement account. A tax-sheltered retirement plan available to individuals who are not covered by any qualified retirement plan.

JEC. Joint Economic Committee of Congress. Established by the Employment Act of 1946, the committee consists of ten senators and ten representatives.

Keogh plan (HR-10). A tax-sheltered retirement plan for self-employed persons.

Macroeconomics. Analysis of the broad aggregate features of the economy.

Microeconomics. Analysis of narrower and more specific features of the economy, such as those relating to individual firms or specific commodities.

New Capitalists. Persons, families, or households owning little or no productive capital, who would be the beneficiaries of universal capitalism in accordance with policies and priorities established by Congress.

Stock bonus plan. A device by which corporations can contribute stock to a trust established for the benefit of its employees. Similar to ESOP, except that only ESOP can use leveraging.

Tax Reduction Act of 1975. The law that established a temporary 1 percent TRASOP provision for 1975 and 1976.

Tax Reform Act of 1976. This law covered many subjects. Its significance for this book is that it established a 1 percent TRASOP provision for 1977 through 1980, with the possibility of increasing the TRASOP to 2 percent if employees contribute $\frac{1}{2}$ percent which is matched by an additional $\frac{1}{2}$ percent contribution by the corporation.

TFT. Louis Kelso's two-factor theory. The two factors are labor and capital.

TRASOP. Tax Reduction Act Stock Ownership Plan. Under this plan, corporations can receive an extra 1 percent to $1\frac{1}{2}$ percent investment tax credit for contributing the equivalent in stock to an employee stock ownership plan.

Trickledown. The theory that the benefits of capitalism will trickle down from the owners of capital to all other levels of society, so that what's good for the capital owners will result in good for everyone eventually.

Universal capitalism. A system designed to give everyone a chance to be a capitalist, mainly by allowing people without savings to own corporate stock that pays for itself out of its own earnings. Used synonymously with "capital diffusion" and "broadening of capital ownership" in this book.

WEFA. Wharton Econometric Forecasting Associates. A nonprofit affiliate of the University of Pennsylvania which provides econometric analysis and forecasting services to government and industrial subscribers.

WEIF. Wage earners' investment fund. The European term for various forms of employee benefit plans.

BIBLIOGRAPHY

Adler, Mortimer J., and Gorman, William. *The American Testament.* New York: Praeger Publishers, 1975.

Andersen & Co., Arthur. "Employee Stock Ownership Plans (ESOPs) —An Approach to Corporate Finance and Employee Motivation." Chicago: Arthur Andersen & Co., 1975.

Boyd, Winnett, and McDonald, Kenneth. *The National Dilemma.* Richmond Hill, Ontario: BMG Publishing, 1975.

Brems, Hans. "An Investment Wage and a Wage Earners' Investment Fund Under Steady-State Growth." *Swedish Journal of Economics* 77 (1975), pp. 13–30.

———. "Profit Sharing and a Wage Earners' Investment Fund Under Steady-State Growth," *Kyklos* 28 (1975), pp. 94–116.

———. Statement and testimony on employee stock ownership plans (ESOPs), Hearings before the Joint Economic Committee, Part 1, December 11, 1976. Washington, D.C.: Government Printing Office, 1976, pp. 521–567.

———. "A Wage Earners' Investment Fund." Stockholm: Swedish Industrial Publications, 1975.

Burck, Charles G. "There's More to ESOP Than Meets the Eye." *Fortune,* March 1976.

Copeman, George. *Employee Share Ownership and Industrial Stability.* London: Institute of Personnel Management, 1975.

Davenport, Nicholas. *Memoirs of a City Radical.* London: Weidenfeld and Nicolson, 1975.

———. *The Split Society.* London: Victor Gollancz, 1964.

Drucker, Peter F. *The Unseen Revolution.* New York: Harper & Row, 1976.

Frady, Marshall. "The Longs of Louisiana." *Sunday Times Magazine* (London), December 7, 1975.

Galbraith, John Kenneth. *Money: Whence It Came, Where It Went.* Boston: Houghton Mifflin, 1975.

Gastil, Raymond D. "The Comparative Survey of Freedom— VI." *Freedom at Issue,* January–February 1976.

Hamrin, Robert. "Broadening the Ownership of New Capital: ESOPs and Other Alternatives." Staff study prepared for the use of the Joint Economic Committee, June 17, 1976. Washington, D.C.: Government Printing Office, 1976.

Hewitt Associates. *ESOPs: An Analytical Report.* Chicago: Profit Sharing Council of America, 1975.

Javits, Benjamin A. *Ownerism.* New York: Crown Publishers, 1969.

Joint Economic Committee. *Employee Stock Ownership Plans (ESOPs).* Hearings before the Joint Economic Committee, Ninety-Fourth Congress, first session. Part 1, December 11, 1975; Part 2, December 12, 1975. Washington, D.C.: Government Printing Office, 1976.

————. "Estimating the Social Costs of National Economic Policy: Implications for Mental and Physical Health, and Criminal Aggression." A study prepared for use of the Joint Economic Committee, October 26, 1976. Paper no. 5 in *Achieving the Goals of the Employment Act of 1946— Thirtieth Anniversary Review,* vol. 1. Washington, D.C.: Government Printing Office, 1976.

————. *U.S. Economic Growth from 1976 to 1986: Prospects, Problems and Patterns,* vol. 1: Productivity. Studies prepared for the use of the Joint Economic Committee, October 1, 1976. Washington, D.C.: Government Printing Office, 1976.

Kelso, Louis O. "Karl Marx: The Almost Capitalist." *American Bar Association Journal,* March 1957.

Kelso, Louis O., and Adler, Mortimer J. *The Capitalist Manifesto.* New York: Random House, 1958. Reprinted by Greenwood Press, Westport, Conn., 1975.

————. *The New Capitalists.* New York: Random House, 1961. Reprinted by Greenwood Press, Westport, Conn., 1975.

Kelso, Louis O., and Hetter, Patricia. *Two-Factor Theory: The Economics of Reality.* New York: Random House, 1967.

―――. "Uprooting World Poverty: A Job for Business," *Business Horizons,* Fall 1964.

Keynes, John Maynard. *The General Theory of Employment, Interest and Money.* London: Macmillan, 1936. Harbinger paperback, 1964.

―――. *How to Pay for the War.* London: Macmillan, 1940.

Keynes, Milo, ed. *Essays on John Maynard Keynes.* Cambridge: Cambridge University Press, 1975.

Klein, Lawrence R. *A Textbook of Econometrics,* 2d ed. Englewood Cliffs, N.J.: Prentice-Hall, 1974.

―――. *The Keynesian Revolution,* 2d ed. New York: Macmillan, 1966.

Menke, John D. *How to Analyze, Design and Install an Employee Stock Onwership Plan.* New York: Panel Publishers, 1976.

Metzger, Bert L., ed. *Pension, Profit Sharing, or Both?* Evanston, Ill.: Profit Sharing Research Foundation, 1975.

Metzger, Bert L., and Colleti, Jerome A. *Does Profit Sharing Pay?* Evanston, Ill.: Profit Sharing Research Foundation, 1971.

Metzger, Bert L., and Diekman, Bernard A., eds. *Profit Sharing: The Industrial Adrenalin.* Evanston, Ill.: Profit Sharing Research Foundation, 1975.

Pillsbury, Charles A. "Note: Employee Stock Ownership Plans: A Step Towards Democratic Capitalism." *The Boston University Law Review* vol. 55, no. 2 (March 1975).

Practising Law Institute. *ESOPs: Employee Stock Ownership Plans.* New York: Practising Law Institute, 1976.

Robinson, Derek. *Income Policy and Capital Sharing in Europe.* New York: Barnes & Noble, 1973.

Rockefeller, John D. III. *The Second American Revolution.* New York: Harper & Row, 1973.

Samuelson, Paul A. *Economics,* 10th ed. New York: McGraw-Hill, 1976.

Schlesinger, James R. "A Testing Time for America." *Fortune,* February 1976.

Silk, Leonard. *The Economists.* New York: Basic Books, 1976.

Smith, Hedrick. *The Russians.* New York: Quadrangle/New York Times Book Co., 1976.

Thomas, Dana L. "Explosive ESOTs," *Barron's,* July 28, 1975.

———. "Mighty Kelso," *Barron's,* July 21, 1975.

Von Hoffman, Nicholas. "What Will Save Us from Poverty?" *Esquire,* December 1973.

Wassner, Neil A. "Employee Stock Ownership Plans, an Idea Whose Time Has Arrived?" *Viewpoint,* Main Lafrentz & Co., New York, 1975.

———. "ESOPs: Can they Work for your Corporation?" *Pension World,* June 1976.

Williams, T. Harry. *Huey P. Long.* London: Oxford University Press, 1967.

INDEX

About the Author

STUART M. SPEISER is senior partner of the law firm of Speiser, Krause & Madole, with offices in New York, Washington, and London. He is the author of fifteen volumes of works on legal subjects which have often been cited as authority by the U.S. Supreme Court and other high appellate courts.

A World War II Air Force bomber pilot and a former commercial airplane pilot, he has represented families of deceased airplane passengers in litigation arising from many of the world's major air disasters. The families of baseball Hall of Fame member Roberto Clemente; John McNaughton, Secretary of the Navy under President Kennedy; and Gordon Dean, first chairman of the Atomic Energy Commission, have been his clients in such litigation. He also successfully represented Ralph Nader in his invasion of privacy suit against General Motors.

His work in aviation death cases required him to project economic statistics into the future in order to prove the losses sustained by passengers' families, since the damage awards are based upon calculation of what the deceased passenger would have earned if he had lived out his life expectancy. This task required him to study econometrics and to calculate the effects of inflation and other economic factors as much as forty or fifty years into the future. He has dealt with the economies of many nations. For example, in the litigation arising out of the world's worst air disaster, the 1974 crash of a Turkish Airlines DC-10 outside Paris, he represented the families of 164 passengers from the United States, Great Britain, Canada, France, West Germany, Switzerland, Sweden, Brazil, Turkey, and other nations.

He pioneered the use of econometrics to determine the legal valuation of human life and to provide the basis for expert testimony of economists in litigation. In 1970, he wrote *Lawyers Economic Handbook,* the definitive legal textbook on the use of econometric projections in litigation.

He has served as trustee of pension and profit-sharing plans, and has also been chairman and chief executive officer of a publicly held corporation. He has appeared on television in the United States and Great Britain and has lectured extensively throughout the United States. He has assembled a notable collection of aviation and photo-realist paintings, many of which have been shown by art museums in the United States and abroad.